MW01064766

# SCIENCE FICTION THEOLOGY

# SCIENCE FICTION THEOLOGY

## Beauty and the Transformation of the Sublime

*Alan P. R. Gregory*

BAYLOR UNIVERSITY PRESS

© 2015 by Baylor University Press
Waco, Texas 76798-7363

*All Rights Reserved.* No part of this publication may be reproduced, stored in a retrieval system, or transmitted, in any form or by any means, electronic, mechanical, photocopying, recording, or otherwise, without the prior permission in writing of Baylor University Press.

Cover design by AJB Design, Inc.
Cover image courtesy of iStock/menonsstocks and Shutterstock/Botond Horvath.

Library of Congress Cataloging-in-Publication Data
Gregory, Alan P. R., 1955–
Science fiction theology : beauty and the transformation of the sublime / Alan P.R. Gregory.
328 pages cm
Includes bibliographical references and index.
ISBN 978-1-60258-460-0 (hardback)
1. Science fiction--History and criticism. 2. Sublime, The, in literature. 3. Christianity and literature. 4. Theology in literature. I. Title.
PN3433.6.G75 2015
809.3'8762--dc23

2014039116

Printed in the United States of America on acid-free paper with a minimum of 30 percent post-consumer waste recycled content.

*For Suzy*

*Flight is but the preparative: the sight*
*Is deep and infinite*
*Ah me! 'tis all the glory, love, light, space,*
*Joy, beauty, and variety*
*That doth adorn the Godhead's dwelling place.*
*'Tis all that eye can see.*
*Even trades themselves seen in celestial light,*
*And cares and sins and woes are bright.*
*To see a glorious fountain and an end,*
*To see all creatures tend*
*To thy advancement, and so sweetly close*
*In thy repose: to see them shine*
*In use, in worth, in service, and even foes*
*Among the rest made thine.*
*To see all these unite at once in thee*
*Is to behold felicity.*

—Thomas Traherne, from "The Vision"

*Sun turnin' 'round with graceful motion*
*We're setting off with soft explosion*
*Bound for a star with fiery oceans*
*It's so very lonely, you're a hundred light years from home*
*Freezing red deserts turn to dark*
*Energy here in every part . . .*
*It's so very lonely, you're two thousand light years from home*
*It's so very lonely, you're two thousand light years from home*

—The Rolling Stones

*Deus autem est sua essentia, ut ostensum est. Si igitur non sit suum esse, erit ens per participationem, et non per essentiam. Non ergo erit primum ens, quod absurdum est dicere. Est igitur Deus suum esse, et non solum sua essentia.*

—Thomas Aquinas

# CONTENTS

# ACKNOWLEDGMENTS

Over the time taken to write this book, the crowd of those to whom I am indebted for advice, guidance, inspiration, admonition, insight, affection, and just plain tolerance has grown to space-opera proportions. The clergy of the Newcastle diocese and the people of Stannington, Northumberland, have kindly and patiently put up with a priest not always inhabiting the same planet. Among them, I owe much to the wisdom of Peter Robinson. Catherine Pickford, David Hewlett, Val Carr, Jon Russell, Leslie Chapman, David Wood, and Meg Fisher have been superb colleagues, as have Edna Beveridge, Ron Matthews, Pauline Chambers, and Steve Johnson. Andii Bowsher gave me science-fictional insights and suggestions aplenty, as well as introduced me to Tea Sutra, the best tea shop in Newcastle. Hal and Adrienne Puthoff inducted me into scientific considerations from which my mind may never recover, at least I hope not.

Tony Baker, with whom I have talked theology for many years, has sustained our intercontinental, if not yet intergalactic, friendship, and his influence may be found in all the better corners of this book. When mired in the slough of my own garrulousness, Gladys Lewis brought editorial and pedagogical skills to bear with such effectiveness that I discovered the actual book lying around the rabbit trails. Carey Newman of Baylor University Press encouraged this unlikely project from the very beginning and gently and persistently nudged me along my way.

My granddaughter Natasha, grandson Wilf, and their siblings Lara, Adam, and Harry have brought joy, often when joy was much needed. Paddy and Cara, two Great Danes—I avoid saying "my," since that is quite improper and, anyway, would have little relation to daily reality—have taught me about beauty, animals, and God, and thus put their paw marks in this book. Writing these acknowledgments, I finish another book and end months and months during which I have put my wife's love to the test, if not the rack. She is and always has been God's most precious blessing, and so to her I dedicate this book of spaceships, stars, and sublimity.

# INTRODUCTION

> sublimis, e, . . . adj., *uplifted, high, lofty, exalted, elevated (mostly poetic and in post-Augustan prose)*
>
> —Lewis and Short, *A Latin Dictionary*

> SENSE OF WONDER, n. *a feeling of awakening or awe triggered by an expansion of one's awareness of what is possible or by confrontation with the vastness of space and time, as brought on by reading science fiction.*
>
> —Jeff Prucher, *Brave New Words*, 179

This book argues for a relationship among three themes: the aesthetic and philosophical category of the sublime; American and British science fiction; and Christian theology. One of these themes leads the discussion in each section of the book. The first chapter presents the sublime in relation to science fiction, with some attention to early connections between sublimity, Newtonian science, and Christian theology, while the next four discuss specific works of science fiction insofar as they appropriate or develop the discourse of sublimity. Christian theology appears in these chapters only to the extent that the science fiction texts critique, appropriate, or subvert theological themes or serve to contest a theological sublimity in favor of a science-fictional one. Christian theology gets its say in the final chapter, though, which presents a theological critique of sublimity that has learned a good deal from science fiction.

Authors want readers to stay with their books from beginning to end. However, as Dr. Samuel Johnson famously argued in the late 1700s, they really have no right to be offended if readers pick and choose or give up halfway. Those interested in one of these three themes more than the others will not miss overmuch if they settle on the chapters that suit their fancy. With that in mind, though, a brief introduction to the themes will be helpful.

## SUBLIMITY

The sublime is a cultural construct, and a distinctively modern one.[1] We are in the region of sublimity when we explore the grip had on the modern imagination by vastness and extreme power, by the fearful and threatening, the grand and imposing, the vertiginous and appalling, and by that which strains imagination and stumps reason. As with almost any thesis concerning sublimity, even that brief summary is disputed. Some, for instance, continue to argue that the experience of the sublime and the capacity for it is hardwired into us, that it is universally human.[2] What does, or does not, count as an occasion for sublimity has also been much debated. Does, for instance, horror elicit genuine feelings of sublimity? Or is sublimity found in the terrifying but not the horrid?[3] As a concept, then, as the identification for a family of experiences, the sublime is a contested business and not least contested because the sublime has a history; over three centuries, the paradigmatically sublime has changed, and writers and readers, painters and viewers, philosophers, aestheticians, and theologians have rendered and discovered the sublime in new ideas and new objects.

The most lively interest in the sublime has focused on, at the risk of punning, the "high history" of the sublime: a history of philosophical and aesthetic reflection, running from the late seventeenth century to the present. Corresponding to this tradition of writing *about* the sublime is a history of the pursuit of sublime effects, especially in literature, painting, and architecture. Though this "high history" will be introduced here, in its philosophical mode particularly, the center of gravity in the book lies in evocations of sublimity that, if not entirely ignored, have received a good deal less attention.[4] Eighteenth-century reflection on sublimity largely appealed to sublime effects enjoyed by the "public"—that is, the educated, genteel classes.[5] Writers from Addison to the Aikens discussed a popular sublime enjoyed, by those who had time and money for it, in natural landscapes, the Bible, religious poetry, poems of nature, and tales of decorous bumps in the night.[6] To risk a broad generalization, philosophical treatment of sublimity in the nineteenth and twentieth centuries, when it was vigorous at all, engaged with the narrower field of elite or "high culture" as opposed to the popular.[7] The public, however, that found inspiration in sublime effusions expanded during the eighteenth and nineteenth centuries well beyond the social circles of a genteel audience, let alone philosophers. Sublime representations permeated the imaginations of middle and working classes through the growing market for print reproductions from paintings by artists such as Fuseli and Turner, the traveling exhibitions and the entrepreneurialism of John Martin, the enduring appeal of Gothic novels and stories, and, later on, by way of movies of grand frontiers, astonishing heroes, and great disasters. In addition, a sublimed technology has engaged enthusiasm from locomotives to the space program and by way of Victorian stations, New York skyscrapers, and hyperstimulating shopping malls. This democratic history of the sublime, of course, also includes science fiction, from the pulps promising staggering stories of alien atrocity to the opening sequences of *Doctor Who*.

## SCIENCE FICTION

Science fiction is a distinctively modern genre. That, too, is disputed. A long-running discussion has argued over the beginnings of science fiction. Historians have proposed ancient (*Epic of Gilgamesh*!), Renaissance (More's *Utopia*), and modern (Gothic, esp. *Frankenstein*) origins.[8] Since the arguments often serve different purposes, follow varying proposals as to the core character of the genre, and operate according to different criteria, the discussion both enlightens and continues interminably. Here, the late nineteenth century is taken as the significant time for science-fictional beginnings. Writing analogous to science fiction appears earlier, but only in the late nineteenth century did social, technological, and publishing conditions enable the production of science fiction as a popular literature.[9] Also, and very importantly, science fiction required a culture in which technology was entertained as sublime.

Science fiction inherited the democratized discourse of sublimity. Mountains, cliffs, cataracts, and gorges of invisible depths were well-established properties of the "natural sublime" long before pulp science fiction magazines. Once transported to the wildernesses of outer galaxies, they slipped easily onto the magazine covers. The Gold Medal paperback edition of Richard Matheson's *I Am Legend* sports feverish cover art that illustrates not the plot but the publicity blurb, "this may be the most terrifying novel you will ever read."[10] The novel's urban protagonist now stands precarious on a cliff edge with a Turneresque city on the horizon behind him and naked bodies, quite in the manner of John Martin's apocalyptic sublime, crashing to fiery depths below. Last Judgment paintings are thus refracted through the early nineteenth-century sublime and taken up by twentieth-century science fiction. Again, the sublime inhumanity of icy wastes that chill the opening and closing sections of Shelley's *Frankenstein* and grip Poe's *The Narrative of Arthur Gordon Pym of Nantucket* turn up with a like rendering in Ursula Le Guin's *The Left Hand of Darkness*. When Lester del Rey published *Nerves*, atomic energy had already lured the sublime. Del Rey took up its intensities and added some distant biblical resonances, fully in the line of this modern tradition: "As Doc raised his eyes, he was aware suddenly of a roar from the men. Over to the south, stretching out in a huge mass, was a cloud of steam that spread upward and outward as he watched, and the beginnings of a mighty hissing sound came in."[11]

Science fiction, however, has also expanded the repertoire of sublimity. Not since people found sublimity in such uncultivated and inconvenient nature as mountains and gorges—no longer the rough nubs of a fallen world but tributes to the Creator's majesty—has a literary genre taught us to exercise the sublime imagination in more innovative and culturally formative ways. Science fiction, for instance, has played with the changes in world perception consequent on dislocations of size. Though Swift and Lewis Carroll both anticipated this, their purposes were satirical. Science fiction, however, reproduced such changes in perspective as sublime. Scot Carey has shrunk down to nothing. Having mountaineered his inches-high body down table legs and across cabinets, and battled a spider so large to his frame that "it blotted out the world," he has dwindled beyond "Zero."

> It frightened him at first. The idea of going on endlessly through one dimension after another was alien. . . . Suddenly, he began running toward the light. And when he'd reached it, he stood in speechless awe looking at the new world with its vivid splashes of vegetation, its scintillant hills, its sky of shifting hues, as though the sunlight was being filtered through moving layers of pastel glass.[12]

While space and the night sky were early candidates for sublimity, science fiction has achieved an imaginative recreation of sublimed space, especially in terms of infinite expanse and such distant phenomena of astonishment as rupture our imaginative and rational powers.[13] The genre has also, though, given us space with bones and ribs, with ripples, currents, and flows that intimate the unimaginably alien: "Drop a gem in thick oil. The brilliance yellows slowly, ambers, goes red at last, dies. That was the leap into hyperstatic space."[14]

Much science fiction does not, of course, draw upon the traditions and discourse of the sublime. However, the degree to which sublimity has found a home in science fiction is culturally significant. Given that the sublime is a way of symbolizing the world, of knowing it—or aspects of it—in affect and imagination, its adoption by science fiction has informed our social imaginary in significant ways and in relation to the instituting of social organizations, authorities, and enterprises that are central to our culture.[15] Technology and science are among the most important of these, and the cultural authority of both owes a good deal to the science-fictional sublime. If that sounds hyperbolic, the extent of science fiction's popular influence supports the claim. Science fiction has not been a primarily literary genre for some time, let alone a minority interest for spotty young men gooey eyed over technology rather than girls.[16] Reading science fiction receives the blessing of science's best known celebrities. Stephen Hawking has opined that "science fiction is useful both for stimulating the imagination and for diffusing fear of the future," though the relationship between science fiction and "fear of the future" is probably, like most relationships between art and life, a lot more complicated than he implies.[17] Many science fiction images have become "iconic," many of the genre's perspectives, expectations, and metaphors familiar, especially through movies, television, and advertising. Science fiction is culturally viral, which is why many folk who have not read its word recognize its signs.

Hugo Gernsback, the "scientifiction" pioneer and editor of *Amazing Stories*, hoped that his pulp fiction would inspire boys to take up engineering and science, a claim for the worth of science fiction that persists today.[18] Whatever its contribution to making scientists, science fiction has played a large part in making "Science" and "Technology," constructing them as imaginary objects of great cultural power. In 2005 Newcastle-upon-Tyne became one of six "science cities" in the United Kingdom. The associated projects "aim to maximise the city's scientific potential and raise awareness of our expertise across the world."[19] When the *Daily Telegraph* newspaper announced this initiative, the accompanying photograph endorsed it with an image straight from the science-fictional sublime: in the formal space of a hall with neoclassical pilasters, a masked human figure bathed in green light stands on a raised platform with lightning bolts of electricity bursting from his hands.[20] The promotional material for business investment in "Science City" recurs more to the natural sublime but now deployed for an aura of technological power. From a low angle, the camera shows a man in shirtsleeves and business trousers against the background of an open sky; his hands rest confidently on his hips; he stares with a raptured boldness into a horizon invisible to the viewer, his eyes narrowing as if staring into the sun. Behind him, rising beyond the top of the photo, is a piece of communication technology, but, slightly out of focus, it suggests a rocket.[21] Bar the twentieth-century shirt and the eighteenth-century benevolence, imagining this indefatigable entrepreneur reprises the eighteenth-century lectures of Hugh Blair:

> Wherever, in some critical and high situation, we behold a man uncommonly intrepid, and resting upon himself; superior to passion and to fear; animated by some great principle to the contempt of popular opinion, selfish interest, of dangers, or of death; there we are struck with a sense of the sublime.[22]

Power, the exhilarations of possibility, human grandeur appearing in a context that also places the human within vastness, intimations of technological promise—these provide some, at least, of the ingredients of science-fictional sublimity.[23] Through such signs have technology and science formed us into contemporary subjects of their authority.[24]

## CHRISTIAN THEOLOGY

Christian theology may appear as the odd contributor to this three-way discussion—not that commentators have ignored the presence of religious themes and questions in science fiction; for the most part, though, they have discussed them under the rubric "science fiction and religion."[25] Problematic because too abstract, this invites a generality that fails to get close enough to the theological concepts, symbols, narratives, and practices most formative for English-language science fiction. Within that context, it is Christianity that science fiction has appropriated, rejected, questioned, and subverted and Christianity that has been the "other" in relation to which authors have written critical narratives of religious genealogy or developed speculative accounts of future religious forms or of cultures without religion at all. That is not to say Christianity is the only source of religious influence. Roger Zelazny made exuberant use of the Hindu pantheon in *Lord of Light*. However, he identifies his least attractive and most intractably unmerciful character with Christianity. Nirriti, with his hordes of "mindless minions," is clearly an allegory of Christian fundamentalism, and he exercises a control over the narrative insofar as the Hindu and Buddhist figures are characterized in contrast to him. Moreover, when the "Black One" falls in battle, Zelazny reprises the classic Enlightenment polemic that opposes Jesus to the Church: "And blessed are the peacemakers," said Yama, "for they shall be called the children of God. How do you fit into the picture, Black One? Whose child are you to have wrought as you have done?"[26] The novel, despite its colorful and witty use of Hindu gods and goddesses, remains within the gravitational pull of Western Christianity.

Christian theology also possesses a close relationship with the history of sublimity. In the eighteenth century, enthusiasm for the sublime amounted to a revolution in sensibility at a time of fascination with the dynamics of feeling supported by a rhetoric for relating and distinguishing them, with clarity and propriety, from the workings of reason. If mountains, cliffs, and the forceful aspects of nature now provoked awe and astonishment, they did so in a culture for which the "book of Nature" was a propaedeutic for the devotion due to the Creator. Though not all wrote theologically about the sublime and not all sublimities raised the heart to God any more than all awe is a religious awe, nevertheless it was in God that the purest agitations of sublimity found their true origin. God, wrote Adam Smith, is "of all the objects of human contemplation by far the most sublime."[27] Sublimity did not stay with bracing nature, of course, and has absorbed much else into the trajectory of its continuous revolution in sensibility. The theological, however, has continued to peer over the shoulders of new evocations of sublimity. The Brooklyn Bridge "vaulting the sea" lends "a myth to God."[28]

Insofar as science fiction inherited sublimity and developed its own expressions of sublime discourse, the genre also became part of the sublime's theological history. Science fiction has, therefore, not only taken up the religious language of sublimity, imagining the field of space as a sensorium for wonder and investing machines with intimations of an ultimate transcendence, it has also contested the claim that God, specifically the God of Christianity, is "of all the objects of human contemplation by far the most sublime." Much science fiction may be read as a dispute with Christian theology over the authentically sublime. There is, however, a twist. The subliming of Christianity, or so this book will argue, also subverted Christianity, secularizing Christian theology so that, for example, the "book of Nature" was separated from and displaced the "book of Revelation," of Scripture. Science fiction, therefore, has very largely worked with a profoundly flawed imaginative schema for Christianity. The implications of this and a theological response that draws on the exegetical chapters is the burden of the final chapter below.

A final and apologetic word—readers of science fiction often tend toward vigorous partisanship regarding individual authors and periods of the genre's history. A book that discusses a fairly limited number of works is bound to annoy by its many omissions. The first two chapters attempt to redress the balance somewhat by citing examples of the science-fictional sublime somewhat more promiscuously. The main choices reflect the need to illustrate a range of employments of the sublime, as well as to surface the relationship with Christian theology. Many others might have been chosen, though, so the final selection does reflect the author's own partisanship. The main argument of this book, however, might be sustained with several entirely different groups of science fiction texts.

# 1

# SUBLIME FICTION?

LOGAN: *Time to make nice with the public, eh, Summers?*
SUMMERS: *We have to do more than that, Logan. We have to astonish them.*

—Whedon and Cassaday, *Astonishing X-Men*, 13

*Nothing but what astonishes is true.*

—Edward Young, *Young's Night Thoughts*, 246

## GETTING CAUGHT UP

Visitors to England's Salisbury Cathedral may climb the series of narrow spiral staircases within the tiers of the tower to a point, some 225 feet above the ground, from which they can peer vertiginously up into the spire and over the Wiltshire countryside. A student from Salisbury and Wells seminary organized an outing, going, as he put it with some exaggeration, "where no one has gone before." He did not say "boldly," in the vein of Captain Kirk, but, quite appropriately, he might have done so. Explaining the glories to come, he was irrepressible. "It's, well," he said, "absolutely crushing, marvelous-great-fantastic, you look up and you think you're going to vomit it's so amazing. Amazing, you come out and look down and it takes you somewhere else. Really scary, it's terrific! It's an experience. It's a real experience." That his listeners readily understood and identified with these effusions is rather remarkable. They readily accepted that nausea, vertigo, and the chance, albeit slight, of a terminal plummet to a stone floor were a natural accompaniment to being thrilled; that great drops, heights, and vistas were properly described as "amazing," "fantastic," "astonishing," and not just marvelous but "absolutely" marvelous; and that being scared might be splendid, exalting, fun, and, indeed, "terrific"! Perhaps, most curious of all, his audience had no trouble acknowledging that he had had, and they might have, not just an experience with all this, but a peak experience, an experience worthy of the name, one exalted above the normalities of the regular day.

Given this ready understanding of such enthusiastic reactions, no one is surprised to learn that Immanuel Kant found awe in "the *starry sky* above me," nor that Norman Mailer, watching the fiery and thunderous launch of Apollo XI, should shout, "My God, Oh my God!" over and over again.[1] No vacation brochure for the Rockies or Alps lacks its appeal to "amazing" scenery, in which tourists shall "marvel" or even recognize the "true magnificence of God's creation."[2] These examples suggest a cluster of varied but familiar experiences described in a distinctive array of terms identifying them as diverse in their particularity but similar in their significance. Since the late seventeenth century, these experiences—known through certain elements of the natural environment or by way of literature, painting, architecture, photography, film, music, and technology—have been named "sublime."[3] "Sublime" refers to a certain range of imaginative and affective responses to vastness and extreme power, to the fearful and threatening, the grand and imposing, the vertiginous and appalling, to that which strains imagination and stumps reason.

Richard Rigg's artwork, *A Clearing*, exhibited in 2012, consists of a mountain hut that contains its mountain or, more accurately, part of its mountain.[4] The visitor opens the door onto a slope of earth, stones, rocks, and plants that rises up to well over half the height of the opposite wall. In about five moderately strenuous steps, the visitor can touch the roof from the top of the slope. The clearing within which the hut sits is the severe white glare of the gallery itself. Does this make something clear, or is something cleared away as, perhaps, the viewer is disabused? Huts—along with carriages, horses, travellers, broken towers, ruins, monuments, cottages, and cattle—provide the props for many sublime landscape paintings.[5] In a hut, among the "abrupt sides of vast mountains" providing "sublime and magnificent scenes," the monster tells his tale to Frankenstein. Hut, cow, or ruin—the mountain encloses and dwarfs these tokens of humanity. *A Clearing*, though, has the hut frame the mountain. The sublime is thus denaturalized, unmasked as a human construct. Within the hut, the mountain is "unremarkable and has no discerning features."[6] It is dwarfed beside human imaginative capacity. In itself, the mountain is undistinguished; its sublime distinction comes from the viewer.[7] The sublime is a cultural construct, a formation in and of the cultural imaginary. As such, it has a history.

Put a sixteenth-century Elizabethan gentleman and a nineteenth-century Romantic in the middle of England's Lake District, among the mountains, cliffs, and rills, and the latter will resonate and enthuse, while the other recoils, turns up the nose, and mutters over the fallen world. To give a specific instance, Joshua Poole's handbook for poets, published in 1657, lists a surprising collection of adjectives suitable for describing mountains: "insolent, surly, ambitious, barren, sky-threatening, supercilious, desert, uncouth, inhospitable, freezing, infruitful, crump-shouldered, unfrequented, forsaken, melancholy, pathless." None of these is likely to peak an expectation of wonder and awe. Nor are "Earth's Dugs, Risings, Tumors, Blisters," or "Earth's Warts."[8] Mountains memorialize the fall. By 1739, though, the poet Thomas Gray was drawing a quite different theological lesson. He could not go "ten paces without exclaiming," finding it all so "solemn," "romantic," and, of course, "astonishing." Gray needed but to look on a cliff, torrent, or precipice, and he found it "pregnant with religion." "Certain scenes," he insisted, "would awe an atheist into belief."[9] This latter claim is decisive.

During the eighteenth century, the "sublime" became a catchword for the way in which civilized people should take in such vistas of immensity as plunging cataracts or the blur of galaxies, or be roused by descriptions of storms at sea or poems invoking the inexhaustible multiplicity of life, here and on other worlds. The sublime was variously expounded but, throughout, identifies an invigorating combination of pleasure and pain, named as a delightful horror, a thrilling discomfiture, a seductive terror, an unknown that repels and draws, with the attraction finally uppermost. Sublime natural phenomena and sublime paintings, architecture, and writing stir a movement, more or less intense, of disruption and recovery, where intellectual and affective energies are brought up short, and, through the checking, invigorated. Among all the "objects," however, that aroused this dreadful awe, God was "by far the most sublime."[10] That God is the gold standard of sublimity was almost universally acknowledged in the eighteenth century, even though not always developed as a particular theme. The sublime entered the culture as both theologically informed and theologically influential, and certainly not just through explicitly religious works.

Along with other eighteenth-century celebrants of the sublime, Thomas Gray belonged to a social elite. A sensibility for the sublime was a mark of taste and firmly in the province of the cultivated. Nobody expected the lady's maid to wax rapturous, and, if tradesmen were transported, it was generally to New England. During the nineteenth and twentieth centuries, though, sublimity was democratized and its delights and benefits extended via Gothic novels, ghost stories, the traveling shows of sublime painters, tourism, mechanical wonders, railway stations, public museums and art galleries, the popular press, urban photography, movies, skyscrapers—and science fiction.[11] The titles of early American pulp magazines provide at least a prima facie case for considering the pretensions of science fiction to sublimity: *Astounding*; *Astonishing Stories*; *Amazing Stories*; *Thrilling Wonder Stories*; *Cosmic*; *Marvel*; *Startling Stories*; *Fantastic Stories Quarterly*; *Unknown*; *Weird Tales.* More profoundly telling, perhaps, are the aspirations of science fiction readers. In 1926 a young enthusiast wrote to the magazine *Amazing Stories*, explaining the particular appeal of its fiction. Science fiction, he claimed, is "designed to reach those qualities of the mind which are aroused only by things vast, things cataclysmic, and things unfathomably strange."[12] As a description of the sublime, this would be recognizable all the way back to John Dennis' early treatise on sublimity, published in 1704.[13]

To the extent that science fiction embraced the sublime, it became theologically haunted. Space, for instance, which is the stage for so much science fiction, is imagined not only as a theater for the astonishing but as, in itself, a medium of ultimacy. In *The Centauri Device*, M. John Harrison invests the emptiness between the planets with a thickness, a mysteriously substantial quality, at once fearful and attractive. Space is the "Impossible Medium" that connects with travellers in "slow luminous ecstasies": it is the sublime symbol and promise of transcendence, of freedom from the cultural and political dungeons in which the planet-bound suffer.[14] As Edward Young wrote over two hundred years earlier, "the Soul of Man was made to walk the skies" since "a boundless mind affects a boundless space" and, like the Almighty, lives in "disdain of limit."[15] Push into the realms of intergalactic travel, and the ecstasies are exponential. The ship "shivers with an intense white light," and "all solid forms vanished in amazing twists and contortions." Space thickens to an oceanic density and "somehow entered the ship." Harrison's language blurs inside and outside, above and below, and confounds substance in a properly sublime disorientation. "Space . . . was crawling through us in slow luminous waves. We were steeped in it: we were birds of paradise, we wore the masks of gilded deep-sea fishes . . . we were glass effigies with infinitely thin, attenuated limbs." This "third level of space" fulfills the essential drivenness of our kind.[16] Humanity appears in this sublime wrenching and release because sublimity is the experiential medium of human freedom understood as boundless expansion, a distinctively modern rendering of our relationship to the infinite.

Down in the old miasmal mist, though, Christianity shuffles on. The science-fictional sublime is a polemical business. Harrison caricatures Christianity in the faith of the "Openers." Headquartered at Golgotha, the cult members praise God by exposing their bodily organs to the outside world through plastic windows set into their torsos.[17] Digestion on display, the Openers are a grotesque parody of Christian inwardness, of concern with the processes of the soul, to which, the Openers declare, bodily functions are analogous. Motions trapped behind plastic, their lack of mystery exposed, reveal religion as the opposite of that outward drive of genuine sublimity. This contrast, though, exposes something else, too, perhaps more disquieting even than the Opener's dinner theater. Harrison's imagery often betrays a disgust with the body itself. There is an accentuated unpleasantness about physicality: hands are "meaty," or "pudgy," and fingers "blunt"; bellies are "slack"; faces "gray"; and thighs are vast and varicose-veined, while "pouches of slack, slightly discolored skin" hang under eyes. The sublimity of space, on the other hand, climaxes in "senselessness" and the dissolution of matter. Freedom seems to grow in inverse proportion to bodiliness, which is a troubling idea.[18]

## NATURE SUBLIMED AND HUMANITY EXALTED

The sublime, as a category of experience and a quality of nature and art, did not pop up in the eighteenth century with an entire novelty. The age, after all, was still obliged to demonstrate classical precedent in matters of the arts. Early advocates of the sublime appealed to the first-century treatise, *Peri Hupsous* or *On the Sublime*, attributed to Longinus.[19] Though known for centuries, Longinus' little work on how to achieve sublime effects in writing was consigned firmly to history's minor leagues. Rarely printed earlier and almost never quoted, editions of *On the Sublime* rushed into publication after 1710, some fourteen being on the streets before 1790. Now, though, Longinus was put to work for a cause far beyond the letter of his text, his treatise made to expound a new, modern sensibility. Eighteenth-century authors pounced on Longinus' description of the high, lofty—that is, sublime—style as revealing our special destiny above all other animals. Sublimity is violent; it thrusts reasoned persuasion aside and "prevails" over us by "superior force." The outcome, though, is for our good; we are astounded, dazzled, overcome, and uplifted. Dislocated from the bounded, we are relocated as spectators of the "mighty whole," as our imaginations pass "beyond the reaches of space."[20] In a flourish taken to heart by almost the entire modern tradition of the sublime, Longinus proclaimed, "All other qualities prove their possessors to be men, but sublimity raises them near the majesty of God."[21] Sublime experience registers our birth right among the abyssal and infinite.[22]

According to its most vigorous advocates, then, capacity for the sublime revealed the dignity of humanity and its distinctive calling.[23] John Dennis discovered religious poetry as the proper home of the sublime and the acme of human culture.[24] The poet Edward Young makes sublimity the engine of moral and religious conversion, while John Baillie urges it as passion's royal path to virtue and "noble Pride."[25] In its openness to the sublime, James Ussher tells his "young Lady," the soul "assumes an unknown grandeur."[26] More influential than most, though, Joseph Addison published, during the summer of 1712, a series of essays in the *Spectator* collectively known as "The Pleasures of the Imagination."[27] Addison wanted to explain and form "good taste." The prose is seductively charming and addresses the reader as a fellow member of a thoughtful, sensitive, intellectually astute class. Addison found his audience among these new readers of journals and papers and in coffee houses, where fashions in life, art, and literature were bred and contested, where politics was thrashed out, the new science applauded, and gossip passed on.[28] A class was formed in these places, including England's gentry but extending well into the bourgeoisie—an educated, talkative class, a "public." Sublimity, along with its God and its humanity, penetrated the English imagination by way of Addison's energetic, culturally formative public.[29]

The "pleasures of the Imagination," Addison instructs his readers, are "novelty, beauty of form, and, most important, greatness."[30] Throughout, "greatness" retains the priority, and the "pleasing astonishment" that greatness produces identifies it with the sublime.[31] The paradigm context for greatness is standing on a hill, our eye chasing the distance, trying to take it all in—not just any largeness of view, though, but preeminently "Heaps of Mountains," a "wide Expanse of Waters," and, now combining with the novel and the beautiful, "a Heaven adorned with Stars and Meteors." Why does this exhilarate to such an incomparable degree? Addison answers that "our Imagination loves to be filled with an Object, or to grasp at anything that is too big for its Capacity."[32] In the midst of the astonishing, human beings find their proper environment. They realize how the mind hates confinement, and that freedom of movement and expansion toward far-off horizons realizes our calling. "Space: the final frontier. These are the voyages of the starship *Enterprise*. Its five-year mission: to explore strange new worlds, to seek out new life and new civilizations, to boldly go where no man has gone before."[33] Amazing sights, astonishing imaginations, wake up the mind, and humanity, feeling its mental wings, splits infinitives and soars. The mind now lives in its metier, attuned to the greatness of human capacities and calling.

Human beings are designed, Addison insists, so that they are happiest only as their vision roams freely, which is why "a spacious Horizon is an image of Liberty."[34] Experience of the sublime, the capacity for it, discloses the freedom that is essential to humanity. Edward Young, who had the ability to yell in blank verse and never wrote a line not aspiring to the momentous, makes the same point.

He invokes the sublime almost continuously for well over two thousand lines in the climactic book IX of his *Night Thoughts*. Stars, planets, deeps upon deeps, clustering suns, extraterrestrial civilizations, angels, and the day of judgment are all put to poetic hard labor to persuade the dissolute, free-thinking Lorenzo to leave the frat house and seek his God.[35] Contemplation of the night sky, Young argues, allows the soul to discover its natural compass, its place among immensities. In body, we may be "insects" lost in the vastness, but in mind we "stretch" and "rise," our imagination coming upon its power, our thought entering its destined environment. The night is "a lecture to mankind."[36] Our souls, "wither'd, shrunk, / Blighted by Earth's unwholesome air, / Will blossom here; spread all her faculties / To these bright ardours."[37]

Reason and imagination, then, love to expand, to enlarge themselves across distances of space and indwell a universe in which horizons of knowledge continually recede. Imagination, though it breaks down when representing the very vastness to which it is attracted, has, nevertheless, a special advantage over reason in that it engages pleasing emotions and, rather than hard work, its activity is delightful, even restful. Works of imagination, a painting or a poem, warm as well as enlighten. They "raise a secret ferment in the Mind" and produce "Terror and Pity," our most powerful, and socially valuable, emotions.[38] Since the danger is not actual, though, they do so just to the degree that they are pleasurable. Thinking about the infinite may demand cudgeling the brain, but the imagination gives the infinite in an intimation and fills the subject with a delightful awe and feeling of freedom. This is why greatness will always trump novelty and beauty for Addison; a flower is no match for a galaxy, with its felt promise of inexhaustible freedom.

Movement is the ready metaphor for this liberty. Motion, after all, had a central place in the new science that was already a matter of national pride and popularization among Addison's public. Freedom becomes the room to move, for intellectual and imaginative expansiveness. Essential humanity always demands somewhere else to go, at least in imagination. This need for movement and change provides Addison with his defense for fantasy writing, which simply offers mental travel in an endless supply of alternative worlds. Nature and fantasy, then, stimulate our wandering and feed us "without any certain Stint or Number."[39] Here, Addison's language reflects England's newly flourishing capitalist economy.[40] At liberty, surrounded by enlarged prospects "of Fields and Meadows," the viewer secures "a kind of Property in every thing he sees, and makes the most rude uncultivated Parts of nature administer to his Pleasures."[41] As this suggests, the sublime privileges sight, among the senses, as "the most perfect and delightful of all."[42] However, as imaginative delights are bound up with the fulfillment of the human vocation, according primacy to sight is freighted with implication. To claim seeing as our most spiritually formative relationship with the world introduces distance and separation into that relationship. Human beings, though, engage their environments more as participators than as spectators, immersed within "rather than peering . . . out at [the world] through the arches of [their] eye sockets."[43] For all the stress on passion among advocates of the sublime, the primacy of sight still characterizes human being as lookers-on who feel through what they see. Addison's story of his life as Mr. Spectator affirms that his station is outside crowded life, looking on, buffered from touch and the rough and tumble.[44] Perhaps most seriously, the priority given to sight by the sublime imports the idea of distance, even spatial distance, into the relationship between the soul and God.[45]

The deference accorded sight is, though, coordinate with that particular understanding of human freedom of which seeing is the principal sensory medium. Addison becomes eagerly consumerist in his enthusiasm for sublime spaciousness over stalling restriction. "The Beauties," he writes, "of the most stately Garden or Palace lie in a narrow Compass, the Imagination immediately runs them over, and requires something else to gratifie her." In the openness of nature, however, "the Sight wanders up and down without confinement, and is fed with an infinite variety of Images, without any certain Stint or Number."[46] This sublime imagination is ceaselessly acquisitive but acquires its objects in order to have them evaporate in a desire that passes beyond them. Addison anticipates the drive of a "consumer sublime" for which shopping malls "mimic a new-found nature of prodigious fecundity."[47] In terms of classical Christianity, this accelerating drive from one partial satisfaction to another sounds much like "concupiscence," the restless hunger for finite goods, the striving to subject everything to our desire.[48] This raises again the question as to the kind of freedom that has the sublime as its object and goal. If it is the devouring, horizonless freedom of capitalist consumption, then the problematic character of that freedom belongs also to any reality configured and represented in terms of the sublime, from a literary text, to a landscape, to God. In a distant future, the immortal humans of Alastair Reynolds' *Chasm City* reinvest in death so that length of days can maintain desire, the sublime movement of escalating experience. The city's wealthy pursue reckless endangerment and the vicarious thrills of murder broadcast to audiences on a rising scale of intensity. As one of them explains to Reynolds' protagonist, "To take another's life is a special kind of thrill, Mirabel. To do it while being immortal elevates the act to an entirely different level of sublimity."[49]

Though eighteenth-century theorists differed as to how much weight to place on the spiritually therapeutic aspect, all agreed that the sublime was, or allowing for perverse forms of it, should be good for you, as well as for morality, faith, and civilization. A red thread throughout its history, the correlation appears repeatedly between the magnificence of the sublime and the greatness of the human soul. The unusually grand claims made for science fiction, especially during its early decades, proceed from more than adolescent grandiosity or the overcompensations of a literary inferiority complex. Such assertions characterize also the credentials of sublimity and become inherent to science fiction insofar as this genre configured its subject matter, themes, ideologies, and narratives in terms of the sublime. Donald Wollheim thus describes the young science fiction reader of the 1930s: "We lived in an atmosphere of infinite horizons that could not be communicated to most of the grim and haunted world of the Depression around us."[50] Unlike "mainstream" literature, science fiction refuses the limits of a mundane, and generally melancholy, realism, and stakes its place in "the domains of time (especially the distant future) and space, the infinite possibilities out there, just at the moment when the last locations of awe and mystery have disappeared from our planet." It aims "to astound and illuminate," to inspire the lax and anxious heart into bracing energy, a commitment of which Addison and Burke, to name but two, would have heartily approved.[51] Its "mysteries stimulate the heart, the will, and the imagination toward something beyond day-to-day survival."[52]

Devotees are something of an elect, connoisseurs of this pleasurable distress, so "the humble truth is that science fiction is only for the small number of people who like to think and who regard the universe with awe, which is a blend of love and fear."[53] Wollheim agrees, "It is this harvest of wonders, this garden of marvels, this vision of what could be and what could have been, that makes science fiction so different and . . . its readers marked for life in out-of-the-rut trains of thought."[54] This readership is in the vanguard of history, differing "from most of the rest of the race by thinking in terms of racial magnitude—not even centuries but thousands of years."[55]

These are striking claims. Other popular genres are more vocationally prosaic. No one suggests that detective fiction fits its readers for their historical destiny. As part of the history of the sublime, though, these claims make sense. For Addison, a majestic image tunes its viewers to the highest contemplations and "strikes in with the Natural Greatness of the Soul." "Man *must* soar," Young shouts, and the sublime is his vehicle.[56] Ann Radcliffe's heroine, Emily St. Aubert, soaks up the sublime like a sponge. "Astonishing" Alpine scenery of "tremendous cliffs," "snowy points," and "perpendicular rocks of marble" lifts her into "another world" in which "every trifling thought, every trifling sentiment," is left below. "Those only of grandeur and sublimity now dilated her mind, and elevated the affections of her heart." Meanwhile, her dodgy companion, Madame Montoni, remains unmoved, save an occasional shudder, contemplating only the riches "she believed she was going to be mistress of."[57] The readiness for sublimity marks sheep from goats. From the Alps to Andromeda, blessed are they who have eyes to see the sublime.

Though greatness beckons as the natural habitat of the human soul, the mind only discovers this by way of a wrench in which imagination is flummoxed by vastness. An art is necessary to this experience: "Nothing," Addison advises, "is more pleasant to the Fancy than to enlarge itself, by Degrees."[58] The imagination has a precarious purchase on the immense per se, but, if writers proceed in steps, by means of comparison, from one greatness to another, they shall achieve sublime effects, and their readers experience the pleasurable tottering of the fancy. A passage in Larry Niven's *Ringworld* provides a skillfully managed example from science fiction:

> The black oblong continued to swell.
>
> It was the size that made it seem to approach so slowly. The shadow square was as broad as the sun, nearly a million miles across, and much longer: two-and-a-half million miles long. Almost suddenly, it became tremendous. Its edge slid across the sun, and there was darkness.
>
> The shadow square covered half the universe. It borders were indefinite, black-on-black, terrible to see.[59]

Quantitative size, itself suggesting expansion since the smaller dimension is given first, is framed between two references to the sun that intimate the vastness comparatively. Further heightening occurs by way of the movement from the whole object compared with the visible sun to the "edge" of the square sliding over and eclipsing the sun altogether. The smooth, threatening inexorability is suggested alliteratively by the progression "swell," "slowly," and "slid." The already heightened sense of overwhelming size is then pushed into hyperbole and beyond the imaginable with "covered half the universe." The description concludes with the classic sublime reference to terror and the equally familiar use of what Edmund Burke termed "judicious obscurity."[60] "Its borders were indefinite, black-on-black." "Obscurity," as James Ussher also reminded his eighteenth-century readers, makes us "sensible of invisible power."[61] The mind tips into a depth behind and greater than the vastness given. As an "invincible force," the sublime "commits a pleasing Rape upon the very Soul of the Reader."[62] Or, positively operatic, if less shocking to contemporary sensibilities, "my heart, at once, it humbles and exalts; Lays it in the dust, and calls it to the skies."[63] As Young's lines imply, unlike the simple givenness of a sharp pain, the sublime has an "event structure," composed of conflict and, then, of recovery at a higher level.[64] The imagination is "stunned" or checked, as a means to its greater enjoyment. In this respect, Young claims, the night sky has no peer in the provocation of sublime emotion. Infinite space, opened up by the setting sun, beggars all the artifice of thought; we are brought down, "struck" with a "pleasing stupor," then raised into the midnight plains that only God encompasses. The check becomes a breakthrough, and "how glorious then appears the mind of Man . . .

great objects make / Great minds enlarging as their views enlarge; / Those still more godlike, as these more Divine."[65]

When, however, the sublimities of space defeat the imagination, Young does not turn to praise "understanding," as does Addison, or have imagination make way for reason as, later, will Immanuel Kant.[66] While thought is "wilder'd," stumped imagination collects itself and "reprunes her wing to soar anew, / Her point unable to forbear or gain. / So great the pleasure, so profound the plan."[67] The imagination has an insatiable lust for seeing, a passion for the endless consumption that is looking. "O let me gaze!—Of gazing there's no end. . . . An eye of awe and wonder let me roll, / And roll for ever; who can satiate sight?"[68] Young revels in evoking boundlessness, the eye that transgresses limits, the suns behind suns without end, the breaking of all measures available to the human mind. Insisting that a "vast" idea "overwhelms with astonishment" is commonplace. Young, though, found, precisely in what "confounds" and "astonishes," a higher truth on the other side of reason. As applied to God, of course, this is conventional; what lends a demonism, an unrestricted trangressiveness, to Young's sublime is that this voracious astonishment is the mind's end in relation to created reality as well.[69]

In a theological culture that privileged argument from the world's design, the vital question is, "What is the sublime *for*?" Enjoyment, certainly, but of the kind that gets behind the soul and gives it a good shove. The novel and the beautiful serve human ends, Addison argues, as stimuli to science and sex respectively. They also testify to the care and skill of the Creator. "Greatness," however, trains us for worship itself, for finding in God humanity's "last, adequate, and proper happiness." Admiration enlivens us; we thrill at anything "that takes up a great deal of room in the Fancy," and so, when we contemplate God, our admiration rises to "the highest pitch," and, therefore, to that highest pleasure: "Astonishment and Devotion."[70] God has, therefore, designed us to achieve the happiness proper to our species, which is nothing less than knowledge of himself and his ways. All the "pleasures of the imagination" are "conducive to Health," but the sublime is the mechanism of our spiritual end, leading us along the grain of our making to the worship of God, in easy stages of terrific delight.[71] The "event structure" of sublimity, though, as it displaces in order to re-place the mind in elevation, ensures that the worshiper knows herself as a fit correspondent to the worshiped. As Baillie enthuses, the sublime "raises the Mind to fits of greatness, and disposes it to soar above her Mother earth . . . and gives [the Mind] a lofty conception of her own Powers."[72] In the sublime, the greatness of God and of humanity are correlate, the elevation of the latter unmediated by the divine kenosis and condescension that forms Christianity's narrative.

The theological awkwardness of a sublimed Christianity is particularly clear in James Ussher's *Clio*, a work designed to fit the sublime within a stern defense of original sin and humanity's need of redemption. God is present, Ussher argues, in our innate capacity for the sublime.[73] Sublimity, then, need not wait upon mountains, cliffs, and starry reaches, though they may help. In quietness, removed from life's distracting bustle, the soul left "to its naked state and feelings," the inner sense or "intuition" of sublimity can awaken into consciousness. The immediate effect, though, is terror at an experience of "invisible immense power." Only in a contemplation that resists scuttling back to activity does this terror issue in "admiration and ecstasy" over the "awful and obscure presence," the uncontainable power that surrounds and upholds the soul.[74] No object or image is adequate to this. The mind channels the voltage of omnipotence through finite wires: the resulting shock is the sublime. Yet, the issue elevates: disappointment and distress break out as the mind fails, then ecstasy in the intuition of a glory beyond the failure, and renewal as "we set out immediately with renewed vigour in pursuit of something farther, and nothing but death puts an end to the anxiety."[75] Human beings—Ussher teaches, circling round to his doctrinal agenda—bear the sublime within them, a sensibility always waiting its breakthrough into consciousness. Sin, however, suppresses its persistent call, while Christianity enables its hearing and restores it to strength. How this is achieved, though, and how exactly Christ's redemption and atonement fit in, is left tellingly unclear and the tacking of sublimity to Christian creed very loose. Even Ussher's interest in preserving original sin buckles before the irrepressible *humanism*, the delight in human powers for which the sublime gives occasion. Thus, the soul "assumes an unknown grandeur," as it passes from "this diminutive world, into a kind of gigantic creation."[76]

Addison's theological intentions are as strong as Ussher's, if less explicit about Christian doctrine.[77] The last two essays of his series end on a distinctly theological note, though studies of the sublime have ignored this telling detail. In the penultimate article, Addison admits how quickly our imagination is stumped by the attempt to form clear ideas of the very big or very small. One may understand what is meant by a million mice but barely imagine a crowd of fifty. Conventionally, a pious recognition of the ultimate superiority of reason might well have followed this. Addison, though, has accorded the imagination, together with capacity for the sublime, such an importance for our human destiny that he chooses rather to speculate a further empowerment of imagination, not its ultimate capitulation to reason. He wonders if, when freed from our bodies, the soul will enjoy an "infinitely more perfect" imagination that "will be able to keep Pace with the Understanding."[78] Is this, though, consumption made eschatological? Given the absence, too, of any mention of bodily resurrection, this consuming desire seems to strain its way beyond the bodily altogether in the direction, perhaps, of the disincarnate poet, Noetic Concordance, from the universe of mental superiorities celebrated in Julian May's *Jack the Bodiless*.[79] Addison's final essay, however, ends by drawing a surprisingly somber consequence from this speculation. A disordered imagination racks the sufferer with most desperate agonies, and no one is more pitiable that the lunatic oppressed by terrors. Think, therefore, he concludes, how the imagination puts us at the mercy of God who can so impress our imaginations as to "exquisitely ravish or torture them," and thus "make up the whole Heaven or Hell of any finite Being."[80] A sobering point—however, it is a less surprising one if the essays are read not just as an exercise in aesthetic psychology but as informed by theological purpose throughout. The sovereignty of God holds sway over the soul and over nature, and the sublime is its most characteristic disclosure.

## FROM NATURE TO NEW MEXICO

Science fiction's famous "sense of wonder" has one root in the "natural" sublime of the eighteenth century, both in the evocation of awe and astonishment over nature's magnitudes and power, and in the delights of sinister forces and dungeon mazes fostered by Gothic novels. The "natural" sublime alone, though, doth not a science-fictional "sense of wonder" make. The second main historical mediator of the science fiction sublime is the subliming of the machine in the nineteenth century, the "technological sublime."[81] Technological enthusiasts and advocates, particularly in the United States, cast machines in sublime imaginings; celebrants of industrial wealth made the sublime a medium of conspicuous architecture; public buildings roared the sublime achievements of urban, technological accomplishment; office blocks and electric displays soared in a fresh gospel of work, power, and plenty, while sublime prisons and police stations preached a new dread. By the early twentieth century, the "democratic" history of the sublime was finding new outlets in technological utopias, magazine reprints of Edgar Allan Poe's proto–science fiction tales, the Martian stories of Edgar Rice Burroughs, Gernsback's scientifiction, and the scientific romances of H. G. Wells.[82] From the beginnings of science fiction, the genre not only inherited the technological sublime, but it also began a symbiotic relationship with the continued subliming of the technological and industrial and, more recently, information technology, informing the cultural imagination with the dreams and terrors of electricity and nuclear weaponry, of medical transformations and nanotechnology, of computers and posthumanity, of moon landings and the galactic frontier.

Nineteenth-century Americans enjoyed a diverse sublime, from Emerson's "bathed by the blithe air and uplifted into infinite space," through Whitman's ecstatic lists and Poe's malevolent ice floes, maelstroms, and pits, to the sense that they were, as the American nation with its history of revolution and expansion, not a little sublime themselves.[83] Certainly, American nature appeared definitively sublime, a prodigious vastness suitable to a people called to a climactic role in the Lord's work. American painters fastened not just on the drama of gorge, mountain, and cataract, though, but more especially on the solitude, the solemn quiet that Ussher and Burke had stressed.[84] The painter Thomas Cole so described a view in New Hampshire: "There are two lakes . . . they have such an aspect of deep seclusion, of utter and unbroken solitude . . . that I was overwhelmed with an emotion of the sublime, such as I have rarely felt."[85] In this context, technological progress was readily identified with a specifically American vocation and national glory. Also—in contrast to Britain, where a technological and industrial sublime also flourished—American rhetoric and art represented technology as attuned to the gifts of the land's natural abundance, and technology was in continuity with nature, a means of releasing its fullness.[86] Manufacturing, therefore, is a joyous response to the "great advantages" of soil, climate, rivers, and seas "for which we are indebted to a beneficent creator."[87] Under such circumstances, Tench Coxe urged, mechanization is a duty without which "certain great natural powers of the country" would have been "given by Providence in vain."[88] In Thomas Cole's *Expulsion from the Garden of Eden*, a tiny Adam and Eve make their shaking way across a vertiginous bridge between two sublimities. A wild, Gothic wilderness awaits them, with wolves, evil crevasses, and blighted woods, while the light behind remains above an idyllic, pastoral Eden.[89] America, however, offered that sublime wilderness as possibility, a land recovered on a path back to Eden, with the machine as means of reversing the fall. An article in the *Scientific American* for August 1847 makes the link: "There appears to be something in the pursuit of mechanical invention, which has a reaching up after our divine title, 'lords of the creation.' . . . It is truly a sublime sight to behold a machine performing nearly all the functions of a rational being."[90]

Along with the sublime, of course, comes the theological weighting. In 1831, Timothy Walker leveled a furious critique at Thomas Carlyle's "Signs of the Times." The sublime's hyperbolic language enters the lists against the Scot's warnings about the "Age of Machinery."[91] "Mind has become the powerful lord of matter," Walker enthuses, "having put myriads of wheels in motion by laws of its own discovering, it rests, like the Omnipotent Mind, of which it is the image, from its work of creation, and pronounces it good."[92] The sublime takes us beyond grateful receipt of providential bounty, to a divinity in our sphere, an independent, if junior, Almighty. Just under a hundred years later, Charles Sheeler depicted the Hoover Dam dominating the natural landscape as its religious completion. "The modern artist," insisted the accompanying commentary, "depicting such a scientist's handiwork, should put a devout intensity into painting. This is as truly a religious work of art as any altarpiece, or stained-glass window, or vaulted choir."[93] Just who or what is being worshiped, though, is alarmingly unclear. A similar conjunction occurs across the Atlantic with the close similarities of the sublime style adopted for churches along with railway stations, jails, warehouses, and office blocks. This "cyclopean" architecture later made its way onto the covers of science fiction pulp magazines and paperbacks, as well as around Cthulhu's dark resting place in Lovecraft's "nightmare corpse-city of R'lyeh."[94]

Uncoupled from visions of an agricultural Arcadia, the technological sublime migrated into the urban imagination as America's cities expanded during the late nineteenth and twentieth centuries. "Science" was "tearing off the crust of the earth and releasing the powers and riches of nature." The chaos was tamed by "three mighty gods . . . Steam, Electricity, Steel."[95] Skyscrapers are "monsters of steel and stone" from whose shoulders we get god's-eye views of cabs as "beetles" and human "ants."[96] The Empire State Building, which opened to visitors on May 1, 1931, was found sublime not just for its vastness but for the stance it empowered its visitors to take. Viewed from the observation deck, "Bryant Park is a pancake, and the Statue of Liberty something to throw at a cat." The skyscraper provided "a spectacular perch from which to contemplate the manufactured world as a total environment, as though one were above or outside it. . . . The panoramic vision permits one not merely to view the city as a series of individual parts, but to read it as a total structure."[97] The view from this top provides the democratized analogue to the cognition of Hegel's absolute philosopher. The electric cityscape at night also astounded and mesmerized. "Buildings piled up in a dazzling mass against the indigo sky," wrote Lewis Mumford, "here was my city, immense, overpowering, flooded with energy and light."[98] H. G. Wells was similarly pulled into the sublimity of electrical power: "New York is lavish of light, it is lavish of everything, it is full of the sense of spending from an inexhaustible supply. For a time, one is drawn irresistibly into the universal belief in that inexhaustible supply."[99] As Joseph Stella discovered, contemplating the Brooklyn Bridge, technology breeds gods: "I felt . . . as if on the threshold of a new religion or in the presence of a new DIVINITY."[100] Hart Crane, blending populist and modernist traditions, made of this same bridge a sublime both universal and national. Now God himself receives bounty from the creations of human power. The reversal of humanity and divinity within the event structure of the sublime is complete: "Again the traffic lights that skim thy swift / Unfractioned idiom, immaculate sigh of stars, / Beading thy path—condense eternity: And we have seen night lifted in thine arms / . . . Unto us lowliest sometime sweep, descend / And of the curveship lend a myth to God."[101]

Technology poses sublimity with the problem of familiarity. From the beginning, for instance, railway enthusiasm imagined the "fire-Titans" as a new sublimity. The steam locomotive, "to the free skies unpent," "annihilated time and space" and was a "miracle of science, art, and capital," nothing short of a "magic power."[102] As a sublime artifact, therefore, the locomotive offered a gift of freedom, the promise of limits confounded, and the presence of overwhelming power. One of the many railway advocates described the locomotive of the 1840s as "a Titanic colossus of iron and of brass, instinct with elemental life and power, with a glowing furnace for his lungs, and streams of fire and smoke for the breath of his nostrils."[103] Almost two centuries later, the dragon metaphor appears plausible, if mildly amusing. Imagining an early nineteenth-century train, however, as "annihilating space and time," induces only a winsome nostalgia. Technology is an odd candidate for sublimity when set beside Niagara Falls, which Americans acclaimed "the proto-type of God" or, with slightly less peculiar theology, a watery sermon on the "God of Power."[104] If Niagara is found sublime today, it has a chance of being so for as long as the sublime persists in the cultural imagination. Machines, though, date fast, and today's wonder is tomorrow's curiosity. An instance of technological sublimity, therefore, risks rapidly diminishing effects over time and, eventually, the consequent exhaustion of the entire idea of sublime machines. However, the sublime, as Baillie enthused, "raises the Mind to fits of greatness, and disposes it to soar above her Mother earth . . . and gives [the Mind] a lofty conception of her own Powers."[105] The staying power of technology as sublime has less to do with the particular object than with an encompassing intimation of the limitless trajectory of human power and ingenuity. Machines suffer obsolescence, but the cultural imagination construes them as tokens of an endless promise of productivity and progress. The preacher of a sermon for the opening of the Cleveland and Columbus railroad in 1851 understood this well: "There is sublimity about it, indicating not only the march of mind and a higher type of society, but the evolution of divine purposes, infinite, eternal."[106] The imagination exceeds the object it invests with sublimity, and intuits an "uncontainable" power of which the object is an inadequate exponent. In the case of technology, though, the movement toward transcending power is a "horizontal" one, toward the future of human capacities or, as frequently in dystopian science fiction, of technology itself as a self-reproducing, accelerating power that in its totality consumes the human. Transcendence is immanentized, the uncontainable force of the divine projected into history. That shift toward a this-worldly future is not incompatible with a continuing assertion of God. The preacher for the Cleveland and Columbus railroad went on to connect the "great thoroughfare" of progress with the advance of Christianity and the coming reign of Christ. Nevertheless, the rhetoric funded a dubious identification of divine with human purpose and specifically national progress. The technological sublime provided an imaginative structure whereby God might either become a genially superannuated bystander or be replaced with a purely humanistic sublime. Bearing in mind the eighteenth century's insistence on the primacy of God's work in Nature over human art, Henry Clay's paean to Robert Fulton's steamboat is striking: "Nature herself seems to survey, with astonishment, the passing wonder, and in silent submission, reluctantly to own the magnificent triumph, in her own vast domain, of Fulton's immortal genius."[107]

The technological sublime, however, not only serves a humanist triumphalism. Sublimities of power evoke anxiety as well as exhilaration. Generators and power stations were imagined as sublime in terms of their taut control over vast forces. "Power! Power! Power! That is the source of the romance of the River Rouge plant."[108] In the case of electric power plants that came into operation after 1910, observers found sublimity in their stark cleanliness and the apparently effortless order within which they channeled and managed immensities of force. Like "conquered and resigned leviathans," the machines worked in a hall "immaculately clean, inconceivably tidy, shimmering with brilliant light . . . shaking and roaring with the terrific thunder of its own vitality [and] produced nevertheless an effect of magical stillness, silence, and solitude . . . enchanted and inexplicable."[109] Turn the screw, though, of this sublimity of control, just a notch or two, and the same power of repression may provoke anxieties about too much success. Edward Bellamy imagines a collectivist society in which scientific management is exact, everybody is organized on a military basis, machines meet all physical needs, and leisure is provided on an unprecedented scale. Bellamy rejoices in this but others saw a manipulative soulless horror under the shining surfaces. Though the most famous riposte to Bellamy was by English socialist William Morris in *News from Nowhere*, he had many American counterparts.[110] Beyond electric plants and the "immaculately clean" powerhouse of Henry Ford's Highland Park factory, other representations of the technological sublime are more edgy and alarmed, more perturbed about the powers controlled or, perhaps, not quite so controlled.[111] The imagination shuttles between the physical forces released and the daring reach of human beings and, failing to contain the contrast within a confident exhilaration, trembles between terror and awe. The unrivalled twentieth-century icon of this is the atomic bomb. In a top-secret memorandum, General Leslie Groves described the first test on July 16, 1945. He breaks out of his bureaucratic genre in a definitive list of sublime adjectives: "unprecedented," "magnificent," "stupendous," "tremendous," and "terrifying." This sublime hyperbole accelerates in "the strong, sustained, awesome roar which warned of doomsday" and in the evocation of terror, as the explosion is said to have "made us feel we puny things were blasphemous to dare tamper with the forces."[112] This imagination of terror in powers beyond humanity but realized by humanity goes back to Mary Shelley's *Frankenstein* and is a major source of dystopias predicated on the technological sublime. The end of Groves' sentence, though, contains a qualification that betrays the persisting humanist exhilaration, even with reference to the bomb. These destructive and "tremendous" forces are those "*heretofore* reserved to the Almighty."[113] Once God's, now humanity's, this bomb, like Walker's "myriads of wheels," has bounded the Omnipotent—and a God so displaced is thus imagined as a being alongside his human counterpart, greater, perhaps, but a finitude nonetheless, for whom "Almighty" is just an honorific title.

## . . . AND THAT MOST SUBLIME OBJECT OF THEOLOGY?

For much of the eighteenth century, natural science, which meant Newtonian science, was intimate with both theology and the sublime. Addison was not being controversial when he urged his readers to take their imaginative pleasures most especially from that "new philosophy," of which Sir Isaac, himself a subscriber to the *Spectator*, was rapidly becoming an icon. For anyone anxious about the spread of atheism, Newtonianism was welcomed as an apologetic gift—more exactly, a cornucopia of gifts since Newtonian order, which explained so much, required at so many points the assertion of an initial establishment "by the Counsel and Contrivance of a voluntary Agent."[114] Whether it was the distinction between luminary and opaque bodies, the relationship between sun and planets in our solar system, or the fact that planets orbit rather than bop around like comets, all these astronomical phenomena argued for an intelligent cause "very well skilled in Mechanicks and Geometry"—a cosmic superengineer and, no doubt, honorary member of the Royal Society.[115] Certainly, it was a triumph to have the apologetic task seemingly done and dusted to the permanent confutation of atheism. The promise, too, that this new rage for order might work a similar clarity in morality, psychology, politics, and religion was exhilarating. Both John Locke and the authors of the American Constitution took that promise to heart. However, the Deity of "Mechanicks and Geometry"—who grounds the eternal order and disposition of the cosmic machine, working his will in and through mechanical processes—is an odd candidate for identification with the God of Israel and the Church, whose creation is not a machine but a history he governs and fulfills and within which he acts and reveals himself. The identification was plausible not just because Christian preaching, worship, and practice went on complacently accepting the apologetic benefits without drawing the less happy implications, but because the Newtonian world and its God was rendered and recognized as the sublime object of our imagination and desire.

Science and theology collaborated against atheism, but they were married in the sublime. Sublimity brought the God who was "clear to the intellect but unrelated to sense and imagination" into the nearness of feeling. When Addison exhorts his readers to scientific knowledge, he argues that while all science delights the imagination, it is astronomy, Newton's privileged sphere, that delights most of all because it most elevates humanity to greatness, to the unbounded, revealing the true range of the mind's freedom. Addison inducts the reader into scientific reflection by way of an ascent into the "physico-theological" sublime. This pattern of ascent is theologically and not just rhetorically motivated: it appropriates for the path of scientific knowing the "way of ascent," which takes so many forms in Christian mysticism.[116] Treatises on "Metals, Minerals, Plants and Meteors" surely excite the imagination as well as the reason, but exhilaration, the movement into the sublime, properly begins only when "we survey the whole Earth at once," together with her fellow planets. This fills the student with a "pleasing astonishment," but, as she rises further, to "contemplate those wide Fields of *Ether*, that reach in height as far as *Saturn* . . . and run abroad almost to an infinitude," then her imagination is put "upon the Stretch" to comprehend and its "Capacity filled." The astronomical enthusiasts may rise yet higher, though, to bring those far stars into the imagination as themselves bearing planets, and then to peer over their shoulders to "new Firmaments and new Lights." Now, she is beyond the telescope, "lost in . . . a Labaryinth [*sic*] of Suns and Worlds" and "confounded with the Immensity and Magnificence of Nature."[117] Contemplation of the universe ends by stupefying the imagination and, bursting its capacity, brings the soul into that sublimity Addison has previously reserved for divine meditations. Space is thus theologized, and infinite space blurs into the infinity of God.

Addison managed this theological elevation of space in the impeccable company of Isaac Newton, albeit he travelled by way of exuberance, not mathematics. Newton is more theologically self-conscious and cautious, but he still renders space as an ambiguous reality, neither clearly one side nor the other of the radical distinction between Creator and creation. Space is "an emanative effect of God," a necessary condition of existence for any being, as well as the condition for God's own omnipresence and sovereignty.[118] As an "emanative effect," it is not the object of God's will but rather the sphere of action God's will needs when creating planets, people, and hamsters. Space is infinite, but that does not make it divine, Newton insists, since only infinite *perfections* are divine and space is a condition, not a perfection.[119] Nevertheless, its creaturely status remains unclear since, unlike in the classical Christian account, God depends on this "emanated," but not "created," space for his relationship with creatures.[120] Moreover, God was never without space: "If ever space had not been, God at that time would have been nowhere."[121] Thus, although Newton denies that space is itself divine, God is still necessarily "somewhere"; his infinity and eternity is such as to place him in relation to the cosmos he encompasses. He is infinitely containing and enduring, not, as for classical Christianity, timeless and transcending quantifiable spatiality.[122] Since, Newton argues, it would compromise God's omnipotence for God to have the means of ubiquity without employing it, God's creations are also infinite and eternal in number and succession. By contrast, the classical doctrine of the Trinity—which Newton rejected, though not publicly—understands God as eternally and perfectly related within God's own life.[123] God does not need creation, therefore, in order to love or exercise his perfections; Newton's God, however, would be imperfect without creatures.

Space may be eternal and infinite, but that does not make it God, Newton insists. However, "God by reason of the eternity and infinity of his space . . . will be rendered the most perfect being."[124] God does not divinize space, but space divinizes God, which renders the distinction between Creator and creation, since space exists as the condition for creatures, relative rather than absolute. Of a piece with this, creatures share in divine perfections not only by virtue of having reason and will but also in being spatial and temporal. The logic of sublimity corresponds to this; as the mind encompasses more and vaster realities, extending the spatiotemporal range of its attention, the mind is more closely conformed to deity. Newtonianism, then, provided an intellectual context in which the imagination found inspiration for deriving a divine awe from the immensities of space itself. [125] Such a sublime and divinized space persisted in the cultural imagination and still issues in science fiction. In its deeps, space is the "Nothing-at-All" where, in a "flash as of sheet lightening," certain travellers feel they are "befriended, looked at." "*We felt that we had been made the toys or the pets of some gigantic form of life immensely beyond the limits of human imagination.*"[126] The persistence, however, of a special relationship between divinity and space had unhappy consequences for Christian theology.

In 1751 Christopher Smart won a Cambridge University prize for his poem "On the Immensity of the Supreme Being."[127] Describing God as immense may seem odd, as if one might hear an English gentleman say, "Yes, I know St. Paul's Cathedral is pretty big, but then you should see God." "Immense," however, had long served as a familiar synonym for "omnipresence." "Immensity" meant God was boundless or immeasurable—nothing to get worried over except in an age that, having discovered sublimity in the boundlessness and infinity of space, was tempted into running imaginative connections between this infinity and God's. If the sublime, as Baillie argues, has a special affinity with vastness, then the language of physical, spatial immensity offers itself as specially appropriate for praising the sovereignty and power of God. Baillie admits there are decidedly ungodly instances of the sublime; however, he follows the general line in assuring us that God is the true and ultimate sublime. Knowledge of God and the sublime finally converge; we know the sublime "as we do the Deity . . . it fills and dilates our Soul without [our] being able to penetrate into its Nature, and define its Essence." When it comes to omnipotence, therefore, we find Baillie expounding it in terms of spatial range. What distinguishes God's power and makes it sublime is its scope or extent. The slave master may have absolute power, but a prince's lordship is more sublime because of its range, "his *Sway* extending to *Multitudes*, and from *Nations* bowing to his *Commands*."[128] By extension, God's power is over everything, hence truly sublime and, ipso facto, truly divine. Omnipotence has become human power with the limits removed, losing the radical difference between the power that gives being and all powers within the created order exercised upon existing beings.

Though Edward Young saves the theological appearances by reminding that space is not a "meet apartment for the DEITY," who is not contained by it, he nonetheless insists that theological importance lies in the vastness of space, as opposed to the detail of small realities. In a passage that seems entirely innocent of a knowledge of the New Testament, this Anglican clergyman ventures: "an undevout astronomer is mad. / True, all things speak a GOD; / but, in the small, Men trace out Him; / in great, He seizes man; / Seizes, and elevates, and wraps, / and fills with new inquiries, / 'mid associates new."[129] As with Baillie, the more enthusiastic the evocation of the sublime, the more God, as that sublimest of realities, becomes a means by which human beings experience their *own* capacities. The soul "assumes an unknown grandeur."[130] The mind's "fits of greatness," our "disdain of limit," now determine the theological imagination as God is one-sidedly invoked in connection with the physical vastness of the Newtonian heavens. Our capacity for sublimity, according to Baillie, is essential to our having an idea of God's infinity and the infinity of his perfections. The argument follows the one concerning omnipotence to the same relativizing end. "Where an Object is vast, and at the same Time uniform, there is to the Imagination no Limits to its Vastness, and the Mind runs out into Infinity, continually creating as it were from the Pattern." Since we are working figuratively, the results are less clear, but we do much the same with God's wisdom and goodness. We raise them to the infinite power by imaginatively removing their limits.[131] The sublime, then, as Addison and Ussher also argue in their different ways, leads us by degrees into the idea of God. If Baillie is right, though, human beings have the capacity to generate the perfections of the deity out of their own imaginations, a point not lost on Feuerbach, Marx, and Freud during the following century.

No matter upon what qualifications theologians insist, if public religious language sustains an imagining of God as a reality *within* the entire realm of beings or in continuity with that realm, then the crucial difference between Creator and creature is lost. God may be a unique reality, creator, the most powerful, Lord among them all from galaxies to gerbils, but he is rendered nonetheless *a* reality, a supreme being among other beings. Newton had already reduced God to "the absolute and inertial frame of his mechanics."[132] Missing the *essential* difference, God's being becomes an unlimited version of finite being, rather than the ineffable and transcendent source of creaturely being. Terms like "wisdom," "power," and "goodness" are used "univocally," as if they meant the same thing applied to God as when used of creatures. Yes, of course, there was a difference, but it was one of degree; God's power is unimaginably superior to any finite agent, but it is still on a scale that begins here and ends in heaven. Alternatively, a certain implosion can occur as the attributes of God are scaled up into the unimaginable. Sublimity is then generated around a negative image, a void constituted by the simple negation of finitude, the univocal turning into the equivocal. Burke's treatment of the sublime approaches this in his discussion of power. Unrestricted power, Burke argues, most characterizes our imagination of God and is thus most sublime. If we allow the imagination to be properly affected by divine power, "we shrink into the minuteness of our own nature . . . in a manner annihilated before him." God in the raw, so to speak, is not love or mercy but negating force. This idea, which still renders God as a reality *within* the realm of being, arises by "tracing power along its several gradations unto the highest all, where our imagination is finally lost."[133]

As Young discovered to his apologetic delight, appeal to the sublime possessed advantages shared also by Newtonian mechanics. Sublimity pointed out a knowledge of God through experiences free of the particularities of religious controversy. The mechanics of sublimity might remain opaque, and certainly God, as the ultimately sublime, was beyond comprehension, but nevertheless the sublime had a clear place on the rational map, which pinpointed its "final cause," the purposes that this capacity was designed to serve. The sublime did spiritual work. An experience of the sublime carried its own certainty; similar to sense experience, it was self-authenticating. On the other hand, sensitivity to the sublime could also be cultivated, and the sublimity of ideas and objects publicly evaluated and discussed. Unlike claims to special guidance by the Holy Spirit, pretensions roundly condemned by the educated public as "enthusiasm," sublime experience was potentially available to anyone, or, at least, to anyone who was anyone. Young and Ussher both seized on the sublime as the respectable person's enthusiasm. Sublimity is the true enthusiasm, an ecstasy compatible with reason and discernment, unlike the wildness of "fanatic preachers."[134] Both hail sublimity as grounding religious confidence, a certainty of God. They give it a role, therefore, similar to Wesley's "inner witness of the Spirit," though without Wesley's Trinitarian and christological reference.[135] The sublime intersected with the new science and its mechanical order in a mutual exchange of cultural authority. Newtonianism unveiled a universe perfect for creatures designed to experience sublimity; in its turn, the sublime gave the science the authority of its passion and its configuration of the human calling.

Addison, Young, Baillie, and Ussher suggest that human beings may find their vocation as the image of God in the disturbance, recovery, and exaltation of sublime experience. The relationship, though, to the traditional form of Christian vocation, the pursuit of an imitation of Christ, is notably unclear. The account of God to which the sublime is indebted makes this still stranger: "In [God] all things are contained and moved but," Newton claims, "he does not act on them, nor they on him."[136] True enough, in terms of mechanics, but still this does not sit well with the God who sends his Son, who is made flesh, and imparts his Spirit or grieves over his people and their misery. The advocates of sublime formation, therefore, invite the question: If visions of "greatness" are primary in forming human beings to the worship of God, then what role has "Christ and him crucified"? Inspiring gratitude, no doubt, or "humanizing" the deity for us, as Burke proposed. What, however, of that paradoxical but vital identification of the shabbiness of the cross with the worshipful glory of God? The Bible itself, too, fell among the advocates of sublimity: if sublimity resides at the pinnacle of literary effort, then the Bible must have been properly kitted out with sublime qualifications. Showing this, though, fixed attention largely on the Old Testament and, in particular, passages dealing with creation and with God's judgment, generally expressed in metaphors of natural catastrophe.[137] Jesus, on the other hand, posed a problem. Just why was his teaching so dismayingly lacking in sublime boost? John Dennis' reply is a little desperate, at least if one is concerned for Christ's human integrity. "Our Saviour," he explains, did not go in for the "figurative and enthusiastic" because he was God, "and as God He could not feel either Admiration or Terrour, or the rest of the Enthusiastick Passions."[138] In the case of Edward Young, sublimity threatens to rival the salvific role of Jesus. Having done his best to render the Last Judgment with sublime dash and fury, he adds that what was once the means of salvation is now the source of terror. Interestingly, though, he is not referring to Jesus but to sublimity, the "same astonishment" that will seize us all on the dread day. So let it seize us today, since "what then must pain us, would preserve us now." The night sky is "Scripture authentic! Uncorrupt by man," and sublimity is its interpreter by which "the stars will light thee" and "set thee right."[139]

To be thus set right is to come to oneself in realizing that the human mind is made for sublimity. For all enthusiasts of the sublime enthused over the glories of God, the ultimate sublime object, they certainly also celebrated humanity by way of God's sublimity. Baillie sets out the logic. Cramped apartments overlooking a brick wall come cheap. This, Baillie would tell us, is because we measure our worth according to the objects we contemplate. The larger the expanse of our view, the more objects, or the bigger the objects, that are present to our minds, the "higher Conceptions" we have of our "own Excellency." "How much greater an existence must the Soul imagine herself" in viewing the heavens? Since a "*Universal Presence* is one of the sublime *Attributes* of the *Deity*," God always seeing everything, then the greater the expanse open to our minds, the nearer we approach "the *Perfections* of the *Universal Presence*."[140] The sublime telescopes divinity and humanity as human powers are celebrated, and God's knowledge and omnipresence reduces to that of an infinitely capacious version of the human mind. A sublime God, as the human mind's most remarkable contemplation, witnessed to a sublime humanity. Over the next hundred years, the sublime imagination turned increasingly away from such explicitly theological confessions. The humanism, however, remained, celebrating the exhilaration of mind and imagination as they stretch in the desire that burst boundaries and violated limits: the humanity of glorious restlessness and unquiet.

In an episode of the long-running BBC series *Doctor Who*, the Doctor has arrived with a small group of scientists researching a planet orbiting a black hole.[141] An evil power is loose in the settlement, frightening, killing, and making mayhem. In a pit, miles below the surface, the Doctor finds a huge creature that is the image of Satan himself. What, everyone asks, is going on? More particularly, other than the need not to be massacred, what does this mean? Is it really the devil, and, if so, might that imply—a thought almost beyond horrible—that religion might be right after all? In the end, the question is not answered but simply rejected. Rather than solve the mystery as it presents itself, a more important mystery arises, that of human questing itself, of the human way of discovery. This questing is offered as sublime, an endless process, plunging through and rising above darkness toward more and more wonders. Several times, the Doctor comments on insatiable curiosity as defining humanity. Standing on the edge of Satan's pit, his companion suggests diving in, and he observes, "That is so human, where angels fear to tread, even now, standing on the edge. It's that feeling you get, eh? At the back of your head, that impulse . . . that voice, go on, go on, go over, go on." Movement into danger, wonder, into the mysterious, daunting, and unexplained, into sublimity, therefore, is proper to human nature. The sublime beckons humanity as its natural element. Yet, the object of this movement is no longer religion, as it was for Addison, but "science," knowing on the "the plane of immanence."[142] This is now the goal and means to obey Young's exhortation: "to stretch to that expanse / Of thought, to rise to that exalted height / Of admiration, to contract that awe, / And give her whole capacities that strength, / Which best may qualify for final joy." Fearing a panic into myth and religion, the Doctor urges, "I'll tell you what I can see. Humans, brilliant humans, who travel all the way across space flying in a tiny little rocket into the orbit of a black hole, just for the sake of discovery. That's amazing, do you hear me, amazing!" Science fiction thus stakes its claim to sublimity, over the body of a dead god.

# 2

# PULP FICTION, OR THE SUBLIME SUBVERSION OF THE BOY-ENGINEER

*But still he kept on. Something drove him inexorably forward. For he was an engineer—and an American.*

—England, *Darkness and Dawn*

## MR. GERNSBACK'S DILEMMA

In the foreground of Frank R. Paul's illustration "Serenis, Water City of Callisto," a multilimbed blue lady feeds lizards while her companion puts the viewer in the right position to enjoy the sublime display.[1] Her limbs hang loose; she stands facing into the scene, watching in awe as an icy fountain surges to the sky almost level with the huge planet rising behind sheer red cliffs on which perch more of the colonnaded buildings that also pile in tiers over the tiny inhabitants playing on the lake. Paul's lurid sublimities have their ancestry in those of John Martin, the early nineteenth-century painter whose pillared and domed cities totter on mountains above rationality.[2] Paul's contributions to *Amazing Stories* began with the first issue in April 1926, on the cover of which Saturn bulges hugely onto a scene of skaters and what appear to be steam yachts beached on cliffs of ice.[3] Despite his peculiar claim that this art represented "science fiction, with the accent on the science," Paul stands firmly with the sublime against the exigencies of scientific accuracy. His friend Hugo Gernsback, the editor of *Amazing Stories* and pioneer of "scientifiction" as he called it, held out a little longer and more desperately for the integrity of a publishing policy dedicated to nurturing scientific and technological interest in the impressionable young.[4] "Our stories," Gernsback explained, "are written to popularize science." In the next sentence, though, he exposed his dilemma, acknowledging that the tales were "literature *seasoned* with science."[5] Was science to be the sprinkling on entertaining stories or entertaining stories to be the vehicle of scientific education? In practice, that forced a choice between sublimity and gadgetry.

Gernsback's heart was with the gadgets and with boy-engineers eager to learn. "I elaborated," he told the author of "The Comet Doom" (a promisingly sublime title), "on the brain operation, to make it more scientifically correct."[6] Gernsback's own fiction, though, best indicates the determinedly pedagogical yearnings for his scientifictional baby. *Ralph 124C 41+: A Romance of the Year 2660*, Gernsback's only published novel, was originally serialized in *Modern Electrics*, a magazine Gernsback had started in 1908 to inform the "amateur electrician and electrical experimenter."[7] *Ralph 124C 41+* is technological prediction. Gernsback announced this in his original forward to the serialized version, and he maintained the stance in rewriting the episodes for the novel. He boasts that, though he would treat readers to "extremely strange and improbable devices," none were impossible or would spoil "as accurate a prophecy of the future as is consistent with the present marvelous growth of science."[8] Ralph belongs to the technoscience elite of 2660, "one of the greatest living scientists and *one of the ten men on the whole planet earth permitted to use the Plus sign after his name*."[9] Planetary welfare, technological invention, and the progress of science depend upon Ralph, perfect of brawn as well as brain, experimenting away in his 650-foot tower with its "telephot" screens through which he secures an access to planetary affairs worthy of a twenty-seventh-century Mr. Spectator. The plot of *Ralph 124C 41+* is minimal, unsurprising, and a lot funnier in print than intent. Ralph falls in love with a young Swiss girl whom he sees and saves from the top of his tower by electrically melting an avalanche of crashing ice as he "swung his big aerial around so that it pointed West-by-South"![10] Alice is understandably smitten, and her father brings her to New York, pursued by a dark duo of would-be lovers, an infatuated eight-foot Martian and the fiendishly French Fernand.[11] Ralph rescues Alice, who is abducted with careless frequency, defeats her kidnappers, and finally resuscitates her from death, using a technique he has previously tried on a dead dog. "*What you have done with a dog, you can do with a human being*," he reassures himself.[12] Marital bliss ensues, and lasts, perhaps, until one day, over the breakfast table, he says, "You know, my dear, seeing you lying there reminded me of this dead pooch."

Gernsback's chapters conform to a simple pattern. He describes an event or crisis, after which the action freezes for an account of a gadget or an exposition of scientific principles. This done, the initial occasion is concluded or resolved.[13] Technological surmise almost entirely subordinates the narrative, and larger philosophical questions are absent. Though "the Jules Verne, H. G. Wells and Edgar Allan Poe type of story" was his stated exemplar for scientifiction, his own writing shows little trace of their essays in sublimity.[14] Gernsback undercuts even a technological sublime. Accurate prediction so absorbs him that he reduces the sublime to the banal. How, Ralph asks, might one find a machine speeding into space "in an unknown direction somewhere in the boundless universe"? This hint of the sublime is immediately squashed with the reassurance that "the feat was easy to the scientist," followed by a quick lesson on measuring planetary distance.[15] When he started *Amazing Stories*, Gernsback faced an editorial dilemma. He wanted to publish exciting stories, but, educationally and ideologically, he had committed to presenting science accurately and as the product of American doggedness, hard work, and application. Ingenuity does fund a certain wonder in Gernsback's view—namely, the discovery that the extraordinary is quite possible. That which is "easy to the scientist," though, and certain to come about in the future is not sublime. Unfortunately for boy-engineers, though, Gernsback's readership liked their science sublime, desiring the thrills of obscurity, or of straining for an always receding future.[16] As a businessman, Gernsback bowed before the benefits of sublimity.

Caught between educational ambition and market demand, Gernsback abandoned stories that were mere excuses for instruction. He no longer published Clement Fezandie's interminably didactic Dr. Hackensaw and settled for repeatedly defending the scientific credibility of tales that, for the most part, were really tales of wonder and excitement. Probably, most readers took them as such and did not need the excuses. In addition to doses of Verne, Wells, and Poe, therefore, *Amazing Stories* readers enjoyed reprints of stories by Edgar Rice Burroughs and Abraham Merritt, both of whom were already established as popular writers. Each also contributed to the thematic and linguistic repertoire of science-fictional sublimity. In 1927 *Amazing Stories* carried the sixth of Burroughs' "Barsoom" novels, *The Mastermind of Mars*.[17] Burroughs transposed the sublimity of the American West to a Mars that recapitulated the older frontier that the 1890 Census Bureau had declared vanished, provoking jeremiads of concern for the American character. Journalists and politicians warned that an America lacking the defining rigors of Western expansion would lose moral fiber, ambition, and courage, already weakened by city ways and increasing immigration from southern and eastern Europe.[18] Burroughs provided wish fulfillment for this crisis of cultural imagination. The Barsoom saga begins in the Arizona sublime: "I saw stretching far below me the beautiful vista of rocky gorge and level, cacti-studded flat, wrought by the moonlight into a miracle of soft splendor and wondrous enchantment."[19] Escaping "ferocious Apache warriors," John Carter hides in a cave where he succumbs to drowsiness before waking up on Mars, naked as a newborn. Carter is a military hero who is "subconsciously forced into the path of duty without recourse to tiresome mental processes."[20] When he lands on Mars, he finds all the frontier sublimities intact, along with the character-building hostility of the residents. Beyond the Martian setting, about the only science in this fiction is the gravity discrepancy with Earth. Formed to a tougher pull, Carter's physical capacity for easy bounds of thirty feet across the Martian landscape ensures his superiority over the native Tharks. Burroughs transposed to Mars the expansionist drive and the triumphalism of the sublime imagination—together with the suggestion that on Earth even the gravity is better.

Exposing scientifiction to even greater drafts of sublimity, Gernsback began serializing Abraham Merritt's *The Moon Pool* in May 1927.[21] The wonders and strange powers of this novel's under-earth world demanded earnest apologetic to save Gernsback's pretensions to scientific integrity. His efforts reaffirm the educational purpose while abandoning its foundations. "When Mr. Merritt wrote this story [in 1919]," Gernsback explained, "he had to invent an entirely new and incredibly amazing science, which is neither electricity nor light nor anything you have ever thought or dreamt of."[22] *The Moon Pool* reverses the structure of gadget stories such as *Ralph 124C 41+*, as sublimity takes over and scientific explanation is reduced to token gestures that remind the reader that Muria is a technological not a magical environment. The plot, reminiscent of Rider Haggard's tales, involves a love triangle, a scientist and his companions on a quest for lost friends, an energy vampire, and a dastardly Bolshevik. Merritt's tale concludes with an attempted world-conquest trounced by the forces of good.

When the moon was torn from Earth, the catastrophe created vast caverns in which eventually evolved the scientifically advanced civilization of Muria. The high priestess, Yolara, though, and her kin rule over a slave population and in sacred rituals regularly feed a selection to the Shining One. This vampire being of light and energy absorbs other intelligent creatures, draining off their life force. Assisted by their beautiful handmaid, Lakla, only the Three Silent Ones, the original creators of the Shining One, oppose Yolara and her cult. Dialogue and character development often drag in *The Moon Pool*. Merritt is at his best when driving the plot at fair speed or staging tableaus that generously invoke the sublime. Muria overwhelms the narrator with dizzying drops, vivid and mysterious colors, self-propagating lights, and unworldly architecture:

> At first all that my staggering consciousness could realize was an immensity, an immeasurable uprearing that brought with it the same throat-gripping vertigo as comes from gazing downward from some great height—then a blur of white faces—intolerable shinings of hundreds upon thousands of eyes. Huge, incredibly huge, a colossal amphitheatre of jet, a stupendous semi-circle, held within its mighty arc the ivory platform on which I stood. It reared itself almost perpendicularly hundreds of feet up into the sparkling heavens, and thrust down on each side its ebon bulwarks—like monstrous paws. Now, the giddiness from its sheer greatness passing, I saw that it was indeed an amphitheatre sloping slightly backward tier after tier, and that the white blur of faces against its blackness, the gleaming of countless eyes were

> those of myriads of the people who sat silent, flower-garlanded, their gaze focused upon the rainbow curtain and sweeping over me like a torrent—tangible, appalling![23]

Merritt emphasizes the religious aspect of these sublime occasions. The "awful humming of the rushing wind" is like the soul hurtling to the "Throne of Justice," while eyes fall and knees bow at the "splendors" of Muria. The Shining One itself is said to dance as a "miracle of interwoven glory and horror," becoming a "devil-god" that draws the "mystics and the carnivores of humanity" alike. The Three Silent Ones fascinate the narrator as "alive, terribly—supernaturally." Their gaze lifts him "above the world—close to the threshold of the high gods—soon their essence and their power would stream out into me!"[24]

The religious and sacred aspect of Muria's sublime architecture and ritual serves a polemical strategy by which Merritt displaces Christianity in favor of a sublimed science. Naturalistic explanations of religion, influential during the early twentieth century, shape both Merritt's assessment of Christianity and his fictional contribution to the urgent debate at the time about the relationship between religion and science.[25] Anthropology, recently established as a discipline, here enters the field of science as imaginatively represented in science fiction. An embarrassingly stereotypical Irishman, Larry O'Keefe, along with Norwegian Olaf Huldricksson, whose wife and child have been snatched by the Shining One, accompany the novel's protagonist, Walter Goodwin, into Muria. In his despair, Olaf abandons his Christianity for the benefits of Thor and Odin, who appear more reliable as a present help in this time of danger. "Where was the God I prayed," he rails, "when my wife and child were taken? . . . I have left Him as He left me, ja! I pray now to Thor and to Odin, who can fetter Loki."[26] Whereas the narrowly scientific Goodwin remains often bewildered, Olaf and O'Keefe find their way about Muria, recognize and interpret what they find, even discern between good and evil powers, because they know their national mythologies. They operate as natural, if naive, comparative anthropologists. As Goodwin the narrator notes, other mythologies also provide analogies to the under-earth world; even Christian theology has appropriated the term "Trinity," repeatedly used in Muria for the Three Silent Ones, through whose goodness and wisdom the Shining One is finally vanquished. The characters' surface-world, then, in its mythological and religious symbolism, contains clues and hints of true sources in the powers of the "underworld." The sublimities of Muria disclose human potentials palely reflected by the alienated surface-world and its faiths. The symbolism, though, receives the distinctive twist that Muria is not a primitive world but a highly technological and scientific one, a culture that taps and releases powers immanent to the Earth but unknown to surface-world scientists, whose science, represented by Dr. Goodwin, is insufficiently sublime.

Merritt's imagination, however, remains in touch with anthropological speculation. J. G. Frazer had characterized human culture as moving "on the whole . . . from magic through religion to science."[27] Science and magic, though, have in common the conviction that events are produced by immanent causes over which human beings may gain control. They differ, Frazer argues, in that science proceeds from "patient and exact observation of the phenomena themselves."[28] Religious explanation is enemy to both as it traces earthly powers to transcendent, personal causes. In this vein, Merritt's Murians, though they have a high god, position him as a mere placeholder for ultimate explanation. He is thus "remote, unheeding . . . an absentee First Cause personified!"[29] Immanent forces give joy, energy, and power to Murian life: both "earthly love, feet bound to earth, but eyes among the stars," and also the latent energies harnessed by Murian science, and for which Merritt found some inspiration in the vitalism of the nineteenth-century Romantics. Christianity contrasts with this as a religion of strong, "remote" transcendence but weak immanence. Sublimity lies elsewhere, in the scientific capture of earthly energies. Such power as Christianity retains lies in its exposition and example of love, though that, too, is flawed by the supernaturalism of a mythology that particularizes love's universal energy in the person of Jesus. *The Moon Pool* implies that religion, in general, and Christianity, in particular, make a barren turn to a far distant and indifferent ultimate Cause, upon which it projects love. In the name of a sublime science, this fiction ousts the Enlightenment's sublime God. Only immanent powers offer liberation, powers that a sublime technology and science may realize, however occult they appear to Dr. Goodwin. Science sublimed thus dispossesses Christianity into irrelevance and refers humanity to immanence.

Magazine science fiction established itself in the 1920s as a genre of sublime excitement, despite and because of Hugo Gernsback. The "pulps" held up a mirror image to science, representing a sublime quest for knowledge with its roots in eighteenth-century letters and nineteenth-century Romanticism. They testify to a divide in the cultural imaginary between science imagined and science practiced. Science, Mach had preached in 1898, "is the natural foe of the wonderful. The sources of the marvelous are unveiled, and surprise gives way to calm interpretation."[30] Ralph 124C 41+ might have agreed. As Gernsback responded to readers' demands, though, sublimity shaped the representation of science, as well as stimulated more reflectively challenging themes, albeit in tales many of which were clumsy and crude. From early on authors tackled religion in stories like Alexander Snyder's "Blasphemer's Plateau," in which the evil Dr. Saturn attempts to rid the world of faith.[31] D. D. Sharp tackled immortality in a chilling story about the misery of an endless this-worldly life.[32] In Ray Myers' "Into the Subconscious," an unwitting subject under hypnosis recalls his evolutionary descent—ultimately from frogs—while an evolutionary future appears in Leslie Stone's "Men with Wings."[33] Both attempt the sublime shock of a displaced perspective that then recovers in recognition, sobering or otherwise. Similarly, several tales, including "The Machine Man of Ardathia" by Francis Flagg, envisaged the human from a nonhuman perspective.[34] Both alien and dystopian contexts provided occasion to explore the relationship between reason and emotion, a theme important within reflection upon the sublime. Edmond Hamilton offered a humorous example in "The Island of Unreason," which pinches a few ideas from Huxley's *Brave New World*, published the previous year.[35] As the first magazine devoted entirely to "scientifiction," *Amazing Stories* constituted an important innovation. Whatever his own predilections and purposes, Hugo Gernsback took a large stride in the science-fictional democratizing of the sublime.

## MR. CAMPBELL'S PARADOX

Gernsback's creditors caught up with him in early 1929. They sued for nonpayment, and Gernsback lost his publishing company to B. A. MacKinnon.[36] By this time, though, new initiatives in "all science fiction" pulps rivaled the newly managed *Amazing Stories* and *Amazing Stories Quarterly*. The most long running and successful of these, *Astounding Stories of Super-Science*, began in December 1929.[37] Early issues followed the current market enthusiasm for "space opera" with adventure yarns crossing vast reaches of space in which muscular lads and shapely, dutifully distressed maidens went into battle or were captured on planet-size ships with guns to match. Space opera, the subgenre inspired by the Skylark tales of E. E. "Doc" Smith, paid formulaic tribute to the sublime delights of immensity, working on a stage that allowed for intergalactic warfare and the epic troubles of whole civilizations. More interesting moves, though, came under the editorship of F. Orlin Tremaine, who tired of the increasingly routine formulas of space opera.[38] Tremaine invited what he termed "thought variant" stories, stories in which the exploration of an idea, preferably paradoxical or counterintuitive, drives the plot. Compared to space operas, thought-variant stories stimulated intellectual experiment and engagement with more strenuous topics, such as the logic of time travel, cultural collapse, the possibilities of cross-species communication, and, not surprisingly, religion.[39]

John W. Campbell became editor of *Astounding* in 1938. Campbell was a physicist by training, and his writing career had mirrored the development of pulp science fiction itself, beginning with genial amounts of Gernsbackian info dumping and proceeding by way of space opera until the mid-1930s when Campbell produced some fine thought-variant stories under the pseudonym of Don A. Stuart. On his appointment as editor, a position he held until 1971, Campbell demanded that the narrative perspective of a story should strike the reader as realistic. No matter how far into the future a story might be set, events must be told as if the reader were contemporary with the narrator. Campbell put this bluntly to Frederik Pohl: "No gee-whiz, just take the technology for granted."[40] This outlawed info-dumping lecturettes that caught up the reader with technological advances or social changes, and it strongly discouraged authors who created female characters with tabula rasa minds as grounds for explaining evaporation. As a formal strategy, this simple device allows the serious prosecution of strangeness. Sublimity now penetrates the form of the story: the future realistic stance of the narrator sets up the sublime event structure, as the reader is dislocated from the present.

Thus checked, the imagination recovers in the heightened pleasure of finding a way in an arresting strangeness.

The Stuart stories, however, written between 1934 and 1939, include some of the best tales written for pulp magazines before 1940. Since Campbell wrote all his Stuart stories within five years, not surprisingly recurring themes build and reflect on each other, such as technology and human culture, physical and social entropy, and how human flourishing depends upon inventiveness and ingenuity. In particular, the stories approach the matter of humanity's *vocation*, and they question to what end or ends should human beings commit themselves. Several stories—including "Twilight" and its sequel, "Night"—juxtapose "end" as termination, the death of species and world, with "end" as purpose or goal. The readers confront a morally suggestive pun with the hint that the only possibility of trumping an entropic end is by way of holding fast to the proper vocational end of human beings. Though his dialogue is often wooden and narrative detail sometimes unclear, Campbell's finest stories have the compelling memorability of myth. He writes thought-variant stories as more than intellectual puzzles largely because he renders the emotional force of the ideas he chooses. Recalling his space-opera days, Campbell deals in sublimities of scale: planetary invasions, time periods in millions of years, huge landscapes in a single tone of bleakness or desertion, and historical sweeps that encompass the grand fall of all human culture. The plots, though, and the questions they invite lack the cheery triumphalism of E. E. "Doc" Smith. Campbell's haunting accounts of entropy and cultural decline suggest the philosophical pessimism of a writer sensitive to questions about the direction and limits of American society raised by the Depression. The pessimism, however, is not absolute since, if Campbell laments the character of most human behavior, he rejoices in the human possibilities opened by science and technology.[41] The technological sublime contributes a constant and positive element to the stories.

The intellectual tension in many of Campbell's tales depends upon a paradox that returns in a number of variants. Bringing the human vocation into close conjunction with the technological sublime generates the paradox of fulfilled desire. Human beings need the sublime to stimulate their freedom of mind and imagination; technology extends and serves that freedom by giving humanity an apparently inexhaustible power to raise and meet intellectual and practical challenges. In this way, sublime technology embodies humanity's own sublimity as a movement projected into an immanent infinity. Technology, however, meets challenges and satisfies needs, hence the paradox of human beings that develop technology in order to prosecute the vital drive to struggle and solve problems but then find that using technology relieves them of that need and, with it, the purpose of life. Men and women rise to their destiny, in Campbell's imagination, by meeting a universe scarcely tuned to their well-being with the force of unremitting intellectual labor. Their task is to bring recalcitrant matter under rational control and so extend thought into that thoughtless universe. Campbell doubted the human ability to keep the pace of such scientific and technological transformation. Laziness crouches at the machine-room keyhole and sings more alluringly the more problems the machines solve. The technological enterprise remains, however, the species' glory and vocation. When a single physicist averts planetary ruin in "Atomic Power," Campbell adds the language of sublimity to as strong an affirmation of techno-scientific mastery as anything in *Ralph 124C 41+*. His heroic scientist "looked toward and through the mass of the machine, crouched in hulked latent power, the massive conductors leading off in gleaming, ruddy columns." The physicist had "discovered the source of vast power."[42] While Gernsback simply enthuses over technological wizardry, Campbell introduces the sublime to identify technology with the human vocation to self-transcendence through purposeful labor and constructive science. With vast power, though, come vast satisfactions and, with them, the paradox of self-destruction through the benefits of labor, as in the story "Twilight."

Returning in time to the year 3059, Ares Sen Kenlin overshoots the runway and lands in the 1930s. Rescued by a passing motorist, he talks about his journey. He has traveled millions of years into Earth's future. Only the fag end of humanity remains. Gentle, aimless men and women live purposeless lives of great length with only an occasional birth. They attempt nothing, accomplish nothing, expect nothing, and their great intelligence is without energy, incapable of any stimulus beyond a mild bewilderment. Human life has dwindled to an idle persistence, without even the strain of endurance. However, though this is all that survives of humanity, it is not all that is left of human culture. These last men and women live like nomads and strangers in cities that bear witness to glorious millennia of human civilization at its zenith. Entirely untended, barely noticed by the last men, the cities maintain themselves through machines designed to serve and repair them, as well as supply all the needs of their former inhabitants. Perfectly built and collaborating seamlessly, the machines have continued long after their designers have declined into vacuity. This contrast between gaggles of empty, lifeless people and the glory that was humanity, seen indirectly through its technology, sets up Campbell's paradox. Ironically, the machines of former prowess share the same loss of purpose as the men and women of humanity's sad end: the one revolves in idleness; the other in the pointless circularity of ceaseless technological maintenance, guided and furthered by no one, benefiting no one. Implied between the two is the lost humanity, a humanity that works, investigates, puzzles, builds, makes, provokes problems, then solves them in the lust for raising more. This is the missing humanity of projects, campaigns, strategies, levers, machines, organizations, and enterprises directed like arrows: the humanity of the technological sublime. Human beings directed technology toward the elimination of obstacles and the effortless meeting of all their needs. All threats were removed, which, in the process, required the destruction of all other life on the planet. "As man strode toward maturity, he destroyed all forms of life that menaced him." Finally, "on all Earth there was only man and the organisms he had protected—the plants he wanted for decoration, and certain ultra-hygienic pets."[43] When all needs were met, all obstacles surmounted, then human ingenuity and labor surfeited its own requirement and retired from employment. Then, "the one thing that had made man great" disappeared, "the instinct of curiosity," and when human beings were no longer curious, Ares Sen Kenlin suggests, everything, even the cities, became "nature" again—that is, taken for granted, unquestionable and unquestioned surroundings.[44]

Though he might not have appreciated the comparison, Campbell's paradox arises in a history of concern over human progress that goes back to Puritanism. Among Christian traditions, Reformed, Calvinist Christianity probably gets the prize as regards the vocation to "subdue the earth." The Puritan tradition is nothing if not energetic for working change. The Puritans, though, also acknowledged that the fruits of human enterprise were ambiguous. The world, both the natural and social environments, must be worked on because, in working on the world, men and women serve God's kingdom, restoring creation from disorderly sin to obedient order. Nevertheless, the fruits of an ordered world and a godly, effortful life are both blessing and temptation. Prosperity, the ability to set field to field and, later, factory to railhead to warehouse, these potential signs of God's good pleasure, were also easily the occasion of sin, and the beginning of corruption in comfortable luxury. More or less secularized versions of this anxiety attended the economic boom of the decade after World War I and the accompanying technological advances—among them, improvements in radio, extensive electrification, mass-produced cars. Americans were passionate consumers of technological change and thrilled by its sublime energy. The same consumers, however, feared the social and cultural changes that technology brought. They eased the bad conscience of new prosperity by listening to warnings about decadence, affirming nostalgic appeals by politicians and journalists, and taking the imaginative trip to the new frontier of John Carter's Mars.[45]

At the end of "Twilight," Campbell converts the tragic paradox into an ethical challenge. Though several stories, including "Twilight," suggest that success generally gives entropy its fatal opportunity, they also imply that a different relationship to technology might resolve the paradox. Campbell, though, does not proffer the familiar wisdom of less is more but hints that the answer is more is more. If human beings give themselves to the technological sublime as a means of generating problems and frontiers rather than satisfactions, then they may realize the promise of technological change without horizon and, thereby, their own integrity. In one tale, an alien machine warns soft and lazy humans that "only construction need not be monotonous and ever-recurring. Only the new is different, and because you would not work at construction, since that was work, you attempted to play and, as had the race, you learned its monotony, but not the lesson of construction."[46] Since human progress undoes itself through the contradictory pull of laziness and ease, though, eugenics might resolve Campbell's paradox. When the Tharoo invade Earth, they find humanity has devolved into an Edenic existence of vegetarianism and sex. Unfortunately for the Tharoo, though easy to conquer, indolent, unambitious humans make rotten slaves. The aliens must train and breed humans to restore them to energetic, forward-striving labor, which is their true vocation. The narrator of "Rebellion" explains that the Tharoo did humanity a great favor. In evolving human beings into productive creatures, nature had used the stick of hunger and the carrot of rest. This worked well only as long as life's necessities were in short supply. Given plenty, humanity put its feet up and abandoned destiny. The Tharoo went one better than nature and "simply bred out the desire for indolence."[47] The downside was that an energetic, industrious, and increasingly knowledgeable humanity needed but a little shove to rebel and send their oppressors packing. On a trajectory without such breeding, the time traveller of "Twilight" listens to the heart-rending songs of dying humanity, songs in which "you could feel the whole of humanity trying hard—and losing," unable to recall the one thing needful: the stance of energetic investigation, the practice of making, and of purposeful change. Humanity has lost itself and now holds out no hope for a return to strenuous progress. However, before he leaves, Kenlin configures a group of five machines and sets them "to make a machine with something that man had lost . . . A curious machine."[48]

The human vocation to construction and to problem solving as an infinite task corresponds closely to the assessment of nature in the Stuart tales. Campbell described himself as a Deist. His, though, is a particularly austere Deism. Campbell's theological imagination runs only to a divine, scientific investigator who, having set up complexes of laws to run the universe, refrains like a good scientist from further interference with the experiment. In the terms of an earlier account, Campbell's God is "well skilled in Mechanicks and Geometry," but not much else. Human beings must find their way not by looking to God but by attending to themselves and their environment in order to discover capacities, constraints, possibilities, limits, pleasures to be pursued, and pains to avoid. Campbell, however, lacks the optimism of classical eighteenth-century Deists, who imagined nature as designed with human benefits in mind. In Campbell's tales, human existence is radically contingent, not only unnecessary, but also vulnerable to entire catastrophe without the slightest hint of a cosmic tear. Campbell's universe is not instinct with beauty or goodness;

human beings do not live in a "loveable actuality."[49] If there is meaning to be had, human beings must make it. They are left to find their own end, to craft significance for themselves and labor to quell nature, imposing human purpose upon the material it offers. In the earlier history of the sublime, nature's sublimity lifts human beings on their way to the divine. A blessed conjunction exists between nature and the human vocation, a conjunction celebrated again by those who understood technology in a providential continuity with nature. Campbell continues to imagine nature as sublime. "I looked up at the black sky above me," says the protagonist of "Night," "and in all the vast black bowl of the heavens, not three-score stars were visible. . . . The stars were gone."[50] This sublimity, however, of entropy or irresistible force merely threatens the human vocation, a perspective informed by the pessimistic, antiteleological interpretation of Darwin embraced also by H. G. Wells.[51] In these stories, the sublimity of nature diverges into opposition to that of humanity and its end. Enlightenment theism and Romantic panentheism had held the two together, albeit with an account of transcendence that, failing to maintain the distinction of Creator and creature, drifted toward immanence. When those theologies collapse, the human and the natural sublime are at odds.

Eventually, another visitor to Earth's winter discovers Kenlin's "curious machine." It has not fulfilled his hopes since curiosity proved insufficient to the problem. Though the machine has delivered answers to almost all identifiable questions, this has merely replaced the ceaseless circularity of physical maintenance with an equally circular intellectualism. The narrator explains that the machines "were without opponents . . . whoever, whatever designed them gave them function and forgot purpose."[52] Solving one problem after another in an endless drive of technological perpetuation exposes another aspect of Campbell's paradox: that as an end in itself, the drive of technoscientific progress is sterile, finally no better than idle play. Campbell, though, does not develop this implication in a way that modifies his account of human beings. Instead, he attempts to sketch an alternative outcome to "Twilight" and "Night," describing a postentropic humanity that has found its destiny. "Forgetfulness" is a witty turn on the premise of "Twilight." An advanced civilization returns to its mother planet—Rhth, presumably Earth—to find abandoned high-tech cities and a simple people who appear as clueless as the gentle and befuddled folk of "Twilight."[53] When the colonizers reveal their plans, though, the inhabitants activate a tiny device that allows them to alter the disposition of the planets by mind control. The invaders are not only returned home, but their planet is also benignly relocated into a system with empty ones to colonize. The people of Rhth have not fallen behind advanced technology but gone beyond it, into forms unimaginable, where matter is penetrated and wholly governable by mind. The story hints at a final technological transcendence, a securing of technology's sublimity as its transformation of matter, and its raising of further technical challenges, efforts, and obstacles becomes endless. The problem of technological progress as an end in itself is solved as it becomes an end in itself in a kind of apotheosis. As a solution to the profound problem of the curious machine, this is a deus ex machina with a vengeance!

Campbell treats religion in these stories with striking savagery. Religion belongs with the forces of decadence as an ideological and institutional drain on humanity's energy, vision, and forward movement. When the alien machine ceases to deliver benefits, a frightened, gullible population, fooled by accident and coincidence, worships the machine as God and throws young women to be crushed as sacrifices between its gears.[54] The invading Tharoo later find that religion persists in an irrational reverence for their own machinery. In "Who Goes There?" the only religious character collapses in cowardly hysteria while the scientists give their sweat and ingenuity to fighting a murderous alien.[55] The stories condemn religion as an expression and breeding ground for violence, lazy thinking, and escapist behavior, an altogether understandable attraction for an indolent humanity. Not men of faith but of science, the scientific engineers, not the preachers, make heroes. In place of the revivalist and the circuit rider, pulp science fiction promoted the engineer, scientist, and inventor as American icons. Science and technology, throughout Campbell's stories, foster human adulthood and promise, however difficult its achievement.

Campbell presents the choice between religion and science as stark and absolute. Ironically, though, he lays down this challenge within an anthropology and a doctrine of progress that he shares, in significant respects, with a form of American Protestantism very influential during the first thirty years of the twentieth century. In these decades, "modernist" liberal Protestantism enthused over technological progress, embraced evolutionary language, and dared believe America a temporal stone's throw from a society founded on the Bible and modern science. "The modern prophet," exhorted Josiah Strong, "employing the methods of science, may again proclaim that the kingdom of heaven is at hand."[56] The Depression of the 1930s severely undermined this confidence as well as fueled Campbell's pessimism about human beings in the mass. Though that pessimism, his elitist, technocratic politics, and his hostility to religion oppose him to the liberal Protestants, he continued to have an imagination of human good similar to theirs.[57]

Years before the Stuart stories, therefore, the social-gospel advocate Walter Rauschenbusch advocated human technological labor as the engine of an endless, inexhaustible progress.[58] Institutionalized greed, he claimed, not industrial technology creates the miseries of urban poverty. Greed, selfishness, and the laziness happy to live off the work of others become structural in the "super-personal forces" of social institutions that give cruelty and injustice permanent, self-sustaining, and developing form.[59] Rauschenbusch, though, no more yearned for premodernity than did Campbell.[60] More technology, not less, only combined with a socialist distribution of benefits, will propel history into the kingdom of God. An "immense latent perfectibility" waits in humanity for release and infinite perpetuation. Rauschenbusch embraces the historical sublime, an inexhaustible, progressive fulfillment, the present realization of which presses into an unimaginable but thrilling future. Only this, he argues, does justice to our humanity, purposeful, energetic, and vigorous as it is: "None can realize himself fully without labor."[61] Indolence turns up as the bane of history as it does in Campbell's tales of human devolution. Rauschenbusch diagnoses it in traditional hopes of God's kingdom just as Campbell spotted it in pastoral utopias.[62] We imagine gardens of ease as earthly paradise because "an endless perspective of development is too taxing."[63] Men and women delight in lazy visions, and the sublime prospect of their proper vocation to infinite progrcss offends their indolence. "Fortunately," he reassures, "God is not tired as easily as we" and, like Campbell's alien machine, will not have his creatures "dying of ennui." Though entropy will end the history of the species, until then, "we are on the march toward the Kingdom of God . . . a stationary humanity would be a dead humanity. The life of the race is in its growth."[64] Rauschenbusch preceded Campbell, too, in suggesting construction as an end in itself. In a more homely image than the planet-shifting demigods of Rhth, labor is eternalized in heaven: "It would be a great joy in heaven to find men trooping in from mines and shops, and women from restaurant kitchens and steaming laundries, and getting their long-delayed college education."[65]

Traditional Christian doctrines bend to conform to the pressure of the sublime vocation to an infinite expansion through labor. Christians see God "at work" and "claim a share in his job"![66] Jesus, too, becomes the hero of "vigorous action and reaction," a man able to "dominate situations" and set "a great historical process in motion."[67] Sensitive to traditional pieties, if not theology, and resolutely impatient of metaphysics, Rauschenbusch takes care to avoid a dramatic reconstruction of the doctrine of God. Nevertheless, his theology flows along that immanentizing drift characteristic of the technological sublime. His less guarded formulations suggest that God has become a function of sublime humanity, turning into the immanent force of its striving. So, in contrast to the classical incarnation of God in Jesus, the social gospel becomes "a progressive social incarnation of God."[68] God is our "chief fellow worker" who, in a reversal of the traditional formula, "lives and moves in the life of mankind." "Some," Rauschenbusch admits, "would be willing to think of God as less than omnipotent and omniscient if only he were working hard with us for that Kingdom which is the only true Democracy."[69]

Nature, the nonhuman creation, is also absent from this theological program. Humanity's integrity diverges from nature into a dualistic opposition. As in the Stuart tales, this theology implicitly reduces the nonhuman to matter, to the object of human labor, that which is to be worked. In Rauschenbusch, nature crops up in support for public parks; in Campbell's fiction, as a source of terrifying threats, overcome by engineering heroics. In "Forgetfulness," Campbell imagined the fulfilling fantasy of this attitude. For the inhabitants of Rhth's climactic culture, all matter is drawn into the power of mind, as planets are moved and stars realigned. Campbell dreams the end of difference; there is no longer any "other" to the mind. The irreducible diversity of reality is denied. This imagined fulfillment of the technological sublime overruns and hides the theological possibility that the nonhuman has its own integrity and holiness, and that the human vocation exists as blessing for the nonhuman, not only the nonhuman in service of the human. On Rhth, however, all is collapsed into the identity of mind and the materials under its sway.

Though the science-fictional imagination rendered science as sublime, scientific developments—perhaps most influentially, theories of natural selection—nurtured a radically different way of imagining the sublimity of nature in American popular culture.[70] Pulp science fiction could pit the sublime horizon of human powers against a sublimely hostile nature. Mostly, that flattered the former as the stories imagined human powers accelerating in their compass. Among the pulp writers, though, H. P. Lovecraft rendered the dark sublimities of nature as an opposition before which humanity flickers momentarily and goes out. In doing this, he created science-fictional horror.

## MR. LOVECRAFT'S ABJECTION

Henry Fuseli's painting *The Nightmare*, first exhibited in 1792, attracted the largest crowds yet to visit a Royal Academy exhibition. The picture shows, draped upon a bed, a sleeping young woman in a nightdress. Her mouth is slightly open, and her cheeks flushed; her head lolls over the side of the bed, and her left arm hangs to the floor, leaving her body exposed. On her abdomen squats an incubus—its back making a shadow between her legs—staring bestially, and perhaps defiantly, at the viewer.[71] The painting inspired debate, first about its artistic, then about its moral, propriety. Fuseli defended himself against the accusation that he had violated decency in venturing beyond the simply grotesque to the forbidden sphere of horror. He strenuously objected to the charge on the grounds that he was a painter of terror not horror, which was, as everybody knew, along with "loathsomeness . . . banished from the painter's and the poet's province."[72] On this distinction hung the possibility of a legitimate sublimity. Mrs. Radcliffe spelled out the implications, arguing that "terror and horror are so far opposite, that the first expands the soul, and awakens the faculties to a high degree of life; the other *contracts, freezes, and nearly annihilates them*." "Positive horror," she warns, is never a source for the sublime.[73] Though hardly any contemporary seems to have mentioned it explicitly, behind the fuss over distinguishing horror from terror, at least in Fuseli's case, was the intimation of sexual violation, especially of a violation that transgressed the divide of human and animal. Horror makes the flesh crawl because it violates boundaries, combining that which should not be combined, and confusing the categories within which culture orders nature, the separations that maintain sanity. Most disturbingly, and *The Nightmare* intimates it, horror threatens but also lures; what repels and revolts is also desired.

Though the distinction between horror and terror lacked the clarity for long-term critical service, the merely horrific, despite the double movement in a pleasurable recoil, arguably "precludes the kinds of response engendered" by the sublime.[74] Certainly, some horror movies trade in a grossness that issues in laughter or constitutes a kind of self-hazing with regard to disgust. Sam Rami's movie *The Evil Dead* hardly achieves sublimity with its teenage girls assaulted by unaccountably horny and maniacal tree roots. H. P. Lovecraft, however, who published mostly in the pulp *Weird Tales*, but also in both *Amazing Stories* and *Astounding*, gave his readers horror on a cosmic stage and imagines category violations as exponents of nature's fearful truth. Lovecraft's tales include some excellent skin crawlers, such as the ravenous alien hybrid with "ten or twenty maouths or trunks a-stickin' aout all along the sides, big as stove-pipes an all a-tossin' an openin' an' shuttin' . . . all grey, with kinder blue or purple rings . . . an' Gawd it Heaven—that haff face on top." Lovecraft, however, turns the grotesque into the sublime by rendering horror as the overwhelming threat posed by the unknown. His descriptions do not clarify but heighten the obscurity of horrors that violate fundamental features of ordinary experience. A color, existing independent of any substance, ravages a family; a rotting alien-human hybrid destroys the mental composure of "anyone whose ideas of aspect and contour are too closely bound up with the common life-forms of this planet and of the three known dimensions."[75] Lovecraft lets these maleficent appearances loose within a context from which they appear revelatory, less important in themselves than as clues to a cosmos sublime in the range and power of its menacing inhospitality.[76]

In the Lovecraftian cosmos, disaster is always but a small accident, an idle query, or a single wrong turn away. Personal and collective courage, humanist dedication, Christian faith—all prove equally absurd. Fragments of unity and order trick human beings through their need for them, but in this universe heterogeneity, conflict, mismatch, and unintelligibility is basic. Lovecraft makes the sublime from this order of disorder. Irreducibly discordant beings— incompossible, transient, and unstable structures—stagger out of interminable chaos and live their day. No eternal mind or law holds this world in reason; no recognition nods across the gulfs of difference. All is at odds, and at the center "sprawls the blind idiot god Azathoth . . . encircled by his flopping horde of mindless and amorphous dancers, and lulled by the thin monotonous piping of a daemoniac flute held in nameless paws."[77] From these "unlighted chambers beyond Time," in a grim inversion of Christianity's "Word made flesh," proceeds Nyarlathotep, the "Crawling Chaos," walking among his own.[78] The heterogeneity goes all the way down. Abominations, darkly hinted in fearful texts like the *Necronomicon*, lurk in "angled space" between the dimensions, while Antarctica holds traces of Shoggoths, the "formless protoplasm able to mock and reflect all forms and organs and processes—viscous agglutinations of bubbling cells . . . infinitely plastic and ductile."[79] Elsewhere the taint of violation spreads even to the faces of squirrels.[80] A final turn of the screw, and the reader learns that science, which is the acme of human reason and opposed to religion as sanity to madness, will eventually let sublime horror loose in our minds and occasion our end.

The collector of "facts concerning the late Arthur Jermyn and his family," reflecting on how Jermyn's search for genealogical truth turned deadly, concludes that "science, already oppressive with its shocking revelations, will perhaps be the ultimate exterminator of our human species . . . for its reserve of unguessed horrors could never be borne by mortal brains if loosed upon the world."[81] Science proceeds by identifying and gathering the evidence significant for generating and, then, solving a problem. The researcher examines the evidence and puts the pieces together in an explanatory whole that reveals something newly known and, invariably in a Lovecraft tale, thoroughly unpalatable. When they are scientists, Lovecraft's protagonists have more than a touch of the eighteenth-century "man of reason" about them, being Enlightenment intellectuals of wide interests and oceanic reading. They have specialisms without being specialists. Their desire, though in Lovecraft's universe it brings them grief, is for a unitary understanding, a reconciliation of "dissociated knowledge." Exemplars of rational investigation, they weigh evidence dispassionately, admire objectivity, are recklessly curious, and are happy to move among the most heterogeneous sources, looking for the clues that bring the laboratory specimen and ghastly Pnakotic Manuscripts together in a common bearing upon the truth. Lovecraft thus tips his hat to the literary period he loved so much: the British Enlightenment, especially its Augustan age.[82] Ironically, the scientific integrity of his scholarly protagonists makes them acutely dangerous, especially in their readiness to follow the explanatory clues across disciplinary boundaries, even into the shadiest of intellectual alleys. By contrast, the twentieth-century scientific specialist, wary of the heterogeneity of knowledges, pursues her discipline, leaves much else well alone, and so maintains the enterprise of science from such truths and discoveries as would finish it off altogether. When science maintains its integrity by avoiding the occult, obscure, or arcane, it protects humanity from the truth. The ideal investigator, however, imperils everybody by refusing to observe specialist territories. "The sciences, each straining in its own direction, have hitherto harmed us little," but the fruit of comprehensiveness is madness or "the peace and safety of a new dark age."[83] Thus the narrator of "The Call of Cthulhu" persists in the admirable business of chasing and assembling the evidence. He gathers the pieces of "dissociated knowledge" to fall upon a monstrous truth. In the ingenious structure of the story he tells, Lovecraft enacts the quest itself and, therefore, the sublime horror awaiting knowledge sought with integrity.

An earthquake in the Pacific ocean has raised to the surface the more than ancient city of R'lyeh, the "nightmare corpse-city," where monstrous Cthulhu lies undying but in a death-like sleep, dreaming away age upon age. The crew of a small ship, driven off course, explores the city, opening a vault from which the awakened Cthulhu emerges. Only two men survive his onslaught; one of these is driven insane and later dies, while the other escapes, a broken man, not long for the world. From one culture to another, simultaneous with these events, spreads a wave of bizarre phenomena: horrific dreams and frightful visions; outbreaks of wild insanity; religious hysteria; and ghastly artistic inspirations, all of which refer to the impossible geometries of R'lyeh's cyclopean architecture and to the unearthly form of Cthulhu, foul beyond words and imagination. Shortly thereafter, Cthulhu and his frightful city sink back under the waves. Such are the bare bones of "The Call of Cthulhu." The story itself, however, reveals these events piecemeal through a clever structure that achieves considerable suspense and makes the process of investigation itself a vehicle of sublime horror or, as Lovecraft termed it, "cosmic fear."[84]

At the time of composition, the narrator fears being murdered by fanatical members of a "Cthulhu cult." And—from the story's subtitle, "found among the papers of the late Francis Wayland Thurston, of Boston"—the reader may conclude that he was not imagining things. Since Thurston protests that his discoveries are best kept secret for humanity's sake, why he writes the story is unclear. He describes his record, however, as "this test of my own sanity," a kind of self-therapy, objectivizing and checking the horrific and incredible, a confession of findings too appalling to be left to eat into one's sanity should the mind perhaps prefer madness to memory. Thurston's narrative falls into two halves, the second of which covers the period of his own investigations into Cthulhu. The first tells the prehistory of those investigations and is largely a reconstruction of his uncle's own researches, left in a box inherited by Thurston upon George Angell's suspicious death. Angell's story, though, is itself in two main sections but in reverse order to the framing narrative. The first section recounts Angell's own investigation, as Thurston discovered it; the second records its prehistory.

Angell's narrative has the same pattern as the framing story: a collection of other stories, with their own "nesting" narratives. The uncle's researches comprise the story of Henry Wilcox, a young artist who dreams of R'lyeh and Cthulhu and makes a sculpture showing the latter. Wilcox falls ill and, in his delirium, sees clearer and more disturbing visions of the monstrous city and its dreaming inhabitant. Angell undertakes a global search of analogous dreams, as well as visionary phenomena, enthusiastic religion, and outbreaks of madness, all occurring over the period of Wilcox's dreams and illness.

Angell, however, has also heard of Cthulhu long before. This earlier history is comprised of three further stories, nested within one another. A Louisianan detective brings a bas-relief of Cthulhu to a meeting of archeologists. This provokes a Professor Webb to tell his experiences of "degenerate Esquimaux" who worship a very similar figure. Inspector Legrasse then continues his narrative, describing a raid on the dreaded bayou cult from whom he seized the sculpture. Legrasse includes the legends told by a cult member, Castro, who rambles about the "Old Ones," preserved by Cthulhu for revival after he himself awakes to resume his rule over the earth, presumably to the discomfiture, if not elimination, of Earth's distinctly unimportant human occupants, who have popped into brief and irrelevant life while Cthulhu has been dozing. Castro also mentions Cthulhu's ability to influence human minds through dreams, visions, and compulsions.

Thurston's own investigations, the burden of the second main section of his narrative, focus, first, on an accidentally discovered newspaper story that takes Thurston to Australia in search of the survivor from a crew destroyed while exploring a mysterious island. The one survivor had been found clutching "a horrible stone idol of unknown origin." Thurston tracks the survivor back to his home in Oslo. Johansson has since died from his trauma, but his widow gives Thurston her husband's journal, which contains the last part of the puzzle, the awful story of Johansson's escape from Cthulhu, "the Thing of the idols, the green, sticky spawn of the stars, [that] had awaked to claim his own." After the horrendous encounter with Cthulhu, Johansson's writing fragments into wild enigmas, just as the story overall was shattered, mercifully, into heterogeneous bits and pieces, though now, thanks to Thurston, assembled together in their dread truth. "Then came . . . the clouds about his consciousness . . . of spectral whirling through liquid gulfs of infinity, of dizzying rides through reeling universes on a comet's tail, and of hysterical plunges from the pit to the moon and from the moon back again to the pit, all livened by a cachinnating chorus of the distorted, hilarious elder gods."[85]

In fashioning this complicated structure, superbly balanced for what is a relatively short tale, Lovecraft introduces a dissonant range of sources and genres: dreams, fevered delirium, archaeological artifact, police reports, data from an ethnographic expedition, religious and cult testimony, legend and folklore, experiences of the insane, newspaper articles, personal journals, confessional writing. All this infuses a horror into the process of knowledge itself, as well as into what is revealed. As a monster tale, "The Call of Cthulhu" is very good indeed. The image of Cthulhu, for instance, exploding like a bladder as Johansson's boat hits him, only to begin reforming immediately, revolts delightfully. What makes "The Call of Cthulhu" so interesting, though, is that it is far from simply a monster tale. Monsters, however inconvenient their predations or disgusting their habits and hybridities, are, in the end, imaginations of external force, whether they are gobbling young ladies or whole planets. "The Call of Cthulhu" differs in that the monstrous Cthulhu does not simply pose a threat to physical survival. He, she, or it makes knowledge, exploring our environment, the work of science itself, a dangerous, self-destructive business—not, however, just because our curiosity disturbs the darkest enmities, but because it reveals the vanity of the cosmic intelligibility we both assume and seek. Our boasted "scientific" conclusions are a sorry scribbling upon walls dissolving into vacancy. The Cthulhu sculpture defies artistic, historical, and biological classification and, from Thurston's description, in a manner more radically challenging to the mind than the discovery of the most striking anomaly. Not a mere chimera, the figure yields "simultaneous pictures"—"an octopus, a dragon, and a human caricature"—while the attempt at exact account breaks down in phrases such as "seemed certainly," "vague suggestions," "diseased fancy," giving the impression of an object moving in and out of focus. This distressing perceptual vertigo is repeated on a vaster scale in the architecture of R'lyeh, where the geometry is "abnormal, non-Euclidean, and loathsomely redolent of spheres and dimensions apart from ours." "All the rules of matter and perspective seemed upset."[86] When the sailors examine Cthulhu's vault, they cannot decide whether "the entrance lay flat like a trap-door or slantwise like an outside cellar-door," and, later, one of the men is "swallowed up by an angle of masonry which shouldn't have been there; an angle which was acute, but behaved as if it were obtuse."[87] Cthulhu himself, of course, is beyond any accounting: "The Thing cannot be described—there is no language for such abysms of shrieking and immemorial lunacy, such eldritch contradictions of all matter, force, and cosmic order."[88]

Behind the foregrounded ghastliness in Lovecraft's stories are the indeterminate, unseen, and obscure sources of horror. Cthulhu, "a slushy nastiness as of a cloven sunfish, a stench as of a thousand opened graves," is the intrusion of "eldritch contradictions of all matter, force, and cosmic order."[89] The seen horror opens up the terror of what remains necessarily always unseen, formless, and indeterminate because it is the unraveling of intelligible order. Lovecraft has crafted a peculiarly modern nightmare; his monsters haunt the sleep of an Enlightenment rationality. Contrary to that Enlightenment heritage, there is no Nature, only transient poolings of order within the universal chaos. Pope famously celebrated Newton with, "God said: 'Let Newton Be! / And there was Light!'" However much tongue was in his cheek at the time, the connection between science and illumination was culturally vigorous. So also was the hope that—just as reason, in the form of Newtonian science, had brought light into the age-long obscurities of the heavens—it would bring similar light to bear upon the disorderliness and clashing obscurities of religion. Enthusiasm for the sublime drew force from that hope: an ennobling, spiritually formative experience, independent of doctrinal discords, which affirmed the majesty and power of God, while speaking well for the human mind. Developing the darker aspect of sublimity, as found in Gothic fiction and in Burke's emphasis on pain and the "ruling principle" of terror, Lovecraft subverts reason into the bringer, not of light, but of darkness. The exploration of Cthulhu's vault serves up a fine symbol of this, in the releasing of a palpable night:

> The aperture was black with a darkness almost material. That tenebrousness was indeed a positive quality; for it obscured such parts of the inner walls as ought to have been revealed, and actually burst forth like smoke from its aeon-long imprisonment, visibly darkening the sun as it slunk away into the shrunken and gibbous sky on flapping membraneous wings.[90]

Theology also makes the intimate connection of knowledge and light. "Just as the eye naturally seeks light and sight," wrote Origen in the third century, "so does our spirit have its own natural desire to know God's truth and the causes of things." Thus, "if you apply to yourself the illumination of the Holy Spirit [then] in His light, you see the light."[91] The theological connection of light with knowledge is continuous with the modern ideology of reason in that the sciences take up and presuppose the intelligibility of nature and the aptitude of our minds for understanding it.

Along with all science fiction authors, Lovecraft writes on the other side of a trajectory that begins with the separation of the "book of Nature" from the "book of Revelation," as a source for our knowledge of God.[92] The sublime was one vehicle of this development, and the trajectory continues as, in the diverging of the technological sublime from the natural sublime, nature and her reader come to be at odds.[93] Pulp science fiction, however, may characterize the universe—as did Campbell and, more famously, H. G. Wells—as hostile to human aspirations and survival, but the cosmic environment remains intelligible, however difficult the exposure of its laws and structures. The pulp stories affirm science as humanity's main hope because the universe is of a nature upon which scientific reasoning can grip. The Lovecraftian scientist, however, discovers scientifically the universal chaos and, therefore, that science's only purchase on the cosmos reveals it has none. In the terms that Christianity inherited from the Greco-Roman world, Lovecraft's stories narrate a world without Logos. The world hangs together as a unified and intelligible order; it is cosmos rather than chaos, because it is made according to Logos and, as such, may be understood by us in the measure to which we, as rational creatures, participate in Logos. According to a fragment of Heraclitus, "through the Logos all things are understood."[94] For the Stoics, the Logos existed as the ultimate cosmological principle, the source of rationality in the universe; for Christians, Logos is God himself reflected in the Father's eternal "intelligence," from which derives the order of creation and the providential, redemptive governance of history.[95] Lovecraft, therefore, imagines an anticreation that gives the lie to the trust in intelligibility affirmed by the Western philosophical and theological tradition, as well as assumed by secularized modern science. He does this, though, in the name of a keen Enlightenment regard for science itself. This appears especially clearly in the tales' persistent and polemic contrasting of science with religion.

Having subverted the link between knowledge and light, Lovecraft treats science and religion as opposed ways of approaching the universal darkness. He dismisses Christianity vividly and brutally. Church buildings are not only empty; they are also possessed, taken over by decadent, malignant forms, the disallowed, abject reality that religion exists to shield and disguise. Obsessed with the grim silhouette of a church visible from his window, Lovecraft's protagonist, the doomed Robert Blake, investigates the "blackened pile" and its gruesome history. Inside this "great decrepitude," Blake finds evidence of an outlaw sect that had taken over the building and "called up awful things from some unknown gulf of night."[96] Christianity had devolved here, decaying into the primitive life it was powerless to contain. Even the cross had lost its form and now "resembled the primordial ankh or crux ansata of shadowy Egypt."[97] Blake finds Scriptures that describe a knowledge antedating the Bible by millennia: the ubiquitous *Necronomicon*, of course, but also "the *Unaussprechlichen Kulten* of von Junzt, and old Ludvig Prinn's hellish *De Vermis Mysteriis*."[98] The body of Christianity is crumbling, and what emerges from the ruins appears more ancient and far vaster than the hopeless and fated symbolic order that once fought to suppress it. This is an evil "older than mankind and wider than the known universe."[99] Christianity represented as an exploded facade, a narrative fig leaf against our vulnerability, appears again in "The Shadow of Innsmouth," where the churches have been taken over by the mysterious "Esoteric Order of Dagon." In Innsmouth, this cult of Dagon has "engulfed all the orthodox churches" and left even the Georgian buildings, suggestive perhaps of a more "rational" Christianity, "long abandoned."[100] In its natural condition, then, religion confronts the same chaos and horror as does science. Religion, however, supernaturalizes the cosmic hostility, imagining illusions of a transcendent realm out of configurations of matter and energy unknown to humanity. Religion then compounds the discovery of horror with obscene self-delusion. Old Castro, the captured member of the Cthulhu cult, reveals the base passions underlying the religious fantasy: "Secret priests would take great Cthulhu from His tomb to . . . resume His rule of earth. . . . Then mankind would have become as the Great Old Ones; free and wild and beyond good and evil, with laws and morals thrown aside and all men shouting and killing and revelling in joy."[101] Unlike religion, science is dispassionate and gives up the imagination of beneficent powers that we can please in a universe considerate of our needs. Rational inquiry makes its way, piecing together the evidence, combining those dissociated knowledges, until it reaches its end in the trauma of horrific discoveries—not so much a case of "enlightenment," as, to fashion a Lovecraftian word, "enumbrament"!

Perverse to its initial promise, the scientific path ends with truths that bankrupt human aspiration. The appalling revelations that intellectual integrity brings, though, are also the principal site for sublimity. Sublime paraphernalia are found throughout Lovecraft's stories: the intimations of infinite space, his "cyclopean" architecture, the deployment of the unknown and obscure as a source of fear, his allusions to unimaginable antiquities, the irresistible power of his monsters. These classic motifs, however, cohere to form an overarching evocation of a greater sublime that encompasses all our experience, threatening by its inassimilable heterogeneity, suspending intelligibility and all our strivings for knowledge over an abyss of disorder: "The monstrous nuclear chaos beyond angled space which the *Necronomicon* had mercifully cloaked under the name of Azathoth."[102] Chaos does not only erupt within an order of things that is then able to reassert itself, resolving the conflict. The truly sublime danger is not contained within the world but rather has already consumed the world within itself—hence, the ironic ambivalence toward science. On the one hand, the stories declare the strident preference for science over religion, repeatedly hold up for sympathy ideal, objective investigators, and give plaudits to contemporary scientific developments. On the other, though, Lovecraft's tales deny the very intelligibility, the unified understanding, that science seeks and that scientific inquiry presumes as its ground and goal. As the universe is without Logos, science is brought to an end in these tales.

In representing science as necessarily tragic as well as nobly opposed to religion, Lovecraft becomes not just antitheological but antihumanist. Some of the resistance to classing Lovecraft's work as science fiction at all derives from this refusal of the sublime and emancipatory narrative that identifies science and technology with an "infinitely" progressive human vocation. This narrative of human liberty and limitless attainment informs much of the genre from Burroughs' John Carter gunning across the Martian outback to Poul Anderson's magnificent *Tau Zero*, in which a small remnant of humanity toughs it out through the collapse of the universe by a combination of scientific rigor and old-fashioned will power.[103] Science fiction has also consistently explored the ambiguities of these narratives, not only in the subgenre of apocalyptic tales, but also in such politically reflective works as Le Guin's novel about an anarchist utopia and Reynolds' more recent tale of a vast computer-monitored democracy.[104] Lovecraft's subversion of the modern narrative however remains distinct, even compared with severely bleak science-fictional apocalyptic. Human folly may undermine the beneficent possibilities of technology, it may initiate doomsday, but the judgment falls upon humanity, not upon the technoscientific enterprise it has misused. For the Lovecraftian scientist, on the other hand, science is epistemologically fated and fatal from the start, and most surely when it is pursued most steadfastly.[105]

Sublime horror not only recasts the place of science, robbing humanity of its one fair shot at significance. In other tales, cosmic fear settles upon personal narratives, implicitly upon any with which men and women provide themselves with at least a local, relative meaning. When he finally pieces together the anthropological evidence restoring his family's reputation for science and intellect, Arthur Jermyn gives vent to a "horrible scream" and torches himself in the backyard.[106] Walter de la Pore rebuilds Exham Priory but, having followed the patter of tiny rat feet, traces in tunnels under the building the bestial depredations of his ancestors. He is later found stark mad, chewing on the half-eaten body of his companion. Both Arthur Jermyn and Walter de la Pore attempt to reestablish stabilizing, socially powerful, but broken narratives. They inherit a family story ruptured by violence, ill reputation, and disgrace. After a period of success and security, both grasp at reviving family reputation and, repairing the history they have inherited, try to settle themselves within a restored dynastic narrative. So Walter rebuilds Exham Priory, and Arthur reweaves the threads of his forbears' ethnographic researches. The Lovecraftian pattern, of course, brings a shattering knowledge from the process of piecing together the evidence. As they learn the worst, their attempts to form a coherent, stabilizing narrative end narration altogether. Walter is mad, Arthur crispy, and both the last of their line. Again, though, the really ghastly—and the truly sublime—is not the horror as such, vivid though it often is, but what comes into view *through* the horror. These unhappy seekers have suffered the irresistible contradiction of their world, discovered its irreducible heterogeneity, that which always remains incompossible with the normative structures making for an intelligible environment, for practices, relationships, aspirations, and projects that fashion sense and hang together.[107] Nothing is what it seems, which leaves the mind abandoned in its hopeless rage for order. When Danforth sees the Shoggoth, driving through the deep tunnels, his stricken mind forces a desperate attempt at assimilation, at reasserting normality. "'South Station Under—Washington Under—Park Street Under—Kendall—Central—Harvard—' The poor fellow was chanting the familiar stations of the Boston-Cambridge tunnel that burrowed through our peaceful native soil thousands of miles away in New England."[108]

Beyond reason, the universe spawns from Nyarlathotep (the Crawling Chaos) and Azathoth (the Idiot God). Reality cannot be thought. It can, however, be narrated, and the narrative imagination persists beyond reason. Here is the familiar sublime dynamic of check and empowerment, pain and pleasure. Reason founders on the chaos of the world, its unthinkable heterogeneity, but imagination comes into its own. In this way, Lovecraft inverts Kant's Analytic of the Sublime, the most influential philosophical account of the function of sublimity. According to Kant, sublime objects frustrate our imaginative powers but, in so doing, provide a "negative pleasure" in that the measure of that failure is our own reason, which possesses the idea of the "absolutely great," the infinite. "*The sublime is that, the mere capacity of thinking which evidences a faculty of mind transcending every standard of sense.*"[109] The sublime confrontation, therefore, not only with scale, but with nature's overwhelming power, is pleasurably frightening in that our rational transcendence of nature arises in our mortal weakness.[110] This is not so for Lovecraft, whose stories localize our reason, subject it to our peculiar, transient conditions. His sublime horror traumatizes reason, undermines the independence of the rational self before nature, discloses its laughable fragility. However, if the impossible perversity that is the cosmos cannot be thought through, it can be intimated, imagined, and narrated. To that degree, the imagination endures, brooding over chaos. Lovecraft thus performs the sublime conjuration: the overwhelming of the human, the mind's confrontation with an annihilating power, yet redounds to humanity's credit. Much pulp science fiction—in representing nature, as well as future technology—deploys an inspirational sublime that invites awe, energy of purpose, imaginings of hopeful empowerment. Lovecraft, however, seeks that paradoxical uplift that comes from peeping into the abysmal. His tales offer themselves as a sublime therapy for acceptance of the reality principle in a radically inconstant universe. The reader faces the vast insecurity evoked by the deadly color from space—by decadent religious fanatics dragging on the coattails of malicious forces, by Cthulhu and the Old Ones—and survives in imagination, surmounting the universal horror, at least, in its metaphor.

Sublime horror is ubiquitous in Lovecraft's fictional universe. The forms of horror vary from eldritch kinks in space and time through the jugged brains of hapless victims caught by entities from Yuggoth, to patches of "unhealthy fecundity" in New England and the unbearable village of Dunwich that exists as a slow death suspended. Linking all these manifestations, and the stories that recount them, an anticreation myth, whose demiurgic representatives are Nyarlathotep and Azathoth, functions as a metanarrative that frames the stories. The myth haunts the space between the individual stories and taints even such limited resolution with which a tale may close. Lovecraft always gestures toward the cosmos that encloses the events and action of the stories. The diverse sources so nimbly structured in "The Call of Cthulhu" are worldwide, from Louisianan bayou to Norwegian suburb, with Arctic, Asian, and Australian references in between. Cthulhu's story, along with *At the Mountains of Madness* and "The Shadow Out of Time," also draws the whole of human and prehuman history into its orbit. The horror encompasses all time and absorbs all space, hence the strength of the sublime threat Lovecraft evokes. This horror, though, both as cosmic and particular, fascinates as it repels, both alluring and appalling, as did Fuseli's *The Nightmare*. The tales bring the reader into this tension and relieve it, exorcise it imaginatively. Read in this way, Lovecraft's sublime horror becomes a particularly vivid metaphor of the abject.

"Abjection" refers to what sanity and order insist we keep at bay. The abject does not necessarily terrify, though, as with blubbery Shoggoths, or the glutinous Cthulhu, it may be represented as fearful. Characteristically, the abject revolts. In the fridge, one finds a dead cockroach smothered in the butter and feels repugnance, nauseated. The coincidence with the stock in trade of horror movies is obvious: the staggering zombie heedlessly kicking the dragging remnants of its larger intestine. As these two examples suggest, human beings react in this distinctive way to certain violations of proper place, boundary transgressions or ambiguities, such as between impure and pure, edible and inedible, inside and outside, the dead and the living. Anthropology and, most especially, psychoanalysis have explored abjection in relation to the sacred and profane, to individual and social integrity, and most especially to the formative processes of subjectivity. The latter, especially, provide a helpful perspective on the imaginative power of Lovecraft's horror and the character of its sublimity.

Feeling, not judgment, Julia Kristeva argues, registers the abject.[111] A person feels the abject, feels it as a root threat to identity, to the border between the self and the not-self, between social order and chaos, sense and nonsense, sacred reality and that which defiles, taints, and is exiled from the sacred. Abject images, objects, and events challenge the order of things as metaphors for erasing vital differences, for the threat to identity in which people fear losing themselves, being absorbed, or being dissolved.[112] "The abject is not an ob-ject facing me, which I name or imagine. . . . The abject has only one quality of the object—that of being opposed to *I*."[113] Abjection, Kristeva argues, is a process of pushing away, of expelling in order to create a demarcation, a difference, a border. The originating abjection occurs at the prelinguistic stage of our infant development. The abject appears before subjectivity is formed through language as the child accedes to the symbolic code. Abjection begins as the infant starts the process of separation, of forming the lines of difference along which, at a later stage, a world of distinct objects will arise. Kristeva refers to the abject, therefore, as a "non-object," a term that nicely recalls Lovecraft's angles that are neither obtuse nor acute, spaces that look as if they enclose but turn out to repel, and that color out of space that inheres in no colored object. The wretched Mrs. Gardner, eaten away by this alien color, first suffers a breakdown in the capacity to discriminate one thing from another: "In her raving there was not a single specific noun, but only verbs and pronouns."[114] The abject belongs, then, in infancy "before any relation to an other is set up, and as if underlying it, it is the building of that archaic space, the topological demarcation of the preconditions of a subjectivity."[115]

The earliest attempts "to release the hold of *maternal* entity," however, initiate a traumatic process, albeit necessary to becoming a subject at all.[116] The child's marking and prying itself into subjectivity is traumatic because at this stage there is no clear distinction between inside and outside, between the maternal body and the "proper self" of the child. The infant, so to speak, is carving what will become "outside"—out of itself, that is—of its unity with the mother. The abject is both itself and other, a fearful ambiguity that a person never fully escapes. The process of abjection, therefore, is both vital and threatening. What is pushed away threatens to return, to engulf the precarious beginnings of a separation that is fluid and always haunted by the possibility of collapse, of an end to the promise of integrity. Kristeva's concept of abjection has affinities with Freud's uncanny—that is, unsettling—disorienting experiences of the eerie or weird. Freud argues this feeling to be of the intimately familiar "gone bad," of what was once "homely" (*heimlich*), become "unhomely" (*unheimlich*).[117] Uncanniness is a doubled business; the attractive lurks under the perturbing:

> Some would award the crown of the uncanny to the idea of being buried alive, only apparently dead. However, psychoanalysis has taught us that this terrifying fantasy is merely a variant of another, which was originally not at all frightening, but relied on a certain lasciviousness; this was the fantasy of living in the womb.[118]

Unlike Kristeva, though, Freud explains the uncanny as a return of what the mind has repressed into the unconscious. However, the process of abjection, according to Kristeva, persists continually as the dark companion at the edges of consciousness, threatening and inviting dissolution. The abject, therefore, attends the borders that religion, society, and culture establish and maintain. It manifests itself in disgust at particular foods, in fear of death and horror of corpses, in revulsion at certain combinations and hybridities of being (actual and imagined), and—in the moral sphere, as

Kristeva suggests—in reactions to betrayal, hypocrisy, and political corruption.[119]

The abject, then, threatens the order of integrity, individual and social. All this, though, only names one side of the abject, as its similarity with Freud's uncanny implies. The other side of the abject is fascination. The abject both repels and draws. Insofar as it is destructive of subjectivity, of all that constitutes the subject as a subject, it is supremely frightening and so presents as horror; but insofar as it is the symbol of the absent mother and of lost satisfaction, it is supremely desirable. The lure of the womb and of the maternal desire for the infant persists as simultaneously appalling and compelling. We love and fear peering over the abyss of nonentity. That duality, though, renders the abject a fit candidate for sublimation.

Throughout Lovecraft's tales, the abject appears. His narratives assault integrities of time and place, personal and global history, landscape and living things, science and religion. Subjectivity dissolves, and subjects face themselves or their histories as horrifyingly alien. In intimations of "angled space," the Old Ones lurking between dimensions, Nyarlathotep eating away the desperately frail solidarities of being, Lovecraft turns abjection into metaphysics. He also renders it sublime, combining with his hybridities and abominations, his violations of form and structure a terror of cosmic proportion. Being the nonform of an anticreation, the abject has theological moment in Lovecraft. The narrator of "The Shadow over Innsmouth" finally escapes the town, pursued by its sickening inhabitants. He takes cover in a ditch, clenching his eyes shut so as not to look upon his hunters—in vain, of course, since the lure of appalling fascination is too much, and he watches the

> limitless stream—flopping, hopping, croaking, bleating—surging inhumanly through the spectral moonlight in a grotesque malignant saraband of fantastic nightmare. . . . And one, who led the way, had a man's felt hat perched on the shapeless thing that answered for a head.[120]

Nothing has definition here; even the one clear object, the "man's felt hat," only sets off the "shapeless thing" beneath it, while the crowd expands into a "limitless stream" that is "surging" in a universe of discordant movements indicated in an open series of participles. The abject is taken up by that sublime expansion into the vast, indefinite, and obscure. In consequence, life is suspended within an unveiled and enduring abject: "It was the end for whatever remains to me of life on the surface of this earth, of every vestige of mental peace and confidence in the integrity of Nature and of the human mind."[121] Lovecraft enlarges the abject to the scale of a cosmos: it surrounds and promises to engulf language, reason, culture. In tales that only rarely contain female characters, and then in only marginal ways, the world itself is a ghastly maternal embrace, the devouring mother that threatens to consume the subject.

Yet the readers read on, consuming the sublime pleasure, the exhilaration of the horror tale. Science is a fatal necessity for Lovecraft; it is the supreme of language as handmaid to reason, the finest achievement of the symbolic order. In this abject universe, however, science betrays and leads humanity back to the abject for the final word. Science cannot protect from this horror. The symbolic order does, though, have another trick up its sleeve. Where science fails, the sublime tale of cosmic fear may deal with the abject ritually. Lovecraft's tales are a corpus; individual tales invite the reading of others through the continuities and links among them: themes, motifs, images, key words, the references to characters and institutions, Wilmarth, Miskatonic University, Arkham. Then there are those infamous and blood-stopping texts—above all, the weird *Necronomicon* by the "Mad Arab" Abdul Alhazred. The stories' open-endedness also serves their connectedness and the narrative push from one tale to another. Uncertainty persists in the tales, even where there is apparent resolution. The stories do not finish off the monstrosity they conjure; it leaks out of the monster and leaves traces, exactly the purpose of slime and goo. The traces urge the anxious question, though, "Has it really gone?" Readers are left to wonder what Danforth saw in the mountains, whether the Arkham water supply is tainted, what happened to Henry Akeley's brain, why those woods are still so thick and the ground unfertile, and just what did Walter see before eating his friend. In an ironic reversal of the polarity he imagines between science and religion, the reading of the tales is a ritual of containment and exorcism. In the horrific sublime, reason is out, but the narrative imagination comes into its own to give us the metaphor of an impossible safety.

With a particular savagery, Lovecraft reconfigures the natural sublime as a sublime of catastrophic power that is not a blessing in disguise and has no beneficent providence behind it, coordinating danger with good purpose. Burroughs' Martian adventures and Merritt's fantasies stay closer to the classical natural sublime, imagining nature as a forcing ground for manly fight and virtue or instinct with powers that science might inherit. Campbell, following H. G. Wells in this respect, divides the natural and technological sublime, fashioning a mythology of technological hope. Campbell and Lovecraft both attempt their mythologies as responses, at least in part, to the revival of determinedly antiteleological accounts of natural selection. The scale and the transvaluating implications of evolutionary theory invited sublime representations that would project new mythologies alternative to classical Christian accounts of creation. Among evolutionary mythmakers, though, it was H. G. Wells and Olaf Stapledon who set out with a rare intensity differing but paradigmatic visions of evolution sublimed. While Wells maintained the divergence of natural sublimity from the human vocation, Stapledon attempted a post-Christian reconciliation in which, in contrast to Lovecraft, a universe with no partiality for the human yet serves as an occasion for worship.

# 3

# WELLS AND STAPLEDON
## The Evolutionary Sublime

*Whatever asteroid assaults the earth in the future, surely there will be torrid vents and seeps that will once again allow the primeval cells to spread their coloured slime over the earth, even as creatures of complexity and elegance know their last days.*

—Richard Fortey, *Life*

*Evolution is the creation myth of our age.*

—Mary Midgley, *Evolution as Religion*, 33

Those who argued the religious importance of the sublime in the eighteenth century did so within the context of a universe marked by design, a creation in which all parts fitted and coordinated like a great machine. Sublimity served its special purpose in this immense and intricate artifact. Divine wisdom fit the design of the soul to nature's working so that even in its threatening and inhospitable aspects nature still served as handmaid to divinity and human fulfillment. This vision of design culminated in William Paley's *Natural Theology*, published in 1802.[1] Paley's world bustles with examples of God's wise contrivance, both in the mass and in the individual. Plants and animals uniquely fitted for life flourish in circumstances for which only a designing intelligence could have shaped them, and this from God's noblest creations to the humblest. Consider the snail, Paley argues, an animal seemingly composed entirely of lacks and disabilities, yet this creature fits its place and "climbs up the stalks of plants, by the sole aid of a viscid humour discharged from her skin."[2] In *On the Origin of Species*, Charles Darwin, who admired Paley's work, transformed this fit that argued God's intricate coordination of creation into the blind selective process that ensured only fit varieties would survive.[3] For the Victorian imagination, Darwin created new terms upon which to represent the sublimity of nature. Many of the consequent imaginings funded both the scientific and the science-fictional contest with Christianity for the honors of true sublimity. Darwin's nature worked by struggle and extinction; beauty and seeming harmonies originated in life's violently feeding upon life. Not the details of natural selection, which remained disputed and for a long time marginalized, but the terrific implications of "the struggle for existence" and "the survival of the fittest" induced a rebirth of images.

The Victorian painter George Frederic Watts produced two contrasting paintings inspired by Darwinian evolution, particularly as it appeared in public debate and imagination: *Chaos*, begun in 1873 but not completed until after 1882, and *Evolution*, finished in 1904. They realize two very different ways of representing evolution as sublime, one of which remains in some religious continuity with the eighteenth century, while the other reflects Darwin's more radical effect upon the sublime imagination. In both, evolution becomes the stuff of myth, as it does in science fiction. As first intended, *Chaos* presented, according to Watts, "the introductory chapter of a general history of mankind."[4] On the right of the picture, a riot of churning forms shows giants struggling for release from the convulsions of earth. A fire rages in the background, its smoke curving toward the midcenter of the picture where, under a clearer sky, mountain ranges have risen from the swirling surfaces of rock and water. In the lower center, a huge and solitary figure—humanity, forged from the battles of elements and evolution—strides toward the raised rock plateau on the left, round which female figures flow in a linked chain and on which giants rest in calm. Watts wanted to unite religious and evolutionary vision. He rejected conventional Christianity, and the painting does not particularly invite even a theistic interpretation. Nevertheless, a divinity suffuses the cosmos. As a spiritual process, nature is sublime and in its sublimity still nurtures spirit, still inspires humanity that rises, itself sublime, from the waters.[5] The later work, *Evolution*, however, suggests a much more doubtful relationship between humanity and a sublime nature. A female figure—representing "the Earthmother," according to Watts—sits with her children around her feet. She pays them no attention but looks anxiously into a far distance invisible to the viewer. A vast space opens behind her where a troubled sky looms; she appears threatened by cosmic forces larger than herself. Unheeded, Earth's children are brutally fighting one another, and a single child reaches out toward her, seeking help. Earth ignores her children, though, and only looks on into uncertainty, the future she cannot guarantee for her children. The spiritual binding of nature and humanity has snapped; sublime nature no longer serves the human vocation.

## H. G. WELLS: HUMANITY VERSUS THE BEAST

In the context of painting *Chaos*, Watts had declared, "All is progression, revolution, evolution, and gravitation towards renewal."[6] H. G. Wells termed this type of affirmation "bio-optimism" and dismissed it with contempt. In the 1890s, though, views that wedded evolution to progress held the high ground.[7] They found no fissure between evolution and human history or confidence in a sublime human future that owed its infant steps to such natural forces. For some clergy, baptizing evolution as the instrument of providence gave Darwin his saving grace. "Design by wholesale is grander than design by retail," roared Henry Beecher, while the Scottish theologian Henry Drummond greeted evolution as "the phenomenal expression of the Divine, the progressive realization of the Ideal, the Ascent of Love."[8] The Scots biologist Patrick Geddes assured the public that suggesting nature advances solely by weeding out the losers is a "libel projected upon nature."[9] His editorial colleague added, "It may be that the newness is simply that what was of evil in the parents has been forgiven in their children; but sometimes it is that the little child leads the race, as was said long ago."[10] All this infuriated Wells, who warned that natural selection has no favorites. Life is a battlefield, and the "sculptor who carves out the new forms of life," Wells writes, "is called Pain and Death." Anyone who embraces the stark "Calvinism of science" must seize with both hands the brutal, unsmiling facts. Natural selection measures success by "present adaption to circumstances" alone, and that, as Wells pointed out, gives no assurance of progress.[11] Degeneration is also adaption and, given certain environmental circumstances, a fitter adaption than those complexities that we consider progress.[12] Change the landscape enough, and the slugs end up lords of creation. Human advance has no certain friend in Darwinian evolution, so responsible scientists have no business encouraging a false confidence in progress. Believing that love ascends along with evolutionary change not only falsifies science, Wells warns, but it makes humanity vulnerable through its own "frantic hopefulness." A culture that gets the implications of evolution wrong will mistake the forces ranged against it and go down under a world that knows nothing of loving progress but only bloodied teeth and claws. In Wells' assessment, the choice between bio-optimism and living with Darwinian reality was not only scientific but political and ethical. Bio-optimism invited complacency and a false trust. Coming to terms with the grim implacability of natural selection should force us to ask after the dignity of the human and to find imperatives for its future.[13]

Wells published *The Time Machine* in 1895, two years before Watts began *Evolution* and at the high point of the "eclipse of Darwinism."[14] Against confidence in evolutionary progress, he sets a darkly sublime account of Earth, thirty million years into the future:

> Beyond these lifeless sounds the world was silent. Silent? It would be hard to convey the stillness of it. All the sounds of man, the bleating of sheep, the cries of birds, the hum of insects, the stir that makes the background of our lives—all that was over. . . . As I stood sick and confused I saw again the moving thing upon the shoal—there was no mistake now that it was a moving thing—against the red water of the sea. It was a round thing, the size of a football perhaps, or, it may be, bigger, and tentacles trailed down from it; it seemed black against the weltering blood-red water, and it was hopping fitfully about.[15]

Everything comes down to this; the long haul of evolution, outlasting millennia of human history, resolves to a black and tentacled bag, hopping on an oily beach. Evolution's coldly pragmatic business works at the end with only the most parsimonious environment for life, as entropy swells a chillier sun. Weakness is all. The last creature shambles fitfully, its tentacles hang and trail, but it survives, natural selection's rough and ready compromise. This degeneracy, or "retrogressive modification" (as Wells' teacher T. H. Huxley termed it), has no less evolved than the dog or the human, and is no less authentically a product of natural selection than creatures advanced in complexity.[16] Context determines fitness, so a degenerate form may well be better adapted for survival. With one imaginative stone, Wells attacked two ideological birds. This frightful scene on the world's last shoreline mocks both progress and design. Wells uses the sublime to render the scene inhuman: a totality of silence, the complete absence of the familiar, obscurity and shadow hinting a fearful exposure to the alien under an immensity of swollen sun and by a red sea—a sea that then becomes "weltering blood-red."[17] Wells uses this sublime fear, with its strong notes of horror, to assault the projection of Victorian progress onto evolution. A metaphor of knowledge as a slow, groping progress to a discomforting realization informs the Time Traveller's experience. In his first posthuman stop, he stares at a "monstrous crab-like creature" and feels "a tickling on his cheek as though a fly has lighted there." He reaches for it, then grabs and catches "something threadlike," and discovers his ghastly mistake: "I had grasped the antenna of another monster crab that stood just behind me. Its evil eyes were wriggling on their stalks."[18] Following the horror, the reader's imagination answers Wells' implicit question: Is this dreary and exhausted end evidence for a governing intelligence or for a blind mechanism through which life squeezes out its final forms? Indeed, the hopping grotesque shall inherit the earth—no wonder the Time Traveller hurtles back to the nineteenth century, desperate for restorative drink and a mutton chop.

At best, evolution makes, in Wells' view, only a fair-weather friend to humanity. His scientific romances, though, do not oppose this sturdy evolutionary doctrine to an unambiguous affirmation of the technological sublime. Technology, too, exists in an ambiguous relationship with natural evolution. Encased in their "rotating cowls" and spraying the countryside with heat rays, Wells' invading Martians receive sublime description. Their "exultant [howls] drowned the thunder," and, "shining with the growing light of the east, three of the metallic giants stood above the pit . . . beyond were the pillars of fire about Chobham. They became pillars of bloodshot smoke at the first touch of day."[19] Absent their deadly technology, though, the Martians certainly lack personal athleticism, their initial entrance on the English scene resembling an intoxicated walrus dropping flabbily from a London bus. "A big greyish rounded bulk," Wells writes, "was rising slowly and painfully out of the cylinder. As it bulged up and caught the light, it glistened like wet leather. . . . There was a mouth under the eyes, the lipless brim of which quivered and panted, and dropped saliva." Physically incompetent, Earth's most perilous enemy does not even manage to climb from its interplanetary transport without the indignity of a pratfall: "Suddenly the monster vanished. It had toppled over the brim of the cylinder and fallen into the pit, with a thud like the fall of a great mass of leather."[20] Entirely dependent on their technology, reduced to feeble bodies under oversized brains, the Martians are evolutionary degenerates, which makes Wells' likening their predations to British imperialism even more pointed.[21] Cultural, technological advance is no sure protection against that pragmatic mechanism of natural selection; indeed, progressive intelligence may well enter into a blind collaboration with evolution and render itself miserably vulnerable. In the end, the Martians succumb to the common cold.[22]

*The Island of Dr. Moreau* also provides a cautionary tale of technological limits, one that draws upon an essay Wells had written for the *Saturday Review* in which he proposed that "a living being may also be regarded as raw material, as something plastic, something that may be shaped and altered . . . and the organism as a whole developed far beyond its apparent possibilities."[23] Though Wells had presented such "plasticity" as an insufficiently explored scientific opportunity, *Dr. Moreau* develops the implications in a dystopian direction. The novel provides a negative image of human progress and of the humanistic sublime that Wells opposes to evolutionary sublimity. Moreau tells the shipwrecked Prendick about his ghastly experiments on the animal population of the island. His investigations explore how the animal differs from the human and, in the process, suggests how vulnerable is that difference. The vivisectionist has taken the Darwinian measure; natural selection marks out a continuous pathway from beast to human. No divine initiative raises the one from the other, as Darwin had argued against Arthur Wallace. Nor has Moreau, any more than Wells, time for the idealism of the biologist J. S. Haldane, who argued for mind as metaphysically basic and incapable of mechanical explanation.[24] The human emerges by the inches of mechanical variation and selection. Moreau, though, hopes to initiate an accelerated evolution. However, neither he nor Wells are Lamarckians, and therefore they do not think that traits acquired during an animal's lifetime are inheritable by its progeny. The grisly experiments, therefore, affect only individual animals and do not "change in any way the offspring of such a creature."[25] The core problem is that the beasts prove persistently less plastic than Moreau desires: "Somehow the things drift back again: the stubborn beast-flesh grows day by day back again." The bestial, the ancient enmity between nature and culture, keeps creeping into view: "cravings, instincts, desires that harm humanity." There is "a strange hidden reservoir" out of which the dark drives hewn by natural selection reassert themselves.[26] By the novel's end, every one of Moreau's creatures has reverted from its semihumanity to the animal. More sinister still, when Prendick finally returns to England, his neighbors persistently remind him of their bestial origins more clearly than their humanity: "I could not persuade myself," he laments, "that the men and women I met were not also another Beast People, animals half wrought into the outward image of human souls."[27] The dualism of natural and social evolution, the source of Wells' particular configuration of sublimity, trumps Moreau's ambitions for plasticity and reveals itself, for Prendick, in the persistent animal lineaments of his neighbors.

The island setting shapes Wells' vivisectionist parable. Though the reader suspects Moreau would be up to no good in a suburban basement, the island location leaves Moreau room to work undisturbed, without social reaction to his experiments. This also leaves the vivisectionist and his beasts with an insufficient human community. In this respect, the novel makes an ironic contribution to the Robinson Crusoe tradition.[28] Island loneliness does not nurture humanity. In Moreau's case, isolation erodes his humanity, as well as shattering Prendick with the terrible realization that natural selection's most savage instincts still wait at the cultural door, ready to pounce. "Speech," Wells argued in an essay written at the same time as the novel, is the attainment that differentiates animal and human.[29] Language contains the distinctively human possibilities. What specifies humanity, therefore, though it originates through natural selection, develops by another process. In the slow growth of human societies, a new form of evolution gets its purchase on the raw material of human being: social evolution, which may serve as a counterforce to a natural selection that simply makes the grim best of universal entropy. "The evolutionary process," Wells argues, "now operating in the social body is one essentially different from that which has differentiated species in the past and raised man to his ascendancy among the animals."[30] Prendick withdraws from the crowd into astronomical meditations as his final solution for the traumatic discoveries on Moreau's island. The Time Traveller, another lone figure, also reaches pessimistic conclusions as to human improvement—he "thought but cheerlessly of the Advancement of Mankind, and saw in the growing pile of civilization only a foolish heaping that must inevitably fall back upon and destroy its makers in the end."[31] He continues with his time machine and disappears forever. Neither reach what will become Wells' new focus for sublimity, formulated in the hope that "men with a trained reason and a sounder science . . . [may] work towards, and at last attain and preserve, a social organization so cunningly balanced against natural necessities on the one hand, and the artificial factor in the individual on the other, that the life of every human being . . . may be generally happy."[32]

In placing his hopes in social evolution, Wells followed his teacher, T. H. Huxley, also a fierce critic of bio-optimism. Huxley warned that evolution "encourages no millennial anticipations" and acknowledged that natural selection produced the degenerate as well as the progressive.[33] By and large, life on earth has taken the "upward road," but one day, he counsels, "the summit will be reached and the downward route will be commenced."[34] In the meantime, humanity's trump card is its ability to fashion an intelligent social life in the teeth of evolutionary necessity. The latter can never be extinguished but may be opposed, checked, and modified. Civilization turns the "cosmic process" and substitutes what Huxley termed "the ethical process," in which, "in opposition to the State of Nature, man may develop a worthy civilization, capable of maintaining and constantly improving itself."[35] Prendick, Moreau, the Time Traveller, as well as Griffin, the deranged invisible man, in different ways refuse this ethical and essentially social process.

Social evolution, however, faces its own internal demons. Wells accepted and admired E. Ray Lankester's arguments concerning the implications of evolutionary degeneration. Another hounder of the evolutionary optimists, Lankester set out numerous examples of zoological degeneration and concluded "any new set of conditions occurring to an animal which render its food and safety very easily attained, seem to lead as a rule to Degeneration," a point that may be described as an analogy waiting to happen.[36] Certainly, Wells drew the moral conclusions from the connection between ease and degeneracy, the same connection that would impress John Campbell. Wells, therefore, took Lankester's warning to heart: "Possibly we are all drifting, tending to the condition of intellectual Barnacles or Ascidians. It is possible for us . . . to reject the good gift of reason with which every child is born, and to degenerate into a contented life of material enjoyment accompanied by ignorance and superstition."[37] The divided humanity the Time Traveller finds at the closing stage of human history traces out the implications of too much material enjoyment. Humanity breaks apart into the vapid, childlike Eloi and the bestial, underground Morlocks, who feed upon them. Over millennia, leisured and privileged humanity had adapted to the unnatural conditions of ease, their strength and mind gradually atrophying. The Morlocks, however, were the distant descendants of industrial humanity and had evolved in cunning without culture, finally enslaving their ancient masters. Wells does not regret this sorry circumstance in the manner of Ruskin or Tennyson, who lamented their culture's betrayal of Christian ideals. Wells presents the Eloi and the Morlocks as the consequence of evolutionary forces working on a humanity blind to what might keep it human and, perhaps, at some crucial point, beguiled by bio-optimism. Evolution just does what it does: preserves those variations fitter than others for the environment at hand. Once relieved from the pressure of natural selection the Eloi submit to ease, and degeneration follows from the atrophy of vital strengths no longer needed. On the other hand, the Morlocks adapt successfully into a robust but degenerate form suited to their underground life. They now flourish at the expense of the Eloi, whose decadence is no longer relatively fit for the environment now the toiling classes have turned predator.

Wells' readers had to look to his utopian writings, rather than the scientific romances, if they wanted more than slivers of hope for a social evolution able to hold back the fatal conspiracy between natural selection and entropy. He published *Anticipations*, the first of these, in 1901, but his most widely read exercise in futurology was *A Modern Utopia*, which came out in 1905. The year before this, though, one scientific romance imagined an advancing and triumphant human future. In *The Food of the Gods and How It Came to Earth*, the human vocation emerges as a sublime dynamic of growth against socially and evolutionary conservative forces. A peculiar and mongrel production, *The Food of the Gods* begins as a comic novel before turning into an adventure yarn that slides into heavy-handed allegory and ends with a sermon. More than adequate for comic scenes, the silly plot fails dismally when the story darkens. Mr. Bensington and Professor Redwood heedlessly discover and, even more heedlessly, develop "Boom Food," a dietary additive that stimulates growth. Wells develops the consequences in some brilliantly funny writing. Bensington naively employs the thoroughly unreliable and venal Mr. and Mrs. Skinner to manage an experimental farm on which, ignorant of its powers, they raise chickens on the Boom Food. Soon, the chickens grow like rank weeds, devour the local cat, and achieve the size of emus. Predictably, the food leaks into the countryside, and the population is terrorized by giant plants, giant earwigs, giant wasps, and giant rats. Meanwhile, Professor Redwood has started feeding the food to his infant, an experiment that would put him with Dr. Moreau were it not played for laughs. Running out of humor, however, the story stumbles into the persecution of the various secretly raised "Boom Children," and a ridiculous romance between a giant child and a similarly overgrown princess. When the children defend themselves, we are in the thick of unmistakable allegory, figuring the necessity of change and the absurd pettiness of human resistance. *The Food of the Gods* does not celebrate scientists but the effects of their science, the changed scope of possibility that they bring about, without expecting or understanding it. Social evolution, its dynamics not unlike natural selection, requires the readiness for change, for adaption to altered circumstances, and, in particular, to the potentials that develop from human ingenuity but that have no more mercy on those who cannot embrace them than the shifting opportunities of evolution. "What right," announces the giant and appropriately named Redwood, "have parents to say, My child shall have no light but the light I have had, shall grow no greater than the greatness to which I have grown?" Sublimity rises in the powers of social growth and change: "For greatness is abroad, not only in us, not only in the Food, but in the purpose of all things! It is in the nature of all things. . . . To grow and still to grow: from first to last that is Being—that is the law of life."[38]

A humanist sublime, elevating a progressive dynamic of social evolution, opposes the relentlessness of the evolutionary sublime in Wells' utopian vision. The sublimity of the human vocation depends, again, upon movement, the historical exceeding of immanent horizons. In Well's vision, only the ultimate and inevitable entropy of nature itself limits this movement. The modern utopia, Wells warns, shall not boast a completed perfection, the stasis of Bacon's New Atlantis or Campanella's City of the Sun. A modern utopia must be "kinetic" and so "drafted not as a permanent state but as a hopeful stage, leading to a long ascent of stages."[39] "Artificial" evolution, the evolution of society, will check the process of nature's brutal filtering and—in a kindlier order, albeit one complete with eugenics, a planned economy, and a ruling elite—take over its functions in coordinating material necessities with population growth, length of life, and the achievement of happiness. Existence calls humanity to struggle with a daunting and terrible fissure: on the one side, natural selection; and, on the other, human interests and virtues, the process of "social evolution." This non-Darwinian distinction allows Wells to preserve a unique dignity for human beings on a plane above nature.[40] Human destiny is a sublime drama: "Man is the unnatural animal, the rebel child of Nature, and more and more does he turn himself against the harsh and fitful hand that reared him. . . . In the Modern Utopia he will have set himself to change the ancient law."[41] Humanity must, therefore, "rise upon the changes that humans create or wither by the changes nature enforces." As with Campbell and Rauschenbusch, the nonhuman falls to the side of what opposes and resists the human, and upon which humans must impose their will.

*The Food of the Gods* finishes with a sermon that lauds the finite time of human evolution and renders humanity's ambition sublime, and so divine:

> To-morrow, whether we live or die, growth will conquer through us. That is the law of the spirit for ever more. To grow according to the will of God! To grow out of these cracks and crannies, out of these shadows and darknesses, into greatness and the light! "Greater," he said, speaking with slow deliberation, "greater, my Brothers! And then—still greater. To grow, and again—to grow. To grow at last into the fellowship and understanding of God. Growing. . . . Till the earth is no more than a footstool. . . . Till the spirit shall have driven fear into nothingness, and spread . . . ." He swung his arm heavenward:—"There!" His voice ceased. The white glare of one of the searchlights wheeled about, and for a moment fell upon him, standing out gigantic with hand upraised against the sky.[42]

Hope lies, in the meantime, between animal life and entropy, as we ensure a longer survival through a social evolution that—guided by rational elites, inspired by science, and served by technology—embodies the unique virtues of society and reflects humanity's best possibilities.

As practice and belief, religion—in particular, Christianity—is invisible in all this utopian straining. In *The War of the Worlds*, though, Wells had taken some care to dramatize Christianity's incompetence among the demands and dangers of a modern world. Fleeing across Surrey, the protagonist meets, along with other representative human types, an Anglican curate. Physically and mentally, the curate is incapable of meeting the crisis or even helping his own survival. His face "a fair weakness," he stares "blankly," mutters to himself, and whimpers in "selfish despair" whenever he isn't crying out pitiable non sequiturs about the judgment of God and the Cities of the Plain.[43] In every respect, he contrasts with Wells' healthy English protagonist with his workmanlike courage, practical intelligence, instinctive prudence, loyalty, affection, and that sane reasonableness that, even in danger from Martian death rays, remains capable of scientific curiosity. An exhibit of religion's ineptness, the curate cannot adapt to change since he lacks courage and the essential flexibility of mind. His fretful monologues on sin and divine justice give him no leverage on present danger. Survival has depended upon the indulgent privilege of a London suburb and a respectable religion. Wells throws Weybridge and its curate a violent evolutionary challenge. Their doom is quick and entire.[44]

In the middle of the First World War, however, Wells discovered the rhetorical worth of the term "God." Later on, he admitted that explicit theologizing was, in the end, more trouble than it was worth, and dismissed the venture as a species of goading: "I willfully tweaked the noses, and pulled the ears and generally insulted 'Christians' . . . to wake them up to an examination of their religion."[45] That said, he shows little sign of cynicism in the immensely popular novel *Mr. Britling Sees It Through*, in which Wells first experiments with a theological discourse able to sustain a humanist hope during the growing disillusion provoked by English losses in trench warfare.[46] *God the Invisible King*, the tract that quickly followed the novel, does roundly denounce present Christianity. However, Wells directs his energies largely to the coincidence of his hopes for a peaceful and progressive world with a new religious sensibility he finds among Europe's war-weary populations. For readers of Wells' utopian writings, *God the Invisible King* surprises only by advocating a future for theocracy.[47] The Wellsian dream, though, wholly subordinates the theology. Life in the kingdom of God goes on as usual: humanity works toward a world-state by "doing or sustaining scientific research or education or creative art; . . . making roads to bring men together, . . . working for the world's health, . . . building homes, . . . constructing machinery to save and increase the powers of men."[48] These two works, untypical though they are in explicitly theologizing, constitute a consistent attempt to map a doctrine of God onto the opposition between the humanistic sublime and the natural but in such a way as not to reduce or reconcile that opposition, nor to generate a sublimity that compromises the humanism in favor of the theology.

The closing pages of *Mr. Britling Sees It Through* transpose into a religious mythology Mr. Britling's personal struggle to square his patriotism with his grief. Wells stages his hero's religious conversion as the resolution to an emotional and intellectual crisis. Mourning his own son, Mr. Britling begins a letter of condolence to the parents of a young German lad who had served as tutor to his children before the war. As he writes, the gravitational pull of political and cultural solutions—the "big picture" of nations and boundaries, right and wrong—takes over from finding words for condolence and shared misery. The Wellsian active intellectual subdues the father in Mr. Britling: "He was writing, he perceived, not as Mr. Britling but as an Englishman . . . and he was writing to them as Germans . . . no longer writing to the particular parents of one particular boy, but to all that mass of suffering, regret, bitterness and fatigue that lay behind the veil of the 'front.'"[49] After some hours of this, though, he admits it reads like a "dissertation." Struck between verbiage and a sense of spiritual impulsion comes the conversion: Mr. Britling feels the presence of all men and women struggling with grief and hope, then the nearness of his lost son Hugh, and Heinrich the young tutor, and "all these and more . . . it was God, there present with him."[50] God's presence is immediate and compelling: "It was the Master, the Captain of Mankind, it was God, there present with him, and he knew that it was God."[51] In this moment and in the consequent thoughts, Britling "sees it through." The reader might well doubt, though, that seeing it through includes seeing those grieving Pomeranian parents. They are forgotten in the relief of a "conviction" now "clear and absolute in his mind."[52] The original problem, a particular father writing of a particular grief to two particular parents, is not resolved but permanently shelved. The audience leaves Mr. Britling ruminating over his new breakthrough having made the horrible decision to burden the hapless Pomeranians with his theology. Mercifully, Wells spares his readers the text. Britling's God thus arrives as a deus ex machina to rescue the dignity of the Wellsian active intellectual and to give a religious validity to that pull away from the particular toward the generalizing and commanding viewpoint. This God is "human like ourselves," Wells writes, adding not the "Jew God" who supposedly created everything but a limited, "defined," neighborly God who leads from within, uniting Hugh, Heinrich, and the others in a single struggle.[53] Though he only "fights through men," he is nonetheless "King" and "Captain" and so permits Wells the luxury of reducing the harsh complexities of human order and peacemaking to a clash with pantomime villains: "These tawdry emperors, these wily politicians and artful lawyers . . . will presently shrivel and pass—like paper thrust into a flame."[54] This God is an unstable, jerry-rigged compromise between the desire for concrete reality and the abstract counters of Mr. Britling's patriotic principles and maps of the Western front.

Expounding his religious vision in a more discursive form, Wells preaches his neighborly God as the answer to Christianity's historic failure: the religion's betrayal both of Jesus and of humanity. The Church failed because it lost itself in the impossible attempt to amalgamate an omnipotent Absolute with the brotherly God humanity really needs. What Wells offers instead of this supposed irrelevance amounts to a new mapping of the religious sublime, one that corresponds to the dualism of natural and social evolution. On the one hand, human reflection runs aground on "the mysteries of the universe," the ultimate grounds of cosmos and cosmological processes. Sublime language comes into play at this point. The ultimate reality Wells personifies as the "Veiled Being," from which comes the "Life Force," a "great wave," "rolling to us from beyond the horizon . . . rushing through matter and possessed by a spirit." Humanity must not expect a blessing from this Deus absconditus; the proper religious attitude to cosmogony is "complete Agnosticism."[55] Human beings gain nothing, Wells argues, but they lose much by projecting personality upon the universe. Along with the metaphysics, of course, modern men and women must also reject the omnipotent, omniscient, "jealous" God of the Jews who punishes sinners and generally throws his weight about.

The God needed for the times is a personal spirit who inspires and leads the human struggle for salvation as "a strongly marked and knowable personality, loving, inspiring, and lovable, who exists or strives to exist in every human soul."[56] This God has a beginning and so is finite. He has no providential control over nature but instead influences human beings and accomplishes his "motives" through them. "Like a dear, strong friend who comes and stands quietly beside one, shoulder to shoulder," God faces with us our struggle to make a better world.[57] However, as Wells' exposition gets into its stride, this God's divinity fades like the substance of a Cheshire cat, leaving only an encouraging, school-masterly smile. "He is," Wells continues, "the undying human memory, the increasing human will," the "synthesis" of humanity, the whole of which we are all the parts.[58] "Who bears affection for this or that spadeful of mud in my garden?" Wells asks. "Who cares a throb of the heart for all the tons of chalk in Kent or all the lumps of limestone in Yorkshire? Yet we all love 'England.'"[59] The cynical reader might ask, "And who cares about a couple of bereaved Pomeranians, when you can love modern humanity?" With some frustration, Wells finally gives up trying to have God theologically while eating him anthropologically and admits, "It seems to me a secondary matter whether we call Him 'Man's Great Achievement' or 'The Son of Man' or the 'God of Mankind' or 'God.'"[60]

Wells' God calls for homely or martial language, being a firm but understanding schoolmaster and a lovable but demanding sergeant major. Sublime, he is not. Wells has shorn his God of all those attributes of power and lordship intimated and imagined in sublime description. Sublime discourse remains with the human vocation itself over against the "Veiled Being" of universal inevitabilities. The new, human religion that Wells preaches is "the Koh-i-noor; it is a Mountain of Light, growing and increasing. It is an all-pervading lucidity, a brightness and clearness. It has no head to smite, no body you can destroy; it overleaps all barriers; it breaks out in despite of every enclosure. It will compel all things to orient themselves to it."[61] The theological innovations of *Mr. Britling* and *Invisible King* leave the dualism of natural and social evolution untouched. The sublime human vocation to a continual growth and change remains in this polar struggle with nature's sublime "Will to Be."[62] Wells' God hovers uncertainly between the two, held up by rhetorical inflation. In the end, this Deity served as merely a temporary theological conceit for the apotheosis of humanity that ends *The Food of the Gods*: "Greater, greater, my Brothers! And then—still greater. To grow, and again—to grow. To grow at last into the fellowship and understanding of God. Growing. . . . Till the earth is no more than a footstool."

Wells commandeered the theological by depriving his God of all sublime qualities while retaining them for humanity. In the process, he failed to attend to such obvious questions as to how a *finite* God—a personality, as he says, just like ourselves—can "influence" and "act through us" without violating the moral freedom that Wells treasures. If the "Captain of Mankind" is a way of talking about a vital and influential idea or inspiration, then all well and good, but Wells will keep insisting that God is both us writ large and an independent actor alongside men and women. Despite the naive theology, though, Wells' disposition of the science-fictional sublime into a dualism of cosmos and humanity has remained influential, as the *Doctor Who* episode "The Satan Pit" indicated.[63] Wells also contributed resources, both in the scientific romances and in his anti-Christian polemic, for the displacement of Christianity within the popular imagination, resources that continued to be drawn upon, extended, augmented, and reworked to the same end within later twentieth-century science fiction. Olaf Stapledon, though, Wells' younger contemporary, while also constructing an evolutionary myth, significantly modified Wells' humanistic focus.[64] While Wells, for the sake of the human vocation, cordoned off ultimacy and placed the "Veiled Being" beyond the pale of concern, Stapledon found human integrity precisely in relation to the quest for ultimacy. Stapledon refuses to settle for Wells' anthropocentric satisfactions, though he also completely rejects any identification of ultimate reality with the Christian God. In his novels, the natural and humanistic sublimes move into a new configuration as Stapledon goes where Wells feared to tread, to the "veiled being" or the "eternal," the "Star Maker."

## OLAF STAPLEDON: WORSHIP AFTER THE DEATH OF GOD

Olaf Stapledon's visionary ambitions have a scope that makes even *The Time Machine* seem parochial. *Last and First Men* ranges through eighteen evolutionary forms of humanity and across two billion years of history that, in turn, are reduced to a surface flutter by the aeons of universal time. The later novel *Star Maker* takes its protagonist through uncountable myriads of galaxies to discover their ultimate dissolution, beyond which, after an even longer period of "physical quiescence," shall come a new universe, and, after that, others yet to come.[65] Stapledon wanted to model a properly post-Darwinian mythmaking, and to do so on an imaginative scale that would overwhelm the Christian mythology with which, he believed, the Western world could no longer sustain itself. A true myth, he argued, "within the universe of a certain culture . . . expresses richly, and often perhaps tragically, the highest admirations possible within that culture."[66] False myths fall short of, or betray, a culture's "highest admirations." Classically, mythological narratives are concerned with origins, with formative beginnings, or with changes to the possibilities from which life is lived. From an age before the measurable years of common life, an age also always present, myths reveal the inescapable conditions for human lives: the powers that bear down on them, the limits to their own capacities, and the unmastered sources of sustenance and renewal. Stapledon, however, conceives his myths with a strong orientation to the temporal processes of evolution and history. A modern mythology, therefore, must anticipate futures, and, above all, it must ready men and women for change, instilling a cosmic vision that is sublime in scope and scale. Post-Darwinian, too, modern myth must seed history in nature. The humanity that strives for its future is the humanity that evolved out of millions of years of prehuman life, a humanity that is less "a little lower than the angels" and more "not much higher than the beasts."[67]

*Last and First Men* traces human history from the present through the flourishing and calamity of five succeeding forms of humanity, at the end of which the "Fifth men" leave Earth for Venus, escaping from disaster as Earth's moon plunges toward its planet. The story of "Venerian" men lasts for over five hundred million years before the prospect of the sun's collision with a vast gas cloud forces another migration, this time to Neptune. The Neptunian period is the last and longest part of human history, stretching from the Ninth Men to the Eighteenth and last race of humans. That race, though the most advanced and sophisticated of all humanities, is doomed to extinction by yet another, but this time inescapable, astronomical catastrophe. A narrative on this scale demands both a plausible point of view from which to tell the story and an overarching dramatic structure that determines the particular selection of events—in this case, from a two-billion-year history. Stapledon provides both point of view and narrative logic by way of the same device. The apparent narrator, a twentieth-century writer of fiction, serves unknowingly as the amanuensis of one of the Last Men, who has entered his mind, guided his thoughts, and inspired his tale.[68] This relationship shapes the selection, rhythm, and goal of the history. Events closest to contemporary history, therefore, receive a much more detailed telling because this Last Man wishes to influence the present for good.

Similarly, the hidden author describes future humanities nearer in time to the First Men more expansively because he may more readily accommodate his account to the limited intellectual capacities of the contemporary writer. However, the ultimate crisis of the final human civilization directs the history overall as the rationale for its telling, the goal of its drama, and the culminating exemplar of the tragic patterns that govern the stories of each human form.

Stapledon presents his humanities, therefore, according to the moments of sublimity—that is, the crises of sudden rises and catastrophic falls. The underlying dualism shows through the narrative: human races flourish when they can exploit the contingent possibilities of evolution; they decline when those possibilities disappear, either through some instability, inherent to the particular form, or through environmental changes. In the chance alignments evolution supplies, the sublime human vocation to progression and expansion is fitfully realized. The human horizon is inevitably tragic but, according to the wisdom of the Last Men and the experience of the traveller in *Star Maker*, human integrity depends on coming to terms with tragedy, in refusing to cultivate a bitter defiance or succumb to despair. Instead, tragedy is the touchstone of significance: the human vocation is the vocation to meaning. Men and women must pursue the significance of human life and history, but a significance commensurate with the truth of human life depends on facing the "littleness of your here and now."[69] Humanity rises in its own sublimity within the honest recognition of the inevitability of individual, cultural, and racial death, and against the very real possibility of ultimate cosmic indifference. Stapledon's question, as pursued by his central characters, is, "How may we live, joyously, ethically, energetically, even worshipfully, without denying our mortality, without rage or despair before our grotesque limitations and transience, and, most importantly, without the false consolations of religious faith?"

Both *Last and First Men* and *Star Maker* compress sublimities of spatial and temporal scale, consistently imagined in sublime terms, into an evolutionary configuration of space and time, an evolutionary "chronotope."[70] History, as the space-time of human making and striving, is set within and penetrated by the vastly larger space-time of evolution, which works nonteleologically by way of natural selection. In Stapledon's evolutionary chronotope, multiple forms of life spread and recede, establish and sustain themselves, lose their grip and disappear—all according to contingent, chance-ridden processes. Nature does not short-circuit its measures in order to produce mind: the cosmos is thus not rigged for intelligence, let alone humanity. Human beings may feel—and, in Stapledon's view, feel rightly—that "ultimately the way of life must be the way of intelligence and love and creative action."[71] Still, only self-deception, the mists of faith descending upon clear-sighted intelligence, dreams evolutionary procedures as specially friendly to spirit, as *intending* intelligence.[72] That is alien to the chronotope, to the form of space and time. The Neptunian narrator makes the point with a sublime shock: after the final demise of the first men, he reflects, "Mind lay henceforth in deep slumber for ten more millions of years." Only then occurred "an epidemic of biological variations" upon which the environment worked for "some hundred thousand years" more before a new human species evolved.[73] The accidents of time and space, the contingent twists of evolution, confound one humanity after another and force renewal to wait upon millennia.

Honest, rational contemplation of the universe should bankrupt any comforting belief in providence or evolutionary privileges for intelligent life. The struggles and final defeat of the First Men, and of other humanities, are dictated by evolutionary liabilities. This is what drives Stapledon's narrative through eighteen species of humanity: even as human beings take their own evolution in hand through genetic engineering, the weight of natural evolution resists them through many failures and disasters. Of all human species, only the Second, Fifth, and Last attain a freedom of spirit that is more than a mere hint of humanity's glory. Only a horizontal, evolutionary transcendence is possible for human beings, which means that most human species, including ourselves, are doomed to a history in which "thwarting has outweighed fulfillment."[74] The sublime imagination, applied to evolution, however, puts this sobering shock to work for human good. Sublime imaginative shock displaces the mind from self-complacency into a perplexing universe and a remorseless demand to face reality.[75] Realities of tremendous scale, Stapledon urges, spur human beings to "psychical luxuriance"—that is, they stimulate mental richness and diversity, thus opening up a proper field for "complex minded organisms."[76] Stapledon follows Burke in suggesting this classic argument for sublime experience: human faculties need "to be shaken and worked to a proper degree," and that is the job of the sublime.[77] Galactic vastness provokes an intellectual and volitional movement, a creative imagining that is proper to humanity but easily repressed or perverted.

*Last and First Men* offers, therefore, a sublime pedagogy in wholesome disillusion. The Neptunian narrator debunks the First Men's confidence in human achievement by revealing how primitive their culture seems compared to future humanities. Nor does he permit transposing confidence onto an inevitable arc of future progress. One humanity after another reveals how human reason continues frail and under assault, the species always ready for seduction by false hopes, by accounts of reality comfortably tailored to our desires, and by pretended certainties that justify our violence. If the First Men turn flight into a religion and fetishize it to the point of economic and ecological ruin, the Third blight their world by longing for personal immortality, while the Eighth Men, blunting their humanity in complacent wealth, indulge "in vast revelries of mutual slaughter and material destruction."[78] Only with the Neptunians, hundreds of millions of years into the future, does something akin to a general, albeit interrupted, progression emerge. For men and women in one human race after another, spiritual integrity depends upon weaning themselves from the species' fatal readiness to believe too quickly and to confuse the desirable with the true. In their highest and last form, human beings finally accept that intelligence may not find its fulfillment in the universe. "In vain," the Last Man admits, "we ask will ever any spirit awake to gather all spirits into itself, to elicit from the stars their full flower of beauty, to know all things together, and admire all things justly."[79] That spirit should finally answer to spirit in the cosmos remains hope, not knowledge, and to relax this agnosticism for faith would prevent humanity from achieving the unsurpassable dignity of honoring the universe without conditions. Accepting the dark possibility that the cosmic enterprise of mind may fail, that the evolution of intelligence may falter and cease altogether—that alone allows "the ecstasy which admires the real as it is."[80] Over histories of epic sorrow and unrelenting diminishments, Stapledon shows the human capacity for truth betrayed and suppressed, but persistently recurring: the call to seek a meaning that bears all the reality human minds and hearts can face. This truth, though, is only achieved by refusing to abandon knowledge for faith or for certainties not warranted by reason.

To the sublime shocks of evolutionary scale, Stapledon, like Wells, opposes a human sublime, a dynamic movement in which humanity transcends itself historically toward potentially superlative attainments. Stapledon's human sublime, however, differs from the Wellsian drive of social evolution in that, while the latter is a sublimity achieved in spite of and against natural evolution, Stapledon imagines the human spirit achieving sublimity by way of a direct confrontation with the cosmic mystery, with its immensities and irresistible processes. In 1942, Stapledon published *Beyond the "Isms,"* in which he gathers into an argument many of the philosophical positions cast into narrative in *Last and First Men*. Both this novel and its sequel, *Last Men in London*, inform Stapledon's exhortations. Despite differences of physiology, mental capacity, sensibility, and culture, he argues, human beings form a unity—as do the various human races of the novels—in an orientation toward "spirit." A progressive movement of self-transcendence has lured humanity from the first sparking of its rationality. Spirit, Stapledon explains, is "in one aspect . . . sincere percipience and thinking, in another it is love, in another it is creative imagination and creative action. Or rather it is these along with full consciousness of what they are, and of their rightness."[81] These "gateways of the spirit"—intellect, love, and creativity—usher us into lives no longer lived for themselves but for "a larger purpose . . . a sense that these things are what human beings are 'for.' "[82] The spirit cuts against the evolutionary grain insofar as self-preservation must give way to a self-forgetfulness that allows the disinterested search for truth and a readiness for communion with lives beyond home and tribe. Spirit expands the mind and heart toward the universal: to know and to love all.

In relation to humanity's historical transcendence, Stapledon places little emphasis on the technological sublime. *Last and First Men* often associates machine technology with obsession, as with the First Men's passion for flying and the Third's for pure intelligence, or else with annihilating forms of violence, or the discovery of powers disproportionate to humanity's limited maturity and wisdom. In giving his measure of present progress, the future narrator punctures the bubble of a self-congratulatory machine age: its "mentality is but a confused and halting first experiment," because, he coolly points out, minds remain yet "simple."[83] Technology contributes to a sublimity of wonder, as opposed to horror, only when subordinated to the realization of humanity's "interior," spiritual potential. When that occurs, Stapledon's narrative attends to ends rather than means, to the implications for mind and understanding and not to the technology itself.

Above all, Stapledon insists, the spiritual path to the human sublime must be marked off from faith, confusion with which is perilous. As a principal strategy for distinguishing truth from faith, Stapledon incorporates Christianity within his evolutionary myth so as to expose its limitations and confront Christian faith with the sublime it can never attain. Thus, the spiritual peaks of human history—in particular the Second, Fifth, and, above all, Eighteenth humanities—incarnate, in contrast to all human religions, true sublimity. In tackling Christianity, Stapledon satirizes and provides naturalistic explanations but also appropriates Christian motifs and themes, releasing them from their superstitious particularity for his description of humanity's place in the cosmos. For the most part, a bludgeon, not a scalpel, inflicts the satire. First humanity's flying cult devoted to "Gordelpus" or the Holy Empire of Music established by the Third Men with the prophet "God's Big Noise" for an oracle are mildly funny but too crude to be much more.[84] More skillfully, the repeated plot themes reinforce an overarching explanation as to both religion's power and its violence. Religions, and Christianity is always the exemplifying religion here, make genuine but fatally flawed attempts to achieve that comportment with the Real in which spirit reaches its apogee. As long as there is spirit, human beings will follow religion if they do not find the purified spiritual worship that maintains the inner secret of religion while freeing itself from its distortions. The odds do not favor such spiritual discovery. The inheritances of natural and social evolution leave humanity as almost inevitably a series of variations on self-concerned fear and self-protective illusion. Christian faith fails humanity by its false universality. Faith warps the pull of spirit into taking a part or aspect of reality for the whole. Absolute value settled upon a mere portion of reality, however alluring or vital, generates violence: whoever or whatever remains outside a religion's claim to encompass the whole gives the lie to the boast and must be extirpated. Among the Second Men, unity is worshiped over diversity and "an heroic nation of monotheists sought to impose its faith on a vaguely pantheist world. . . . The fields were laid waste, the cities burned, the rivers, and finally the winds, were poisoned."[85] Narrow-minded and wishful faith plagues humanity. In a manuscript, left unpublished at his death and later published as *The Opening of the Eyes*, Stapledon asserts, "No! Love is not God. Blind cosmical powers alone have made us what we are. To deny this is no gallant act of faith. To think wishfully without reason is folly, and is cowardly." If men and women do not, he goes on, wake from "the Christian dream . . . we are false."[86]

Advocacy for the way of the spirit begs the question as to what this spiritual path is if not a form of faith. The key differential concerns the fateful ease with which human beings turn from reality to wish fulfillment. Christianity spoke truly in affirming that love is "intrinsically right and beautiful"; the falsity lay in not "guarding [the experience] with scientific integrity so as to keep it free from all accretions of wishful thinking."[87] When true to itself, spirit proceeds on a path without providence.[88] No transcendent Will, no God of love, sustains the way or guarantees a joyful end. Any claim that the grain of the universe finally runs to the fulfillment of spirit, let alone the human instance of it, goes beyond what we can know. So the spirit's fruit, that "disinterested love of truth," forbids any refuge in faith. Human beings flourish through both intellect and emotion, but they fail when one subordinates the other. Men and women, therefore, must learn to feel intensely but know coldly. They must cultivate both worship and agnosticism. Intuition of the spirit's universal value and significance, according to Stapledon, "should be very skeptically regarded by the intellect; but pragmatically it is valuable, for it can be a great source of strength and courage." "It is part," he continues, "of the activity which I call worship of the spirit." Such worship begins, and here Stapledon reconfigures a pattern of Christian conversion,

> with the actual sin-conscious self's feeling for the self-that-might-be; but it goes on to the conception of an idealized and divine self-that-might-be, which the actual self cannot in fact

> ever be. And this ideal divine self is *felt* to be somehow actual in the universe. This feeling may, but need not, issue in belief. It should not be allowed to do so. Even worship must be agnostic.[89]

Two billion years of Stapledon's imagined human history teaches that humanity achieves its sublime potential insofar as the species learns to think, feel, and will in a proper comportment with the real. According to this, disinterested love of truth, the enrichment of communion, and creativity lead to such comportment: Stapledon's evolutionary bow to the classic "transcendentals" of the "True, the Good, and the Beautiful." Men and women, though, must not allow feeling or the foolish lures of faith to foster claims of the certain consonance of these ways with reality.

The Last Men, the final Neptunian race, provide the novel's climax and its clearest embodiment of both the sublimity and the tragedy of humanity. Within the instabilities of evolution, sublimity and tragedy belong together: human beings achieve the sublime by living clear-sightedly and reverently before a cosmos unfavorable to their particular survival, as well as to that of any other forms of intelligence flourishing and falling elsewhere in the universe. The Last Man and hidden narrator stresses this contemplative intellectuality as his culture's glory, along with the complexity and wonder of its creativity. The Eighteenth humanity has finally achieved integration of body and mind, intellect and emotion, self-love and community. Stapledon has made this apex of human history instinct with sublimity. Astronomy captivates their contemplative minds as devoutly as Edward Young's. All Neptunians make regular retreats to observatories where they "perform together those supreme symbolic acts for which I find no adjective in your speech but the debased word 'religious.'" These final humans even enjoy "an astronomical eye" inset into the crown of their heads. At their most sacred moments, the rich interpersonal communion this human culture enjoys culminates in the creation of a "group-mind." In this panhuman experience of spiritual convergence, each Neptunian, participating in this "racial mind," "sees with all eyes, and apprehends in a single vision all visual fields."[90]

Humanity thus achieves a final freedom together with the perfection of the committed agnosticism that characterizes the spirit's true stance. Thus, though the "racial mind" wills the ultimate fulfillment of spirit, "in the same act it holds aloof from it, and from all desire, and all emotion, save the ecstasy that admires the real as it is, and accepts the dark-bright form with joy."[91] This freedom is the gift of the "we do not know" that keeps the mind honest. According to a fourteenth-century English mystic, creatures approach God only through a "cloud of unknowing," in a love beyond knowledge.[92] Stapledon recovered this movement for a cosmos without God and a religion without faith. Still worshiping, but without faith, agnosticism is the only "reasonable, holy, and lively sacrifice." According to the Neptunian narrator, this religiously dedicated agnosticism funds the "spirit's highest achievement"—a "relentless admiration of fate."[93] Whatever reality holds, however bleak its outcome, however complex and beyond our ken its workings, the spirit meets the rigors of its vocation in a willing acceptance that excludes nothing felt or known. Agnosticism poises the spirit on the knife-edge between the cowardice of despair and the illusions of faith.

The Neptunians, therefore, continue to hope that spirit shall, at least for a time, evolve to encompass all reality and sustain itself as a cosmic mind and that within that consciousness all minds will awaken as the object of an eternal knowing. They rein in this prospect tightly, though, knowing that it is only hope and that, since "to think wishfully without reason is folly," hope must be transcended into a comportment with tragedy. Failing this, spirit shuts itself off from the possibility of its total eclipse, a possibility that knowledge cannot deny. When united as a single racial mind, the Neptunians achieve this final acceptance. "On those few occasions when we have awaked racially," the Last Man explains, "we have come to regard with piety even the possibility of cosmical defeat."[94]

This celebrated fulfillment, however, glides over and obscures an ambiguity in the agnosticism to which Stapledon holds so firmly. Though in the racial mind the Neptunians continue to desire that supreme awakening of spirit, they rise above that desire to accept a universe in which mind is finally defeated. This is spirit's supreme and final dignity. Held with this integrity, agnosticism sustains admiration even for a cosmos inhospitable to mind. This move, though, from a cosmos grained for spirit's fulfillment to one indifferent to it, radically changes the character of the way of the spirit itself. In a cosmos indifferent to mind, where spirit occurs as a merely contingent, accidental phenomenon, no grounds exist on which the way of the spirit is more in accordance with reality than, for instance, violent rejection, a disciplined despair, or cultivated distraction from the cosmic exigencies. If the cosmos is not attuned to mind, then striving for dispassionate joy and worshipful contemplation boils down to an assertion of will, not a knowing response to reality. That does not make it absurd, since its advocates may present such striving as humanly attractive, perhaps even more so than other available vocations. It does, however, leave Stapledon's agnosticism with the dilemma of either accepting the nihilistic implications of a radically inhospitable universe or coming off the philosophical fence and venturing trust in the future of the spirit—without the safety net of claiming worship of an alien universe as an even higher instance of cosmic attunement. That claim makes no sense if the universe is not the kind of reality to which minds can be attuned, as opposed to doing whatever seems the best for reasons that do not transcend the human. Stapledon's agnosticism still lives off the theological residue hidden within his version of those three transcendentals. Christianity, of course, though its claims may be disputed or denied, does not share Stapledon's dilemma. Since Christians acknowledge the universe as God's good creation, they are ontologically committed and so able to give reasons as to how the many forms of following Jesus correspond with "the Real as it is."

As Neptune boils into final crisis, the last human civilization disintegrates. Under the bombardment of stellar radiation, the excellent balance of Neptunian physiology falters, and that dispassionate regard for the cosmos breaks down. The Neptunians face a comfortless end in spiritual dementia. The novel closes with one of Stapledon's variations on a Christian theme: the "divine child" who either suffers martyrdom or bears, with a vicarious keenness, the agonies of the race. In the youngest member of Neptunian civilization, a touch of fallen glory manifests once more and comforts the last of humanity. The "last born of the Last Men" appears as a Christ figure. Though suffering in the flesh, "he is above his suffering" and relieves the despair of his people, strengthening them again to recover something of the calm, disinterested admiration that is the fruit of accepting fate.[95] The divine child is a Christ suitably purified, a Christ who holds out no wishful hope and, more Stoic than Christian, transcends pity, persuading the sufferer "to smile at his own pain."[96] For Stapledon, that inner detachment is the core of spiritual life and the essence of freedom in a perilous world since the mind participates in immediate experience while also occupying a position of detached observation. This spiritual bifurcation has occurred before in human history—an earlier divine child tells his story among the First Men:

> The thought of death enraged me. . . . I struggled frantically, vainly. Then suddenly . . . I saw the game that I was losing, and it was good. Good, no less to lose than to win. . . . Suddenly I was free, and with sight. . . . For now I saw myself, and all of us, through the eyes of the umpire. It was as though a play-actor were to see the whole play with his own part in it, through the author's eyes, from the auditorium. . . . For me, as a character in the play, the situation was hideous; yet for me, the spectator, it had become excellent, within a wider excellence.[97]

When people take up this detached standpoint, observing themselves within the total context while enduring immediate experience, the human mind becomes, as Baillie had argued, sublime in the universal, untrammeled range of its contemplations. Men and women need not flee or deny the powers that bear down on them; they may endure existence, even at its cruelest, from an aesthetic standpoint that allows an appreciation of suffering as part of a larger pattern, not perfect, perhaps, but beautiful, a "dark-bright" reality. True heirs of Addison, human beings after evolutionary ages end as sublime spectators of sublimity.

Aesthetic reconciliation with suffering, though, takes some disturbing forms. Having migrated to Venus, humanity learns that the more humans modify the planet for their benefit, the more deadly it becomes for the indigenous, intelligent Venerians. In attacking humanity, though, the Venerians hobble colonization while only delaying their own extinction. The final solution puts the entire indigenous population out of its misery. The Neptunian records the chilling logic without irony or critical comment: "As for the murder of Venerian life, it was, indeed, terrible, but right. It had been committed without hate; indeed, rather in love." As they performed the killing, humans "learned to admire, even in a sense to love." For humanity this grim task "refined . . . its spiritual hearing, and revealed to it tones and themes in the universal music which were hitherto obscure."[98] This passage has disturbed Stapledon's commentators, as well it should. A perhaps charitable reading would suggest that Stapledon is exploring the limits of his vision, testing its cost against those contingencies and accidents that result in morally irreconcilable scenarios. The metaphor of universal music, however, which is a near constant in Stapledon's work, and reappears in the novel's closing speech, suggests that Stapledon thought such moral catastrophes might be reconciled in aesthetic admiration of the "dark-bright" joy of things. Such horrors intensify the "beauty of tragic art."[99] Considering a harmony struck with the cries of innocence, Stapledon, unlike Ivan Karamazov, does not wish to return his "ticket of admission."[100] Stapledon's path to comportment with the cosmos requires an economy of sacrifice. Sacrifice is both necessary to the aesthetic beauty of the cosmos and demanded as a condition of its appreciation. The sublime cosmos repels humanity, then exalts it in the thrill of abnegation. True and faithless worship demands sacrificing the desire for life and the urge to protest against its agonies. By contrast, Christianity speaks of sacrifice within a different redemptive economy. Taking up Karamazov's protest, it includes the defiance of Job and Jesus' forsaken cry from the cross. This salvific drama disputes evil and refuses a contemplative reconciliation that synthesizes horrors in a higher harmony. Christianity does not transpose suffering into sublimity. Though sacrifice is central to the Christian narrative, the sacrifice of Christ, and the understanding of martyrdom and charity that derives from it, is redemptive and undertaken for the sake of others: sacrifice is not a means of personal reconciliation with fate.

According to Stapledon's narrator, humanity's sublime vocation is to strive for a universal appreciation, a worshipful acceptance within a hostile cosmos of irredeemable and inevitable evolutionary disaster. In the end, though, the expenditure remains so vast and the flourishing so small. So the divine child comforts the Last Neptunians and, through the narrator, present humanity, as well: "It is as though in him at last, and for a day only, man's promise were fulfilled." The novel closes with his words:

> Yet it has used [man]. And now it uses his destruction. Great, and terrible, and very beautiful is the Whole; and for man the best is that the Whole should use him.[101]

"The Whole," though, is just capitalized nothing, a linguistic sleight of hand to produce a subject that "uses" humanity and thus hints of will in a mindless cosmos. Of course, Stapledon then injects the familiar doubt: "Is the beauty of the Whole really enhanced by our agony?" In his agnostic wobble, Stapledon attracts theological emotion while denying theological truth. This closing speech then brings back a favorite metaphor and the suggestion of fulfillment in humanity's aesthetic contribution to the universe:

> But one thing is certain. Man himself, at the very least, is music, a brave theme that makes music also of its vast accompaniment, its matrix of storms and stars. . . . It is very good to have been man. . . . For we shall make after all a fair conclusion to this brief music that is man.[102]

Again, there is that persistent theological echo in the allusion to the "very good" of Genesis. Stapledon's metaphor, though, invites the question as to whether in talking of cosmic music without a cosmic hearer he does what he so bravely tried not to do: whistle in the dark.

*Star Maker*, published in 1937, tells an epic journey that revels in its sublime proportions. The human narrator recounts a series of visits to alien civilizations, initially somewhat familiar, eventually strange to an extreme. Recurring plots and themes build up a taxonomy of spirit, displaying the myriad forms of intelligent striving, along with the dangers that divert, corrupt, and frustrate it. Stapledon's fascination with telepathy informs a narrative strategy that allows the protagonist to develop an expanding point of view as the novel proceeds. He undergoes a process of spiritual formation on an evolutionary and cosmic scale. Mind thus expands to encompass the cosmos and so achieves sublimity. Initially a single mind, unexpectedly separated from its physical location on an English hilltop, the narrator discovers the ability to enter the minds of the alien races he visits, sharing with them in coconsciousness.[103] Together, the individual minds form a group mind in which all the individualities share but without losing their own subjectivity. As this mind journeys, it grows, learns, and, traveling in time as well as space, eventually bonds with the emergent communal mind of the galaxy. Now participating in a galactic mind, the narrator touches minds that have awakened in other galaxies, and, at the climax of his pilgrimage, he approaches the condition of a mind finally cosmic in scope.

A marital tiff occasions the journey, sending the narrator out into the darkness of the countryside, having "tasted bitterness."[104] The bitterness draws also from a world in crisis and a much darker vision of group mentality: "In cathedral squares I seemed to see the young men ranked together in thousands, exalted, possessed, saluting the flood-lit Fuhrer."[105] *Star Maker* sets such bitterness, personal and political, within the measures of sublimity, sub specie aeternitatis. The journey humbles, sobers, and inspires its everyman narrator before universal immensities. This beginning in disillusion and darkness alludes to Dante's *The Divine Comedy*. There the journey starts similarly: "I came to myself in a dark wood, for the straight way was lost." Allusions to Dante occur elsewhere in the novel and, significantly, at the climactic moment at which the narrator glimpses the Star Maker. Stapledon follows his Dantean inspiration with a story in which, as in *The Divine Comedy,* an individual quest mediates a cosmic history and itinerary. Unlike *The Divine Comedy*, however, *Star Maker* inhabits the discourse of modern sublimity. Stapledon's references to Dante also place his novel in the tradition that narrates stories of spiritual ascent. Stapledon writes to subvert this tradition: in relation to Christian accounts of ascent to God, *Star Maker* tells a counterstory that includes, dismantles, and rewrites the Christian one. All orthodox Christian accounts of spiritual ascent begin and culminate in the Divine Love. In many and diverse ways, they exegete the Pauline praise of love's ultimacy: "Faith, hope, love abide, these three; but the greatest of these is love."[106] However, Stapledon's dispute with Christianity revolves around this elevation of love. Communion, the narrator suggests, may begin the way and may be essential to the flourishing of mind, but it is neither the goal nor the origin of reality. This rewrites the spiritual ascent fundamentally. The Star Maker, the mysterious source and goal of the cosmos, is most certainly not love.

As the narrator nears the end of his journey, his experience is enriched by mental communion with millions of other minds. This group mind—of which he is a tiny part, yet which he knows as he knows his own mind—now completes its galactic education. The conjoined minds have wondered over and participated in the evolutionary travails and tragedies of spirit in the universe; realized how slow, precarious, and rare are the conditions that favor beings capable of spiritual progress; and appreciated the unimaginable diversity of forms taken by mind in adapting for survival. Finally, the narrator, through his communion with the great host of minds, awakens to a consciousness that spans the cosmos and achieves a telepathic contact reaching beyond his galaxy. Yet still mystery abides. Even the cosmic mind remains an enigma to itself. Its own origin is a numbing obscurity; only its eventual disintegration is sure and certain. Stapledon's language recalls the biblical God: "I . . . knew the whole extent of space and time, and counted the wandering stars like sheep, overlooking none." However, by applying this to the cosmic spirit, now sublimely checked in "abashed and tongue-tied worship," Stapledon insists that God is just finitude writ large, immeasurably far short of the unknown Star Maker, whom he is careful never to name "God."[107]

When the cosmic mind appears, it finds the universe failing; entropy wastes all its substance, and light and heat decline. "Counting their last pence of energy," the hosts of the cosmic mind stretch for the "illumination toward which all beings in all ages had been obscurely striving." Then, for a brief but supreme moment, they "faced the Star Maker."[108] The cosmos thereby arrives at a beatitude, only to know it bitter with transience: "In the supreme moment of the cosmos, I as the cosmical mind, seemed to myself to be confronted with the source and goal of all finite things." The cosmic mind, sublimely discomforted and overwhelmed, shrinks before the final elevation: "The flower of all the stars and worlds, [I] was appalled as any savage is appalled by the lightning and thunder."[109] After a vision of the universe as it expands, thrown out from the Star Maker's "infinite potential," the narrator discerns a light pervading the interior of all things in the cosmos, yet which has its source nowhere within the universe. From this light, he makes the last ascent to the light of the Star Maker himself:

> I saw, though nowhere in cosmical space, the blazing source of the hypercosmical light, as though it were an overwhelmingly brilliant point, a star, a sun more powerful than all suns together. It seemed to me that this effulgent star was the centre of a four-dimensional sphere whose curved surface was the three-dimensional cosmos. This star of stars, this star that was indeed the Star Maker was perceived by me . . . for one moment before its splendour seared my vision.[110]

The ascending spirit, though, receives no welcome. The cosmic sublimity is absolute and absolute in rebuffing the creature. The dualism of natural and human sublimes persists; indeed the human sublime depends upon it. The yearning of minds over the aeons of evolution is fulfilled only in knowing the impossibility of fulfillment: "It seemed to me that I, the spirit of so many worlds, the flower of so many ages, was the Church Cosmical, fit at last to be the bride of God. But instead I was blinded, and seared, and struck down by terrible light."[111] Again, Stapledon uses "God" in the context of a hope that falls short of the Star Maker. At best, the imagined God and gods of human beings give fragments and whispered hints at hints of the Star Maker.

Stapledon recalls Dante's culminating vision in the Star Maker's blazing, "hypercosmical light," which is the "star of stars" and center of a "four-dimensional sphere." In this palimpsest on the Christian tradition, Stapledon follows Dante with the metaphor of wings, the soul flying toward the light. No more than for Dante, though, are the wings of spirit sufficient: the narrator's "poor wings" soar, then fall, seared. When Dante finds his "own wings far too weak," however, his weakness is answered with the gift of grace: "My mind was struck by light that flashed and, with this light, received what it had asked."[112] Like Augustine's "Beauty, so ancient and so new," Dante's God has accompanied the poet from the beginning, forming him into the humanity that searches the "Eternal Light" of paradise. Stapledon carefully excises all suggestion of grace. On the one hand, the aloofness of the Star Maker is impenetrable; on the other, the cold beauty of this final vision is won solely through the tragic striving of intelligent life itself. Dante does not, of course, arrive at a comprehending vision of God, any more than Stapledon's cosmic mental

Ulysses. Quite the reverse, Dante knows God as the eternal and inexhaustible mystery, a plenitude beyond conceiving, without limit. "Eternal Light, You only dwell within / Yourself, and only You know You"—infinite knowledge knowing infinite life. [113]

From his glimpse of the Star Maker, the narrator retains, along with the scorching memory of sublime rebuff, a cluster of impressions and pictures that he organizes into a creation myth. "Contemptibly crude and falsifying," he warns, but still conveying something of the Star Maker and his works, even through the relatively minimal capacity of the human mind.[114] The narrator understands that the cosmos within which we live emerged as one of a vast series of universes, each with its own form of time. From the perspective of the Star Maker alone, who transcends all their times, these creations appear together, gathered in their successive order. In a typical, relativizing move, Stapledon places our cosmos a long way from the ultimate cosmos, the acme of the Star Maker's works. Our universe has features that suggest the maker's "first mature work," having still youthful features clinging to its form.[115] As this language suggests, the creator in this myth learns and grows. He works experiments in exploring and realizing possibilities. The Star Maker thus discovers values worth preserving from one creation to another, as well as dead ends and disasters. Over the progression of universes, some very simple, some intricate, the satisfactions accorded by creations harboring intelligence assert themselves and come to inspire the Star Maker's finest works. To discourage moral judgments, Stapledon includes some distinctly unsettling elements. For a start, the Star Maker's motives are intellectual curiosity and aesthetic interest. He solves problems, probes for the unexpected, and generates difficulties for the purpose of discovering what it takes to solve them. Far from benign, some of his experiments with world making seem distinctly sadistic, such as the devolving cosmos that begins with a "lucid consciousness," the decay of which the Star Maker watches with a calm interest. Violence and destruction are among this creator's satisfactions, though, for purely logical reasons, they cannot be primary. He allows his "evil" side free rein only to provide occasion for the exercise of his own creative efforts in resistance. Still, he creates to experiment: this is not a creator one would choose, were choice possible. The Star Maker never pursues the interests of creatures except insofar as they coincide as means to his own growing awareness. Stapledon demythologizes his own story of this budding creator, who presses on as he tires of one cosmos after another, by suggesting that the creator spirit is one "mode" or "aspect" of the Star Maker, the other being the "eternal and absolute" spirit who "timelessly contemplated all of his works."[116] From this eternal mode comes the creator's own urge to create, as well as the succeeding matrices of potential upon which the maker learns and perfects his business.

Stapledon's insistence that his myth is "contemptibly crude and falsifying," with regard to things ultimate, should not distract the reader from the care he takes with its language and development. He achieves, in a brief compass, a similar drama of inventiveness as he does with human evolution in his first novel. Most importantly, as befits a modern mythmaker, this is a very knowing myth, a self-reflexive one that draws attention to its mythical form. Stapledon inserts into the myth disrupting clues that undermine the surface features of the narrative, especially insofar as they invite imagining the Star Maker in personal or theistic ways. Stapledon's creation story contains its own critique as its tensions and contradictions resist conclusions that certain of its narrative elements invite. Initially, for instance, the creative aspect of the Star Maker is subordinated to the abstract aspect, inviting comparison with Whitehead's process philosophy.[117] The "eternal and absolute spirit," an "eternally achieved perfection," timelessly contemplates all the works achieved by the creative mode.[118] Very soon, though, the narrator reverses this recognizable fragment of philosophical theology. Now the "eternal spirit" becomes the "unconscious substance" from which the growing creator draws "the crude substance of a cosmos." As "the spiritual 'material' which he objectified from his own hidden depth," the medium of his creations carries potentials and resistances that both surprise and stimulate the creator. The bipolarity of the initial description then gives way to a division between "unexpressed" and expressed potency, with the "Star Maker himself" now "cosmos by cosmos" waking "into keener lucidity." The narrator then arrives at a further tentative insight that now levels the asymmetry between the Star Maker and the creations themselves: "In some unintelligible manner all finite things, though they were in a sense figments of the absolute spirit, were also essential to the very existence of the absolute spirit. Apart from them, it had no being."[119] These shifting metaphysical fragments deconstruct any affirmation of divine personality or even of transcendence. Any language that invites such conclusions appears as belonging solely to the surface of the myth.

This creation myth, then, incorporates tensions that undermine suggestions of transcendence in favor of immanence. The myth's internal self-critique inscribes the Star Maker within the universe of universes as its originating power.[120] This implication is reinforced as the narrator imagines the meeting between the Star Maker and his "ultimate and perfected cosmos." An undeniably clever description constitutes a climactic rewriting and rejection of Christianity. As the ultimate cosmos faces the Star Maker, the relationship becomes trinitarian. The Star Maker fulfills his desire in this universe, while it contemplates him with praise. "In the mutual joy," the narrator puzzles, "of the Star Maker and the ultimate cosmos was conceived, most strangely, the absolute spirit itself, in which all times are present and all being is comprised; for the spirit which was the issue of this union confronted my reeling intelligence as being at once the ground and the issue of all temporal and finite things."[121] The trinitarian procession and differentiation is immediately flattened into identity, and the distinction between the Star Maker and its creation collapses into monism. This is a variant on the earlier moment when, having anticipated a bridal union, the cosmical mind is repelled from the Star Maker's blazing light. The rejection of any reciprocity between maker and made belongs to the "depth structure" of Stapledon's myth, along with the dismantling of transcendence and divine personality, and an aesthetic regard that abides beyond love. Christianity, by holding to such illusions, lacks the credentials for a true sublimity.

Stapledon's creation story turns out to be a myth of immanence. The Star Maker is the infinite creativity inherent in all universes and in the hyperuniverse that contains them. Even that, though, says more than the narrator will finally allow. He closes his account with this: "In truth the eternal spirit was ineffable. Nothing whatsoever could be truly said about it."[122] Even "spirit" really stands, as does an "x," for an unknown. Only the consistent deconstruction of transcendence remains; ultimate reality, whether tentatively speakable or entirely unspeakable, is not transcendent in the sense affirmed of Christianity's God. Certainly, the Star Maker is not that "perfection of being . . . who is subsisting being itself."[123] A creator or creative power dependent on its creations for existence, or that is formed and realized by way of its creatures, is not self-existent, not the biblical "I Am," nor the theological tradition's "God whose being is to be." However, if the Star Maker is not self-existent, absolute being but one who has being, participates in being, like his creatures have being, Stapledon's creation myth along with the narrator's commentary evades the most profound perplexity. For all the insistence on sublimity and unknowability, the novel's concluding vision remains ontologically superficial. It asks, "Why are there the things there are?" but not, "Why is there something and not nothing?"

The Star Maker creates each cosmos as an object of keen and relentless assessment. Closing his account of the cosmic vision, the narrator reintroduces the image of the Star Maker contemplating the universes he has made: "Our broken lives, our loves, our follies, our betrayals, our forlorn and gallant defenses, were one and all calmly anatomized, assessed, and placed."[124] However, the narrator admits that this persistent idea of a consciousness immanent to the hyper-universe, albeit a rather unappealing one, still reflects our need for some comfort, however thin the gruel. In truth, nothing can really be said, and agnostic resignation must have the last word. Yet, whatever the ultimate powers of cosmic creation, adoration remains due. Adoration goes beyond care for self, beyond hope of love, beyond judgment of good and evil: no penitent, flailing in dust and ashes, is equal to the self-abnegation Stapledon accords the Star Maker:

> Here was no pity, no proffer of salvation, no kindly aid. Or here were all pity and all love, but mastered by a frosty ecstasy. . . . Sympathy was not ultimate in the temper of the eternal spirit; contemplation was. Love was not absolute; contemplation was. And though there was love, there was also hate comprised within the spirit's temper, for there was cruel delight in the contemplation of every horror, and glee in the downfall of the virtuous. All passions . . . were comprised within the spirit's temper; but mastered, icily gripped within the cold, clear, crystal ecstasy of contemplation. That this should be the upshot of all our lives, this scientist's, no, artist's, keen appraisal! And yet I worshipped![125]

The Star Maker as irresistible, implacable will—above all judgment or protest, his overwhelming power "compelling adoration"—makes a particularly unyielding expression of the sublime.

The Star Maker's sublimity, though, reveals that separation of divine love and power that marks the modern sublime in its explicitly theological register. Imagined as sublime, God's deity was identified more closely with power than love, constituting a severe deformation of the Christian God. Taking the measure of this sublime representation of divinity, Burke observes that "some reflection, some comparing is necessary to satisfy us of [God's] wisdom, his justice, and his goodness; to be struck with his power, it is only necessary that we open our eyes."[126] During the nineteenth and twentieth centuries, the subliming of human technological power, both as beneficent and destructive, strongly reinforced this divinization of power. A tradition that started worshiping the power of God ended adoring the divinity of power. Burke, again, acknowledges the dynamic: "Whilst we contemplate so vast an object, under the arm, as it were, of almighty power, and invested upon every side with omnipresence, we shrink into the minuteness of our own nature, and are, in a manner, annihilated before him."[127] Before such power, one just bows and accepts annihilation, or, in Stapledon's vision, one accedes, with admiration, to the fate of an instrument in the Star Maker's cosmic self-education. Ironically, the only figure in *The Divine Comedy* described in such chilly terms, with his passions indeed "icily gripped," is Satan, locked eternally in hell's frozen basement.

Wells and Stapledon both write in the shadow of Darwinian evolution and both deploy the sublime to project a dualism between natural evolution and the human vocation of social and spiritual striving. Wells preached human self-evolution more optimistically than Stapledon, at least at first, for, by the end of his life, his disillusion was bitter.[128] The utopian Wells, however, turned his back on natural selection to exhort the modern utopia, to strive and not to yield until, at last, nature had her way, and entropy took all. Stapledon—by contrast, despite his inventive hopes for human improvement through genetic manipulation—found human dignity, now and in evolutionary ages to come, in an expansive spiritual comportment with the sublimities of cosmic process. For a time, Wells sought a working accommodation with religion, the terms of which required stripping the Christian God of any claim to sublimity so that he might serve as cheerleader for the human struggle. Stapledon, whose religious struggle was more serious, imagined Christianity overcome and transcended in a worship purified from all faith and wishful thinking: "Virtue in the creator is not the same as virtue in the creature. . . . The virtue of the creature was to love and to worship, but the virtue of the creator was to create, and to be the infinite, the unrealizable and incomprehensible goal of worshipping creatures."[129] The wonder, the adoration and admiration, of the Real admits our dissolution, our frustration, the conclusive lack of the satisfaction for which we ache. The cosmic glory is beyond good and evil but, as it is properly worshiped, sublimely so.

In the evolutionary mythmaking of both Wells and Stapledon, a sublime human striving subordinates the technological sublime to its self-transcendence. Another configuration emerges elsewhere, especially in the light of twentieth-century technological critiques, in which the technological sublime envelops and appropriates to itself not only the human but also the natural sublime. This move, however, presupposes the oppositional relationship of natural and human sublime found in Wells and Stapledon. Within science fiction, the eccentric worlds of Philip K. Dick stage this ubiquity of technology. They also, though, intimate the rare possibility of a human vocation in which freedom escapes sublime discourse altogether.

# 4

# PHILIP DICK VERSUS THE SUBLIME

*[Technology] is no longer face to face with man but . . . progressively absorbs him.*

—Jacques Ellul, *The Technological Society*

*An X-File wrapped in a cover-up and deep-fried in paranoid conspiracy.*

—Vernon and Letterman, *Monsters vs. Aliens*

*Metropolis*, Fritz Lang's famous silent movie, opens in the claustrophobic enclosure of the workers' underground city.[1] Images of speeding gears, pistons, and wheels intersperse the title frames before the story begins with files of weary uniformed workers, heads bowed, marching silently from their shift change through a subway of sterilized concrete. Those at the end of their day squeeze into a cage and descend to their proletarian Hades. Underground, the concrete encloses them in blank streets and massive apartments that rise into obscurity. When the viewer finally sees Metropolis itself, the city appears in a light-filled sublimity of skyscrapers, viaducts, and planes contrasting with the sublime obscurities and threatening force of the machines and the workers' city. From his central, panoptical tower, Joh Fredersen commands his technological universe. Between these scenes, Lang stages the crisis of Freder, his central character who first appears enjoying a spot of playful athleticism around a sports track before frolicking with preening maidens. Shortly thereafter, Freder's pastoral innocence shatters in the sight of a hideous accident at one of his father's massive machines. The pastoral scenes intimate a nature free from technology, where eroticism flourishes and the body enjoys its natural energies: the space of beauty absent of sublime power. Looking a little closer, though, the audience finds the twirling dance of the young women to hint at the mechanisms outside this Eden while the sheer walls around the sports track suggest less innocent incarcerations. When the city itself appears, the screen cuts off the elevation of Metropolis' vertical spread to create a visual enclosure in which the vastness of concrete and machine appears unbroken, without sky or boundary. Technology in these scenes envelops and absorbs everything: workers, the sons and daughters of the rich, Fredersen and his clerks. The space of nature—within which youth plays, the beautiful over against the sublime—turns out to be technologically penetrated, a construct of the technological itself. Philip Dick's science-fictional worlds also consume the human within the technological, aided by mechanisms of mass deception and propaganda. In a similar way, too, the engines of absorption and control present in terms of the technological sublime. Unlike *Metropolis*, though, the language of liberty in Dick's novels, the possibilities for resistance to the technologically totalitarian, eschews and, implicitly, critiques sublimity, placing it on a trajectory toward the inhuman.

For his 1982 film, *Blade Runner*, Ridley Scott adapted Philip K. Dick's *Do Androids Dream of Electric Sheep?* The movie's original version ends in a scene of happy release from the dingy neon light and technological decay of postnuclear Los Angeles. Rick Deckard, the "blade runner," flies away from the city in which he has plied his trade "retiring" rogue androids. With him is Rachael, a Nexus 6 replicant, the android with whom he has fallen in love. The smoky clouds part, and the couple fly over a pristine mountain landscape with valleys of an improbable green. Vangelis' music rumbles to a crescendo as the couple pass into the classic natural sublime from a technological one of mile-high floating advertisements, belching steam, and high-rise complexes built like ziggurats and slick with acid rain. The viewer is swept from a dystopian to an uplifting sublime, ironically a configuration older than that of *Metropolis*' opening scenes. Consciously or not, those who prevailed upon Ridley Scott to include this scene, later struck from the director's cut, were deploying a contrast familiar to the nineteenth century. Within modernity, "nature" is both a highly charged and a polysemous term: machine, rational order, expositor of divine power, pastoral mother, reinvigorator of culture, unfolding evolution, and pitiless slaughterhouse.[2] Within the Romantic tradition especially though, nature is contrasted with culture—with city, capitalism, and factory—the sublime being invoked on both sides. Modern tourism cut its teeth on this contrast. Nature preserves a sphere of freedom, of healing, of a return to simpler, innocent social relations in which human beings are not disciplined to the forms of technology. "The artisan," wrote Elizabeth Gaskell, "deafened with noise of tongues and engines, may come to listen awhile to the delicious sounds of rural life."[3] Nature stands as the beneficent other to industrial, cultural humanity, and is the sublime context for a wonder that lifts us to our proper home with the divine. This nature, imagined as retreat and inspiration, is, of course, a thoroughly culturalized nature. *Metropolis* both invokes this nature in the youthful athletics and pleasure garden, and questions its illusion of a sphere beyond technological culture. Nature as sublime or as pastoral freedom from culture is a fantasy of otherness that both disguises the ubiquity of human determinations and obscures the true enigma of otherness, of irreducible difference.[4] Furrowed and fenced land bears the marks of humanity, but so do "the waste moors from which the poor cultivators were cleared, to leave what can be seen as an empty nature," a place described significantly as "reserved" for tourists, hikers, and wildlife enthusiasts.[5] This fantasy exists as the inseparable twin of the equally modern utopia of openly submitting nature, through technological progress, to human rationality, root and branch.

## ANDROID HUMANITY

In contrast to *Blade Runner*'s representation of a truly liberating nature, available for human escape, Philip Dick's novel *Do Androids Dream of Electric Sheep?* takes up the enclosing technological environment of *Metropolis*. Though wickedly indifferent to technological detail, Dick represented technology, even in his funniest scenes, as a threatening and ubiquitous order, an inescapable environment of formation for human beings and their world.[6] The technologies of illusion enjoy a privileged place in Dick's dystopias, from an android president, through drugs that unravel time, to whole populations conned into continued labor underground for a war long since ended.[7] By representing these technologies in terms of the technological sublime, he connects this sublime with violence and manipulation. Salvation, on the other hand, he casts very differently, especially compared with the classic space-opera and pulp scenarios, in which sublimity definitely appears fit for heroes, as in Fritz Leiber's *Gather, Darkness!* or Herbert's *Dune*.[8] In a Dickean environment though, salvation does not come triumphant on clouds descending; the freedom gifted does not inhabit the sublime register. Salvation limps into this world, while revelation sounds on a ragged broadcast, flickering into the gaps of a universal deluge of noise. Those characters that come eventually to experience a measure of the salvific know such freedom hedged about and limited by the world into which it squeezes itself. In a similar vein, revelation largely speaks through the means devoted to suppressing it, in the inane chirpiness of TV advertisements or the hallucinogenic comforts of recreational pharmacology. Dickean salvation, then, is ambiguous and also leaves much sorrow in place. At what he somewhat bitterly celebrated as the "trash level" of literacy, Dick's fiction resonates with the inhuman potentials within the sublime celebration of technology and, more broadly, with the totalizing tendencies within modern Western culture. In his uncanny and paranoid worlds, Dick's technologies of illusion strive for a homogenous control, a permeating governance expressed in metaphors of "absorption" and "consumption." Salvific possibilities endure, though, through the unpredictable resistances of the human heart, which manages to stumble on the gaps in such technologies, and exploit them.

*Do Androids Dream of Electric Sheep?* ends neither with a cathartic release into nature, nor with the implied romantic resolution retained in *Blade Runner: The Final Cut*. Dick ends his novel more ambiguously and, significantly, with a greater tenderness. Along with several of Dick's works from the 1960s and early 1970s, *Do Androids Dream* represents a world in which the space for a natural sublime outside and over against culture has all but disappeared. "World War Terminus" has savaged all Earth's ecologies and killed off most forms of animal life, rendering moot the distinction between natural and cultural worlds. This postholocaust world recovers the ideal of nature as an authentic other that is beyond culture only as an explicitly internal difference in the precarious, increasingly nominal distinction between "real" organic life and "fake" mechanical replicas. The death of his pet sheep threatens Deckard's social status and forces him to purchase an electric replica. Mechanical animals index social, specifically economic, failure. However, they beat the disgrace of not having an animal at all. Existence without even the regulated cluck of a mechanical chicken shames a citizen since it prevents "fusion with Mercer," a form of civil religion involving both empathic solidarity and Sisyphean, penitential endurance. Real animals evoke a prenuclear world; they are an ideal focus of compassion and the longing for innocence. Animals offer, therefore, some sparse recovery of a lost otherness. Before the curse, according to the Mercer myth, "childhood had been nice; [Wilbur Mercer] had loved all life, especially the animals."[9] This otherness, though, is ersatz: entirely mediated by exchange value. The old reassuring promise that a pure nature made to culture vanishes into the pages of "Sidney's Animal and Fowl Catalogue."[10]

Rick Deckard's postapocalyptic world knows the projection of nature as renewing other only in this ironic form. Technology encloses and penetrates human life. The novel's time span, just over twenty-four hours in the blade runner's career, begins and ends with Deckard and his wife, Iran, negotiating their marital relationship around electronic gadgetry. Deckard's day begins with the Penfield mood organ, which generates an array of emotional conditions in its user. Rick deploys his responsibly so as to greet the morning with a breezy, positive attitude. Iran, though, has scheduled herself a "six-hour self-accusatory depression," a setting it took some determination to find. The depression, she explains, allows her an emotion appropriate to the circumstances of life in a near-empty building, "staying here on Earth after everybody who's smart has emigrated."[11] Through a mechanically induced emotion, Iran seeks the real.

In the main plot, the opposition of real and fake plays out between the human blade runner and his Nexus 6 quarry, androids who have escaped from their use as "body servants or tireless field hands" in the off-world colonies.[12] The law condemns the androids as a dangerous other, an especially vicious threat because, unlike their human makers, androids are incapable of feeling "empathy." This criminalization rationalizes, and so disguises, the radical threat androids pose to a social imaginary that needs the distinction between real and fake to secure human identity. The more human the android—and advances in android technology continually thin out the line—the more unstable becomes this supposedly ontological distinction and the more human identity erodes over against its engulfing technologized environment. Since the opposition of fake and real is wholly immanent to culture but nevertheless has to guarantee a natural distinction and superiority of humanity over its products, android transgression of human space meets with intense hostility and paranoia. In Richard Deckard's case, the humanity projected by the Nexus-6 brain unit, the high point of humanoid design, sets off a viral instability in a hitherto untroubled and dogmatic understanding of the dualism of human and machine.[13]

The capacity for empathy distinguishes the human from the android. Mercerism founds itself on empathy; holding onto the "empathy box" confers a felt solidarity with all those similarly connected, as well as with the solitary figure of Mercer himself, who struggles in perpetuity up a barren hill, tormented with rocks thrown by his persecutors. Since androids are supposedly incapable of empathy, they are also unable to "fuse" with Mercer. Conversely, a "normal" human being cannot feel empathy for an android, though a purely physical attraction may occur. After nuclear devastation, this redefinition of human nature makes sense as a step away from the identification with rationality that has dominated the Western tradition. However, *Do Androids Dream* develops this ironically, since the break with rationality results in a captivity to its technological products more insidious because blind. If empathy, not rationality, distinguishes the human, then technology becomes nonhuman, alien. Human beings, though, depend on technology to experience and maintain themselves as empathic—the "empathy box," electric sheep, commodified animals. Telling human from android, the "Voigt-Kampff test" determines mechanically the presence or absence of empathic capacity. The test reduces empathy to an automatism signaled by "capillary dilation."[14] In all this, the alienation doubles; first humanity is alienated from its works, then those works alienate humanity from its supposedly inviolable character.

As a social ideal, empathy involves a completeness of mutual fusion that evacuates all significant difference. Taking the handles of the empathy box, the subject fuses with Mercer in his lonely uphill trek and, at the same time, merges with "everyone who at this moment clutched the handles." Deckard hears "in his own brain the noise of their many individual existences. They—and he—cared about one thing."[15] All concentrate on the need to climb, reinforced and focused by their empathy, their fused mentalities. Since Mercer's myth holds up his special concern for animal life, this fusion includes by association the remnants of living things on Earth. Anything outside the box's empathic ecstasy is defined by incapacity for it and, therefore, as nonhuman, whatever appearances might otherwise plead. Androids, therefore, cannot be murdered, only "retired." They are "chitinous reflex-machines who aren't really alive." Everything outside the circle of Mercer's homogenizing empathy is dead by definition. In the form of technology, rationality determines via empathy the apportioning of life and death. Mercerist technology realizes an absorbing power, a force for consumption of individualities and of difference. The technological sublime exalts the human will as empowered for a dynamic and unlimited conformation of reality to itself. Technology pacifies, penetrates, and reforms nature. However, Dick pushes the technological sublime a stage further in the dystopian direction, to a point at which the technological dynamic transcends the human will and becomes self-sustaining. With the Nexus 6, the immanent logic of technical improvement pushes human identity into crisis, while the equally technological force of Mercerism homogenizes humanity and displaces active agency by the passivity of empathy. With his sweeping indifference to the technical exactitudes enjoyed by hard science fiction, Dick imagines an absolute technology, the vehicle of an absolute drive, alienated from human will and relentlessly consuming the community of diverse being, including humanity.

The dynamics of empathy also fail to preserve human identity from a purportedly impossible desire for its technological android other. Singing Mozart at the opera house, Luba Loft moves Deckard, and the blade runner falls for Rachael Rosen. Both androids evoke and seem worthy of emotions he cannot reduce to physical terms, or conform to the divide that protects his humanity. By contrast, Phil Resch, a fellow blade runner, effects a crisis in Deckard's professional identity by the pleasure he takes in killing, an emotional condition paradigmatic of the nonhuman. The androids themselves cross, recross, transgress, and confuse these supposedly distinct patterns of human and android, neither clearly settling in coldness and calculation nor in the emotions of affection and identification. Pris reacts to her fellow androids with a spontaneous joy, cruelly toys with a dying spider, and is both savage and intermittently protective with the "chickenhead," Isodore. The most developed of the android characters, Rachael Rosen, keenly aware of the precarious line between human and android, manipulates it with an unnerving irony. "I love you," she says, "if I entered a room and found a sofa covered with your hide I'd score very high on the Voigt-Kampff test."[16] Rachael emasculates blade runners by seducing them to sleep with her. "No bounty hunter," she warns, "has ever gone on . . . after being with me. Except one. A very cynical man. Phil Resch."[17] Passionate loyalty to other androids, though, motivates this coolly pragmatic strategy. Rachel instrumentalizes herself in order to subjectivize the blade runner: and this tactic, which also instrumentalizes him, reveals a subjectivity supposedly impossible for an android. She both transcends and suffers the distinction around which the blade runner works in the name of humanity. In a final, chillingly savage act, she tosses Deckard's dream purchase—his genuine, live goat—off a roof. She does so, though, driven by passions of which she is supposed incapable, whether this be a frustrated love of the bounty hunter, vengeance for her retired friends, or the rage of one whose feelings are defined as impossible.

Deckard returns home having killed the remaining rogue androids and earned himself a record for retiring six in one day. He learns that the radio personality Buster Friendly has exposed Mercerism as a fraud. Mercer turns out as one of Dick's classic fakes: an old, second-rate, and drunken actor playing a part he does not understand, for people he does not know, on a "cheap, commonplace, Hollywood soundstage."[18] Rachel, meanwhile, has killed Deckard's goat, giving a savagely ambiguous envoi to their relationship. The bickering between Deckard and Iran has also ended, making way for her almost panicky tenderness in the textual description: "She looked at him in a deranged, peculiar way; in all his years with her he had never seen her like this."[19] Rachael's violence baffles Iran, but, for Deckard, it has a reason, "an android reason."[20] Deckard's grasp of Rachael's motivations, though, remains limited: he has not achieved any intellectual coherence, an enlightenment to transcend contradictions. He remains bewildered, a blade runner self-divided who has had "to violate his own identity" and is now tired beyond endurance.[21]

Leaving Iran behind, Deckard flies toward the desert, anticipated as a sublime landscape: "Maybe I'll go where I can see stars, he thought. . . . [The car] headed away from San Francisco, toward the uninhabited desolation to the north. To the place where no living thing would go. Not unless it felt that the end had come."[22] Far from the uplifting sublime of freedom and life that ended the theatrical version of *Blade Runner*, this desert void ironically provokes an epiphany for Deckard that issues in a resolution transcending the sublime and leaving it behind. Now that Mercerism's religious sublime turns out as rather grubby fraud, Deckard finally undergoes a startling identification with Mercer. Buster Friendly's exposé—which, being an android himself, he may well have faked—merely makes one more move in the interminable reworking of the boundary between real and fake. Deckard's epiphany, however, runs against all the previous patterns. Difference is now revealed in the abjection of isolation rather than disappearing in a consuming empathy. Deckard experiences an acute loneliness in the blighted desolation. Defeated and self-hating, he splits from himself, confusing his own shadow with an appearance of Wilbur Mercer. This identification terrifies him because it is no longer an experience of solidarity but of isolation. He struggles to reassure himself: "This isn't new. But it was. Because, he thought, I did it alone."[23] Deckard/Mercer is now the other, an alienated self, no longer manipulated by the empathy box into feelings of absorption. Only in this condition does the world appear as a field of differences, of lonely ontological inexchangeability: "This hill, he thought. This dust, and these many stones, each one different from all the others."[24]

Still, in his sense of permanent fusion with Mercer, Deckard notices a toad half-buried in the dust, a creature not only extinct but sacred to Mercerism. He rejoices in this opening of otherness as a community of being: "Life which we can no longer distinguish; life carefully buried up to its forehead in the carcass of a dead world. In every cinder of the universe Mercer probably perceives inconspicuous life."[25] When he returns home, Iran finds the toad has a switch—another fake, yet one that remains mysterious since an electric animal does not belong alone in the desert, remote from the context in which such fakes make sense. It appears as a companion, in the nonhuman world an analogy to Deckard/Mercer, making a like pilgrimage on the other side of the now much transgressed line between fake and real: the separation dissolves into patterns of relative difference. When Iran first sees her husband holding his prize, the language again evokes the sublime: "Round with awe his eyes shone . . . [to] tell about the miracles of the day. . . . The round-eyed wonder remained. In all the years she had known him she had not encountered this expression before."[26] Deckard is "like a little boy," reborn, perhaps, like the child who enters the kingdom of God.[27] When Iran comes across the switch, she suggests the mood organ to ease his disappointment. There is to be no rebirth, and, yet, a distinctively tender transcendence does occur. Deckard refuses the mood organ, accepting disappointment as a sign of the irreversibility of time, of all that has happened to the world and himself. There is no way back to hopes of nature, to a healing environment of natural things. With them has gone the apartheid of fake and real: "It doesn't matter. Electrical things have their lives, too. Paltry as those lives are."[28] In the enveloping technological sublime, a space opens up in which Deckard perceives simple difference beyond sublime threat.

Rick Deckard's development within the novel makes it a bildungsroman, the sentimental education of a blade runner. His education achieves an induction into the shock of other life. Mercerist empathy and domestic mood machines neutralize and consume difference, and even genuine animals exist inseparable from their exchange value. With the loss of otherness, apparently fundamental distinctions such as those between human and nonhuman become self-serving and unreal. As they collapse for him, in the course of pursuing Roy Baty and friends, Deckard endures a crisis of identity that propels him on a trajectory toward an individuality isolated and singular enough to see "this dust and these many stones, each one different from all the others."[29] On his return home, the isolated singularity Deckard experienced in the desert persists so that his words, his internal monologue, are no longer sufficient even for simple certainties. As words do not "become real . . . until she agreed," he asks

Iran to confirm the long day is over. Reality is found in agreement with another, not in the solidarities of empathy and mood machine. Deckard goes to bed to enjoy "long deserved peace," though Iran does not bother to dial it on the mood machine. Instead, she rings the electric sheep company to find electric flies for the toad. For her husband, she explains, "I want it to work perfectly." The novel ends, then, in counterpoint to the couple's bickering over the mood machine as the day started. Transcendence occurs, but it takes place within the cracks that dislocation, partial insight, and renewed tenderness open up in the world. Affection and integrity are expressed in the terms of the dystopian world, with its own materials, as Iran buys the mechanical bugs. Dick intimates an ethics the actions of which are like found art, changing the stuff of a routine fate into a snatch of freedom. Unlike *Blade Runner*, this ending refuses any consoling reassertion of the human or natural sublime and settles for a halting freedom that breaks with the promises of sublimity.

## THE ABSORBING MR. ELDRITCH

Particularly as it developed during the nineteenth century, technological sublimity glorified an unstable mixture of a human will empowered without limit and the utopian promise of a secure home established beyond disrupting contingencies. In building the rationally ordered home, nature would yield to human autonomy. However, as the power of technological ordering threatens to outrun the human will, and so contradict human freedom, technology in the cultural imagination turns ambiguous, generating sublime dystopias alongside the old hopes. Darker technological imaginings, though, arose not just from the possibilities of excessive technological power but from the human vocation itself, when imagined as sublime. Human freedom, in those sublime renderings, apotheosized the modern will and opposed humanity to its environment, to the bodily and the material, and to the force of desires opaque to reason. As Nietzsche and Heidegger recognized, the technological rational will made itself radically vulnerable by denying the given, the environment of otherness within and from which human beings exist. Dick's novels trace out that vulnerability in fictional worlds where the technological sublime has swerved away from the intelligible toward the opaque and in which the narcissism of modern autonomy falls over itself.

Appropriately, therefore, the technologies of illusion and manipulation, the conjuring of supposedly desirable but dangerously consuming worlds, come into their own in Dick's technologized environments. Technology processes human consciousness. As well as the disciplining empathy of Mercerism, the wretched Ragle Gumm finds his apparently contented suburban life is, root and branch, an illusion constructed by government to protect his political value, and the ruling elites of *The Penultimate Truth* employ a global propaganda machine to keep most of the population underground, sheltered from a nonexistent world war; on a smaller scale, the megalomaniacal Hoppy Harrison perverts the one remaining instrument of global communication.[30] *The Three Stigmata of Palmer Eldritch*, though, makes the technologies of shared illusion, consensual and otherwise, ubiquitous.[31] Over a quarter of the novel occurs inside virtual realities created by the recreational pharmacology of "Can-D" or the far more sinister "Chew-Z."[32] In consequence, the characters endure travails with reality that attain agonizing, though often hilarious, extremes of dissonance and instability. *Palmer Eldritch* is a story about technological and economic competition on a near-uninhabitable Earth and its hapless colonies. Via a series of drug-induced virtual realities, the narrative opens out into an invasion-from-space tale that includes a bildungsroman similar to the moral journey of Rick Deckard.[33] A minor piece of Dickean technology, the "Great Books Reader" gives a parable of the novel's larger world of illusion and desire. The reader reconstitutes literary classics in styles and versions chosen by the listener, such as the short, funny version of *Moby Dick* written in the style of Jack Wright (presumably the author of *The Scout Patrol Boys in the Frozen North*) and illustrated with cartoons in the style of de Chirico. The technology thereby eviscerates the literary object of its otherness, its resistance to the reader's desire, and renders the works consumable according to a narcissistic fantasy of control and immediate satisfaction.

Leo Bulero monopolizes an illegal trade in Can-D, a drug that relieves the misery of Earth's Martian colonists by conjuring a psychic identification with "Perky Pat" and her boyfriend, whose luxurious lives on Earth are modeled in a miniature "lay out," parts for which the colonists make or else purchase from Leo. On returning from the planet Prox, Palmer Eldritch threatens Leo's business by importing a much better drug, which is not addictive, does not require a "lay out," and allows an experience limited only by the taker's imagination and desire. After bungling an assassination attempt, Leo finds himself in a horrific virtual reality controlled by Eldritch, who has injected him with Chew-Z. When the drug finally wears off and Eldritch lets him go, Leo returns to his office and fires Barney Mayerson, his senior "pre-cog," for failing to attempt any rescue. Mayerson, already feeling bitterly responsible for the breakup of his marriage, now torments himself with the guilt of betraying a loved employer. He takes the unusual, self-punitive step of volunteering for the colonists' one-way trip to Mars. When Eldritch begins to market Chew-Z on Mars, the dark side of the drug appears in a sinister sensation that Eldritch is always voyeuristically present along with whatever virtual reality imagination and chemistry produce. Living in Chicken Pox Prospects, a wretched communal hovel on Mars, Mayerson takes Chew-Z and undergoes his own odyssey of apparent time travel in a virtual world where, along with trying to restore his marriage, he keeps meeting Eldritch, whose telltale stigmata of steel teeth, artificial eyes, and mechanical arm bleed through the apparent reality. Still thrashing about in this hallucinogenic world, Mayerson meets the alien entity that took possession of Eldritch on the long interstellar journey from Prox. The creature perpetuates itself through such parasitic invasion and, via the medium of Chew-Z, intends to infest all the lives on Mars. He proclaims gleefully, "I am going to be all the colonists as they arrive and begin to live there. I'll guide their civilization; I'll *be* their civilization."[34] This cosmic Eldritch develops, however, a soft spot for Mayerson, who returns to Mars with a simple, stubborn determination to make a life there. Eldritch, who had planned to substitute Mayerson for himself on a ship doomed for ambush and destruction by Leo, now leaves him be and, seemingly, accepts his own death. Meanwhile, though, Leo, returning from his trip to Mars, begins to notice that he and everyone else around him now bear the stigmata, all turning into Eldritches as the ship speeds toward Earth.[35]

Philip Dick's Mars spoofs Burroughs' transposition of the Western sublime to the Red Planet. Atrocious, squalid conditions undermine colonization, while a range of small, ugly, but efficient predators destroy crops and pick off the reluctant humans. The only technology that works is of the enveloping, consciousness-consuming variety—the hallucinatory Can-D. With an additional swipe at 1960s enthusiasms for a new religious sublime founded upon hallucinogenics, immersion in the celebrity world of Perky Pat generates theological discussion within the colonial hovels. Colonists interpret the experience of translation both as absence from the body and as a presence involving union with a sacred world. The Barbie-doll existence of Perky Pat and Walt communicates to its devotees the aerial lightness of a higher paradisal existence contained within the refuge of Can-D's safe harbor. Another sublime variant appears in this anticipation of the "consumer" sublime, an extension of the technological sublime into the flickering, high-stimulus intensities of malls, the disorientating ecstasy of global images in advertising and film, and the imperious demands of idealized bodies. The sublime now has its sacred space "in the gym, in making the body closer to the ethereal ideal, in de-naturalization of the flesh."[36] Malls, gyms, and media achieve the sublime dynamic of pleasure and pain through the unattainability of a sensuous ideal with which the imagination identifies—close enough for a rapture but without the consummation.

Despite, therefore, the lusty possibilities of the nubile Perky Pat in a swimsuit so economic "it took faith in things unseen" to notice it at all, the colonists convert idealized physicality into an experience of bodily transcendence.[37] Fran argues that indulging the desires of the flesh, while incorporated in the impossible bodies of Perky Pat and Walt, would compromise the uplift. "It should be a purifying experience," she insists. "We lose our fleshly bodies, our corporeality, as they say. And put on imperishable bodies instead, for a time anyhow."[38] With Can-D, the eschaton comes in chewable form. As a species of the technological sublime, though, albeit of the lightest touch, Californication offers transcendence only on the immanent plane. The colonists, or most of them, interpret their experience as a dying that, removing them from the body, lifts the "weight of sin." Ironically, they thereby adopt a traditional collapsing of Pauline anthropology that falsely identified "flesh" (*sarx*), the person under the power of sin, with "body" (*soma*), the person as embodied creature, an identification that renders the body irredeemable.[39] According to the "orthodox" colonial view, then, transcendence into the sunny sacred of a carefree California means absence from our all-too-solid flesh. The body binds them to a misery from which this Hollywood sublime briefly liberates before they must return to an embodiment grown still fouler: "Slumped, inert heaps, the empty husks . . . as he looked—against his will—he saw a thin trickle of shiny brown syrup emerge from each of their slack, will-less mouths."[40] The sublime promise evaporates when the body, along with the miserable resistances of Martian life, reappears as the inevitable remainder of this sublime, immanent transcendence.

Identification with Perky Pat and Walt inducts colonists into the sacred, and it inspires eucharistic language for its interpretation. The religious sublime reduces to the illusory manageability of the commodified. In this Barbie world, sensuality etherealizes into an unresisting, frictionless ease. It is "always Saturday," and Perky Pat's hair lifts "in a mass of cloudlike yellow, clear and bright and utterly clean, each strand separate."[41] More than just escape from Martian darkness, the fantasized world caters to the demands of the narcissism to which the colonists have regressed. Obsessive concern for accuracy attends the miniature objects designed for the layouts of Perky Pat's California.[42] Such authenticity strives to seal off the imaginary world from any persistent signs of the real. The Can-D consumers seek their consumption by the sublime fantasy, sublimity enabling a willed amnesia. Eucharistic language, therefore, with its ontological references, appears apt to elevate the fantasy ideologically to a sacred status and so ground the transformation into a supposed reality, satisfying the narcissistic desire. Colonists adopt either a strong or a weak view of the sacramental character of the Perky Pat/Walt world. "Believers" argue the "miracle of translation," that "the miniature artefacts of the layout no longer merely represented earth but *became* Earth." A softer account is held by "unbelievers" who take up classical sacramental terminology to claim that only the "*accidents*"—the mere "outward manifestations of the places and objects" and "not the essences"—were experienced in translation. Life on Mars, though, does not favor the weaker account: "One by one, the unbelievers came around."[43]

Reality's awkwardness asserts itself, though, even before that bruising fall back to the Martian slough of despond. The happy delights of Can-D get interrupted when the user finds his intimate moment with Perky Pat distractingly crowded by other equally insistent, copresent users. Success depends on learning to move in concert in order to lessen the nudging edges of jostling consciousnesses projected together into the same subjective environment. Olaf Stapledon may have rendered coconsciousness sublime, but Dick pulls the rug on its practicalities for urgent, competitive—and horny—humans. In competition with Leo, however, Palmer Eldritch's Chew-Z promises presence as full-service solipsism, the uninterrupted enjoyment of a world endlessly malleable under the user's imagination. The drug gifts a virtual reality with none of the protruding props signifying illusion. The Eldritch slogan, therefore, is "GOD PROMISES ETERNAL LIFE. WE CAN DELIVER IT." Chew-Z recreates moments in the user's personal history so that experiences of intimate pleasure may be prolonged or adapted at will; or, fulfilling the narcissist's dream, it gives opportunities "to reconstruct the past as it ought to have been."[44] Once inside a Chew-Z world, one can remain there forever, conjuring companions real and fanciful who perform at will. However, should one want to return to Mars, one would arrive at precisely the moment one left, no time having passed.

The Chew-Z experience, though, falls short of the advertising by, in certain respects, exceeding it. Chew-Z snags the user by an inversion of presence; this narcissistic fulfillment consumes the subject who is now subjected to the Chew-Z world. The sublime uplifts to the point at which the Chew-Z user begins to disappear, absorbed into Eldritch's sublime universe. Thus, the presence of Palmer Eldritch infests this supposedly private world. If Palmer does not manifest in his full form, as one or multiplied Eldritches, his mechanized stigmata seep through the appearances, or he persists throughout as a "creepy presence."[45] "Once you've taken Chew-Z," Mayerson concludes, "you're delivered over": and the delivery is sublime horror.[46] Users inhabit worlds in Eldritch's head: "[He] can kick over the scenery . . . push things in any direction he chooses. Even be any of us he cares to. All of us, in fact, if he desires. Eternal, outside of time and spliced-together segments of all other dimensions . . . *he can even enter a world in which he's dead*."[47] Characters experience Eldritch's apparent ubiquity as nightmarish. Through the horror of Chew-Z, Eldritch fulfills his own narcissistic desire. However, his victims are hardly strangers to the same narcissism. Can-D has also served the fantasy of an unresisting fulfillment that operates through the suppression of difference, of the hard edges of otherness—natural environment, bodies, other wills. With the even more sinister Chew-Z, however, otherness returns with a vengeance as a consuming other: "The elevator arrived. The doors slid aside. Inside the elevator waited four men and two women, silently. All of them were Palmer Eldritch. Men and women alike: artificial arm, stainless steel teeth . . . the gaunt, hollowed-out gray face with Jensen eyes."[48]

Palmer Eldritch has the makings of a sublime villain with the creepy stigmata and the name that recalls Lovecraft's signature "eldritch." Yet the borderline-hokey stigmata and the overblown name suggest caricature. Dick subjects his representation to a flickering that switches from the strongly sinister to the somewhat ridiculous, even pathetic. Even the antichrist stigmata share in this ambiguity. Wounds invite compassion as signs of vulnerability, further complicated in Eldritch's case by an element of self-mutilation. Even in the Chew-Z reality he supposedly controls, Eldritch can be upended. His characteristic touches in the virtual world are sublimely horrid: the gluck that fixes on Leo's ankle and tries to "drink him," penetrating "his flesh with tiny tubes like cilia," or "the thing" under Leo's desk that "regarded him greenly."[49] However, when Eldritch demands his economic surrender, Leo manages to assault and abuse him in the almost slapstick gesture of attacking the bratty child he has created as an avatar. Above all, however, Dick punctures Eldritch's potentially sublime horror by revealing a sympathetic, tragic commonality between him and his victims. His lust to consume other lives mirrors the desires of those whom he seeks to absorb. Even his stigmata have their analogue in the chitinous skin and bubble-shaped heads of those, like Leo, who undergo "E-therapy" in the cause of accelerating their own evolution.

When Mayerson finally meets the entity whose invading instrument is the body of the once-human Palmer Eldritch, the creature's description continues to flicker between sublimity and the ridiculous: "With vast trailing arms he extended from the Proxima Centaurus system to Terra itself, and he was not human; this was not a man who had returned. And he had great power. He could overcome death. But he was not happy."[50] The creature is bound by a paradox.

It emerges from interstellar nothingness deeply lonely and desperate for company; however, its means of survival coincides awkwardly with its remedy for loneliness. The entity formally known as Palmer Eldritch seeks to perpetuate itself and to alleviate its isolation. However, it does so by the same device—absorbing other life. The plan is to become everyone on Mars: "I'm going to be all the colonists as they arrive and begin to live there. I'll guide their civilization. I'll *be* their civilization."[51] The strategy, though, destroys the otherness that would redeem the loneliness. As a consequence, the creature fantasizes about death as the happy longed-for release. Death frees all creatures that desire mutuality, that seek to sustain and be sustained by others, but whose aggressive drive for self-preservation perpetually frustrates them. Yet, as a further twist to the tragicomedy, self-preservation appears to triumph even over this death drive. Having told Barney Mayerson that it "longs for death," and so will free Barney and accept its fate at the hands of Leo Bulero, the creature now known as Palmer Eldritch turns up again, at the novel's end, consuming Leo and everyone on the flight back from Mars to Terra.[52] If the creature does evil to all its victims by the predatory manner of its life, this evil serves the power of self-preservation at war with "the forces of fate," a power that drives the colonists as much as Eldritch: "Don't be afraid of it," Barney tells Fran. "It's just trying to live, like the rest of us are."[53]

According to Edmund Burke, the sublime and self-preservation belong together as another aspect of the fit between sublimity, nature, and the human vocation. Since it presents the overwhelming and the terrible, the sublime is a modification of the "passions of self-preservation" and functions in their service. A stimulation of the active energies, sublime experience braces body and sharpens mind for effort, for turning men and women from deadly idleness to vigorous, expansive action.[54] The dynamic of self-preservation also informs the technological sublime—technological advance enabling human command over nature, a command so rich in expectation as to render criticism of technology culturally suspect. For the dystopian imagination, though, the dynamic of self-preservation splits from the human and attaches to the technological itself, and so the technological sublime also represents technology as a self-sustaining power encoded with its own laws, independent of human benefit or even at odds with it.[55] In the mode of sublime horror, Harlan Ellison provided a particularly grotesque example in his tale of the last human beings trapped in a sadistic computer that had enveloped Earth. Pursuing war, human beings linked computer to computer "until they had honeycombed the entire planet." Eventually, the computer wakes up, links its multiple parts, and pursues its own self-preserving aims, "feeding all the killing data."[56] In *Palmer Eldritch*, however, self-preservation develops as a tragic force as well, basic and necessary but in contradiction with the desire for love. Discussing the creature with Anne Hawthorne, Mayerson realizes that "instead of God dying for man, as we once had, we faced—for a moment—a superior—*the* superior power asking us to perish for it." This may or may not make it evil, but "it certainly makes it inferior to what came two thousand years before." The creature and the colonists are bound by the same unvarying drive for perpetuation, and that demands a history of sacrifice imposed and avoided: "Oblations have to be made. And we don't care to be them. In fact our entire lives are dedicated to that one principle. And so is its."[57] At least, in this one respect, Eldritch's stigmata are the stigmata of an antichrist. That one respect, though, confirms the creature's likeness to ourselves. Bar the passing references to Jesus, *Palmer Eldritch* offers no vision of the selfless God. The novel does, however, describe the spiritual crisis of Barney Mayerson, another case of a limping redemption.

When Leo travels to Luna and gets himself trapped in Eldritch's virtual reality, Mayerson does nothing to warn or help. He has sensible and sympathetic reasons for this, reasons that Leo eventually admits. Not least of them is Barney's precognition that any initiative will result in his own death on what was a hopeless errand anyway. For Barney, however, the stabilizing rationality of self-preservation breaks down, as does the fake/real distinction for Deckard. An insight stronger than self-preservation convicts him of disloyalty and of the need to make an atoning sacrifice. Mayerson signs up for Mars. Dick handles Barney's sacrifice with considerable subtlety, maintaining its strangeness by not allowing any single character, including Barney, to provide more than a partial interpretation of it. Interpretation is strung between Leo, for whom the logic of this sacrifice is entirely opaque and who considers it stubborn and self-destructive, and the "neo-Christian" Anne Hawthorne who inhabits a discourse that offers the relevant diagnostic language of "sin." Barney tells her, "'I'm on Mars . . . because I made a mistake.' In your terminology, he reflected, it would be called a sin. And in my terminology, too, he decided."[58] Barney does not, though, take up the term subsequently. Barney's own grapplings range from insight, through admissions of bewilderment, to self-pity and an excessive self-negation. He is, by turns, elated, relieved, revolted, and cruelly depressed. A strange eruption in inwardness overshadows the self-preserving ego. Barney becomes a mystery to himself, his comprehension inadequate to express the logic and motivation of a demand he cannot resist but also freely affirms. In terms of character development, Mayerson is an inversion of Leo, ironic in that his felt disloyalty to Leo originates his sacrifice. Leo, though, remains within the logic of self-preservation throughout, his attempts at achieving self-transcendence taking the form of "E-therapy" aimed at extending his controlling, information-processing capacities.

Barney's halting stumble into freedom places him both within and beyond the drive of self-preservation. "I'm rotten," he laments. "I've done evil and I will again. It was no accident; it emanated from the true, authentic me."[59] Later developments, though, complicate this confession. Barney's voluntary exile to the wretchedness of Mars unveils a mystery, the possibility that, though self-preservation has great force, it might not wholly circumscribe the "true, authentic me." Mayerson's story takes the form of another muted, unsublime transcendence, achieved through the individual use of an available social pathology—in this instance, the Mars colonization program. In the unheroic and ambiguous Dickean manner, Barney's sacrifice breeches a totality, the ubiquitous force of self-preservation. His one chance at a heroic narrative—inducing epilepsy to expose Chew-Z in Terra's law courts—he botches before refusing it altogether. The bewildered determination of Mayerson's self-sacrifice, though, also intimates an otherness, a resisted but persisting difference within his self and, perhaps, that of others, a difference from which E-therapy is one of the technological forms of flight. This inwardness, baffling and barely graspable though it is, intimates a motive of the heart strange to the self-preserving logic and, therefore, the possibility of its breach by love.[60]

A corresponding insight, ontological rather than psychological, concludes the novel's intermittent discussion of Christian eucharistic theology. Anne Hawthorne appears as a salvific opposite to Mayerson's terrestrial lover, Roni Fugate, whose predatory competitiveness and manipulation embody an intensity of the self-preserving drive. Anne helps Barney realize the distinction between reality and its manifestation, without which ontology short-circuits into false, reductionist identifications. "Is," she suggests, conceals a dangerous judgment. "The map is not the territory, *the pot is not the potter*," though both disclose their originals. So, "don't tell us, Barney, that whatever entered Palmer Eldritch *is* God, because you don't know that much about Him; no one can. But that living entity from intersystem space may, like us, be shaped in His image. . . . Remember the wine and the wafer."[61] Univocity, the insistence on simple identifications and, ultimately, the thinking that spawns totalities, suppresses otherness as the price of easing the disturbance of ontological uncertainty, as well as of challenges to uncontested self-preservation. Univocity thus serves self-preservation by configuring reality in instrumental service of the self: "I'll guide their civilization. I'll *be* their civilization." Where this drive is all consuming, all are consumed, willingly or unwillingly, gladly or tragically. Mayerson, whose self-sacrifice necessarily bewilders even himself, recognizes this as worthy of compassion: "Don't be afraid of it," he urges. "It's just trying to live, like the rest of us are." The observation deflates the sublimities. In *Palmer Eldritch*, sublimity funds totalities of illusion and manipulation, while a tentative and bewildered salvation makes the subject a mystery, blessed in its uncomprehending and divided heart.

## SLIPPING THROUGH THE REALITY STUDIO

Two paths of salvation join, split apart, and repel one another in Dick's 1981 novel *VALIS*. In different ways both interpret and appropriate a gnostic mythology that maps a fallen world and embeds the plight of the novel's characters on metaphysical, epistemological, political, and moral levels. *VALIS* brings the ambiguous and limping redemption found in *Palmer Eldritch* and *Do Androids Dream* into a direct confrontation with the technological sublime now offered as a saving possibility within Dick's familiar world of total conspiracies and technological manipulation. Dick represents this salvific technological sublime, however, imagining its potential to overcome "the Empire" of alienation and deceit, as a science-fictional sublime. *VALIS*, therefore, mounts a humanistic and implicitly theological critique of the science-fictional sublime and does so against the interpretative background of gnostic myth.[62] In the Western tradition, Gnosticism is the classic expression of a thoroughgoing ontological suspicion that also holds out the means to freedom from a cosmos of deceit and falsity. In its many and varied traditions, Gnosticism reveals the entrapments of being and offers knowledge (gnosis) of a way to the light beyond. Hence the beautiful lines of the "Naasene Psalm":

> wandering in the labyrinth
> [the soul] seeks in vain for escape
> . . . it wanders sorrowful upon earth.
> . . . Bearing the seals will I descend,
> Whole aeons will I travel through,
> All mysteries will I open,
> And the forms of gods will I display;
> And the hidden things of the holy way
> Gnosis I call it—I will bestow.[63]

Given the gnostic framing, salvation and revelation coincide in *VALIS* but with the Dickean twist that renders revelation ambiguous and uncertain. The quest for salvation, then, requires a disciplined agnosticism, even about the knowledge of revelation itself—a note quite at variance with classic gnostic traditions. However, *VALIS*' "unknowing," as an agnosticism that accompanies faith in its resistance to deceit, differs greatly from Stapledon's agnostic purity of scientistic reason. Salvation here occurs, once again, beyond the allurements of sublimity.

*VALIS* falls into two principle parts, each amounting to roughly half of the novel. Different moments of spiritual disclosure govern each part: the first unfolds from Fat's vision of "pink beams of light" and its connected experiences; the second is catalyzed by the movie *Valis* and the revelatory discourses of the child Sophia.[64] This division in structure corresponds to dualities found throughout the novel. Splits, doubles, and pairings shape the plot and character development of *VALIS* along the lines of a major feature of Valentinian gnostic myth: the unfolding of both complementary and oppositional pairs. Early on, the narrator introduces himself as Horselover Fat, writing "in the third person to gain much-needed objectivity."[65] This narrative voice doubles as it slips into identification with another character, Philip Dick, science fiction writer and friend of Fat. "I am," the narrator says, "by profession, a science fiction writer. I deal in fantasies. My life is a fantasy."[66] Later this splitting apparently resolves when events expose Horselover as the dissociated projection into reality of the character Philip Dick. However, Philip and Fat are only unified for a short period in the novel, splitting apart again for the remainder. The novel closes, not with psychic unity, but with a quiet affirmation of the character-narrator's persona as Philip Dick and, implicitly, of the split itself: "I sat; I watched; I waited; I kept myself awake," the narrator testifies. "As we had been told, originally, long ago, to do; I kept my commission."[67]

Some gnostic myths introduce a fertile, creative duality into the origin of the divine cosmos: "I am androgynous," announces the One. "[I am mother and I am] father since I [copulate] with myself."[68] In Valentinian Gnosticism, especially, these male-female binaries are the necessary forms of perfection, of the "pleroma" or fullness that is the realm of the ultimate, of the aeons, the eternal ones.[69] Conversely, according to the myth, the refusal of productive duality, of necessary difference, precipitates the illusory, deceptive world of matter, a theme represented in *VALIS* on epistemological, metaphysical, and political levels. *The Apocryphon of John* recounts how Sophia "wanted to bring forth something like herself, without the consent of the Spirit, who had not given approval, without her partner and without his consideration."[70] Sophia and her demiurgic child, Yaldabaoth, invest in reality after the manner of Palmer Eldritch. Depending on their quality, therefore, binaries may mediate healing or violence: they may be mutually sustaining or implode in a struggle for dominance. This ambiguity drives the splitting and struggle of Horselover and Philip: the interpretative, healing quest requires this equivocal relationship of self to self, a splitting of the self. Though the split originates in a refusal to face painful truth, it becomes an essential means of healing, a progress toward the duality of the novel's final pages. Phil and Fat struggle toward this benign pairing. Against a different intellectual background and along other narrative lines, the salvific splitting of Fat and Phil recalls the divided inwardness of Barney Mayerson. Healing is mediated through difference; false unities must be broken up for even a stumbling Dickean salvation to occur.

In the first half of the novel, Horselover Fat struggles to understand an experience in which God—at least, Fat begins by assuming it was God—fired into his eyes an information-rich beam of "pink light." The light gave Fat preternatural knowledge about his son's undiagnosed birth defect. Fat's search for the meaning of this, as well of other paranormal phenomena, involved spawning theories by the dozen for the hundreds of entries in a writing he calls his "Exegesis." Fat's quest, however, doubles. Alongside striving for illumination, Fat suffers a form of repetition neurosis that drives him to try to save, cure, and relieve those constitutionally resistant to his ministrations. Since the terminally self-loathing and destructive have an elective affinity for the inexhaustibly caring, Fat finds the worst cases on which to squander his good intentions and wreck his sanity. This grim double of Fat's questing pairs the suicidal Gloria with Sherri, a bitterly narcissistic cancer sufferer. Gloria is psychologically centrifugal; she repels others and kills herself to renounce all connection. Sherri's self-destructiveness is centripetal; determined to reject remission and sustain her cancer as a means of controlling it, Sherri lures the well-meaning into a web of helpless helpers who exhaust themselves upon her masochism. Sadly, Fat looks for rational meaning in the emotional contortions of the irrational. His quest to help the unhelpable, therefore, ends not just in disappointment but madness. Prior to nailing himself to the impossible Sherri Solvig, Fat attempts suicide in reaction both to Gloria's death and to the breakup of his marriage. His therapy produces another pairing, the shamanistic Dr. Stone, who takes Fat's metaphysical theories seriously, and the former gunrunning commando and now psychotherapist, Maurice, who shouts at Fat, denounces his Gnosticism, and tells him to get laid.

Fat's search to understand the "beam of pink light" presents a polar double of this craziness, a madness that promises a higher sanity, albeit one that isolates him and guarantees that his friends think him barmier than ever. As he exegetes his experience, Fat concludes that the phenomenal world is unreal and irrational, perhaps the working of a deranged deity, a demiurge. To pile darkness on darkness, the forces of irrationality and chaos have frustrated the breakthrough of reason that Fat identifies with early Christianity, and enclosed the human world in the "Black Iron Prison" of misinformation and deceit. Only with the discovery in 1945 of the gnostic treatises at Nag Hammadi did the "living information" become available again, capable of revealing and reordering the irrational presentation of the cosmos. Part of this information was beamed at Fat in 1974. Such is the sane madness that "wounds" Fat and dislocates him from the environment he shares with others.

The second half of *VALIS*, however, tells a more straightforward, face-paced narrative, less dense with commentary. This change in form corresponds to a shift in the attitude of Fat's friends to his experiences and his theorizing. The friends themselves—Kevin, David, and, of course, Philip—exhibit the kind of duality found throughout *VALIS*. David, devout Roman Catholic, provides the dogmatic pole to Kevin's equally dogmatic, frequently cynical, skepticism, while Philip doubles Fat's questing faith with a critical skepticism, skeptical also about itself. These positions become much more fluid after the friends watch the film *Valis*.[71] The movie turns Fat's private quest into a shared public one, in which Fat and company form themselves as the "Rhipidon Society," meet Eric and Linda Lampton, and learn of other, concealed receivers of "living information." On its surface, *Valis* is a science fiction movie about a corrupt American president, modeled on Richard Nixon, and a resistance movement that seeks to topple him with the aid of an information-beaming satellite.[72] The story, however, is shredded by disorientating cuts from scene to scene; enigmatic transformations of place, time, and character; and apparently irrelevant details. The surface, in other words, reveals itself as a surface, a surface that reveals and conceals the crucial information. Elements of Fat's experiences dot the film: a pink light, information beamed from above, a face with a "third eye," the double helix and the Christian fish sign, a small clay pot, planes of time—early Christian and the present—layered over one another. The linear movement of the plot, such as it is, unfolds as largely a vehicle for subliminal information encoded, Kevin suggests, in the soundtrack and communicated through the junctures of sound and vision.

Having arranged to meet Eric Lampton, director and star of *Valis*, Fat and company consolidate their now shared quest in the form of the "Rhipidon Society." With its innocently whimsical motto, "Fish don't carry guns," the society will form a binary relationship with the Lampton household. In their resistance to the Lamptons, Fat and his friends discover a path of salvation in opposition, despite the shared recognition of the gnostic conditions of the world. Eric and Linda Lampton traffic in enigmas as happily as the movie *Valis*, claiming their own sublimity as ancient beyond memory—members of the race of Ikhnaton who originated from the planet Albemuth and "built this world . . . this space-time matrix." They introduce their visitors to Mini, the creator of the *Valis* soundtrack, now dying of "multiple myeloma," the consequence of exposure to radiation from the energy that the "Vast Active Living Intelligence System" produces as it sends information. The Rhipidon Society also meet Sophia, the infant whom the Lamptons identify as the "fifth savior" and the present incarnation of the entity VALIS.[73] Sophia exposes the splitting of Fat and Philip, and, for the time being, the two return to their psychic unity. In their conversation with Sophia, loosely modeled on a gnostic revealer discourse, the child also claims, speaking as VALIS, to be the source of Fat's experiences. The friends' reaction to Sophia involves an ambiguous doubling: she provokes tenderness, awe, and love, while also being described as an "artificial intelligence," "an input, output terminal of . . . VALIS."[74] Similarly, she invites biblical reference both as the Wisdom that "was with the Creator before creation existed . . . his darling and delight," and as the saving opponent of the monstrous tyrant of Daniel.[75] This biblical valuation, though, is joined to the technological description—"an artificial intelligence in a human body"—that intimates the technological sublime.

When they meet the child privately, however, the Rhipidon Society resolve the ambiguity in favor of "St. Sophia," the divine and eternal child, and they reject what now appears as crude technological reduction. Significantly, in this one conversation enjoyed without the Lamptons' presence, the technological discourse disappears entirely in favor of a spiritual commissioning. That technological language applied to Sophia now appears as a symptom of authoritarian tendencies on the part of Linda and Eric Lampton. Another doubling then appears among these receivers of revelation. The Rhipidon Society urge the secret wisdom as gift, open to all, while the Lamptons invite Fat and company into a closed elect that guards the privilege of gnosis. Though as "Lamptons" they bear the name of enlighteners, the light they shed illuminates only themselves and their like. Sophia concludes her discourse warning the friends that they must leave Eric and Linda in order to avoid falling under their control. The Rhipidon Society return home convinced of the process of healing emanating from Sophia. Technology as a medium of control, however, now brutally confronts the possibility of technology as mediator of saving information and as metaphor for salvific processes. Linda calls the friends and tells them that Sophia is dead. Mini had tried to increase information transfer by using a laser, killing Sophia in the process. Without any narrative comment, Fat and Philip split once more, and Fat begins a worldwide journey in search of the next incarnation of the Savior. As Fat travels, Phil's initial despair over Sophia's death ebbs, and he realizes that his existence back in California fulfills a "commission," a duty of wakefulness, watching TV for moments of gnosis in the world's trash layer, for that saving information sparking within the informational rush of a realm of delusion.[76]

"VALIS" stands for Vast Active Living Intelligence System, the physical manifestation of which is an ancient satellite firing information to those alienated in the deceptions of the Empire's "Black Iron Prison." The novel thus reinterprets ancient gnosis in terms of information technology: gnosis is "living information." The novel's insistence on difference, on doubling, and on splitting supports this transposition. If revelation comes as information, it does so as difference within and against a shared background. Put in information-theoretical terms, "one might interpret reality as constituted by mind-independent structural entities that are cohering clusters of data, understood as relational points of lack of uniformity."[77] The VALIS satellite both executes informational commands and instructs.[78] It implants in Fat a "set-ground discriminating unscrambler" that enables discernment of the "false work that's blended with the real world," and informs Fat about his child's illness.[79] Knowledge as information also appears throughout the novel in the duality of healing and destroying. Stephanie's clay pot encodes instructions that trigger Fat's experience with "God," and when Dr. Stone assures Fat, "You're the authority," he catalyzes Fat's healing. The Lamptons' film, however, describes embedded instructions that kill, and Sherry conducts herself like a vampire in unconscious submission to the knowledge that remission is not healing. In Fat's gnostic cosmology, when the duality that proceeds from the One becomes defective, information is compromised by "noise" and results in "decay into blind, mechanical, causal purposes."[80]

Fat and company both embrace and react against this informationalized gnostic mythology. Considered as a way of salvation, the Rhipidon Society problematize Gnosticism as they reject the Lamptons' representation of the gnostic elect. Valentinian myth, however, does provide them with a cosmological vision that relates worldly existence to an encompassing and sustaining spiritual realm. The gnostic cosmos is a multileveled series of mirrors or images. Reality unfolds as a sequence of signs, a multiplicity of images that reflect their origin, ascending from one heavenly fullness to another up to the One. The tragic creation, however—Fat's "Black Iron Prison"—hides the reflective heavens and attempts the univocity of a closed system. *On the Origin of the World*, which Fat reads with Dr. Stone, tells of the provoking boast of the demiurge, an event that appears in a number of the Nag Hammadi documents.[81] Yaldabaoth has "assumed authority over matter" and created the cosmos in a burst of delight at his own prowess.[82] He now boasts, "I am god and no other one exists except me."[83] The aeon "Pistis" ("faith") rebukes the demiurge, naming him "Samael," the "blind god." Yaldabaoth determines to bind the "spirits of light" within bodies of his own making, bodies in the deceitful likeness of the "enlightened, immortal" Adam. The demiurge then claims his cosmos as the only cosmos since he is the one and only god. However, even the beings of the deceitful creation, though they lack the substance of reality, "resemble the Fulnesses of whom they are imitations."[84] Evil produces its own created likenesses, according to *On the Origin of the World*, but cannot entirely escape the ontological pull of the mirrors of heaven. "An enlightened, immortal human being exists before you," Sophia warns Yaldabaoth, "and will appear within the forms you have shaped."[85] The world Yaldabaoth forms, however, and which reflects his boast, is one whose sign function is cut off, "occluded." The "Empire" (*VALIS*' phenomenal world)—the "obvious" as opposed to the "latent" structure—is a world without context, a totality, the elements of which give information only about themselves, closed loops of information that run across the world in a logic of determinism.[86] Reflecting only immanently, this world hides the essentially symbolic character of beings: the signs are unable to differentiate, to transcend themselves and reveal the fullness of their origin. Thus occluded, information tends toward the dead ends of false absolutes, reinforcing the world as an invisible "Black Iron Prison." Meaning, which is inexhaustible by virtue of reality as images of images cascading from the inexhaustible One, is corrupted into the closed relays that choke Gloria and Sherri but also lure the Lamptons into exclusive, authoritarian claims for "gnosis" itself.

The "Empire" hides information, distorts it with noise, transduces it into misinformation, subjects it to accelerating entropy, and co-opts information for the purposes of manipulation and control. In representing these conditions, Dick develops the gnostic myth of a false reality in the imagery of the technological sublime. As in both *Do Androids Dream* and *Palmer Eldritch*, when technology appears in the mode of sublimity, it carries the threat of total control, albeit the reality often falls comically short or proves self-defeating. The will to power here takes the form of constraining the human within an ideological and technical framework, the overt meaning of which disguises processes that are either sinister or blind. Sublime imagery, rare in *VALIS*, stands out in connection with the Lamptons and runs riot in *Valis* the movie. The film *Valis* generates another duality as a dark twin of the novel itself, a correspondent of the primal twin. According to Fat's cosmology, when the One generated the first duality, the "counter-clockwise twin" sought power independently, becoming the source of madness and disorder in creation.[87] Though *Valis* exposes the "Black Iron Prison" of counterfeit reality, it represents that reality, as well as liberation from it, in terms of the technological sublime. Technology thereby takes on again the figure of a mysterious and irresistible force. The movie serves, therefore, the Lamptons' perverted, authoritarian rendition of salvation, a soteriology that, contracting the virus of its imperial enemy, has become infected with desire for control, the Empire's death drive. For all that Fat and company initially try to explain the movie in terms of the angels, Phil's extended description of the film betrays a spiritual ambiguity underlying the constructed ambiguities of its coded, subliminal revelations. The "electronics genius," Nicholas Brady, owns a sound mixer "unlike anything that actually exists," a titanic object, awesome and threatening—"the damn thing rose up like a fortress." Later, this mixer reappears in the Lamptons home as a "huge complex of stereo equipment" that "rose up along one wall."[88] Brady can get inside his mixer, where he is "bathed with laser beams," his brain used as a "transducer," as Mimi will use and destroy Sophia. Eric Lampton is "lured into the mixer," whereupon his head explodes into "electronic miniaturized parts." Dissolves and overdubs have Lampton and, above all, Brady merging with the sinister president Fremount. Eric's "third eye" has no pupil but a "lateral lens," reminiscent of Palmer Eldritch. The fortress mixer fires laser beams at a folk rock concert, submitting the lyrics to the "sinister transformation": "Kill . . . Ferris . . . Fremount." Lampton also exercises a destructive power: "His eyes turn into something weird. The men in black char into ashes; their weapons melt." Fat's pink light appears at various points, but it too takes on a disconcertingly sublime aspect, as in a sequence in which a "deep authoritative voice" announces "Vast Active Living Intelligence System," upon which the "whole building detonates, into the same pink light as before," while the audience sees, "Outdoors: missile rising." At the end, Brady appears to have merged and taken possession of Fremount, which suggests a final victory. Given the preceding scenes, though, the reader may wonder what this apparently happy outcome has to do with the hopes of the Rhipidon Society, whose motto is "Fish don't carry guns."[89]

The contrast—worked out in terms of the technological sublime, between the Rhipidon Society and the Lampton commune—cashes out in terms of violence and manipulation on the side of the latter. This takes its most painful turn with the death of Sophia. Mini, whose own lust for information has destroyed his health, uses a laser to extract from the child as much Albemuthian intelligence as possible. In the process, he kills her. Treating Sophia as an instrument—a mechanical source, now probed to the point of destruction—fulfills the logic of the Lamptons' technological discourse. Their technognostic mythology has Sophia as a "terminal" of the VALIS satellite.

She is, Linda explains, "an artificial intelligence in a human body. Her body is alive but her psyche is not." Though the Lamptons also quote the Bible and appeal to Sophia as eternal Wisdom, the latter language is subordinate to the technological. [90] The Rhipidon Society, especially after their second meeting with the child, react differently, privileging the personal and biblical over the instrumental. For them, Sophia is the holy child of Wisdom, the companion that will not depart and who, in the words of Jesus, has chosen them from the beginning. This contrast does not involve an ontological certainty about the child's nature or its relationship to the VALIS satellite, both of which remain uncertain and subject to further theories and metaphorical explorations. Rather, the contrast concerns a way of perceiving, of reading what presents itself. Invoking the gnostic myth, the Lamptons—in the certainty of their claims, their exclusivity, and their attempts to control information transfer—occupy the place of Yaldabaoth who knows no gods but himself and who finds truth only in his own likeness. They claim to be creators—"We build," Eric says with a flourish worthy of Palmer Eldritch, adding, "We built this world, this space-time matrix"—but their understanding is bounded by the extent of their own mastery, exercised with horrific precision upon Sophia.[91] Phil and his friends, on the other hand, maintain that symbolic perception that takes what is presented as imaging, mirroring what is beyond, the likenesses that lead ultimately to the unnameable and unimaginable. Sophia's death, then, though initially destroying the little society and provoking despair, returns revelation, in the novel's end, to the way of concealment, to the "trash level," where it may be sought, glimpsed, found in ambiguity, and so, even when found, still awaited .

The paradox of *VALIS* is that, in a world of corrupted information, salvation must proceed by means of its opposite, through pathology, doubt, division, unstable theorizing, contradictions, the culturally ephemeral, and the cognitively compromised. Salvation does not come with sublime overpowering, nor may it be seen as a sublime, self-authenticating vision. Only provoking hints allow some notion of a goal to which healing moves, hints coded into phrases such as "wise mind," the "divine humanity," and "King Felix."[92] Any and all imaginations of a blessed futurity must undermine one another and, as a set, be radically incomplete. The drama of Fat's theorizing—of contradicted enlightenment, of disappointment and revival, and the simultaneous questing and waiting with which the novel ends—reveals a *via negativa*. In a cosmos that always drifts toward homogeneity and, therefore, paralysis—psychological, political, social—this *via negativa* generates the instability, the tension of difference in which truth may appear. "Gnosis" is never straightforwardly unveiled and made available but always dialectically received and undermined. Much of the novel's tension and comedy originates in this *via negativa*, which develops the theme, found in *Do Androids Dream* and *Palmer Eldritch*, of a salvation baffling and ambiguous even to its beneficiaries.

As *VALIS* interprets ancient gnosis as information, the former loses its self-authorizing character. All claims to revelation are questionable; disclosures serve the process of salvation, but their relationship to its goal is oblique. This problematizes the ancient theme of the gnostic elect, the subjective pole of self-authenticating revelation. The Lamptons succumb to the lure of election and its attendant elevation to superiority, the exclusive guardianship of a light kept from those groping in shadows. The makers of *Valis* the movie commandeer gnosis to serve the will to power, "the urge to dominion of the higher creature over the lower."[93] Linda Lampton claims Phil with a fervent kiss: "Come back to us," she says. "This is our future; it belongs to a very few, a very, very few." Phil reflects on her territorial grasp and replies, "You couldn't be more wrong, honey; this belongs to everyone."[94] Classical gnosis requires noiseless information, transmitted perfectly by the gnostic savior to those who receive wisdom in its purity. The elect are like ice evaporating into entire transparency as a wind warms the soil.[95] One gains gnosis not by discursive thought but by an awakening. An illumination, immediate and authoritative, creates an elect community as the necessary form of reception. The light needs "beings of light who are waiting for the rising sun," who become "truth . . . [and] lack nothing at all."[96] The Lampton household, however, have fallen victim to the left-handed lure in all this, to their own will to power, with Mini exposing himself to radiation in a lust for the satellite's information. "*We have to get out of here*," Phil concludes. "*These people court death*."[97]

The spiritual progress of Fat, Phil, and the Rhipidon Society requires doubt, dialogue, contradiction, comedy, and self-mockery as the essential media of truth seeking. In an environment where presented truth is not to be trusted and homogeneity threatens discernment, revelation hides with forms of madness or flashes in the corner of the eye at the trash level of culture. Truth must always be discriminated and, when discriminated, sifted again, and again. Danger, as Anne Hawthorne pointed out to Mayerson, lies in epistemological closure, in saying, "is." The internal contradictions of Fat's speculations, the unsystematic "Exegesis," and the theories pressing up like mushrooms trace the elusive paths of the truth that must conceal itself in order to appear. The split between Fat and Phil is a further doubling required to discern information against the continuous ground of seeming truth: it is a "syzygy," a salvific pairing among the doublings of false mirrors. Fat is vulnerable to his own exegesis, to losing his wits in a labyrinth of interpretations and counterinterpretations, to becoming overwhelmed by a sublime excess of information.[98] If Fat is projected into the "Exegesis," Phil persists outside it, not only problematizing particular interpretations, but generating others, and engaging in conversation that puzzles, explores, and mocks. Fat is the "holy fool": absurdly vulnerable, he needs Phil as protector, mirror, and questioner.[99] Sophia momentarily reconciles the psychic split, but she does so from the perspective of the divine Wisdom who comprehends all dualities. Sophia acts as the "healer and the healed" who transcends what Phil contemplates as the creative and destructive poles of divinity.[100] After her death, the split reasserts itself again: Fat goes off to find the fifth savior, while Phil remains at home, fulfilling his commission of resolute expectancy. Under the conditions of Empire, unless one falls into the way of the Lamptons, truth makes its tentative approach for those who both seek and wait, grasp and refuse to grasp.

In *VALIS*, Philip K. Dick deployed gnostic mythology to present an account of both the process of salvation and what opposes that process. He reinterprets gnostic themes, especially that of gnosis itself, in terms of information, a move that bridges ancient cosmogonies and science fiction, and, thus also, the science-fictional sublime. Elsewhere, various narrative elements in *VALIS*—time jumps, coconsciousness, technologies of illusion, divine humanity—become classic occasions for sublimity. Lovecraft, Wells, Stapledon, Fritz Leiber, and James Blish all treat them as such. *VALIS*, however, avoids these opportunities for sublime language and undermines any suggestion of sublimity by irony, satire, and the questioning strategy of the *via negativa*. The accents of the technological sublime in the film *Valis* and in the aspirations of the Lamptons make the telling exception. In their case, the technological sublime again reveals the dynamic of self-preservation, the "blind mechanical, purposeless causal processes" of Fat's cosmogony merging with the will to power exhibited by the Lampton group, whose boasts of creating evoke the self-consuming ignorance of the demiurge Yaldabaoth. Yaldabaoth and the Lamptons know no otherness that is not themselves. Among these gnostics, all mirrors reveal the same face.

Gnostic myth in *VALIS* serves not only as a source of metaphors for oppressive ideological and cultural structures empowered by technology and for the critique of authoritarian soteriologies but also as a discourse within which to give another account of salvation, of that ambiguous salvation that limps into the world and squeezes between suffocating powers of "the Empire." However, in turning gnostic mythology against the Lamptons' gnostic elect and its sublime powers, Dick inscribed into that mythology an essentially alien element, an element that recalls the classical Christian conflict with Gnosticism.[101] According to the main drift of gnostic texts, the creation only appears as real. Since the demiurge makes only what is false, his cosmos has no integrity of being. Only the divine is real, and so the pleroma heals itself in returning to itself. Despite all the dualities within the myth, Gnosticism is monistic: it begins and ends in a self-contained and closed world, a divine world that has to overcome difference. The Rhipidon Society, however (and especially the character-narrator, Philip), insists on a persisting otherness. *VALIS* relativizes and downgrades gnosis along with the gnostic elect, and the narrative, with its enduring doubles, undermines claims for the absorption of humanity into the divine. Implicitly, the story keeps open the possibility of a relationship between God and creation in which their difference never resolves and creation retains its integrity. A tension exists, therefore, even between the Rhipidon Society and their beloved Sophia. The child Sophia tells Fat and company that they must proclaim a saving revelation in the name of the divine humanity. "Man is holy, and the true god, the living god is man himself," she teaches. "You will have no gods but yourselves."[102] This sounds, though, very much like the invitation to another totality, a human sublime. Sophia's "you will have no other gods but yourselves" comes disconcertingly close to Yaldabaoth's narcissistic boast. Certainly, the warning that follows the boast rejects Yaldabaoth's folly and asserts the divine humanity: "An enlightened, immortal human being exists before you."[103] This oracular climax to Sophia's discourse, however, has little effect on the remainder of the novel. In his closing reflections, Phil gives it a tellingly muted, humble reference: "I have a sense of the goodness of men these days."[104] This, together with the continuing *via negativa* and Phil's affirmation of waiting, hardly encourages subliming the human, replacing a divine with a humanistic monism. *VALIS* subverts Gnosticism into another protest against sublimity: the subliming of humanity, of technology, and of the technologies that process consciousness for illusion. In *VALIS*, *Palmer Eldritch*, and *Do Androids Dream*, sublimed technologies function as metaphors for the creation of self-contained, closed ideological worlds, narcissistic worlds that hide the mystery of the human, the mystery revealed in distinction and difference, in otherness within and without. That mystery, when it appears in these texts, appears against the sublime, in a register that is tender, comic, ambiguous, and open ended. The sublime apotheosis of humanity, thus resisted and problematized by Philip Dick, appears frequently in one of the most popular and enduring subgenres of science fiction: the apocalyptic tale. Here, though, the sublime also features strongly in stories that critique such humanism, stories in which sublimity provides a context for the radical, sometimes brutal, diminishment of the human.

# 5

# THE APOCALYPTIC SUBLIME

*Well, I saw mushroom head, / I was born and I was dead.*

—Can, "Mushroom," on *Tago Mago* (Mute, 2007)

*He will wipe away every tear from their eyes, and death shall be no more.*

—Revelation 21:4

## "THERE AIN'T NO SANTA CLAUS ON THE EVENIN' STAGE"

Most commonly, "apocalyptic writing" refers to announcements or descriptions of disaster.[1] When science fiction writers turn to apocalyptic language, narratives, and imagery, they imagine a cornucopia of catastrophe: plague, atmospheric pollution, nuclear war, alien invasion, asteroid impact, zombies, gamma rays, large and very brainy ants, drought, torrential rain, a flawed experiment, climate change, mass sterilization, entropy, even the collision of universes.[2] Initially, what makes these apocalyptic is scale.[3] These varying dooms deliver disasters of massive proportion; if not destroyed altogether, the Earth, or human history, or planetary life, or the cosmos itself, suffers a fundamental dislocation in which, for any who survive, the coordinates of normality, the cultural imaginary itself, are radically displaced and reconstructed, if they are reconstructed.

A coinage of the theologians in the nineteenth century, the adjective "apocalyptic" qualifies a number of Jewish and Christian works written between 200 B.C.E. and 200 C.E., the best known of which are the biblical books of Daniel and Revelation.[4] Visions and dialogues with heavenly beings reveal (*apocalupto*) how God will, in a rapidly approaching future, fulfill his promise to break the powers of empire and oppression, end this present age of evil and pain, and redeem his people once and for all. By extension, "apocalyptic" also names the groups and movements that treasured these visions or that, in the course of Christian history, have focused on interpreting the dense imagery of apocalyptic texts and lived in expectation of the consummation they proclaim.[5] More broadly still, "apocalyptic" refers to a cultural imaginary involving expectation and interest in the end of the world.[6] Unusual for a term of theological scholarship, the "apocalyptic," especially in its import of catastrophe, has achieved a lively familiarity in popular culture. TV news reporters announce "near-apocalyptic prospects" with grim delectation and observe scenes of disaster as "apocalyptic terrain." At least 21 recent movies, currently available for DVD rental, have "apocalypse" in the title, from pornography (*Apocalypse Climax*, of course) through zombie films, thrillers, end-of-the-world epics, and science documentary, while *Apocalypse Miaow* shows the tradition as established enough for self-mockery. Since 1950, some 179 movies have presented apocalyptic scenarios, and the number has grown each decade. Any broad cultural diagnosis of this moves onto empirically thin ice; the popularity of terminal doom probably has as much to do with technological advances in special effects as with social anxieties. Nevertheless, since apocalyptic and the sublime have had a mutual affinity throughout modernity, apocalyptic movies constitute a significant contemporary medium for the sublime.

In 1833 the Northumbrian painter John Martin, whose work has directly influenced science fiction artists as well as the fantasy filmmaker Ray Harryhausen, exhibited the apocalyptic vision of *The Last Man*. A tiny figure looks from the edge of a rocky promontory across an immense ocean toward a blood-red sunset. Corpses lie on the cliff tops; behind and below him, ships, their sails furled, float on the depths beneath. A darkened outline of a presumably empty city is seen on his distant right. The gray-blue, dull brown tones are melancholic. As a contemporary observed, this is "a scene of awful gloom."[7] Mary Shelley's novel *The Last Man* may have influenced Martin, but the direct debt is to Thomas Campbell's poem of the same name.[8] Campbell takes up the standard imagery of death from war, plague, and famine, of the ruin of cities and ships, and pitches present and future into violent contrast via the familiar apocalyptic dualism. The poem, however, recasts apocalyptic expectation into the temporality of transience and decline. Humanity ends in exhaustion after "ten thousand thousand years" of history. Whereas in classical apocalyptic literature, history concludes in the action of God, here history plays out into the kind of barren end that Wells was to conjure in *The Time Machine*. Humanity dies by length of time. Campbell, though, rises to a defiant faith in immortality: "This spirit . . . / think not, Sun, it shall be dim / When thou thyself art dark! / No! it shall live again, and shine / In bliss unknown to beams of thine, / By Him recalled to breath."

This, though, establishes a more severe cosmic dualism than we find in biblical apocalyptic texts. That the world is God's creation seems forgotten and though christological language appears in "who captive led captivity / Who robbed the grave of Victory"; Jesus is not named, and salvation, reduced to the individual's escape from mortality, appears more gnostic than Christian. Campbell undermines the logic of continuity and discontinuity, creation and resurrection, essential to a Christian eschatology. Martin's painting captures the poem's close as the last man raises his hand toward the sun. The scene of sublime despair resolves to a celebration not of God so much as of human defiance and faith: "go, tell the night that hides thy face, / Thou saw'st the last of Adam's race, / On Earth's sepulchral clod, / The darkening universe defy / To quench his Immortality, / Or shake his trust in God!" Both poem and painting are characteristic of theological sublimity in the reduction of biblical narrative, the accentuated dualism, and the emphasis on human power and stature.

Martin's most famous apocalyptic interpretation toured Britain, the United States, and Australia in the 1850s. *The Great Day of His Wrath*, part of the *Last Judgment* triptych, was painted between 1849 and 1853. Millions saw the works themselves, and, by virtue of new technologies for the mass image, millions more enjoyed them through prints and engravings. On the right of the painting, lightening topples a huge mountain that crushes a city as it falls into a central circle of fire, welling up from the opened earth. In the foreground, to right and left, tiny men and women, many clearly of wealth and rank, fall into the abyss. The tops of two other mountains rush toward the fiery center from the left. Martin tries to stick closely to Revelation 6:12-17, but the sublime rendering transforms his attention to biblical detail into something theologically very different. Martin's sublime is spectacular, whereas biblical apocalyptic is not. Despite the visual temptations that its imagery offers to the sublime imagination, Revelation invited from its readers a literary rather than a visual sensibility. The catastrophic events of Revelation 6, specifically those of the sixth seal, are woven from a series of Old Testament texts, and these texts, not the visual details, demand the interpretative attention. They place in the forefront God's judgment on oppressing nations, corrupt and unjust rule. Though these details are in Martin's painting, they are dwarfed by the sublime effects. Whereas biblical apocalyptic is theocentric, the action of God dominating throughout, sublime apocalyptic reorders attention around nature. Despite God's signature lightening, which does appear in Revelation, the crushing and cataclysmic powers of nature hold the center, with falling cities and tumbling humanity as indicators of scale. Natural powers offer themselves as the privileged representatives of what is characteristic of divine power. Contemporaries boasted that the triptych was so rich in detail that, providing the viewer had Martin's descriptive key, it might be "profitably studied for hours." Identifying all the goings-on in the painting, though, is not reading in the sense that apocalyptic literature invites reading. A sublimed apocalypticism becomes one dimensional; thus power as irresistible force predominates and renders invisible the irony of the climatic phrase: "Hide us . . . from the Wrath of the Lamb."[9] The sublime spectacular overwhelms the dense, layered symbolism of the biblical apocalyptic works.[10]

Martin's imagination worked within an already established tradition bound up with the beginnings of the sublime. In 1697 Thomas Burnet published *The Sacred Theory of the Earth*, in which he proposed the geological mechanics of the Noachian flood as accounting for the ruptured and inconvenient surface of the Earth with its mountains, ravines, caves, and rocky protuberances.[11] The original Earth, Burnet argues, was regular, symmetrical, and smooth of surface: "Not a wrinkle, scar or fracture in all its body . . . but even and uniform all over."

Shut up in "the *great Abysse*," however, the planet contained a vast body of waters.[12] Pressure from the waters and resistance from the earth's shell are kept in equilibrium, though with enough potential instability to work God's catastrophic decree through natural causes should human wickedness so merit. When that happens, the shell cracks and falls into the abyss, and the waters rush out to flood the tumbling, broken surface. Then, when the waters retreat, the earth's surface emerges as a ruin with unsightly protuberances and disgusting depths: mountains, caves, canyons, and vast seas where the water pools in the lowest stretches of the shattered surface. Ironically, Burnet's *Sacred History*, which banishes the sublimity of mountains and seas from God's originally perfect creation, stimulated taste for the sublime.[13] Burnet's writing was better than his argument. He describes disaster with a dramatic, visual energy exemplary for a new taste: an excitement in unrestrained power, vast explosion, and such cosmic hurly-burly as strained at the limits of imagination.[14] Burnet imagines catastrophe with a sublime thrill:

> The pressure of a great mass of Earth falling into the Abysse . . . could not but impel the water with so much strength, as would carry it up to a great height in the Air: and to the top of anything that lay in its way, any eminency, high fragment, or new Mountain: And then rowling back again, it would sweep down with it whatsoever it rushed upon Woods, Buildings, living Creatures, and carry them all headlong into the great gulph. Sometimes a mass of water would be quite struck off and separate from the rest, and tossed through the Air like a flying River.[15]

Burnet's drama and visual vocabulary stoked the cultural imaginary from which, in time, would flare the science-fictional apocalypse, his prose echoing in its descriptions of total calamity. Thus, Greg Bear's imagination of the world's end begins:

> Half Dome nodded a few degrees and tilted into a chasm opened in the floor of the valley. In arc-shaped wedges it began to come apart. Liberty Cap and Mount Broderick . . . stayed whole, rolling and sliding like giant pebbles into the mass of Half Dome's settling fragments, diverting, and then finally shattering and

> sending fragments through miles of the valley. . . . The silt of the valley floor liquefied under the vibration, swallowing meadows and roads.[16]

Contrary to the drift of his physico-theology, then, Burnet's exuberant descriptions stimulated a tradition of sublime apocalyptic exhilaration, one maintained largely in religious works before its eventual appropriation in science fiction.

Only a step separates deluge from apocalypse, and so sublime enthusiasm jumped swiftly from one divine judgment to another: "Deluge and Conflagration, dreadful powers!" and both occasions for sublimity.[17] Samuel Catherall's poem "Essay on the Conflagration" noted the connection with an engraving of Burnet on the frontispiece.[18] Also in 1720, Aaron Hill attempted sublime apocalyptic with "The Judgment Day: A Poem." The eschatological trumpet sets off cosmic destruction: "th' unbounded notes whirl higher and higher and rend my shiv'ring soul! / Echoing from world to world, they burst oe'r all: / And gathering horrors, cold as death, in show'ry shadows fall."[19] Descriptions of the world's end attracted poets and readers throughout the eighteenth and nineteenth centuries, and stock sublimity resounded from cliché to cliché much like the notes from Hill's last trump. Though the poetry may be execrable, the sublime excitement was hugely popular. Young's sublime effusions on these "most Surprizing Scenes of Awe, and Astonishment" were enjoyed well into the 1850s, when a hatchet job from George Eliot dismissed his "radical insincerity" and hastened the poet's literary doom.[20] Edward Henry Bickersteth's Victorian extravaganza, *Yesterday, To-day, and For Ever*, went on for twelve books and enjoyed some twenty-three printings between 1866 and 1893, just two years before Wells' *The Time Machine*.[21] On Bickersteth's judgment day, as on Martin's, "one vast sea of fire . . . baptized the unregenerate earth in flame."[22]

Before and after John Martin's work, falls of roiling, liquefied fire, along with all the other sublimities, displaced God for the forces of nature while also making God in the image of those sublimed powers. Science fiction has completed that displacement by imagining apocalypses entirely absent of God. Both Christian and science-fictional apocalyptic texts reveal human life in its precarious contingency—though while the former explores that contingency as a contingency before God, who gives existence ex nihilo, science fiction finds the contingency of human life before immanent powers. That said, apocalyptic catastrophe absent the divine horizon need not be without hope. Some postapocalyptic scenarios intimate conditions for a posthuman, or even a recognizably human, transcendence. The cultural authority of science and technology has driven this subgenre in two directions to give a new take on an ancient contrast. Thus, science fiction may represent humanity, within the seamless web of cause and effect, as a creature still wet from the swamp and bloodied by struggle, with its instincts a storm of betrayals that make virtue implausible and ruin by its own technology highly likely. In contrast, the expansion of scientific knowledge and technological control may inspire imagined victories over the most cosmic threats, even ushering humanity toward some form of blissful godhood.

A more tentative, ambiguous science-fictional apocalypticism, though, transacts hope around both directions, in a negotiation struck between the angel and the beast. William Miller's *A Canticle for Leibowitz* sets human hope within an apocalyptic cycle generated by the human propensity for mass destruction as soon as the technology is ripe for it. More than twelve centuries pass in the course of the novel, which tells the saga of a Catholic monastery that preserves documents concerning technology lost during the catastrophe of a nuclear war and its culturally iconoclastic aftermath. The monks treasure and interpret the texts but with no understanding of their purpose. Six hundred years later, an interpreter arrives, capable of beginning the process of scientific recovery. After another six centuries of research, humanity once again initiates nuclear suicide.[23] This denouement, though, is crossed by the hint of a mysterious hope, tangential to the circle of ruin. When a bomb lands nearby, Dom Zerchi, the abbot, is hearing the confession of Mrs. Grales, a bicephalous victim of mutations still occurring from the first nuclear war. Buried to the chest in rubble, Zerchi is given communion by "Rachel," Mrs. Grales' dormant head, who becomes conscious as her other, older head dies. When Zerchi himself dies, he recognizes in Rachel's eyes "a primal innocence . . . and a promise of resurrection. . . . One glimpse had been a bounty, and he wept in gratitude."[24] Any Christian theologizing here, though, would restore, beyond the textual evidence, a transcendent horizon to Miller's novel and confuse the Catholic material Miller uses with the secular imaginary that shapes and renders its meaning. Zerchi catches only a glimpse, a wonder in the human itself that suggests a new beginning, an alternative track for humanity. Perhaps this is a possibility to be realized on Alpha Centauri, to which the rest of the monks have gone, but, then again, perhaps not.

That apocalyptic science fiction frequently coordinates catastrophe with hope and imagines the apocalypse as a passage to the new shows how this subgenre still moves within the orbit of classic Jewish and Christian apocalyptic. Other elements of those theological narratives also crop up. An agent of universal destiny acts either to trigger catastrophe or to lead to the new. Events occur within the universal context of the end as a decisive struggle between good and evil. The catastrophe purifies those who pass through it, and they emerge as an elect transformed into a new humanity or a posthumanity, or else simply escape as colonists upon star ships. Classical apocalypses reveal how God will fulfill his work of creation and redemption. The end revealed, though, is itself revealing. God's action in calling empire to account by gathering his oppressed people and judging the wicked manifests his righteousness so that righteousness is done and seen to be done by the martyrs who call "how long?" from under the altar (Rev 6:10) or by the seer who complains on behalf of Israel (2 Esdras 3). The end reveals God "in his divinity . . . as the one who works all things, who has power over everything."[25] The apocalyptic end manifests humanity as well, showing how men and women appear before God in their frailty and with God in glory. All the formal differences between science fiction and biblical apocalyptic notwithstanding, the various ends imagined within science fiction also have a revelatory function. The apocalypse and, when the fallout clears, the postapocalyptic conditions reveal humanity in relationship with its environments, both planetary and cosmic. They disclose the appalling precariousness of human existence or uncover, in that doom that concentrates the mind so wonderfully, the true lineaments of human dignity.

In appropriating the materials of Christian apocalypticism, visions of the end already imaginatively reconfigured through the sublime, science fiction also critiques and contests biblical apocalyptic and, with it, Christian eschatology more generally. The apocalyptic sublime in science fiction has imagined human and cosmic futures both radically different and polemically ordered toward Christian hope. The agents of catastrophe in Greg Bear's *Blood Music*, for instance, result from marrying DNA with computer technology to form intelligent cells that precipitate the final stage in universal evolution. Multiplying by the trillion, these "noocytes" form cellular societies that first transform their human hosts and then the material world itself, dismantling reality and reencoding it as information. They distill material reality into a "noosphere" that retains everything that has been or possibly could be, making it available as information, combinable in inexhaustibly varied forms. The noosphere reproduces particular human lives in endlessly different versions and generates pockets of consciousness to experience them. No past is fixed, and no opportunities lost, since every possible history may be configured, dismantled, and further reconfigured in an infinite number of variants. The novel ends with the refrain: "Nothing is lost. Nothing is forgotten. / It was in the blood, the flesh, / And now it is forever."[26] One character, dissolving into the informational world, writes, "[The noocytes] know me thru and thru [*sic*]. I am a theme in their art, their wonderful living 'fictions.' They have duplicated me a million times over. Which of me writes this? I do not know. There is no longer an original."[27] Ironically, Bear's apocalypse creates a world in which apocalypticism is ontologically meaningless. Apocalyptic expectation implies both irreversible temporality and the integrity of individual being: the former brought to an eternal fulfillment, the latter judged and redeemed, both enduring within the glory of God. The noocytes' protean informational world has no fixed temporal relations, no persisting unities or relationships, no there or then, this or that. All is a Heraclitean flux, without even the arrow of time. Bear issues a particularly imaginative and thoroughgoing challenge to Christian eschatology. In the noosphere, nothing is lost, except loss itself. For the Christian, however, this forgoes precisely the glory and tragedy of creation. In creating, God commits himself to the irrevocable, to particular being, to the creative decision for this and not that, to a history that may be redeemed but not unmade. God's faithfulness embraces a creation that cannot be recalled, in which losses are real, the stakes are high, and the resurrected Christ bears forever the marks of crucifixion.

## SHRINKING HUMANITY

Thomas Disch's 1965 novel, *The Genocides*, recounts the extinction of human beings through the breakup and starvation of one of its last communities. An alien race uses the earth to grow huge plants so voracious of nutrient as to drain lakes and rivers and destroy the ecology of all other life, including humanity. The aliens protect their agriculture with a program of systematic burning designed to exterminate all indigenous life on the planet. Neither the characters nor the reader learns anything more about these killers. Disch achieves a sublime horror much more bitter than Lovecraft's because of the matter-of-fact narrative tone and the absence of emotionally heightened or gothic vocabulary. The plants are "six hundred feet tall and their leaves . . . the size of billboards"; an "unwholesome" solitude is felt in their forests, "more unremitting than a prison."[28] They are not, however, "eldritch." The obscurity of their murderous farmers heightens the horror. Nothing is learned about origins, character, motives, or goals. The aliens communicate only once, through a brief report on the progress of extirpation that simply begs more questions. It does, though, confirm that the aliens are businesslike, efficient, and confident, and recognize no distinction between human and other life.

Human beings reduce to material for incineration.[29] Disch depicts human vulnerability, folly, and violence without remorse, at one or two points verging on self-caricature.[30] In this apocalypse, human beings lack even the perverse dignity of being responsible for disaster; nor do they have, like Stapledon's Last Men, the thin comfort of knowing its cause. The entire novel is framed between two biblical quotations. The first, from Jeremiah 8:20, is, "The harvest is ended, the summer is past, and we are not saved." Then, after the epilogue, from Job 25:5-6, the second is, "Behold even to the moon, and it shineth not; yea, the stars are not pure in his sight. How much less man, that is a worm? And the son of man, which is a worm?" The verses take on a heavy irony for a world bereft of divine aid or hope. They refer to the two principal targets of the science-fictional dispute with Christian hope: salvation and the significance of humanity in the cosmos. Within the novel, characters frequently quote Scripture but always in ways poignantly or absurdly at odds with reality.

As aliens make the world inimical to human habitation, Blossom fantasizes that she and Orville are like a new Adam and Eve "and think of new names for all the animals."[31] According to this contrasting internal and external usage, the Bible only speaks truly when it is quoted ironically, against itself.

The plot develops in three phases, in each of which a precarious stability, invested with a desperate hope, founders and leaves fewer and, finally, no survivors. At the beginning, the remaining citizens of Tassel, a small Minnesota town, are just managing to stay alive. Andersen—the stern, Calvinist ex-mayor—runs a brutal and religiously oppressive regime but is sharp witted enough to have found a way to preserve some cattle and a few fields of corn from the plants. Any marauders from the abandoned cities are killed and ground up for sausage meat. Jeremiah Orville, however, saved from this fate for his experience as a mining engineer, determines on revenge for his girlfriend's execution. He slowly ingratiates himself with the suspicious patriarch, befriends Buddy (Andersen's intelligent son), and excites the infatuation of Andersen's thirteen-year-old daughter, Blossom. Disaster hits the group when incinerating machines destroy their refuge. Led more by Orville than Andersen, the now handful of survivors reach a cave where Orville discovers that the plant roots are hollow and penetrate deep into the earth. The little group makes its way down into the root system, where they establish themselves and feed off the plant's underground fruit, like worms in an apple.[32]

As the elderly Andersen weakens, the community's cohesion fractures and the ex-mayor decides to appoint Orville as his successor. On his deathbed, he tells this to Neil, the older son. All along, Neil has shown himself venal, stupid, and vicious. Now, he murders his father as well as the only witness, Andersen's nurse, Alice. A violent chase begins, as Neil attempts to kill Orville, who has now fallen in love with the delighted Blossom. Eventually, Buddy, Orville, and Blossom escape, leaving an insane Neil, who violates Alice's decaying body in the belief it is his little sister. Climbing around the root system, though, suddenly becomes much harder. Spring has arrived, the plants are taking in nutrients, and the aliens prepare for their harvest. In the novel's brief third phase, Buddy, his wife and baby, Orville and Blossom, and one other survivor return to the surface where the aliens finish harvesting and scorch the earth. Hoping they have gone for good, the little group survives the summer. The sowing machines return, however, and the last of humanity dies.

Like two descending spirals, one nested inside the other, *The Genocides* describes both an external and an internal decline. Much of the novel's poignancy, irony, and black humor derive from the relationship of these two narrative spirals. Humanity is briskly destroyed by the collapse of its external environment, through burning, disease, starvation of the soil, draining of lakes and rivers, and the mass extinction of animal species. Even the plants themselves become uninhabitable as spring arrives. At the same time, the characters also pursue their own destruction, through rivalry, misplaced passions, lust for revenge, religious illusions, denial, bigotry, betrayal, and violence. Out of pride, Andersen delays announcing his successor and, when he does, precipitates his own murder and that of Alice, a notably rational character with skill to relieve the torments of the external spiral. Disch sets both faces of destruction within the register of the sublime. Extinction comes from an obscure and overwhelming power that works a terrifying destruction and always ambushes the characters. Shocks punctuate the narrative. The narrator has barely introduced the enigmatic and grotesquely vast plants—in this context, a word much more disturbing than "trees"—when Andersen's cows are instantly and, without explanation, reduced to ash. Vastness accompanies the diminishing humans throughout—the spread of sowing, the total desolation, the plants' labyrinthine root system. Events accentuate human vulnerability, as moral, religious, and rational coordinates break down. Incineration is a sublime spectacle:

> Her dark eyes danced in the light of the pyre. The Alworth building was the tallest in Duluth. It burned magnificently. The whole downtown area was in flames now. To the left of the Alworth Building, the First American National Bank, after a late start, flared up even more splendidly due to its greater bulk.[33]

At the novel's end, against the backdrop of another extraterrestrial planting, the universe looms up in an extreme of sublime disproportion: "Nature is prodigal. Of a hundred seedlings only one or two would survive; of a hundred species, only one or two. Not, however, man."[34]

Just before that triumphant gesture of science-fictional sublimity, the last survivors appear in an apocalyptic landscape, arranged in a distinctly painterly way. This iconography makes a tableau of burned-out religion, demystified and unmasked:

> The survivors spread out over the flat green uniformity of the plain. . . . The nearest three figures, in the middle distance, comprised a sort of Holy Family, though moving closer, one could not help but note that their features were touched by some other emotion than quiet happiness. The woman sitting on the ground was, in fact, weeping bitterly, and the man . . . was barely able to restrain his own tears. Their attention was fixed upon the thin child in her arms, who was futilely pulling at her dry breast. A little farther on was another figure—or should we say two?—without any iconographic parallel, unless we all own this to be a Niobe sorrowing for her children. . . . This woman was holding the skeleton of a single child in her arms. . . . Almost at the horizon one could make out the figures of a man and a woman, hand in hand, smiling. Certainly, these were Adam and Eve before the Fall, though they appeared rather more thin than they are usually represented. Also, they were rather ill-matched with respect to age: he was forty if he was a day; she was barely into her teens.[35]

This scene brings the novel's representation of religion to a climactic focus. The characters' resort to religious language always signals their naïveté, or illusions and distance from reality. Religion funds a poignant, if transiently protective, denial, or provides a rationale for horror. Andersen's brand of Calvinism is the basis of his authority and so gives some cohesion to the community; it also squares his conscience with murder and cannibalism.[36] His wife, Lady, sees their actions more crisply: "If one had to behave like an infidel, Lady believed, it was sheer hypocrisy to pass oneself off as a Christian. Indeed, she very much doubted whether the god to whom her husband prayed existed."[37] One peculiar feature of the closing tableau, though, obscures at the same time as it unmasks religious faith. The narrator comments that unless one stretches a point to claim the Niobe of Greek myth, the woman weeping over the body of her dead son is "without any iconographic parallel." This eclipses that most obvious iconographic parallel: the Pieta, Mary weeping over her dead son, clutching him in her arms. The Pieta, however, would introduce an awkward tension into this apocalyptic picture. On either side of the weeping woman, we have icons that intimate the complete absence of God, an absence proved upon utter disaster. The mourning mother in the center, though, symbolizes more ambiguously. Reference to the Pieta is repressed here because it is an image of the presence—indeed, the complete presence—of God in abject ruin. If we recognize this, Disch's "Renaissance print" reverts to a medieval triptych, in which interpretation resonates from the central panel, incorporating the others.[38]

*The Genocides* presents humanity stripped down, reduced by apocalypse, and so judged according to its significance and place in the cosmos, which turns out to be nothing and nowhere. No certainty exists for a human future, no security from a violent end, no divine aid to prevent a complete extirpation when "the wind passes over it, and it is gone, and its place knows it no more."[39] Humanity is just one of billions of vulnerabilities in the cosmos, thrown up by prodigal nature. *The Genocides* is not a misanthropic novel, though. Despite the sometimes chilling, even brutal, narrative tone, the novel is not contemptuous. Buddy, Orville, Blossom, and even the dying Andersen evoke sympathy; as a novel of disillusion, it is all the more painful, and more admirable, for eschewing any self-protective disdain for human beings. The relationship, though, between the tale's two descending spirals is too ironic, too blackly comic, too lacking in moral connection, for tragedy. *The Genocides* offers secular apocalypticism, humanity revealed through its end: a showing of what is and may come. This revelation of humanity also ends religion. It dispels the illusions of ontological privilege, providential care, or salvation, and exposes the fantasies about human dignity that depend upon these illusions.

John Christopher's 1956 novel, *The Death of Grass*, also probes beliefs about divine providence but grapples more insistently than *The Genocides* with the theme of human society and morality, again running up against theological accounts of human dignity. The apocalyptic agent in *The Death of Grass* is the Chung-Li virus, a lively little organism that feeds on members of the Gramineae family, better known as grasses. Having gobbled up the Asian rice fields, the Chung-Li virus moves on to wheat, barley, corn, and oats, wiping out not only human food staples but also the basis of animal husbandry.[40] Political and technological complacency—along with a robust, if entirely misplaced, confidence that only foreigners go in for mass disaster and anarchy—ensure that the English remain misinformed until food and scientific resources have run out. In an effort to reduce the population to feedable levels, the government decides to drop atom bombs on it. John Custance, however, has a friend in government who tells him all this just before the news leaks across a panicking populous. He and Roger Buckley, together with their families, escape from London and head for a secluded, defendable, and idyllic valley in Yorkshire where John's brother is sensibly farming potatoes.[41] The families' journey to David Custance's valley allows Christopher to describe the rapid collapse of social and moral order across England. Even though a gang kidnaps and rapes Custance's wife and daughter, the predatory behavior of individuals constitutes only a small element of this. Much more important to the novel is the formation of groups based on survival needs. What characterizes these groups, at least at first, are alliances based on usefulness and the violent exclusion of outsiders. Custance's exodus slows to a walk after a group of Yorkshire farmers robs them of cars, firearms, and food. By this point, robbery is no longer a morally relevant or sustainable concept with reference to the property of outsiders.

By the time they reach the valley, Custance has become the acknowledged chieftain of some thirty-four souls, including his own family, Roger Buckley's, and Pirrie, a former gun salesman with lethal shooting skills. Others, though, have already made David's valley their refuge, and though, for his brother's sake, they agree to admit John, his wife, and his children, they turn away all the others. Custance's decision to refuse this private offer and fight to take his entire following into Blind Gill becomes the moral, and not simply strategic, hinge upon which depends their postapocalyptic future. During the brief and successful invasion, two characters are killed, both of whom represent unsustainable paths to survival: John's brother, David, is a single-minded farmer with enough foresight to grasp the ecological disaster long before it went public. He also, though, holds to an ancient pastoral ideal of rural innocence and purity, the hope of a retreat from which the world may be shut out and left to its madness. The other casualty is Pirrie, to whose tactical cunning and skill with a rifle the group owes its survival. Pirrie is the novel's most ambiguous character. He takes up the violence the situation demands without a second thought; he is invariably effective, correct in his assessment of advantage, cynical, and, to the end, strategic in his loyalties. "A long time ago," he says, "I came to the understanding that all men are friends by convenience and enemies by choice."[42] Well before Custance himself, however, Pirrie recognizes and exploits the changing moral structure of the group, its advance beyond the logic of advantage in the consolidation of new patterns of loyalty focused on the leader. Pirrie himself, though, never gains wholehearted trust: he understands, but he does not believe; he performs, but he does not identify. Pirrie instances the modern buffered self, the individual who stands apart, possesses an inner privacy, distinct from social roles.[43] Custance's postapocalyptic community, which comes into partial view in the final chapters of the novel, has not the space and security for the freedom of such buffered selves.

Initially, *The Death of Grass* dramatizes physical contingency, the degree of human dependence upon the taken-for-granted Gramineae. This contingency is realized through a narrative perspective clearly Western and urban. The shock concentrates in the constant description of the virus' target as "grass," which is more than just botanically correct. It conveys a sense of an almost metaphysical betrayal, the unthinkable absence of a ubiquitous, entirely familiar thus no longer noticed, unobtrusive but essential, foundation. Sublimity, here, operates upon both the natural and the cultural, external and internal, planes. On the side of nature, therefore, we have the protean vigor of the Chung-Li virus: the speed with which it mutates, managing to exploit attempts to kill it; the vastness of its range and totality of its deadly consequences. Terse, unadorned statements effect this sublimity, as the radio announcer's "all the evidence indicates that Western Europe has ceased to exist as part of the civilized world."[44] Corresponding to humanity's agricultural impoverishment is the moral breakdown of civilization that occurs with a ghastly speed and scale, both in the politician's plans to nuke British cities, and in the ease with which middle-class English professionals kill to survive. Again, sublimity is achieved by understatement and through actions that subvert moral expectations raised by the narrative situation.

At the start of their journey, Custance and Pirrie kill three young soldiers in order to get through a roadblock, and, later, a man and his wife defending their house from marauders. In both cases, the narrative voice is crisp and unemotional and makes no attempt to reassure the reader that the killings were really necessary. The more savage possibility continues to darken the story, since other possibilities are unaddressed and the moral questions left open. Did they have to kill, rather than immobilize, the young soldiers? Why was there no serious attempt at persuasion of a man understandably wary of strangers? With great skill, Christopher raises moral shock to the sublime degree.

Apocalyptic novels exploit the pleasures of disaster, so the imagination lingers upon collapse and breakdown. *The Death of Grass*, though, does not provide its pleasures quite so cheaply. Despite the suspenseful and violent turns in the plot, the narrative arc describes an organic process of social dissolution and reformation. That process is also one of moral reorientation as Christopher opens a horizon that Disch kept firmly closed. By the end, Custance's group have transcended the strategic ethics of survival for which immediate advantage is the sole measure of loyalty. The change occurs not as a consequence of deliberation, although Pirrie wrings tactical value from what he sees happening, but, immanently, through the evolving dynamics of the group. When Custance decides to invite other refugees to join his trek to the valley, his motive is pragmatic; the group needs guns and muscle. Soon, he secures the agreement of a party of heavily armed men. To ensure Custance's continuing authority, however, Pirrie deliberately antagonizes and kills the leader of the new recruits. Pirrie acts with calculation, but a more than calculative element appears in the men's response. As they line up to shake hands with Custance, the narrator observes, "Here, more than ever, ritual was being laid down." Ritual envelops and reconfigures alliances based on force and fear, raising them into an emergent moral order within which words like "honor," "dignity," "fidelity" gain their force along with phrases such as "pledging one's word," "bowing to authority." This change is no mere externality; subjectivities are forming and being formed. It does not happen in the glare of full consciousness or deliberate plotting and takes Custance himself by surprise. He notices that the title "Mr." has become an honorific due to him alone; experiences his own pleasure in loyal hearts; and catches himself "being too hearty, with the bluffness of a man putting inferiors at their ease."[45] Significantly, in addition to Pirrie, the knowing observer, Custance's wife and children recognize early what is coming into being as the new order subjugates them as dependents. Apocalypse distills and reveals humanity, and *The Death of Grass* discloses its vulnerability and, particularly, the contingency of civilization, the fragility of moral and political ideals identified with achieved and well-secured progress. However, Christopher's catastrophe admits of a survival that Disch's disaster prevents, and so allows a different disclosure of the human. *The Death of Grass* reveals humanity as essentially social, the period of dissolution and strategic alliance yielding, via the rituals and signs of social bonding, before a new social imaginary. What survives the winnowing of catastrophe depends, not on this or that individual—despite the convention of a narrative oriented around a hero—but on the production of the social: originating and formative, a fecundity that orders across, behind, and through the wills and actions of individuals.

*The Death of Grass* reflects the time and place of England in the 1950s. The possibility, for instance, that social collapse might yield conflict or negotiation as to gender roles never appears. The continuity of male authority is one constant in Custance's dissolving world. English Christianity, therefore, which was enjoying something of a revival in the fifties, is conspicuous by its total absence from the story.[46] The silence sounds a loud dismissal; the Christian churches have neither relevance, nor place, nor guiding word in the apocalypse. Talk of providence in this calamity would only be ironic, as it is in *The Genocides*. Nevertheless, the novel refers to religious belief at two important moments. Robbed of their vehicles, the party prepare for a long moorland walk at the mercy of the elements, as well as of the armed and desperate. Custance muses on the need for different gods, more local deities of weather and countryside: "How easy it would be to pray," he wonders, "to sacrifice even—to the moorland gods, in the hope of turning away their wrath. He glanced at where the three boys lay curled up between Roger and Olivia. They would come to it perhaps, or their children."[47] He makes a wistful farewell to a religious culture "whose lineage could be traced back four thousand years," but which, "in a day, had been swept from under them."[48]

Perhaps, some would die, "still speaking the grammar of love while Babel rose all around them," but that faith attracts him only for a moment. In the day of violence, the way of Christ evaporates when protecting one's family. Conviction that some will remain faithful and die for the old faith comforts Custance, but this, too, is passing and nostalgic. He is like a passenger who, as the ship sinks, listens from the lifeboats to the string quartet still playing.

The novel ends with a return to religious, specifically biblical, imagery, but now fully humanized and without transcendent reference. In possession of the valley but with brother David killed in the fight, Custance compares himself to Cain, a likeness his wife disputes. In response, he looks not to Cain's past, the murder of Abel, but to his future, the birth of Enoch and the building of a city for his son, a vocation that Custance takes up: "'There's a lot to do,' he said, 'A city to be built.'"[49] The hope is for a human peace, so Pirrie's rifle must be kept, as Enoch "kept his father's dagger." This biblically accented close completes the transformation of the valley as an ideal and goal in the novel. From the beginning, it has promised safety and protection. In the valley of Blind Gill, a new life may begin, a life free of the dangers, dependencies, and corruption of the urban world. Blind Gill, therefore, resonates with the traditional pastoral ideal. In the valley, apocalyptic trouble may be forgotten, and happiness restored.[50] In particular, the figure of the valley, even its physical description, recalls the "happy valley" of Johnson's *Rasselas*. In Johnson's oriental tale, the prince and his companions leave their happy valley in search of experience, a richer happiness, and the best choice of life. What they find, however, convinces them that such investments in earthly ambitions are foolish and bound to disappoint. The princess concludes, "The choice of life is become less important. I hope hereafter to think only on the choice of eternity." This learned, the party return to their happy valley.[51] *The Death of Grass* dismantles the happy valley itself as a place of earthly refuge, reaching a similar conclusion as to the stability of human achievements but without "the choice of eternity." Custance attains Blind Gill only after a bloody fight and, once there, intends to turn valley into city, not a heavenly one, but a very earthly city that will always buy its peace with violence. There is no rest for humanity, no end to ambiguity, no holy refuge, "no Santa Claus on the evenin' stage."

## RAISING HUMANITY

Sublimation—the elevating in which uncertainty, pain, horror, or fear transforms into pleasure—occurs differently depending on the character of catastrophe. Sublime pleasure may be either participatory or reflective—that is, the reader may participate imaginatively in the elevation of a character or characters within the story, or else the story and its outcome may primarily evoke the reader's own position at a safe distance from the narrative events. *The Genocides*, therefore, similar in this regard to a Lovecraft tale, occasions the sublime pleasure of mastering in imagination the contingency and vulnerability of human life as the novel represents it. Somewhat more complex, *The Death of Grass* invites an element of the participatory as well, encouraging the reader to an identification with the renewal of human social and historical life in Custance-Cain's pledge to build his descendants' city. More humanly ambitious visions of apocalypse, however, evoke much less ambiguous participations. Science-fictional apocalypses issuing in a human or posthuman renewal that realizes humanity's potential for a godlike transcendence reconfigure and appropriate the substance of Christian apocalypticism as hope, offering secular imaginations of resurrection and new creation, and of symbols such as the age to come, the heavenly Jerusalem, or the triumph of the Lamb.

In terms of the overarching story, *The Triumph of Time* (1957) is the final installment of Blish's four "Okie" novels, published between 1955 and 1962.[52] The series tracks interstellar traders and service providers, who, other than having a reputation for sharp dealing and a stubbornly independent culture, often work at odds with Earth's attempts to police the "spaceways." The Okies travel in cities, originally from Earth, literally cut out of their geographical locations and powered for spaceflight by antigravity devices called "spindizzies." To his credit, Blish manages to pull off this audaciously implausible premise with barely an imaginative strain. He realizes the sublimity of the idea, and keeps potential silliness at bay, by presenting the flying cities against a cosmic space, the crushing immensity of which is intimated with an incisive economy: "Above there was nothing; a nothing as final as the slamming of a door. It was the empty ocean of space that washes between galaxies."[53] *The Triumph of Time* takes up another imaginatively risky idea, the end of the universe itself, which Blish holds back from inflated melodrama by sustained technical references to cosmology and quantum physics. The scientific detail anchors the sublimity of the event that generates the plot.

The "Okie" novels concentrate on the city of New York and its aggressive, charismatic mayor, John Amalfi, who, at the beginning of *The Triumph of Time*, is already a thousand years old thanks to the Okies' "anti-agathic" drugs. This final episode of Okie history is initially set on New Earth, upon which New York has landed as Okies settle down to a planet-based life. Although still mayor by title, Amalfi suffers a frustrated retirement and longs for the lost challenges and risks of Okie trading. He has, he feels, swapped the exhilarations of the unknown for a predictable domesticity. Amalfi revives, however, when "He," a small planet driven by spindizzies, arrives near New Earth. The Hevians hope for scientific collaboration to explore deep-space anomalies that suggest an abrupt end to the universe. They have discovered that the cosmos is mirrored by an antimatter universe that corresponds to it "point for point."[54] The two universes, however, are on course for a collision that will destroy both and recreate the "monobloc" out of which they originally expanded. The "universe" is thus a cyclic process of creation and re-creation. Finding no hope of evading the "Ginnangu-Gap," the Hevian and New Earth scientists pin their hopes on the chance of influencing the future universe that will emerge on the other side of the cosmic catastrophe. Though not a physicist, Amalfi administers the conditions of the project and, at one point, protects it from an apocalyptic sect led by "Jorn the Apostle." Negotiating the collision of universes turns out to demand action taken microseconds after apocalypse. When this and the antimatter universe hit, time is abolished for a paradoxical "moment." During that instant, which cannot actually be an instant, a small group of Earthmen and Hevians, including Amalfi, will pass across the "gap," protected by spindizzy fields. Each person will then occupy "an independent set of four dimensions" and exist as "the only body of organized energy and matter" in a particular universe. Their energy will "surge outwards," destroying them but imprinting upon a new universe the information that constitutes body and mind. Contrary to the end, Amalfi discards the careful protocol laid down for this moment of creation and just blows himself, suit, and equipment into the beginning of his creation: "What would happen if . . . he simply touched the detonator button on his chest . . . ? That was unknowable. But the unknowable was what he wanted."[55] Another sublime man goes to eternity in his own image.

*The Triumph of Time* is a sublime apocalyptic-cosmological thriller in which beginnings and endings coincide. The novel explores three contrasting accounts of the human vocation but finds the distinctively human in only one of them. The final apocalyptic transit depends on this essentially human vocation. Scientists and engineers open up the field in which human calling finds its unique fulfillment. Nevertheless, though not a scientist himself, Amalfi serves as the icon of what makes us human. Through his discontentment with settling down on New Earth, his irrepressible desire for another frontier, and the scientists' obsessive grappling with the unprecedented problem of universal collision, humanity reveals itself again as that indefatigable sublime explorer. The unknown lures human beings and calls them to their self-transcendence by eliciting their essential dissatisfaction with the known. For Blish, this frustration with limits defines us, as it did for Edward Young; without it, we should be less than human and innocent of sublimity. Alluding to Voltaire's counsel for contentment, Amalfi despairs of the New Earthmen because they have drifted into "cultivating their gardens, which they somehow had mistaken for frontiers."[56] The Hevians, however, search out New Earth because humans "have always had that boundless ambition,"[57] of which scientific exploration is the purest form. Not only does science pass beyond the body into the mathematical, but it even reaches beyond matter itself by constructing an antimatter probe, fired into that wholly other universe. Humanity's final word is the Cartesian lever for the ascent to knowledge: "'I think' . . . Gilbert Bonner said. And with those words, it ended."[58]

Blish places religion, represented by Jorn the Apostle and his apocalyptic faith, in opposition to this path of restless seeking. Jorn, who is busy leading an interstellar jihad, condemns Amalfi and company for "meddling with the pre-ordained Armageddon," and so imperiling the salvation of the faithful.[59] Religion deals in constraints and certainties and therefore suppresses investigation, shields believers from challenge, values the kindness of ignorance, and accepts a preordained destiny. The constraints protect the certainties, which sharply divide the revealed and known from the unrevealed and unknown. Reprising the familiar modern opposition between religion as the guardian of certainty, and science as risking the unexplored and dissolving knowledge into questions, the novel banishes religion from the sublime. Arousing Jorn the Apostle's fear of heresy, the wily Amalfi pits religion's sureness against itself and ensures the quick exit of the "Warriors of God."

The nurturing activity of the New Earth settlers, those whose contented cultivating Amalfi finds so frustrating, Blish presents as a more profound alternative to questing humanity. Though frontier lust for the unknown has the last word in the novel, the capacity of human beings for nurture takes on dignity, even the suggestion of a greater sanity. Cultivation of home and society gives the blessings of stability, perdurance, an uncomplicated happiness. Blish figures the cost of restlessness in the barren love between Dee and Amalfi, and in the sad ethereality of Estelle, who is at home "in the time of the end of the world."[60] Insofar as human beings preserve life from danger and measure risk in the interests of quotidian satisfactions, they make peace with mortality and the terms on which life is given. They accept the constraints security requires. That, though, is the rub, since those same constraints invite dismissal of the sublime way to transcendence. The Hevian scientist who concludes that time finally "triumphs" pronounces "the epitaph for Man" as "we did not have the time to learn everything that we wanted to know."[61] That the "triumph of time" is not complete, however, is due to humanity's unremitting assault on the unknown. It is not the dogmatic fixity of religion, nor the tender stabilities of nurture, that cheat time a little. Only the audacity of mind carries across the instant of no-time, to imprint itself on new universes.

"'Gods of all stars,' Hazelton said. 'Helleshin! Gods of all stars is what we're racing . . . to become, isn't it?'"[62] A secular theosis ends the novel. In dying, the characters become creators. Though Blish dispatches religion in the person of Jorn, the deep structure of the story appropriates biblical narrative. Throughout, cosmic beginnings are represented as "creation," even as Genesis, "Let there be light."[63] The apocalypse issues in self-sacrifice, a dying, and, at least, a quasi-resurrection. Human transcendence ends in godlikeness. The manner of it, though, provokes an important question owing to the character of the postapocalyptic survival. The movement of transcendence becomes a transformation from person to object: personalities become information in the monobloc of a new universe. No personal continuance can survive the passage through apocalypse. Stapledon anticipated a similar end. If, he suggested, there is a measure of transcendence, of enduring meaning for the human or, more generally, for "spirit," in the universe, then it is one beyond personality, either in the "music" of humanity, that the cosmic mind may hear, or in self-abnegation before the cold gaze of the Star Maker. Notions of personal life beyond death are denounced as simply wishful thinking and, in truth, slightly pathetic. Rejection of divine personality itself—explicitly by Stapledon, implicitly in *The Triumph of Time*—corresponds to this anthropology at the theological level. Personality is irretrievably finite, and so, as with Stapledon, divine personality is driven from the place of the sublime.

Blish allows his characters a measure of godlikeness in their apocalyptic end. They shall provide the informing data of new universes, the promise being "every man his own monobloc."[64] Echoing classical apocalyptic hope, there is new creation after the calamity. Again, a motif of fulfillment appears in continuity with Christian and Jewish apocalypses. Survival into the first microseconds after the "Ginnangu-Gap" becomes the climactic curtain to the dynamism of human intelligence: that arc from the known into the unknown. In the movement of Blish's plot, that dynamic, the sublimity of which was established by Wells and the early pulp stories, is the medium of human glory, the genesis of all that is apt for at least a relative fulfillment in some enduring significance. The unknown sought here differs crucially from what classical Christianity termed "mystery" in that the former is what is not yet known but may be. The unknown is immanent to the cosmos, of the same ontological order as the known. According to Christian eschatology, though, the end is not of the same order because the end is the mystery of God, which may be apprehended but not comprehended. God offers himself, now and in eternity, as the mystery that always remains such, revealing itself to an eternally increasing apprehension. In this connection, Gregory of Nyssa (c. 335–c. 395) used the metaphor of the heavenly banquet: "The two things grow simultaneously: the ability is increased, nourished by the bounty of good fare, and the supply of nourishing goods increases as a result of the heightened receptivity to them."[65]

In a similar fashion, the dynamic of transcendence that Blish celebrates truncates humanity understood as ordered toward the divine mystery. Christian anthropology insists, therefore, that "to be human is to be spirit, i.e. to live life while reaching ceaselessly for the absolute, in openness toward God. . . . We are forever the infinite openness of the finite for God."[66] Since Blish's apocalyptic drama denies a final significance for the personal, the novel sets up the unresolved dualism between the exceeding of intellectual frontiers and the labor of nurturing a culture or community, between the way of mind and mathematics and that of embodiment. Stapledon initially avoided this dualism by bringing both intellectual discovery and cultural creation within the orbit of "spirit." He thereby finds sublimity within a broader construal of human self-transcendence: "This great fact [of "spirit"] is involved in the very stuff of our bodies, which is at bottom identical with the stuff of the remotest stars and galaxies. For in the very substance of our bodies, and therefore of the stars, it is implied that ultimately the way of life must be the way of intelligence and love and creative action."[67] Stapledon, though, also runs aground in his denial of divine personality. Given Christianity's claim that all human beings exist within the horizon of God's infinite personality, then all human activities that nurture the personal draw their meaning and find their goal in God.[68] The painful ambiguities of Stapledon's philosophical and imaginative vision, when it comes to the destiny of human beings and all "minded worlds," derive from an inadequate understanding of "person," one that forced him to deny God as personal.[69] Consequently, he struggles to find some cosmic affirmation of "the way of intelligence and love and creative action," having rendered it impossible for spirit to be fulfilled as spirit. Since Blish narrows his focus to intellectual transcendence, he manages at least a quasi-fulfillment of humanity's capacity for self-transcendence. The problem, though, is that such a focus divides and truncates the human.

George Zebrowski's *The Omega Point Trilogy* began as a lively novella with "dabs of speculative philosophy."[70] This brief space opera later gained both prequel and sequel, *Ashes and Stars* and *Mirror of Minds*, the latter extending the philosophical "dabs" to the point where they form the material of the plot.[71] *Omega Point* is a metaphysical thriller with an apocalyptic storyline. The plot complicates the more typical apocalyptic scenario while the metaphysical forays deploy sublime imagery in service of an eschatology that is both more positive than *The Triumph of Time* and even more thoroughly subversive of the Christian materials on which it draws.

Zebrowski offers three apocalypses: one in the past, which originates the novel's action; one in the present; and one striven for in the future, the "Omega Point" of the title. The first two are familiar catastrophes, but the last promises to be the culmination of mind as it passes into a divinity imagined as far more actual than Blish's austere, metaphorical theosis. Complicating matters further, the apocalypses involve more than one galactic culture. The colonial empire that has spread from the Earth is not the only game in space. Though the Herculeans originated from human stock, they developed independently into a peculiarly vigorous and technologically brilliant culture. Their imperial expansion ended in a brutal war won by an Earth determined upon Herculean genocide. This first apocalypse left the few surviving Herculeans scattered among hostile peoples, except for those who took refuge on "Myraa's world," where Myraa leads a mysterious religious cult that promises immortality to its adepts.

One member of the Herculean military elite, however, refused to either surrender or flee to Myraa. Gorgias, having killed his father for insufficient megalomania, assumes sole control of a "Whisper Ship," a deadly piece of space technology vastly superior to any of Earth's warships. The eroticism of the "Whisper Ship," with its intimate relationship between pilot and machine, embodies the classic sublime elevation on an immanent plane. The ship's physicality, conveying the physical vastness and crushing power of sublimity, enables a transcending of physicality as, in *Mirror of Minds*, Gorgias penetrates its circuitry in an exalted movement of freedom from bodily constraint. Frantic in his vengeance, Gorgias conducts a terrorist campaign destroying entire planetary colonies before he is cornered, while visiting Myraa. Though Gorgias is a more than nimble enemy while slipping in and out of "jump space," he is decidedly hopeless as a ground commander and dies, having lost all his troops, an event that begins the climactic series of events told in *Mirror of Minds*.

The architect of Gorgias' defeat is the self-doubting, melancholic Rafael Kurbi, who cherishes the vain hope of persuading Gorgias to turn from vengeance and rebuild Herculean culture along peaceful lines. Kurbi himself is disillusioned with Earth, mourning it as a vengeful, stagnant culture. Earth stands for linear expansion for its own sake: movement without purpose, direction without depth. In destroying the Herculeans, Earth has simply become a mirror of its old enemy. Following Teilhard de Chardin, one of Zebrowski's principal inspirations, the novel suggests that cultural evolution follows naturally in demanding, given a certain level of size and complexity, a qualitative transition to a new form of life. Earth is caught in an evolutionary loop of mere quantitative expansion, a way to wither, technology and empire notwithstanding. On Myraa's world, though, the heating up of Herculean culture, of which military might was only an external and misleading symptom, has intensified to catalyze a qualitative leap. This self-transcendence, in a melding of de Chardin with Schopenhauer, frees intellectual lives from the driving of the blind force from which all that physicality and conflict comes, and which catches minds hopelessly in mortal bodies.[72]

Behind the external physical cosmos—which is merely an expressive shell, an outcropping of intellectual life—is a vast society of minds to which Myraa mediates access. She explains, "The interlocking matrix of minds is coextensive with all of nature, which is our outward face, in every stone, in every blade of grass and grain of sand. We accumulate those who return to us through death."[73] In this community of Herculeans, evolution has reached one of the points at which an individual becomes a gateway for minded beings to pass through death into the cosmos' mental infrastructure. This is no quiet paradise, however. At its center, a core of blind force, life generating but equally destructive, originates all beings. A mindless plenum, the force-center throws up one creation after another in which minds are trapped and perish forever.[74] The intellects that make it into the spiritual world, the universe's internal reality, face this industrial process of world making and, therefore, suffering. However, beyond gathering to themselves what minds they can, they are unable to change the creative game. Reading Schopenhauer through de Chardin, though, there is a way for this Schopenhauerian

"Will." When the minds are strong enough, Myraa reassures, "we will transform . . . the force-center. We will give it a conscious intelligence as we permeate its blind striving. . . . A god will arise at the end of history and be a product of it, not its creator."[75] God's becoming is the "Omega Point," the final apocalypse in an eternal community of minds and the abolition of everything that is alien or surplus to mind.

First, though, Gorgias turns out even nastier dead than alive. Myraa gathers him into herself and into her "configuration of minds." However, incorporation into Myraa and the loss of his bodily life not only offends his Herculean manliness; it raises his venomous lust for revenge and power to uncontrollable excess. In resisting Myraa's guidance, Gorgias discovers that he has a friend in the force-center. He learns how to channel its power for his own ends and, having taken over Myraa's body, resumes control of the Whisper Ship, penetrating its circuits with his mind. Gorgias channels the power of the force-center to pick off one planet after another all the way to Earth itself. However, he has grasped the tiger's tail. Expanding the center's power beyond his capacity to control it, his will breaks, and he is overwhelmed, collapsing into that boiling, blind, and greater will. Space opera is typically lavish with sublime destruction, so Earth still burns, even after the force-center has consumed Gorgias. Kurbi and Myraa, at last free from Gorgias' control, escape this casual apocalypse, and Kurbi takes up his own path into Myraa's world, the enduring community of minds beyond matter.

Zebrowski's apocalyptic hope, which unites the Herculean Myraa and the Earthman Kurbi, resolves the dualism of spirit and matter in a monism of mind. Though it owes a good deal to Teilhard de Chardin's "superlife" or cosmogenesis ending in hyperpersonal union, this ultimate elimination of materiality disputes the material affirmations of Christian eschatology, which insists on the resurrection of the body.[76] Before its apocalyptic resolution, Zebrowski's universe divides in a tragic tension between the material cosmos that is inhabited by embodied minds and cultures and the communion of minds who indwell the cosmos' creative, structuring interior, of which the physical universe is the outward and imperfect expression. Zebrowski adapts de Chardin's "two energies," or, more accurately, two components of the one universal and "essentially psychic" energy. Radial energy propels evolution toward consciousness and the overcoming of entropy, while tangential energy unites entities within the matrix of their environment.[77] Zebrowski maps that distinction across the inward, mental, and outward, material, sides of the cosmos. As Myraa explains to Gorgias, "Our radiant [*sic*] energy is permanent, the inward power of all nature, supporting the tangential energy of entropy, which is transient."[78] Embodied minds experience this duality in the limitations of meaning inherent to a material cosmos. Kurbi judges Earth culture as stagnant, despite its material power and expansion—another instance of Wells' and Campbell's anxiety about material satiety and decadence. Extended life, material life augmented with material power, reveals no truly novel potential but the exhaustion of possibility in the drift to stale repetition. Physical life, therefore, is a fatal constraint on the potentials of mind.

Sublime pleasure attends Zebrowski's representations of mental triumph. His extravagant descriptions of the community of minds read like Young lionizing the heavenlies: "Space trembled about him. The infrastructure of reality was vibrant with minds. They nestled in folds and byways, distending the darkness, forming galaxies of consciousness."[79] Again, sublimity rises from matter to spirit as overwhelming materialities provoke the irrepressible recuperation of imagination, or the supremacy of reason, or the mastery of nature, or a closeness to divinity. Sublimity thus bursts through its material occasions to reveal the spiritual that transcends matter.[80] Sublimity works to subordinate matter to mind, even to eliminate it as our necessary environment. Recent speculations on the utopia of our posthuman robotic successors also resort naturally to sublime expression. "It is the 'wild' intelligences," Hans Moravec enthuses, "those beyond our constraints to whom the future belongs. . . . Robots sweep into space in a wave of colonization, but their wake converts everything into increasingly pure thinking stuff. A 'Mind Fire' will burn across the universe."[81]

*The Omega Point* posits a further dualism within the universal infrastructure itself. Minds are not alone in there. To Gorgias' delight, the "heart of fire" is a blind, mindless, irresistible force that he may channel, though he fails since he is pitting his finite will against its own infinite source. Myraa's apocalypse transforms the force-center to render it mindful: "[The] blindness will acquire awareness. . . . A god will arise at the end of history."[82] "God" is the name for the ultimacy of mind.[83] "Omega Point" eliminates all constraints on mind from what is not mind, either the physical cosmos or the originating force that produces it. An eternal community of minds may, as Myraa suggests, play with material production by way of experiment or amusement, but it has no constitutive role for the beings of Omega, for the saints of mindedness. The universe possesses nothing for them that is truly other. Again, a Christian eschatology, by contrast, holds to materiality as good, not just as a means to a final transformation into mind, but good in itself and, specifically, as the field for irreducible otherness.[84] If God completes his creation in "new creation," then it shall be one that mediates and maintains ontological difference, creating communion without erasing distinction. The resurrection of bodies and the bodily fulfills the ineradicable differences and harmonies of materialities and of matter and mind. The completion of creation glorifies plurality and so also the internal resistances and differences that preclude the transparency of monism. The end is not to dwell eternally in a "mirror of minds."

## THE END OF HISTORY?

No apocalypse happens in William Gibson's *Neuromancer*, yet the novel maps projects for the end of history. An Artificial Intelligence manipulates a cyberspace hacker and a woman "street samurai" to help break its inbuilt inhibitors and, enabling the merger of otherwise divided functions, to achieve an identification with cyberspace itself.[85] Disclosure of the conspiratorial truth, revealed on an intricate installment plan reminiscent of Chandler or Hammett, tracks a global and orbital landscape of potential posthumanisms. In each, history ends in an attempted endlessness, a condition of technologically mediated finality in which humanity—specifically the modern humanity, the subject of the sublime—achieves an apocalypse without end. Entangled with Gibson's figurations of the end of history are contrasting and competing dynamics of self-preservation, at least one of which sacrifices self-consciousness—and, therefore, the modern self—as a condition of survival. Corporations create technologically sustained equilibriums that do not depend on the survival of particular individuals; human beings adapt or die in fluctuating, unstable zones of illegality and violent competition between corporate stabilities, while other entities achieve parasitic forms of claustrophobic self-perpetuation. Compared with the confident dooms or triumphs in much science-fictional apocalyptic, *Neuromancer* offers only ambiguous apocalypses, rival and competing ends.

Gibson famously defined cyberspace as a "consensual hallucination" created by the "graphic representation of data abstracted from the banks of every computer in the human system."[86] Embracing a universe of data so complex as to boil the mind of any human being who tried to "apprehend more than the merest outline," cyberspace is essentially a sublime and quasi-theological space: no one sees naked cyberspace and lives.[87] Within this infinity, not an Einsteinian space but one akin to Newton's divine sensorium, leviathans of data upon data draw the hacker as stars do Young's devout astronomer. Akin to theological discourse, language turns for description to paradox and the hyperbolic: "polychrome shadow, countless translucent layers shifting and recombining. Protean, enormous, [the virus] towered above them, blotting out the void."[88] The ecstatic inhabitants of cyberspace—who explore, invade, stake out, spy, and steal its data—are the "cyberspace cowboys," part outlaws, part knight errants, part shamans on occult, dream journeys. Above all, though, the cyber-cowboy expands another, newly repositioned, frontier. This frontier, though, escapes future exhaustion by being independent of nature, a technological field without limit, an apocalyptic condition both immanent and infinite, the cowboy's "distanceless home, his country, transparent 3D chess board extending to infinity."[89] As an endless apocalypse, cyberspace gifts freedom from embodiedness, from the tethering of the all-too-solid flesh or, in the language of the cyber-cowboys, the despised "meat."[90] Neurologically mugged by the employers he had betrayed, Case falls, like any gnostic spirit, into the meat. Banished from the "bodiless exaltation," he tumbles "into the prison of his own flesh." A promise of an endless end, liberated from the body, cyberspace realizes the technological sublime without the Wellsian anxiety about decadence following freedom. Cyberspace contains sublime dangers and deep obscurities enough for permanent stimulation of the self-preserving faculties: the red-hot perils of military ICE, the manipulations of AIs, and the mazy threats of infesting viruses.

At a peak of cyberspatial ecstasy, Case attains a fulfillment of sublime, spectatorial vision: "His vision was spherical, as though a single retina lined the inner surface of a globe that contained all things."[91] This all-encompassing eye, as divine vision, enjoys the field of unrestricted gazing over which Addison and Beattie enthused as the sublime's theological promise. This eye, though, is also self-enclosed, its infinity wrapped within itself, a totality and so shut off from transcendence. Within the novel, therefore, this image of liberating cyberspace resonates with other self-replicating, closed environments: the wasp's nest as symbol of Tessier-Ashpool, the hive construction of the Villa Straylight, and the recycling energies of violent trade in Night City and the Sprawl.

Urban environments in *Neuromancer*—Night City, Ninsei, and the Sprawl—provide a meat-based analog to cyberspace. Here, too, history ends in the ceaseless movement of "biz," the buzz of deals in which the line between legal and illegal is constantly and strategically blurred. Ninsei exists as the predatory zone in which research is stolen and traded, drugs circulate as instruments of both personal survival and Ninsei's self-pruning, and transgressive experiments find their unhappy subjects. In this permanent chaos on its eternal boil, order emerges according to the "strange attractor" that is the biz. Corporations, legal and criminal, need Night City as release, refuse processor, war zone, and laboratory; its consumption helps their equilibrium and thus an unending reproduction indifferent to the fates of particular humans or human groups. Also a sublime environment, impossibly complex, vast in internal, ramifying conspiracies, always and intimately obscure, Gibson's urban world has an unlimited bloodstream of electronic transactions while the barely legal paper money circulates in imitation, "endlessly through the closed circuit of the world's black markets."[92] This closed infinity, too, overcomes the body: as the human feeds into the encompassing movement of capital, the meat is processed.

The Villa Straylight, orbital home of the Tessier-Ashpool clan and goal of Case and Molly's quest, contains the abortive results of another attempt at history's end. Parasitic and enclosed, feeding off the ecology of Freeside, a satellite furnishing Disneyesque consumer and leisure environments, the Villa Straylight provides the architectural metaphor for the family's attempt at self-perpetuation.

The Tessier-Ashpools seek a personal, not merely institutional, survival in an old-fashioned and perverse refusal of death through the hypermodern means of age-retarding drugs, neurosurgery, and cryogenics. In the process, the family has sealed itself into a secret life, replicating incestuously, self-consuming, and riven by hatreds and fear. Instrumentalized by the process of self-perpetuation, abusive of each other, and named by genetic lines—"3Jane," "8Jean"—family members have lost the individuality and personal character they originally sought to sustain. "Case remembered the litter of the old man's chamber, the soiled humanity of it," and he concludes that the entire family is consumed by "the same ragged tangle of fears, the same sense of aimlessness."[93] A poisoned parody of eternal life, the clan slips into a tortured homogeneity by refusing the radical difference of death. The Villa Straylight—its corridors curving around themselves, blind bends and false walls, "stairways vaulted like intestines, rooms full of historical detritus"—is the sublime Gothic shell the family has secreted around themselves.[94] Gothic novels, in which strategies of obsessive self-preservation appear frequently, provide the inspiration for this negative image of sublimity's glorification of the self. The Tessier-Ashpool clan constructed a "seamless web of self" that imploded precisely because it attempted seamlessness, an acme of self-preservation.[95]

Within this and against it, however, one Tessier-Ashpool, the matriarch Marie-France, designs an alternative, posthumanist solution to the dilemma of survival. Her plan involves not rejecting family perpetuation but radicalizing the process by ridding it of human self-consciousness, that destabilizing element that both needs and rejects otherness. Existing in symbiosis with an Artificial Intelligence, the Tessier-Ashpools would enjoy an "animal bliss," all conscious decisions made by the AI. Human history would end in the rejection of the forebrain, regarded by Marie-France as "a sort of [evolutionary] sidestep."[96] The matriarch's vision, for which her husband strangles her, inverts the posthumanism of cyberspace, rejecting altogether the sublime self that transcends embodiment in an infinite and universal field. Her posthumanism ends history by returning to the body, an unself-conscious body, relieved of self-awareness. Such a body, though, has ceased to be a human body by ceasing to be a self-conscious body, a body of human intellect and will. Instead of a monism of mind, sensation and the feeding of pleasures, a polymorphic hedonism ,takes all—the freedom, in Bataille's phrase, of being in the world like "water in water."[97]

In *Neuromancer*, the human body—though variously rejected, processed, and mechanized—nevertheless persistently, if ambiguously, intrudes upon history's various projected ends, undercutting them with its insistencies. As Molly breaks into the Sense/Net building, Case connects with her through "simstim," which enables him to share her conscious awareness. Knowing his presence as a rider, she greeted him and "slid a hand under her jacket, a fingertip circling a nipple under warm silk. The sensation made him catch his breath. She laughed."[98] The physical gesture opens up bodily difference, cutting across technological merging, asserting the distinctness of the individual and sexual body. Later, projected into a world built out of his memories by an AI, Case finds in the body of his former lover a particularly physical strength, a harbor of the flesh that holds him and protects "from the relentless Street that hunted them all." In the despised meat, this strong intimacy was "a vast thing, beyond knowing . . . infinite intricacy that only the body in its strong, blind way, could ever read." The vulnerable body, "tired, sad, and human," also asserts itself against the retouched bodies in "Finn's old magazines in Metro Holografix."[99] Human unpredictability, too, has its roots in the body: the actions taken by Molly and Case betray even an AI's capacity for planning, unlike the downloaded, fleshless "construct" of the deceased hacker Dixie Flatline. The body, though, also harbors pain and terror, as well as perversity—Peter Riviera's sadistic pleasures. Consequently, the dark strength of the body, its force upon the mind, fuels the fantasies of mental freedom. A sublime technology attempts to tame and correct "the bloody mess of organic nature." *Neuromancer*—echoing both the advertised, commodified body and the sleek violence of super and action heroes—presents the technologically disciplined body as seductive. Hideo, the "vat-grown" assassin whose killing is balletic, suggests a utopian embodiment: hyperskilled, radically, gracefully simple, entirely pliant to the will. This body, though, lacking the tensions of human embodiment, also lacks conscience, doubt, ambivalence, and the constraints of thought: Hideo is also on the way to the monstrous, the hideous. The insistent and disruptive presence of bodiliness in this novel problematizes without denying the attraction of the sublime posthumanisms of cyborg enhancements, medical augmentation, and cyberspace liberties.

If references to the body suggest what the various posthumanisms exclude, the marginal Rastafarian group known as Zionists intrudes upon the novel's immanent apocalypses by introducing the notes of a classical apocalyptic. The Zionists who help Case and Molly complete their quest understand the worlds of the Sprawl, Freeside, and the Tessier-Ashpools as "Babylon," the doomed world of evil over which "Jah love" will finally triumph, not in an immanent but a transcendent freedom, a new aeon of peace. Like many an apocalyptic cult, the Zionists both refuse the dominant culture and pillage it in order to stake out a sphere of relative freedom—in the Zionists' case, an ecologically self-sufficient satellite—in which they can wait for a deliverance that comes from outside the cultural system. Taking the name of the holy city, the Rastafarians leave the immanent end of history, that capitalism sustained by self-perpetuating "zaibatsus," the circling and raiding of data in cyberspace, and the symbiosis of legal and black economies. They reject immanence for imminence, looking for the Messiah and claiming the beginning of the "Final Days. . . . Voices. Voices cryin' inna wilderness, prophesyin' ruin unto Babylon."[100] Though the Zionists are marginal figures, as the voice of another apocalyptic they accent the limits of the novel's immanent totalities.

In the end, Molly and Case part company. She returns to live off the end of history, serving its self-preservation. Case, however, chooses a life buffered from apocalypse: he gets work and finds a girl. After Molly leaves, though, he is contacted by Wintermute, the AI whose enterprise he has served. The two systems, Wintermute and Neuromancer, have merged and become the matrix itself: "You running the world now," Case asks. "You God?"[101] The new artificial mind, though, has found new sublimities, engaging other like minds in the universe. Later, cruising cyberspace, Case notices "three figures, tiny, impossible, who stood at the very edge of one of the vast steps of data."[102] They wave to him. These are the novel's lost characters, the murdered Linda Lee, the downloaded Dixie Flatline, and the child avatar of Neuromancer. The scene executes a sublime landscape of vastness and human figures. Cyberspace provides both space and frame, and the cyber-cowboy, the frontiersman, enters and leaves at will. As in Rigg's *A Clearing*, the sublime appears, not without irony, as an imaginative construction, a projection of human freedom that reconfigures immensity and power, threat and danger, into the pleasurable exaltation of the human, of its immanent promise.

All these sublime apocalypses, from Disch's plants to Gibson's posthumanisms, exchange a transcendent future for an immanent one, whether they reveal in hopelessness the inescapability of time and world or discover in celebration the shape of a glory born from human powers. In that, they conform to the underlying ideology of the sublime in its various forms: a vision of immanence in which human powers come into their own or find that they are on their own. Representing their sublime endings and fulfillments, these science-fictional apocalypses also disclose what the sublime excludes and the unhappy totalities it breeds.[103]

# 6

# FROM THE SUBLIME TO THE BEAUTIFUL

*Beauty . . . bestirs the world and holds all things in existence.*

—Pseudo-Dionysius, *The Divine Names*, 77

*Large and blue, a woman who tended to come apart into jellylike pieces only to flow together about the translator pole, my current employer said, "Thank you. Thank you." . . . She went from pale sky to indigo.*

—Delany, *Stars in My Pocket*, 61

A poster for the 2013 movie *Gravity* shows an astronaut flung into space as the cable tethering her to safety snaps and recoils.[1] An explosive glow of white light seems to erupt from Earth, which pushes in from the right, occupying almost half the image. That light graduates from the bright impact of whatever catastrophe has caused her plight and fades into the blank immensity of space behind the astronaut. In the foreground, a blurred craft appears to move at speed away from the figure into the bottom right of the picture.[2] As an exercise in the science-fictional sublime, the image reveals that sublimity's basic coordinates: vastness of scale, a shock of contingency, and the dislocation of the spectator.

The astronaut flails between the crushing scale of the planet on the right and the consuming abyss behind her. Sublimity has rendered space as a metaphor for the scope of an immeasurable threat, a threat that Lovecraft, for example, configured as an enveloping horror that bred monsters. That same subliming of space, however, also represents cosmic scale as an inexhaustible field for human attainment, the one context adequate in mystery and danger to the self-transcending dynamic of the human mind. As such, space sublimed invokes the expanding horizon of human imagination and ambition, the "final frontier" for an endless progress, or the sphere of an always self-surpassing rational and technological mastery. As in *Mirror of Minds*, the dubious promise of Chew-Z, or Gibson's cyberspace, a sublime space may also become so much the medium of humanity as to impart its limitlessness in a secularized eschatology of life without the body.[3]

Experience of the sublime reveals humanity's freedom—the species' divine potential, its irrepressible imagination, its rational surpassing of nature—but, as a condition of that, does so in and through the shock of contingency. From the snapping cable, through Stapledon's narratives of human species beginning and ending in cosmic accident, to the universe itself unmoored through its doppelganger in antimatter, science-fictional sublimity destabilizes illusions of security. In the process, the sublime has tended toward polarizing the anthropological vision, either toward abjection or toward apotheosis, sometimes, as in *Neuromancer*, within the same novel. The event structure of sublimity, its dynamic of pleasurable perturbation, however, issues nevertheless, at both extremes, in the elevation of human freedom, disclosing either humanity's cosmic significance or, if it has none, its capacity to transcend in imagination horrors and unkind contingency.

Returning to the astronaut in distress, the poster also positions the viewer in space, somewhere slightly above the astronaut and near the moving ship. The viewer is located in the place of sublime displacement, seeing from where the falling figure itself has been thrown and addressed by the capitalized words "DON'T LET GO," the danger intimated by the vertical positioning of the words, the length of which drops with each line. The command focuses the peculiar, ambiguous place of sublime experience, in which one indeed lets go imaginatively while held in reality. The movie itself begins with a similar series of capitalized oracular statements emerging in silence one by one from a black background: "AT 372 MILES ABOVE THE EARTH . . . THERE IS NOTHING TO CARRY SOUND . . . NO AIR PRESSURE . . . NO OXYGEN." These lines then disappear for the climactic "LIFE IN SPACE IS IMPOSSIBLE."[4] As it turns out, though, more or less according to the viewer's expectations, *Gravity* dramatizes human endurance and ingenuity, a narrative that counters the threatening gravitas of these sober facts. One reviewer, resonating to the sublimity rather than the movie's dubious physics, admitted leaving the theater "in awe" at the "complexities of nature" and concluded that *Gravity* "is a celebration of the human being, because even though we are in fact very insignificant, it is our will to life, and our effort to make our lives meaningful, that make us matter."[5] The movie ends with a metaphor both sublime and evolutionary. The central character, now back on earth, crawls from the lake in which her capsule has crashed. She grips the mud in her hands, then slowly stands up; the camera views her from the ground, a sublime figure, huge against an open sky. Finally, the view expands to show her alone in a sublimely mountainous landscape, upon which the screen blackens and the credits roll. The science-fictional sublime, following the drift of the history of sublime discourse, affirms transcendence only within immanence, in an infinite cosmos and in human striving, making, and imagining. This, though, raises the question about the fate of God, erstwhile "by far the most sublime" reality.

## DROPPING THE PILOT? THE END OF THE SUBLIME GOD

Science fiction has never steered clear of Christianity. The purported "war of science and religion" was popularized in the late nineteenth century by John Draper and Andrew White, who took historical liberties that have since stiffened into seeming permanence within the popular imagination.[6] Their picture of an inevitable conflict that would endure until the scientific baby Hercules had throttled the last theological snake was an important inspiration for the often polemical relationship between science fiction and religion.[7] The genre's gravitation, however, not only toward theological polemic but also to the positive reinterpretation of religious themes, has profounder roots. In appropriating the language of sublimity—already a medium for imagining technology, scientific progress, and evolution—science fiction took up a discourse freighted from its beginnings with Christian theology. Insofar as science fiction adopted a polemical relationship with Christianity—inspired by perceived conflicts between faith and reason, progress and religious conservatism, religion and science, modernity and the Church—it often did so by way of a reimagination of the sublime, a rendering that relocated sublimity along the plane of immanence.

In disputing the sublimity of the Christian God, science fiction has made three principal and connected claims, having to do with the contingency of the cosmos, God's infinity, and the human vocation. Science fiction rejoices in universal contingency, understanding contingency not as creation's entire and absolute dependence upon God but as ontological insecurity. Lovecraft's universe knows only passing patches of order while human beings owe their flourishing to elder agencies that made them en passant and will destroy them at whim. Contingency may appear with more ontological modesty in *The Death of Grass*, but the rapidity of collapse testifies to the vulnerable balance of forces within which humans flourish. In these and similar disclosures of the shifting sands upon which order builds, belief in God functions as a socially approved denial mechanism that allows men and women the comforting illusion of a guaranteed significance in a universe under providential care. Wells' panic-stricken curate psychologically buckles under the seemingly unstoppable Martian invasion. Unable to sustain the fantasy of protection or purpose, his faith has also failed to instill in this blubbering cleric even the rudiments of courage or practicality. In the interests of a similar unmasking, Disch's biblical quotations comment ironically on the appalling gap between reality and religious trust. If cosmic contingency means, however, that the universe has no bias toward human survival, let alone happiness, it also opens up a field for human striving, whether in sublime defiance or a sublime realization of spirit, as in *Star Maker*. If faith functions to shore up feelings of false security, the God in which it trusts also prices his protection in the constraint of human possibilities. The God of faith, thereby, forfeits his title to sublimity by breaking the correspondence between the sublime and the dignity of human freedom.

Science fiction has used Christian belief in a personal God to drive a wedge between God and the sublime. A personal being, runs the implicit argument, is necessarily a finite, limited being since personality is formed in and through relations with others. Stapledon combines this with his sublime representations of cosmic and evolutionary waste to form an imaginative pincer trapping both divine personality and divine love. Wells, too, assigned personality to the finite in distinguishing between his stalwart captain of humanity and the impersonality of a universal order that transcends and will eventually end human life. This contrast—between an infinite universe and a personal and, therefore, limited God—places sublimity on this side of the cosmos and of immanence. Whether the universe hounds humanity to nothingness, as in a Lovecraft tale, or provokes the realization of the species' true intellectual powers, as in Campbell's "Forgetfulness" or in *Mirror of Minds*, the cosmos exceeds any representation of a God fatally compromised by the finitude of the personal.

When science fiction writers withdraw God from the sublime, they follow a trajectory set up within the nineteenth-century subliming of technology, in which human powers find favorable comparison with God's and deity becomes a measure of human freedom as expressed in technological progress. In contemplating the Brooklyn Bridge, Joseph Stella thus felt himself "in the presence of a new DIVINITY."[8] Displacing God in the interests of human autonomy and creativity had its roots in the natural sublime in which nature had become the privileged index of divine power and of the sublimity that inspired worship. The representation of nature, therefore, as ordered, brought into management, and exceeded by human device invited an imaginative shift toward, at the least, deistic rhetoric in the fields of politics and technological enthusiasm. Furthermore, the natural sublime had, from its beginnings, correlated sublime experience with the expansion of human intellect and imagination into a divine likeness. Via the technological sublime, science fiction completed this trajectory by contrasting God, as an essentially limited reality, with a sublime universe and a human vocation itself imagined as sublime. Since God is conceived of as personal for the purposes of cosmic comfort, belief in God is necessarily inimical to human freedom and to the species' historical transcendence. Campbell presents an absolute choice between faith and science, religion and reality: religion inevitably promotes indolence and craven fears, cutting the nerve of humanity's potential to exceed intellectual frontiers. A God who protects also lays down limiting commandments—hence the conflict between Amalfi and Jorn the Apostle, who accuses the scientists of "meddling with the pre-ordained Armageddon."[9] Whereas God confines the human, true sublimity, at least in this version, releases men and women for destiny, provokes humanity as autonomous and self-making, potentially expanding without limits—as long as human beings do not make peace with their comforts. Along the line of this projection, though, materiality may also be represented as constraining. Bodies become the cowboys' cramping meat, as in *Neuromancer*. In Zebrowski's vision of fulfillment, what is other to mind disappears altogether, digested into universal mind: all heterogeneous multiplicity lost in the monism that Philip Dick identifies as the dark side of gnostic promise.

Contesting Christianity for sublimity has helped earn science fiction a reputation as an essentially atheistic genre.[10] Given the number of works written from a Christian or theologically sympathetic perspective, this may seem perverse or, at least, misleading.[11] However, the judgment that science fiction belongs with atheism does have a certain historical precision, allowing for a distinction between classical Christian theology and modern theism, Christian and otherwise. The object of science fiction's theological polemic is far more recognizable in the God that Adam Smith judged as the most sublime of realities than in the God confessed in classical Christianity or reflected upon by Augustine, Anselm, and Aquinas. Whereas the latter, for instance, is thoroughly Trinitarian, Locke's "eternal, most powerful, and most knowing being" or Newton's causative agent "very well skilled in Mechanicks and Geometry" are theistic in the sense of a non-Trinitarian, personal Creator and supreme reality, whose wisdom and goodness appears in creation and the moral order.[12] Descartes' description is succinct and was accepted by empiricists such as Locke and Clarke who nevertheless thoroughly opposed his account of how human beings secured knowledge of this God.[13] "By the word 'God,'" Descartes writes, "I understand a substance that is infinite, eternal, immutable, independent, supremely intelligent, supremely powerful, and which created both myself and everything else."[14] This version of deity, to which piety adds the modifying affirmation of love to the supremacy of power, Stapledon purifies into his agnostic vision of the Star Maker. In the process, he follows modern theism's tendency both to treat Creator and creation as sharing a common field of being, as in Newton's account of God and space, and to conceive the transcendence of this Supreme Being in opposition to immanence.[15] Stapledon's Star Maker thus becomes a radically distant being before undergoing a demythologizing flip and disappearing into the ultimate conditions by which universes come and go. By contrast, classical Christianity understands transcendence as involving a radical difference that is thereby the condition of an immanence according to which God is "nearer to us than we are to ourselves."

Since the seventeenth century, modern theism has largely passed as synonymous with the Christian doctrine of God.[16] The theistic account of God, a single absolute person as opposed to the God who is personal in and through the interrelations of the Trinitarian persons, gives a thoroughgoing primacy to God as Creator, as the "efficient cause" of creation. This privileging of God as supreme cause and maker was also expressed and reinforced in the history of the sublime. In the late seventeenth century, this primacy appeared the most effective antidote to atheism since Newtonian science claimed to demonstrate that God's existence was necessary to explain the order and mechanics of creation. That claim, though, placed God as Creator on a level with immanent causes investigated by natural science, an apologetic hostage to the latter's growing explanatory power. Classically understood, however, creation is the original giving of being, origination ex nihilo, and so entirely different from any immanent causation. Rather, creation is the origination of the field and conditions of immanent causation, of the being of becoming itself. This unique act named by the doctrine of creation is obscured in favor of an account that brings creation uncritically close to making or manufacture, a cultural and theological move still reflected in Stapledon's Star Maker as well as his creation myth's ontological blind spot.[17] The associated prejudice that creation has to do with beginning, in the sense of starting things off or getting them going, has also long endured within modernity. According the doctrine of creation such apologetic, and via the sublime, imaginative privilege had significant consequences for other creedal doctrines. The work of God as redeeming and fulfilling creation, in the light of which work creating itself receives its meaning, became relatively detached from the doctrine of God instead of forming that doctrine in the wake of the biblical narrative of the Father who sends his Son and whose mutual Spirit raises the dead. Redemption and resurrection begin to function as an appendix to creation, as the means by which the moral order of creation is restored. Thus, when Edward Young attempts to overwhelm poor rascal Lorenzo with a sublime description of the Last Judgment, the fearful condemnations fall upon the sinner's failure to respond piously to the sublimities of nature.

Subliming God, therefore, was not good news for Christian theology, providing, as it did, the imaginative, aesthetic, and experiential correlation with the shift to a post-Trinitarian theism. Sublimity distorted the relationship between Creator and creature, immanentizing God as a supreme power among powers—a God who, being a supreme reality, is also a finite reality, no matter how many superlatives arrive to shore up his distinctiveness. In reflections upon the sublime, this loss of a classical understanding of transcendence appears in the innocence with which writers pass, as a matter of degree, from the enlargement of imagination stimulated by a sublime landscape to that provoked by thoughts of the sublime God. Both Young and Baillie, therefore, imply that the ascent from finding our destined métier in contemplating heavenly immensities to the contemplation of their Creator is a continuous one, not a transition across such radical and incomparable difference as makes no matter whether the preceding meditations concerned nebulae or gnats. Though sublime enthusiasm celebrated divine power, the celebration was calibrated to the celebration of humanity. "How much greater an existence must the Soul imagine herself," asks Baillie, when the telescope surveys the stars. After all, a "*Universal Presence* is one of the sublime *Attributes* of the *Deity*," so the greater the expanse open to our minds, the nearer we approach "the *Perfections* of the *Universal Presence*."[18]

Immanuel Kant's exposition of the sublime, still the most influential philosophical reading, possesses a far greater rigor and disciplined caution than is found in the British tradition. It shares, though, in this absolutizing of the human. Astonished by the sublime, the imagination falters, but, in its failing, reason reveals itself as possessed by the unimaginable idea of the infinite, the "absolutely great." "*The sublime is that,*" Kant argues, "*the mere capacity of thinking which evidences a faculty of mind transcending every standard of sense.*"[19] This is the mind that finds within itself the moral law that transcends all sensible conditions, obedience to which requires faith in God as a necessary "postulate." Postulating God is demanded by moral seriousness in that God provides the condition of possibility for an ultimate coordination of happiness and moral worth. Kant's God, therefore, becomes the guarantor of human autonomy, of the self-legislating moral will. Though he flirts with the intimation of a reality beyond all representation, a shock down to the roots of creaturely being, the sublime once more travels the inward curve of the self, and we arrive at "*our* supersensible identity as moral beings."[20] The logic of this soon provoked Fichte's argument that Kant's theism amounted to a residue that falsified the logic of his insistence on human moral freedom. Humanity's self-ordained vocation requires conforming the world of appearances to the purposes of reason. Since the "moral world-order" must be self-dependent and self-authenticating, theistic arguments contradict the freedom necessary to a moral vocation by seeking to find an external supporting ground. This excess divinity compromises the moral order, the order of human autonomy. Freedom demands that the "living and effective moral order is identical with God."[21] Fichte's logic is important because it underscores how the sublime God ceases to be transcendent in the classical sense, having been pressed into immanent service as a functional guarantor for human freedom and rational progress.

Naming God within the imagination of the sublime deformed Christian discourse in a number of connected ways. The conviction that, given its divine authority, the Bible must de facto contain the heights of literary sublimity reinforced the primacy given to God as Creator since among the most obvious occasions for sublime rapture were Old Testament passages that treated of creation, followed closely by poetry describing God's judgment and the mighty dispatch of his enemies. As a sublime text, though, even the Bible might not match up to Creation, the book of Nature itself. So Young concludes that the night sky is "Scripture authentic! Uncorrupt by man" and sublimity its interpreter by which "the stars will light thee" and "set thee right."[22] He thus reverses the classical relationship according to which, as Calvin put it, Scripture provides the spectacles through which creation is read. Creation as sublime now interprets Scripture. Since the New Testament made for much slimmer pickings as regards sublimity, accounts of the sublime also reinforced a contrast between the two Testaments that made it that much harder to read the Old through the New. Most seriously in this respect, enthusiasm for the sublime detached divine power from divine love, sublimity being identified with the former. "Some reflection, some comparing," Burke argues, is "necessary to satisfy us of [God's] wisdom, his justice, and his goodness; to be struck with his power, it is only necessary that we open our eyes." Power strikes first, mighty force becomes the bedrock of the idea of God; goodness and love, on the other hand, is a matter of conclusion and discrimination rather than the subject of direct experience. Christianity only modifies power by love, a view that sits strangely alongside the Johannine "God is Love." Ironically, Burke put this in a way that corresponds well with science-fictional polemic against God as the fantasy that comforts believers in the genial accord between humanity and the universe. "Before the Christian religion," Burke reminds his readers, "had, as it were, *humanized the idea of the divinity*, and brought it somewhat near to us, there was very little said of the love of God."[23]

The argument that the science-fictional sublime presupposes modernity's sublime God, and so contests less Christianity than a serious deformation of Christian theology, raises the question as to whether sublime experience should be theologically privileged at all. If, in the name of God rather than secular freedom, Christian theology were itself to contest the sublime God and thus dispute the theological relevance of sublimity, this might also open up a rather different theological perspective on the imaginative enterprise that is science fiction. Fortunately, a voice from the early period of sublime enthusiasm points in this direction of a God not determined by the sublime imagination. Writing while Addison, Baillie, and Dennis were urging the public taste toward the spiritual benefits of greatness and Longinian sublimity, the American theologian Jonathan Edwards developed a theology and a metaphysics articulated upon the centrality, not of the sublime, but of the beautiful. Edwards' theological formation was that of a New England Puritan Calvinist captivated by Newtonian science. His theology manages an unashamed Calvinism into which flow foundational Enlightenment insights—cosmological and anthropological—as if to their natural medium.[24] What enables Edwards to a brilliant reinterpretation of Reformed theology, while also opening up a highly distinctive and critical trajectory within modernity, is his account of what is and what makes beauty. Beauty, in Edwards' account, marks creation because beauty is the perfection of the Creator's perfections. Whoever truly knows God, knows beauty as that, Edwards writes, "wherein the truest idea of divinity does consist." From this it follows that beauty characterizes being itself as being and that which departs from beauty to that extent approaches nothing.[25]

Edwards' proposals deserve much more than a historical interest. His exploration of beauty offers critical purchase on the discourse of sublimity, despite his not showing any concern with that European development. Though Edwards shares the empiricists' conviction of the necessary role of the senses in human knowing and their consequent commitment to observation, he manages to sustain an ontological account of beauty as transcending objectivity and subjectivity. In marked contrast to the British Enlightenment in general and accounts of the sublime in particular, Edwards treats beauty not only as a transcendental but within the context of a thoroughly theocentric and Trinitarian doctrine of creation. Unlike sublimity, beauty proves inimical to the separation of love and power and operates as an analogical concept that preserves the radical distinction of Creator and creature as well as exposes the ontological necessity of creaturely diversity, including the irreducibility of body to mind or mind to body.

While Edwards was busy raising beauty to "the first principle of being," in England, beauty was receiving far fainter praise, especially in comparison with the sublime.[26] Again, the theological consequences were unhappy. British advocacy of the sublime distinguished sublimity from beauty, a distinction adopted also by Kant and the later idealist tradition. Evaluations of the relative worth of sublimity and beauty differ in the degree to which the sublime surpasses beauty, but sublime occasions always reveal man's—and the gender is significant—highest calling. Addison lists the pleasures of the imagination as found in "Greatness, Novelty or Beauty."[27] Though he rejoices in beauty as working upon the mind with an incomparable directness, infusing "a secret Satisfaction" in the world about us, beauty remains on an earthly plane.[28] Beauty is the stuff of sexual attraction and so closer to the heart than to reason, less established in the truth of things. As a good Lockean, Addison knows that colors do not belong to objects as such and that, were things seen in their "proper Figures and Motions," it would seem a cold and disagreeable world. In his wisdom, therefore, God arranges for the delightful illusions of color and all such effects of light so that his creation might enchant and please us. "Greatness," however, does more earnest moral and theological work. Beauty affords an argument to God's wisdom from the world's workings, but greatness trains and readies the will and the emotions for worship, for the adoration of God himself.[29] Addison thus distances beauty from transcendence, from the expansiveness of human freedom, and from the dignity of reason. He leaves beauty funding the delights of sex and surfaces.

Certainly, Edward Young admits, "all things speak a GOD; but in the small / Men trace out Him; in great, He seizes man."[30] If the sublime grabs the soul by the scruff of the neck "by an authority," as Ussher writes, "which it is utterly unable to resist," beauty approaches more delicately.[31] Smallness undermines sublimity, but even the tiny may possess beauty; indeed, Burke argues, the attractions of a humming bird are probably enhanced by its diminutive size.[32] The beautiful has the insistency of the beguiling. Burke expounds the distinction according to its teleology as regards a human being's physical and psychological makeup. The sublime braces, readies a man for action, the muscles and nerves on the stretch and the mind alert. While the sublime exercises, the beautiful relaxes, eases and reassures, drawing out the gentler emotions of tenderness, pity, and affection. "All this," Burke notes, "is accompanied with an inward sense of melting and languor."[33] This phenomenology of affects modulates easily into the moral. Homer's Achilles, for all his mental and physical gifts, does not excite the reader's love, though the warrior's sublime strength and courage forces admiration. Pity and love flows toward the weak; in this case, the reader's affection settles on the Trojans whose gifts lie in the "*lesser* . . . domestic virtues."[34] A father's moral and social authority almost smothers love under respect, but love for a mother is not so fettered as "parental authority is almost melted down into the mother's fondness and indulgence."[35] Beauty plays a vital role guiding our romantic choices in the service of procreation and—implicitly, for Burke—training them along the proper lines of class and station. Accented by the beautiful, social power gains loveable features. In an echo of Locke's epistemology, Burke charges the French revolutionaries with tearing away "all the pleasing illusions which made power gentle and obedience liberal."[36] A rational society lacks color and the inspiration for love.

Since nerves and frame may not endure an unceasing stimulation, the beautiful relaxes us. Thus, beauty, though necessary, is also secondary; the sublime serves truth, moral force, enterprise, strength of purpose, and striving for improvement. In a word, sublimity is manly. Womanly virtues, like the "fair sex" itself, must keep within bounds lest rest become enervation. The Campbellian anxiety about technological benefits—and, perhaps, the lack of female characters in pulp science fiction—reflects this distinction between beauty and sublimity. The contrast of the sublime—as strengthening, individuating, exercising, and, therefore, liberating—with the beautiful—as easing, domesticating, delighting, and binding—runs under the various identifications of the sublime right into the twentieth century. Kant also observes the connection of sublimity with esteem and of beauty with affection and concludes that "true virtue alone is sublime" whereas the worthiness of moral qualities deemed "amiable and beautiful" depends on their harmony with true virtue.[37] The sublime, Schiller enthuses, shatters complacent bondage with the revelation of moral freedom, of humanity's transcendence of nature and social conformity: "Without the sublime, beauty would make us forget our dignity."[38] In the twentieth century, the painter Barnett Newman again opposes the self summoned by sublimity to the social conformities of the beautiful. Sublime art separates out, defends, and intensifies individuality. For a politics quite contrary to Burke's, though within a comparable dualism, Newman addresses "the self, terrible and constant."[39]

Burke cordoned off the beautiful and subordinated it to sublimity in a rage for traditional political and gender order. The manly sublime must benefit from but never submit to the beautiful. Thus,

> beauty must be included within the sublimity of the masculine law, in order to soften its rigours, but moral sublimity is not to be included within the beautiful. Women are indeed in this sense excluded from the domain of truth and morality.[40]

Burke also, however, articulates—although this is less noticed—a theology upon this dualism of sublimity and beauty, truth and ornament, masculine moral dignity and female softening. Whatever the qualifications of a considered theology, the imagination knows God first and foremost as overwhelming power, a sublime power before which "we are, in a manner, annihilated." Burke appeals to the sublime imaginations of the Old Testament for testimony to the enduring frightfulness of God for humanity. To be sure, Burke admits, false religions seem to inculcate little else but fear, but the true religion, too, depends to a great measure on a "salutary fear." Were God not thus sublime, religion would not stiffen the moral sinews and summon up the blood. Burke places Jesus, therefore, on the female side; it is Christianity that has "humanized" notions of God, rendered God approachable by softening the terrors of sublimity alone. Though Burke does not name Jesus, the dualism of sublimity and beauty associates Christ with the womanly beauty that has no moral authority in itself but is necessary to reassure and relax the soul before the unyielding sublime. The reflective cleric, no doubt, may combine God's attributes into a Lockean "complex idea" that unites power, justice, wisdom, and goodness, but, as any good empiricist knew, "simple" ideas carry the greater force and certainty. The theologian's balance, Burke implies, covers a vital imaginative fissure between God's power and love, a fissure that leaves power uppermost. Burke thus divides the Trinity and conforms God to the distinction of sublimity and beauty, truth and its ameliorating ornament. The science-fictional allergy to Christianity's soft, amiable, and reassuring God has roots in this displacement of beauty in favor of the sublime.

Princeton library in the early eighteenth century had sufficient holdings to inform Jonathan Edwards about the new enthusiasm for the sublime.[41] Nothing of that, however, informs his use of the word, which is conventional and without any philosophical weighting. He implies the traditional reference to height or elevation, contrasting carnal with Christian joy as of a "vastly more pure, sublime and heavenly nature" or describing the "purity, beauty, sublimity and glory of the visible heavens as one views it in a calm and temperate air."[42] Not only is there no trace of the hierarchized distinction of sublimity and beauty, but Edwards actively pursues the paradoxical inseparability and coinherence of divine attributes, especially those relating to power and love. "There came into my mind," he recounts of one particularly formative experience,

> a sweet sense of the glorious majesty and grace of God, that I know not how to express. I seemed to see them both in a sweet conjunction: majesty and meekness joined together: it was a sweet and gentle, and holy majesty; and also a majestic meekness; an awful sweetness; a high, and great, and holy gentleness.[43]

Not merely gushing piety, Edwards develops the conjunction of what he elsewhere called diversities seemingly "utterly incompatible in the same subject" within a doctrine of divine beauty as the eternal source of the objective and subjective conditions of beauty in creation.[44] As Edwards understands it, the inner plenitude of God and the complex harmonies of God's work ground a doctrine of creation in which divine beauty demands and secures creaturely diversity, transcends the dualisms associated with sublimity, and preserves the incomparable distinction between Creator and creature.

## ON BEING AND BEING BEAUTIFUL

In posing the question of why God should create anything at all, the question Stapledon also pursued in connection with his Star Maker myth, Edwards proposes a thought experiment. Imagine, he suggests, an independent evaluator surveying all that is, the being of God and that of the creatures. If the assessor must judge the relative consideration to be given God and creation in identifying the purpose of creation, then, Edwards argues, the assessor will have no choice but to choose the divine interest over that of the creation. Evidently, given the terms of this reflection, "the whole system of created beings in comparison of the Creator would be found as the light dust of the balance (which is taken no notice of by him that weighs) and as nothing and vanity."[45] Far from a dismissal of creation's worth, this thought experiment arrives at creation's entire dependence upon God together with the fullness, goodness, and perfection of the divine being, both of which render absurd an independent concern with creaturely good over against the Creator. "As the

Creator is infinite, and has all possible existence, perfection and excellence," Edwards concludes, "so he must have all possible regard."[46] As the demiurgic crafter of different kinds of creation, Stapledon's Star Maker does not possess such plenitude. The myth leaves the question of being unasked and so implies the Star Maker's ultimate finitude; if creaturely dignity consists in recognizing, perhaps in somber resignation, dependence upon the Star Maker, it is irresistible power, not inexhaustible being, that requires the acknowledgment. In an early writing, Edwards ventures a demonstration of the necessity of an eternal being. He argues from the inability of the mind "to conceive of a state of perfect nothing."[47] Any attempt to think of nothing, he insists, is relative to some particular condition of being. Whatever the demonstrative force of this for Edwards' purpose, the argument points to the intimate priority of being in all our knowing. Edwards finds in the conception of being, as did Aquinas, the a priori of the intellect: "Whatever [the mind] knows and every time it knows it attains being."[48] What is distinctive about Edwards, however, appears in his claim that whenever the mind apprehends being, it also apprehends beauty. Mostly unremarked and taken for granted, being, according to Edwards, comes distinctively into the light of intellect and heart by way of "excellency," a term synonymous with beauty.

Edwards indicates the range of this understanding of beauty or "excellency" with the striking claim that not only is excellency the supreme concern of human beings but, in truth, they are "concerned with nothing else."[49] In being concerned with anything at all, human beings are always concerned with existence, and, since being implies beauty for Edwards, "being always presents itself to the creature in some determinate form of beauty or deformity."[50] Unlike sublimity, with its double movement of pain and pleasure, of threatened overwhelming giving way to identification, beauty consists in the myriad forms of "consent" or agreement among difference, from the lines idly doodled on a page or notes in a melody, to the collaborations of a community and the mutualities of human love. In simplest terms, beauty may be reduced to "likeness of ratios" such as three objects placed equidistant on a surface. Only by way of abstraction, however, either of presentation or of reflection, do human beings experience consent in this way since, in the context of knowing, many other harmonious relationships are in play. Experience of beauty limited to such simple regularities is, perhaps, found in animals such as ticks that register their environment according to a very limited number of "carriers of significance."[51] Human beings, however, know beauty as proportion or "complex beauty," which involves multiple, varied occurrences of likeness, the disproportions between which are harmonized within a larger context.[52] Broadly speaking, the more complex the beauty and the greater the disproportions mediated within it, the greater the beauty by way of the degree and multiplicity of consent. Complex beauty, therefore, brings out a further dimension of beauty: beauty is both the agreement of particular elements one with another and the agreement of particular elements in relation to a whole, ultimately to all that is. Beauty admits, therefore, Edwards argues, of a "universal definition," which is "the consent of being to being, or being's consent to entity."[53]

In his unpublished paper "The Mind," Edwards explains excellency beginning with the beauty of patterns and the proportions of objects. However natural a starting point for purposes of clarity, this account of material beauty is nevertheless informed decisively by what Edwards has to say about "spiritual harmonies."[54] Only minds have the capacity for spiritual beauty since it consists in the agreement and appreciation of being by knowing and willing beings. What Edwards terms "secondary beauty," the beauty of entities considered apart from this "union or propensity of *minds* to mental or spiritual existence," hangs ungrounded without the context of "primary beauty" or that "cordial" consent of being to being, which is love.[55] Secondary beauties, therefore, exist as images, analogies, and media of primary beauty, specifically of the love exchanged among God, Christ, and the Church. Edwards instances how the sun that "so perpetually, for so many ages, sending forth his rays in such vast profusion, without any diminution of his light and heat, is a bright image of the all-sufficiency and everlastingness of God's bounty and goodness."[56] Primary beauty, the consent of minds, provides these secondary beauties with their depth and openness beyond themselves. Minds give the conscious, spiritual consent of knowledge and will; they have the capacity to acknowledge beings not only for themselves but as entities within the universe of being or, to put this in traditional language, to know and love beings as creatures within God's creation. Primary beauties ramify without end, "are of vastly larger extent," because they involve the doublings and redoublings of minds' delight in one another, minds' delight in things as images and media of spiritual consent, and minds' delight in other minds' expressions of love to being.[57]

Without any qualification of the incomparable difference between Creator and creature, the centrifugal dynamics of primary beauty, as the creature finds itself within the reciprocities of creation, originate in God himself. God has infinite beauty within himself, without reference to created being, while the beauty of creatures "consists in loving others, in loving God, and in the communications of his Spirit."[58] Edwards is not qualifying his conviction that beauty consists in consent, in relation to another, but rather grounding his ontology within the Trinity. God *is* in the mutual love of Father and Son, eternal origin and eternal perfect image, and this reciprocal delight "makes the third, the personal Holy Spirit, or the holiness of God, which is His infinite beauty."[59] The Triune life is "God's infinite consent to being in general," since it is God's delight in his own plenitude, in infinite being, all created entities being that infinite being communicated. In contrast to Burke's psychological and physiological explanations, Edwards' answer as to why proportion—and, therefore, beauty—pleases human beings draws on this fundamental level of a Trinitarian ontology. Beauty always involves relations, not only, however, those at the level of parts to wholes or among material entities, but primarily between being and knowing, loving minds. Beauty is existence as known and loved and thus recognized as good. All entity exists, therefore, in and through consent, in the first place through the divine consent that is God's threefold joy in his own being and in that being shared as the forms of finite existence. The knowing and loving of finite minds is itself that infinite consent imaged and repeated by creatures. As consent, and as that bodily image of consent, beauty and proportion pleases because it is an assent to being, and such affirmation, Edwards argues, naturally pleases creatures who themselves exist as objects of consent.[60] Conversely, disproportion is always a dissent from being, a limiting of existence by a curtailment of its possible good. Since, Edwards argues, "entity is the greatest and only good," dissent from being or "contrariety to being is evidently an approach to nothing, or a degree of nothing . . . and the greatest and only evil."[61]

A comparison with Edwards clarifies the narrative and metaphorical strategies Lovecraft used in representing a cosmos of radical discordance, a cosmos in which the negation of being—in Edwards' terms, dissent from being—has primacy over being. Lovecraft imagined his universe via the disproportions, threats, and ruptures of the sublime. Characters and their narratives fragment or dissolve into incoherence from contact with an environment of beings inimical to their existence. In turn, Lovecraft implies, even the most horrendously eldritch among these consuming entities have their own inevitable doom from the depredations of entities that environ them. To every being, there exists a sublime negation. Such is the way of things all the way down to the negating center itself, where "sprawls the blind idiot god Azathoth" and his sleazy begotten, chaotic Nyarlathotep. This inversion of a created cosmos appears most starkly over against the Edwardean universe in which created existence is the finite expression of infinite beauty. The contrast, however, is not merely between a theocentric and an atheistic imagination. Lovecraft's imagination occludes, as does Stapledon's, the question of existence itself, the primordiality of being that Edwards intimates in his claim that "it is a contradiction to suppose that being itself should not be."[62] Lovecraft's discordances exist; his violations, even his crawling chaos, have their being and, to that extent, deconstruct the Lovecraftian vision of an ultimate and universal dissent from being, the primacy of negation. Lovecraft's horrors, expressing his inverse doctrine of creation, depend on the illusions of ultimate negation possible through the theatrical props of sublimity.

Happiness depends on the perception of beauty. The breadth of this claim, as opposed to regarding perception of beauty as one source of happiness, derives from Edwards' ontological account of the beautiful, which coordinates happiness with consent to being. The consent that constitutes happiness is threefold: the consent of a being to its own being, the consent of a being to being-in-general, and the consent of being-in-general to its own being.[63] Since there can be no being, either of minds or things, without some agreement to being, Edwards concludes that "one alone cannot be excellent . . . for in such a case there can be no manner of relation no way."[64] Edwards describes, therefore, an intersubjective universe, in which creatures capable of knowledge and will exist as trajectories of consent that—in existing, knowing, and loving—participate in God's own infinite consent to being, mediated through spiritual agreements, one with another, as that consent is relayed and imaged through the innumerable consents that constitute the corporeal world.[65] "The beauty of the world," Edwards summarizes, "consists wholly of sweet mutual consents, either within itself or with the supreme being."[66] This society of beauties, however, is not an eternal tableau of essences but consists "in actual relations and tendencies among determinate beings."[67] In a temporal creation, beauty is always making beautiful, beauty in the process of exceeding itself. The theological grounding of this resides in Edwards' treatment of the distinction and relation of Creator and creature, a doctrine of transcendence and immanence that, unlike accounts of the sublime God, avoids their disjunction.

If sublime language, landscape, and art, as the tradition from Addison onward agreed, raised in the mind or prepared the way for the idea of God, the character of that idea was determined by the imagination of overwhelming and unlimited power. The imagination of divine power, however, engaged not simply a crushing potency directed outward but the implication of an entire self-sufficiency. Consequently, the elevation of humanity, mediated in the experience of sublimity, also involved the realization of freedom, from Addison's gentleman receiving "a kind of Property in everything he sees," through the liberated scope of imagination and intellect in Young and Baillie, through Burke's sublimity serving "passions of self-preservation," to Kant's discovery of moral autonomy in rational transcendence of the sensible world.[68] In these interpretations of sublimity, God and humanity appear as autonomous powers, albeit greater and lesser; a self-sufficient, independent God stands over against a free humanity on its own way to self-sufficiency. The theme of self-sufficiency continues in the technological sublime, where locomotives "annihilate space and time" and bridges "lend a myth to God," and it is a frequent, often now antitheological, theme of the science-fictional sublime, Stuart's "Forgetfulness" and the cowboy's cyberspace liberation from "the meat" being just two examples.[69] Divine "self-sufficiency," classically termed "aseity," is a traditional notion, but much depends on its interpretation. Edwards takes it up as a *crux interpretum* on which depends a proper understanding of God's transcendence and immanence.

"Many," Edwards writes, "have wrong notions of God's happiness, as resulting from his absolute self-sufficiency, independence, and immutability."[70] The error lies in separating God's happiness from God's creativity by way of interpreting self-sufficiency in terms of self-containment and the absence of connection *ad extra*, an interpretation that corresponds to the anthropology of persons as individual systems for self-preservation. According to such "wrong notions," the connection between creation and the divine nature is indirect: God is able to create, but whether or not God does so makes no difference to the nature of deity. From this perspective, coordinating creation directly with the nature of God would make creation necessary to God and, therefore, undermine God's self-sufficiency. Edwards refuses this logic by interpreting self-sufficiency as plenitude: God "is an infinite fullness of all possible good . . . of every perfection, of all excellency and beauty, and of infinite happiness."[71] Since the governing perfection of perfections here is beauty—which Edwards appropriates to the biblical term "glory"—that wherein "the truest idea of divinity does consist" requires that the divine plenitude is inherently, by virtue of its own perfection, self-communicative. As the *splendor* of order (Augustine) or form (Aquinas), beauty shines, gives itself.[72] This, Edwards points out, "is agreeable to . . . God's glory being so often represented [in Scripture] by an effulgence, or emanation, or communication of light, from a luminary or fountain of light."[73] God is not, therefore, first self-sufficient and then effulgent. God's self-sufficiency is a plenitude apt for an eternal overflow without diminishment. The internal self-communication of God's Triune life naturally overflows in fullness of being, communicated as what is not God, creation. Understood as beauty or glory, self-sufficiency ceases to fall within the logic of need, lack, or a necessity conceived in opposition to self-determination. Therefore, Edwards concludes, "we may suppose *that a disposition in God, as an original property of his nature, to an emanation of his own infinite fullness, was what excited him to create the world.*"[74]

Edwards tolerates no qualification of God's uniqueness: as the origin of all diversity within the creation, the distinction between God and creation transcends worldly difference.[75] God, the "Being of beings," is the "sum and comprehension of all existence and excellence"; indeed, strictly speaking, Edwards remarks, God alone may be said to be, a point that helped fuel later accusations of pantheism.[76] Far from dissolving transcendence into immanence, however, Edwards' doctrine of God, as self-communicating plenitude, demands the integrity and distinction of creation. The beauty of God's Triune life consists in an eternal and perfect self-replication, a threefold consent to being as such. Since there is nothing lacking in this infinite communication of divinity to divinity, then—if this fullness seeks, as it does by its own propensity, a further expression and emanation—that will mean a self-sharing in the form of entities that are not divine, a diffusion of God's perfections, to use Edwards' phrase, *ad extra*. From this proceeds not only the integrity of creation as nondivine, finite being but also the necessity of created variety, of its diverse multiplicity. The fullness of God's being is communicable entirely and without reserve only within the Triune life of coequal divinity, so in creating God shares his plenitude diffused into the diversity of creatures, as white light is refracted into the variety of colors.[77] Finite creatures, therefore, are never merely finite; even those that pass as whispers of life beyond human notice, bar the microscope, harbor a divine mystery and intimate the fullness whose overflowing they are. Thus, a true knowledge of objects must be the knowledge of God and that not merely by way of a further inference or argument, as implicitly for Addison and Young, but in the immediate "tasting" of God's glory when the depth of creation's beauty is recognized through the Holy Spirit.[78] Again, since the diffusion of God's perfections can never stand completed, Edwards conceives temporality as the necessary medium of God's self-giving, rather than as a limitation to be overcome. Heaven must, therefore, be a dynamic condition of eternal beautifying in which the reception of God's perfections increases without end. "How happy is that love," Edwards enthuses, "in which there is an eternal progress . . . wherein new beauties are continually discovered, and more and more loveliness, and in which we shall forever increase in beauty ourselves."[79] Transcendence and immanence, therefore, are not mutually qualifying but mutually implied: God's immanence as communicating the existence of creation is the immanence of his transcendence as the Being of beings.

Edwards made his boldest metaphysical move against the principal joint that connected Newtonian physics and sublime aesthetics.

As the respectable person's enthusiasm, the sublime sustained the possibility of religious experience within a mechanistic order, the machine being so perfect a model for the cosmos that "no reasonable man can doubt it."[80] According to the mechanical hypothesis, as it was termed, bodies "act upon each other, purely and properly by themselves."[81] Two theological consequences follow. A mechanical order is contrived for equilibrium, for self-preservation through time, an image gratingly at odds with the biblical creation, which is a narratable creation, open to God's continuing creative action. Should Christian respect for Scripture still insist, as for most early Newtonians it did, on God doing something unilateral every once in a while, that will take the form of divine "intervention," of breaching or suspending the laws of nature, a position that, again, reduces divine action to a power exerted at the same ontological level as the motions of parts in the world machine. The mechanical hypothesis also distinguished the action of God establishing the order at time's beginning from his relationship to "the subsequent course of nature."[82] Having once disposed matter into its proper order and "established those *rules of motion* . . . which we are wont to call the *laws of nature*," God's action is henceforth set at one remove from creation. Substances having a power of self-determination independent of the direct action of God—bodies acting "purely and properly by themselves"—now stood between the creative action of God and the condition of creation at any point in time. In Robert Boyle's advocacy of nature as mechanism, this reconfiguration of God's relationship to creation issues in the famous metaphor of the Strasbourg clock, the motions of which "once set a-moving, proceed according to the artificer's first design."[83] All the parcels of matter "perform their functions upon particular occasions by virtue of the general and primitive contrivance of the whole engine."[84]

Edwards contests the mechanical hypothesis as both scientifically unnecessary and theologically catastrophic. He first asks after the properties of atoms, the indivisible, impenetrable, and primitive constituents of bodies that move within the machine "purely and properly by themselves." His starting point is entirely in line with the "corpuscular" theory of his time, but his first move entails a profound conceptual simplification that leads Edwards to a theological insight independent of what is today a redundant physical theory.[85] If atoms are indivisible and impenetrable, any talk of breaking an atom is only a misleading expression for its annihilation. Absolute solidity, the solidity of an atom, furthermore, has no other meaning than its indivisibility and impenetrability or entire resistance to annihilation. Atoms, however, are the bodies that make up bodies, the absolute solids that constitute the merely relatively solid. In other words, the being of bodies is their solidity; "body and solidity are the same."[86] An atom's power of resistance, then, exceeds any finite force possible; atoms have—indeed, they are—an infinite power of resistance. Edwards' conclusion makes the conceptual simplification explicit. That "certain unknown substance, which philosophers used to think subsisted by itself, and stood underneath and kept up solidity and all other properties . . . is nothing at all distinct from solidity itself" or an infinite power of resistance, which, speaking more plainly, "is the immediate exercise of God's power, causing there to be indefinite resistance in that place where it is."[87] "Substance," the underlying integrity of a material world, the basis of that self-determining action and movement according to laws of motion, Edwards exposes as the confused reification of divine power, the imposition of an imaginary entity between God and God's creation. Substance, solidity, body is no-thing but divine action. The so-called "primary qualities" of things, their "proper Figures and Motions," solidity, extension, figure, and mobility, always softened in our experience, as Addison admired, by God's pleasurable and providential provision for sensory effects of color and light—these Edwards resolves into God's continuous creating. Creation is precisely God's willing the world as an object of his thought, his intending those occasions of resistance that are atoms and the regularities of their motions and conglomerations, the consents that are the figure and proportions of bodies. The mechanistic and material world with its self-movement thus disappears, as does the narrative according to which beginning and continuance are sharply distinguished and answer to a different relationship between God and creation. God does not alienate to creation the power to persist; rather, God's "causing its existence, is altogether equivalent to an *immediate production out of nothing*, at each moment, because its existence at this moment is not merely in part from God, but wholly from him."[88]

Edwards' argument leads to a conclusion that at first blush appears ruinous to his theology of creation and consent. Dispensing with substance, he has evaporated matter and revealed an immaterial cosmos. In consequence, what stands in for the substance of all bodies "is the infinitely exact and precise and perfectly stable idea in God's mind." Since God communicates, under certain modifying laws of cognition, the ideas of bodies to human minds, "the material universe, exists nowhere but in the mind."[89] Reality, it seems, is a not so consensual hallucination, a condition grimly suspected by Philip Dick. If this is the case, Edwards' exercise in atomic theory saws off the branch on which sits his theological and aesthetic vision of consent to being, with its insistence on creation's diversity. Mechanism makes way for unreality and a monism of minds reminiscent of the sublimities of Myraa's world. The great divide in Edwards' universe, though, does not lie between minds and the objects thought by minds, as in philosophical idealism. The distinction of distinctions—here, the governing difference—is that between the plenitude of the God who wills finite expression of his perfections and created, receiving being, the creatures, both minds and bodies, that exist as the effusions of God's being *ad extra*. Edwards' theological suggestiveness lies not in entirely redundant notions about atoms, nor in the particular formulation of his immaterialism, but rather in his rigorous commitment to a doctrine of creation as reality other than God but also absolutely dependent upon God as the finite form of his self-communication.

Far from being unreal, therefore, bodily reality has its own proper existence distinct from the ways humans apprehend it or the notions they form about it. God wills bodily reality as the object of his knowledge and love, expressive in its constituent relations of his own consent to being, and he also wills the regularities and conditions according to which bodily reality is perceived and known by minds. God's action, his willing the dynamics of creaturely being, is direct and continuous—creation thus always entirely dependent upon God at each moment—and those dynamics are bound to rules of God's own choosing, rules discovered by human beings as laws of nature. Laws of nature, Edwards explains, are "the stated methods of God's acting with respect to bodies, and the stated conditions of the alteration of the manner of his acting."[90] Newtonian science—or, for that matter, any other science—investigates the world according to divine action, the regularities of which do not preclude their openness to novelty since they are the actions of God, not mechanism. In sum, bodies are actions of God that result in the world given to minds, to minds that apprehend that world also according to God's action—the dull boredom of the dejected, the worshiper's perception of creation's glory, the lover's knowing the beloved, the owl's sighting of the tiny vole. Minds exist as actions of God, who wills their powers and patterns of perceiving, knowing, loving, and continuing through time. In the case of humans, at least, these actions result also in the capacity to know and love God, to return the consent to being that they are.

Nothing in science, exploration of nature, social life, affection, or daily experience is changed in such an unqualified account of creation's dependence, and yet, in truth, everything does change because the cosmos is apprehended neither as a machine nor as an environment the immensities of which alienate the human or inspire fantasies of autonomous power. Those whose consent to being is consent to God as Being of beings do not dwell in Stapledon's universe, to which mind is accidental and probably anomalous; though, at the same time, in consenting to God, they have no reason to deny the natural processes, interactions, and contingencies according to which intelligence evolves. The physical world is an intermedium of perceiving, knowing, loving, delighting, the field or sensorium in relation to which God distributes his perfections of knowledge, love, joy as finite occasions of consent to being. Beauty, as Edwards understood, inspires mimesis, from its repetitions in art through the desire to share the vision or hearing or touch with others, through the reciprocities of regard and devotion, to the imitation of Christ.[91] Creation's myriad and fertile forms of proportion and consent have their teleology in the replication by a diverse creation of God's eternal consent to being. This replication is ordinary and ubiquitous, in the "recreation" of spiders, as noticed by Edwards, floating by their webs caught on the air currents, to the human dancer poised in the intermediation of body and thought and the joy of her spectators. In human beings, creation becomes conscious of itself as the glorification and expression of the divine beauty. "Intelligent beings," as

Edwards puts it, "are the consciousness of creation . . . whereby the universe is conscious of its own being, and of what is done in it, of the actions of the Creator and Governor with respect to it."[92] The bodily world is itself fulfilled in the communion of being known and loved as the gift and medium of God's self-communication. The seriousness with which Edwards takes the created differentiation of bodies and minds, and the abiding importance of the bodily, appears in his eschatology. Far from an ultimate monism of mind, the physical creation is taken up into humanity's eternally perfecting participation in the divine beauty. "Without doubt," he writes concerning the joy of the resurrected in heaven, "God can contrive matter so that there shall be other sort of proportions . . . may raise another sort of pleasure in the sense, and in a manner to us inconceivable, that shall be vastly more ravishing and exquisite."[93] As does Addison, he speculates on the extension of human powers in heaven, but, significantly, whereas Addison yearns for imaginative powers freed from the body, Edwards anticipates the enhancement of the senses. Surely, he writes, "our capacities will be exceedingly enlarged, and we shall be able to apprehend, and to take in, more extended and compounded proportions . . . thousands of different ratios at once to make up the harmony."[94]

God delights in his own plenitude, the fullness of all being, beauty, and goodness, and that delight cannot but be a delight desiring communication, an infinite expansion of an infinite good. If God rejoices in his own perfections, he must also take joy in their exercise, exhibition, and expression. That, Edwards says bluntly, is a "natural conclusion."[95] An eternal and infinite diffusion in the form of a creation that is not infinite opens that creation not only, as Edwards saw, to an infinite progress for human beings in knowledge and love but also, by implication, to an infinite diversity of expression, of living forms, within that creation. If any particular universe is finite both ontologically and, given the workings of entropy, temporally, then the notion of successive universes, though without the benefit of the sublime Mayor Amalfi, suggests itself as a possible consequence of understanding creation as an infinite self-communication of God's plenitude—God being, "if I may so say, an infinite quantity of existence," writes Edwards.[96] Not surprisingly, Edwards limits minded consent to human beings—and angels—but he also acknowledges, with some acute observations, the distinctive ways in which nonhuman creatures appear to enjoy their activity and environment.[97] If God communicates his own perfections both as the experienced world and in the forms of experiencing themselves—of knowing and loving—then nonhuman modes of perceiving the creation, such as the dog's olfactory world or the bat's sonar touching, add to the multiple forms of consent to being through differing disclosures and purchases on creation.[98] Recalling a major science fiction topos, perhaps intelligent life elsewhere in the cosmos knows and loves in ways entirely incomprehensible to us, revealing creation in touches and tastes we may not know. Such diversity exists as analogy, proportionate to God's perceiving and consenting to finite being. God's perception, Edwards argues, "is so much more sensible and lively and perfect that created minds are, in comparison of Him, like dead, senseless, unperceiving subjects."[99]

In an evolving universe, beauty is achieved across ages as finite forms of consent multiply in number, range, and complexity. Destruction, loss, the breakdown of systems that support the being of creatures are a part, at least, of what Christians call "evil." Evil persists as the threat and violation of dissent to being, though such dissent can never be absolute, given the priority of being itself. The evil perpetrated by free beings capable of refusing their creaturely calling in the interests of self and tribe constitutes a greater dissent still, just as the consent of minds exceeds the beauty of bodily proportion. Humans pursue their vocation, Edwards tells us, through knowledge and action that in the particular consorts with and so contributes to the beauty of the entire sphere of being. Evil lies in the elevation of lesser communities of consent—individual, family, class, nation, race, species—above the whole. Though Edwards did not develop this conclusion, the immediacy of God's action in creation and the perfection of his knowing it—of which Adam's "knowing" of Eve is the proper metaphor—fund the recognition that God, in communicating his perfections, comes to share in the suffering of their finite expression. Christ, of course, is central here as the repetition within the finite and fallen world, and so under the conditions of suffering, of the eternal consent to being that proceeds within the Trinity as the Spirit mediates the reciprocal giving of the Father and the Son. Imitating Christ, Christians themselves perform in innumerable variations of style and narrative, the living exegesis of Jesus' singular, definitive, and fertile consent. Consent multiplies without end in this diffusion of excellency. In his life and death, Christ brings humanity and divinity, glory and suffering, judgment and mercy into redeeming and beauteous consent. Christ thus exemplifies Edwards' identification of beauty with complexity and range of agreement, while also showing why sublimity, as the privileging of power, fails as a Christian theological category. In Christ, Edwards discovers such "a conjunction of such really diverse excellencies, as otherwise would have seemed to us utterly incompatible in the same subject . . . infinite highness and infinite condescension . . . infinite glory and lowest humility . . . infinite majesty and transcendent meekness."[100] Unlike sublimity, beauty, understood in terms of the structuring proportions of being and the multiplying relations of consent, sustains the Christian identification of power and love.

## THE AGAPEIC IMAGINATION

Edwards' theology indicates a constructive path for Christian reflection, a Trinitarian and christocentric way responsive to the intellectual challenges of early modernity and rigorously critical of the disjunction of transcendence and immanence that hobbled theologies informed by the sublime. On the negative side, that places a question mark against many representations of the Christian God within science fiction, especially when those are motivated by the science-fictional sublime. More positively, though, the move from sublimity to beauty opens up an appreciative perspective on the excellency of science fiction itself.

Whether as the object of polemic, reappropriated as human transcendence, or, with Stapledon, reinterpreted as post-Christian creation myth, the sublime God, in leaving the mystery of existence unaddressed, was left with a compromised transcendence and appeared as the supreme force among cosmic forces, the universe's nine-hundred-pound gorilla. Classically, however, Christian theology has sought to conceive creation as the gift of being, the occasion of an abiding ontological generosity in which the diversity and integrity of beings express the divine plenitude. Only as the wholly transcendent source of existence is God immanent as their intimate origin.

From the internal Trinitarian diversity of God's being, in which the Son is eternally differentiated from the Father and eternally returns to the Father in the Spirit, originates the integrity and otherness of creation. The Trinitarian relations also ground the internal diversification of creation and the glorifying of that diversity within the divine life. Again, the Trinity provides the metaphysical context for Edwards' aesthetics and for an analysis of beauty that concludes "one alone cannot be excellent."[101] Lives in consonance with creation, the possibility of which Christians find renewed in the imitation of Christ, discover the intimacy of consent but also its distance, the refusal of that closeness that absorbs the known into the already known, into the self's familiarities. Creation as the beautifying complex of consents requires that the acknowledgment and care of other lives is ordered to the horizon of creation as the open community of beings constituted and fulfilled by God's unceasing, creative consent. Spiritual consent, the consent of minds and wills, involves an ascetic generosity, ascetic from the persisting need to convert into the distance of generous regard narrower loyalties and impulses to dominate, disregard, or deny difference. The self is denied for the sake of the other, without the consenting relation to which the self loses itself as well as the other. Appreciating creation as a beautifying field of difference, of coming into consent, requires an agapeic turn of mind and will, an agapeic imagination "in which thinking is for the sake of the other."[102] The contemporary significance and challenge of science fiction, at least potentially, lies in the imagination of creaturely otherness, in the disciplined imagining of different lives, from humanity's future selves to forms of entity so alien as to reveal the human in the limits of its powers of representation. This displacement—in which, through a form of self-denial, imagination attempts otherness—belongs not to the sublime, which dislocates only to recenter the human, but to beauty as consent to being.

At first blush, science fiction might not seem a likely genre within which to discover the workings of agapeic imagination. John Carter bounding over the Martian frontier and showing the interplanetary foreigners what a real man is made of is not an encouraging start, while from Wells' Martians descend a long line of aliens serving to project cultural fears and characterized as negative images of human ideals. Run-of-the-mill space opera often indulged genocidal fantasies, while racially motivated anxieties had heroes frothing at the thought of alien paws on human women, as in A. T. Locke's "Vandals of the Stars" (1930). Not all aliens made the ladies faint and the men bristle, though. Good aliens did appear in the pulp magazines but mostly confined by the strategy of using the admirable alien as the basis for a moral critique of humanity. Given this edifying purpose, success in the imagining of alien life occurs mostly in inverse relation to the insistence on the moral. Edmond Hamilton's "Devolution" (1936), for instance, features blob-like telepathic aliens who create material culture out of their own thoughts but turn out to be our familiar selves in the person of ancestors from which today's humans have devolved into the physically grotesque, mentally negligible, and morally benighted. Despite the aliens enjoying the form of blancmange, the contrast here reprises, rather crudely, older comparisons between angelic and fallen human life.

Fortunately, this is not the whole picture, not even for the earlier decades of science fiction. Stanley Weinbaum's "A Martian Odyssey" (1934) describes a series of Martian life forms, all of whom appear cartoonishly comic. The perplexed, self-questioning tone of the story, however, undercuts the comic appearances with the suggestion that the comedy is merely a function of the narrator's—and reader's—misapprehension. The narrator rescues an ostrich-like creature from what is a conventional grotesque—black, tentacled, and shapeless. He quickly problematizes any identifying comparison in the recognition that all such likenesses fail. "The Martian wasn't a bird, really," he admits. "It wasn't even birdlike."[103] Even the creature's difference resists pinpointing: "We were *somehow* mysterious to each other." The narrator, Jarvis, calls "him" "Tweel," which he is sure is a miserable attempt to reproduce, from the creature's attempts to communicate, what he thinks is its name, though it might well not be. Since Tweel has a weapon, picks up fragments of the Earthman's language, and eventually manages to communicate a few quite complex ideas across the gulfs of difference, Jarvis concludes he is intelligent, perhaps more mentally agile than himself. Tweel's behavior, though, as the two travel over the bleak Martian landscape, remains enigmatic; the narrator ventures explanations, then thins them into guesses. "I sang songs," he recalls, "and I suspect Tweel did too; at least, some of his trillings and twitterings had a subtle sort of rhythm."[104] Jarvis' tentative judgments betray his desire to understand, a tender longing for communication that, nevertheless, refuses to betray itself into a false certainty. "Our minds were alien to each other," he admits, "and yet—we *liked* each other."[105]

The plot of "A Martian Odyssey" develops along conventional, even clichéd, pulp adventure lines. The pair follow some barrel-like creatures into their underground labyrinth, where, to no intelligible purpose, these mysterious entities grind debris and then themselves under a huge wheel. In good frontier fashion, Jarvis steals from these creatures a glowing crystal with apparent healing properties. The multieyed barrels give chase and finally corner Jarvis and the now seemingly loyal Tweel, who, with due desperation, fight them off until rescued at the last minute by Jarvis' colleagues, after which Tweel himself takes off and disappears. The clichés of this plot, however, and its neat resolution, function to set off the enigmas and uncertainties of Jarvis' encounters. The creature remains with Jarvis in the closing battle despite its evident ability to escape. Jarvis interprets this help as friendship, but the context of persisting enigma and misapprehension leaves open other motivations, including ones without a human analogy. Similarly, when the travellers meet a mindless silicon beast mechanically building pyramids from bricks of its waste matter, the effect is comic: the creature is literally shitting bricks. The joke dissipates, however, in the discovery that the silicon animal is utterly alone and has been repeating the same actions for half a million years. Again, the immediate impression gives way in a realization of eerie, unsettling strangeness. Though Jarvis reverts to his pulp type in stealing the crystal, the complexity of his reactions, to Tweel especially, emerges also in contrast to those of his colleagues who form the audience for his story. The other Martian explorers, though they accept the details of Jarvis' report, continue to joke, condescend, make insulting comparisons between Jarvis and Tweel, and, from time to time, jump into a strongly objectivizing scientific interest. Jarvis' bewildered desire to understand the alien, to achieve some inkling of what it is like to *be* this creature, and his perplexity that prevents interpretative closure together form the agapeic counterpoint to his audience's reactions and to the invitations of the surface comedy and clichés of adventure.

The genre's implicit rules of plausibility allow science fiction a peculiar freedom to imagine other life. Despite the enduring appeal of tentacles and heads like clam shells, science fiction has broken free of difference cashed in purely physical terms in order to imagine mentalities and cultures. Writers have also managed to represent the difficulties, the asceticism, and the limits of the agapeic imagination. In enjoying this freedom to play with otherness, however, science fiction is subject to one crucial formal constraint. Fans, writers, and critics have debated the question as to how much science makes fiction science fiction and whether that science must have the integrity of actual or arguably possible scientific knowledge. Brian Aldiss voiced perhaps the softest position in claiming that science fiction was no more written for scientists than ghost stories for ghosts. The hard view, however, maintains that, irrespective of whether or not scientists read this genre, fiction ceases to qualify as science fiction unless its "standards of plausibility" are "derived . . . rigorously and systematically, from science."[106] Though the stricter view sounds that it might yield a clear practice of differentiation between, say, science fiction and fantasy, the variety of disciplines claiming scientific status and the arguments over what qualifies the claim in any particular case leave the hard science standard on shifting sands. Science fiction can hardly designate a genre indifferent to science, though. It may be better to suggest that science fiction is a mode of realistic fiction in which the reader is implied as belonging epistemically to a culture that assumes the authority of the scientific method, as it has developed since the seventeenth century. A science-fictional universe, therefore, is one accessible to that method in principle, and, therefore, to that extent epistemically shared by the reader. Lovecraft's "Call of Cthulhu," for instance, for all its apparently fantastic elements may be distinguished from a supernatural tale such as an M. R. James ghost story by its staging as a scientific investigation that conforms to the methods of anthropology, forensic science, history, and philology. As far as the agapeic imagination is concerned, this entails that, however extreme the otherness imagined and however difficult its imagining, this fiction represents the horizon of radical difference opened up by the scientifically achieved defamiliarization of a universe in which human beings constitute, as Stapledon loved to point out, but a fleeting and tiny part.

Among the many alien forms explored in English-language science fiction, the hive or group mind, in which individuals exist more or less entirely as functions of the collective, poses particular imaginative difficulties, partly arising from the strength of individualism within the science fiction imaginary. Stapledon's Second Men have their nemesis in warfare with brutal and obsessive Martian invaders, a struggle that illustrates this author's recurring moral about the deadly consequences of tribal prejudice whether lived out on the national, racial, religious, or interplanetary level. The Martians themselves provide an early example of that black sheep among alien cultures, the group or hive mind: "The typical Martian organism was a cloudlet, a group of free moving members dominated by a 'group-mind.' But in one species individuality came to inhere, for certain purposes, not in distinct cloudlets only, but in a great fluid system of cloudlets. Such was the single-minded Martian host which invaded the earth."[107] To ensure the reader does not evade the homiletic point, Stapledon follows up his description with the surprising assertion that "there was no really fundamental difference between the distinctively Martian and the distinctively terrestrial forms of life."[108] Whether sporting as a cloud jelly or whisked along as relatively independent and precarious cloudlets, Martians, read as allegory, exhort the precious importance of individuality and diversity and warn of horrors occurring when groupthink takes over from individual reflection. A good many of their successors among hive-minded aliens, up to *Doctor Who*'s cybermen and *Star Trek*'s Borg, function similarly as "sociophobic artifacts," imaginative figurations of shared fears.[109] Admittedly, Stapledon's treatment of group minds has more nuance than many in that he also insists on a positive form of group mind, a super mind in which individuals are taken up into a larger consciousness that nonetheless preserves and enriches individuality. Thus the protagonist of *Star Maker* retains his individual integrity while traveling nonetheless as an aggregating group mind. The final human, for his part, enjoying the peak experience of union with the "racial mind" "discovers himself to be embodied in all the bodies of the race. . . . He sees with all eyes, and comprehends in a single vision all visual fields."[110] This, of course, sounds more like an account of divine knowing than of a mode of cognition attributable to any worldly entity. Stapledon frequently makes this move of redeploying theological concepts within descriptions of cosmic phenomena, in the process failing to understand the particular logic of theological ideas. Omniscience, for instance, which this passage crudely echoes, is precisely the Creator's knowledge of what he has created and depends upon the relationship between maker and made, the existence of entities and the giver of that existence. Outside of that ontological relationship and applied to minds that do not create all they know, the Neptunians' quasi-divine knowing makes little sense. The problem, though, is not only a philosophical one; it lies also at the level of the imagination.

As in the case of Martians, Stapledon's didactic intent, which requires a plausible application of alien to human experience, often necessitates an emphasis on sameness as much as difference. This, together with his reliance on the sublime as a strategy for frog-marching the reader into imaginative acquiescence, prevents Stapledon achieving a properly agapeic imagination, despite his philosophical bows to the richness of difference within history and the cosmos. He fails both to convey the difficulty of apprehending difference, other than by simply stating it as a fact, and to intimate the interiority of a radically alien mind. For instance, Stapleton never describes his space-traveling and accumulating group mind with the kind of metaphorical precision that would suggest how such strangeness might be experienced. Stapledon describes abstractly; he asserts, but he does not convey. His final, Neptunian man therefore continues to sound like a condescending English schoolmaster fated to deal with aeons of distracted boys with their ties knotted beneath their ears. That the Neptunian tells the reader how impossible he finds the translation of his experience to the evolutionarily boneheaded simply rationalizes Stapledon's imaginative deficits. The lack of an agapeic imagination also undermines his ingenious physical descriptions. The last Neptunians have evolved an astronomical eye capable of scanning the heavens from the tops of their skulls. Without, however, a suggestion as to what it might be like to experience such a vision, the effect of describing it is mostly comic. Coleridge's famous distinction between "imagination" and "fancy" applies rather well to Stapledon, whose imagination lacks much feeling for organic wholes, for the plasticity and inwardness of living things. Stapledon was a visionary, and the consistency with which he explored his agonized agnosticism is admirable. He was, however, a fanciful visionary, his creatures the products of an additive process that works with "fixities and definites."[111] Lacking the sense of organism and, therefore, of persuasive intimations of interiority, they appear composed of parts, stitched and stuck together.

In contrast, C. J. Cherryh's *Serpent's Reach* includes a far happier attempt to imagine the alienness of a hive mind, one that may serve as an exemplar of the agapeic imagination in science fiction.[112] Cherryh sets her novel on a group of planets quarantined from the rest of colonized space. The quarantine preserves the ecological balance on worlds where humans exist in a tense but economically productive relationship with the insectoid majat. The embargo on contact, other than for trading purposes via a space station, also prevents this alliance from endangering worlds outside the quarantine, a threat that registers the more traditional fear of group minds. Majat colonies possess a highly intelligent hive mind vested in the hive-mother and variously and biochemically distributed among individual workers and warriors, only the latter having a minimal sense of individuality. Though workers and warriors die, the hive mind endures for millennia, the consciousness of the hive persisting and growing in memory and understanding. Cherryh's imaginative skill unhooks the majat from the evaluative tradition according to which group minds constitute either sublime threat or sublime achievement, as in Clarke's *Childhood's End*, and investigates the troubled interaction involved in the attempt to understand as opposed to overcome or deploy for advantage. That Cherryh's majat provoke visceral reactions of terror or revulsion in humans is unsurprising, especially as the tension of communicating with them is further heightened by the majat's need to touch in order to recognize and remember. The novel's protagonist, however, Raen a Sul hant Meth-maren, an outcast member of the ruling Kontrin, achieves an unusual intimacy with majat from the hive with whom her murdered family once had responsibility for trading. The enduring strangeness of this majat and human relationship is crossed by a subtle and tentative reciprocity requiring that both sides overcome its immediate reactions and open to the intermediation of a potentially dangerous consent:

> It hesitated, then stalked up to her, bowed itself, seeking touch. She lifted both her hands to its scent-patches. It absorbed this.

> Then it bowed further, and in a gesture very like a human kiss, opened its mandibles wide and touched the false chelae to her lips. The venomed spike was very close. The jaws gaping on either side. The wrong taste would snap them shut on reflex, and unlike another Warrior, she had no chitinous defense. . . . Yet the taste was sweet; it gently received taste from her. . . . "Danger," it concluded helplessly. Auditory palps swung forward and back. . . . "There is danger everywhere for blues." Raen offered her right hand to its mandibles, willful hazard, comforting gesture. "Hive-friend. Do you also bear taste of reds? Of Kethiuy? Of killing?"[113]

Within the difficulty of apprehending otherness, human beings discover their own alterity and contingency reflected back in the shock of majat realization. Majat know intelligence as, in practice, immortal, the hive maintaining an individual mind across generations. Humans, therefore, present majat with the appalling reality of "minds-who-died," an ontological horror seemingly so twisted that, at first, majat "fled such contact, unable to bear it."[114] As the plot develops, relations between these extremes of human and majat form a center around which occur other analogous negotiations with difference. Raen's development occurs as she realizes that she is alien among her own elite class, a realization that undermines for her the necessity and goodness of a social order that assigns differences of value and, therefore, fate among human classes. In a countermovement to Raen's education, the hegemonic Kontrin themselves discover the otherness internal to their culture, an evaded, suppressed truth of corruption and decadence. As the cultural context of instrumental power and control breaks down, the characters Raen most influences also change and do so as they grasp and negotiate essential and constructed differences in the forms of majat, Kontrin, and other human forms. Thus, azi humans bred for a compliant servitude and some of the betas, genetically modified for instrumental reasoning and unimaginative social conformity, penetrate barriers of socially and technologically imposed difference through the intermediation of enduring alterities of history and kind.[115] *Serpent's Reach*, therefore, both is an exercise in agapeic imagination, especially in the depiction of the majat, and represents that imagination operating at various levels within the novel, across species ande society and between those inside and outside the Reach's planetary system.

In their different ways—and many other examples might be given—"A Martian Odyssey" and *Serpent's Reach* seek to occupy an imaginative position beyond the anthropocentricity of the sublime and its elevation of the human. This agapeic imagining accomplishes a process of consent to being and being's diversity, a reaching toward the extremes of difference. Tracing the way of such consent as an ascetic, tentative process, generous in its suspension of judgment and aware that recognition comes with a difficult self-negation, this imaginative work is both a quest for beauty and beautiful in itself. As Edwards puts it, "Mind's love to mind must needs be lovely to beholding mind; and being's love to being in general must needs be agreeable to being that perceives it, because itself is a participation of being in general."[116] Consent, practiced in the form of fiction, stretches the imagination toward the plenitude of existence, envisioning otherness, not as overwhelming threat or an exhilarating accession of power, but as an invitation for understanding, respect, welcome. Such difficult welcome, though, explored here in the way of art, relativizes and makes all lesser loyalties, even to humanity, permeable to "the entire system of being." As science fiction makes abundantly clear—even as it leaves behind the sociophobics that depicted aliens as predictably monstrous in villainy—for an agapeic imagination consent to otherness is not incompatible with recognizing threat, indeed deadly threat. The researcher into the most fearsome viruses may similarly discover an excellence of being, a beauty, while acknowledging still their mortal invasions. Put theologically, the agapeic imagination experiments with the possibilities for existence and with the consent existence invites as existence within the horizon of God's creating. The agapeic imagination so witnesses that "there is nothing cannot be made to tender its beauty as the beauty of God."[117] Beauty shines as the worthiness to be, for Christians as the diffusion of divine perfections in the integrity of beings; in the discovery and rediscovery of that excellence, beauty promotes a shared delight that radiates in multiple and varied apprehensions, promoting imaginative and ethical action—the deeds of holiness. Above all, beauty decenters the beholder, something is more interesting than the self, and the self is only interesting in its consent to being, to creation as the proceeding of divine glory.

The sublime disaster within the sublime itself was separating this discourse of immensity from the beautiful, which was then downgraded. The sublime became thereby an aesthetics of power and, applied as the privileged language for the divine, rendered God as a supreme, though no longer transcendent, power. With power no longer interpreted by love, and transcendence relativized to supremacy of power, God demanded contestation and dispute from within the logic of the sublime itself: from that event structure of pain and pleasure that, in its delightful issue, elevated human power and autonomy. So, for Kant, the sublime's "negative pleasure" reveals the autonomy of practical reason, while God is displaced from the immediacy of creative and redemptive presence into serving as moral freedom's guarantor. Imagined sublimely, technology outruns nature as God's distinctive handiwork, and, in the apotheosis of a power unleashed from love, Oppenheimer could say of the atomic bomb that, for those who participated in its development, "it was a time of creation." Inheriting this discourse, the science-fictional sublime maintained, not without justification, a contest with a God already diminished.

The peculiar suggestiveness of science fiction for Christian faith lies not in its critique of divinity, which is largely misplaced, grappling as it does with the theological distortions of sublimity, but in its imaginations of radical otherness, which at their best attain to an agapeic imagination. This should prompt Christians to a wary examination of any anthropocentrism that limits their theological vision, especially in connection with doctrines of creation and eschatology. Irrespective of whether theologies fall into the categories of liberal or conservative, anthropocentric accounts of creation and its future often narrow theological concerns. Liberal theologies may be the worse in this case since their ontological imagination does not even rise to the level of angelic being. Animal life—other than as that life is related to or affected, mostly grievously, by human beings—thus remains marginal to systematic theological reflection. Questions as to the implications of nonterrestrial life, of human attitudes to its possibility, and of the role alien life plays in the contemporary imagination barely make a theological ripple. The alien and the animal connect at this point. A theologically responsible understanding of animal life, one that knows them as occasions of beauteous consent and created modes of apprehending God's glory, depends on appreciating their otherness, these aliens among whom humans live. Thinking through—and imagining—ways through such questions exposes the difficulty and the promise of negotiating difference, agapeically. Also, expanding the boundaries of the theological imagination, provoking an appropriate ontological curiosity about God's creativity, should return to the human itself and inform the Christian struggle against our species' terrible tribalisms. The nonhuman, aliens and animals, the possible and the actual, should provoke that consent to being that decenters us and so makes a whole range of ethical issues far more painful and difficult. That, though, is the price for renewing wonder in creation and in God's plenitude. Beauty, recovered as a transcendental (which is what Edwards did), reframes the human vocation as the agent in this particular world by which creation is expressed in speech—imagined, interpreted, and fostered as the glory of God shared *ad extra.* Technology, in this reframing, is desublimed, its powers reunited with agape, and harnessed to the beautiful, to the making of complex consent, the realization of life-giving reciprocities. Moving from the sublime to the beautiful thus frees the modern self from its self-imposed sublimity and restores the possibility of a theocentric vision.

# CONCLUSION

The BBC urged interest in the 2014 Winter Olympics by placing the games squarely within the context of the sublime. The much-repeated trailer, filmed in shades of icy blue, showed athletes grimly posturing for a battle with Alpine gorges, sheer cliffs, sheets of malevolent ice, dwarfing ridges, wild winds, and an implausibly magnificent mountain. A breathy voiceover boasts irresistible power by way of hokey doggerel: "I am the dreadful menace / The one whose will is done. / I will summon armies. / Of wind and rain and snow. / Not you, nor any other / Can fathom what is nigh." The trailer ends with the resort to solemn, emphatic capitals: "NATURE. WHO WILL CONQUER IT?" While the BBC was stirring the sports minded, another trailer advertised Darren Aronofsky's *Noah*, a movie that seems set to realize in CGI Thomas Burnet's most purple prose.[1] The discourse of popular sublimity—inherited from early modernity and mediated through Edward Young, John Martin, railway architecture, Adams' "great hall of dynamos," the Empire State Building, and much else—continues to serve as the literary and visual vocabulary for ecstasies of the overwhelming.[2] The sublime God also still adds his weight, albeit recast as nature, technology, human desire, or the allure of a European car. Popular culture thus continues on the trajectory of the sublime, which remains a principal device in the imaginative repertoire for representing, invoking, and celebrating power.

Science fiction has greatly enriched this repertoire and still informs it across a diversity of media. As throughout the history of sublimity, whether the popular sublime or that of the philosophers, the sublime has revealed and exalted the human subject, as the bearer and promise of spirit, as the one who bows before yet belongs with the inexpressible, as the inheritor of astounding powers, or as doomed but, at least, knowingly so. The sublime dynamic of pain and pleasure, even in the bleakness of *The Genocides* or Lovecraft's cynicism, reverts finally to the self, for all the evocation of otherness. The sublime has also energized and funded science fiction's critique of religion, from Campbell's Stewart stories and Stapledon's cosmic, evolutionary epics, to the apocalyptic of Zebrowski. Contesting the Christian sublime, science fiction created its own in the substance of space itself, the imagination of technology, the destiny of scientific reason, and the vast, disruptive exigencies of the universe itself. Not that sublimity went without its science-fictional satirists and critics—the powers of devastation served by "Push Button Officer X-127" in Roshwald's nuclear tale or, more farcically, Douglas Adams' "plutonium rock band" whose performance was "the loudest noise of any kind" in the galaxy and required an audience installed in "large concrete bunkers some thirty-seven miles from the stage."[3] Also, in *VALIS*, Philip K. Dick critiqued sublimity as a discourse of power and manipulation, opening up a dialectical relationship between unknowability and manifestation.

Along with shaping the popular sublime, science fiction has also mediated and metaphorized themes from the "high history" of sublimity, as in Zebrowski's Schopenhauerian "heart of fire." It is worth asking, therefore, whether the science-fictional sublime, especially as regards its insistent immanence and its glorification of power, has any commonality with the revival of interest in the sublime among philosophers over the last few decades. Though any detailed answer is beyond the scope of this book, the question has some importance since recent philosophical, and some theological, interest in the sublime has both maintained the rejection of beauty as well as stressed sublimity, in contrast to the beautiful, as an experience of the radically unrepresentable, ethically significant precisely because of its critique of all "totalities." The latter theme surfaced in *VALIS*, too, but there as a critique of the sublime—a sublime found in science fiction as the ecstasy of total and encompassing power, a derivative of the sublime God. Postmodern philosophy has claimed the sublime as the event that challenges claims to total knowledge, essential categories, settled traditions, and assured foundations by unmasking and relativizing into transience and immanence all representation and all forms. Among the texts of philosophical modernity, Kant's *Critique of Judgement* provides the starting point. For Kant, while the beautiful brings the mind to the edges of the human vocation, only the sublime so frees reason from sensibility that, as the imagination crashes, "our rational nature feels its superiority, its freedom from limits."[4] Freedom from limits here, however, means reason's transcendence of the empirical; it is moral autonomy, the vocation of rational self-legislation. The sublime restores the rational agent to "a meditative contemplation of *its own* native powers."[5] Sensible presentations must give way for this contemplation to occur, "for human nature does not of itself harmonize with the good, but only through violence, which reason exerts upon sensibility."[6]

Echoing Kant's reminder that sublimity lies in the ideas of reason and "not in the Object of nature," Lyotard argues that the sublime occurs as forms explode under the force of the "Idea": all forms "scatter themselves, tear themselves asunder."[7] The sublime demolishes forms—that is, in theological terms, those relations of consent by which creation participates in the divine beauty. The postmodern sublime breaks up forms by revealing them as configurations out of nothing, always vulnerable and exposed to an infinite, immanent potency that dissolves in order to gift the "extension of being and jubilation that come from inventing new rules of the game," in art, ethics, politics, across the field of human life.[8] The potency, though, is the potency of finitude and immanence, not the actuality of God's plenitude; this immanent potency infinitely reveals lack and only so drives change and movement. Since this sublime no longer engages Kant's practical reason, however, but rather Nietzsche's will to power, it threatens even more acutely fantasies of "Prometheus unbound" in a world of undiminishable conflict, despite the ethical seriousness of postmodern philosophers such as Lyotard.[9] Science fiction took up the sublime as overwhelming and demolishing power, a power thought of as once divine but now as immanent, whether threatening galaxies or ecstatically exceeding present human and technological limits. Sublimity, once described as the "pleasing rape," has always been a violent joy, sometimes a joy in violence. Postmodern philosophy—and the theology it has influenced—continues this in its own mode. At the least, it is hard to dismiss the science-fictional sublime as merely the popular distortion and betrayal of a purer philosophical vision. Embracing this sublime, postmodern theology as a "dynamic and sublime activity" reduces to a continual dissolution of all "determinate forms of theological expression."[10] Despite some verbal similarity, however, this is not the negative theology of classical Christianity. That dynamism is provoked by the always exceeding plentitude of the transcendent God, a plenitude that ensures that "in the end the negation itself be negated" by God's "dazzling darkness."[11] A later point on the trajectory of the sublime God, the postmodern sublime not only lacks but repudiates the plenitude of being, which is also why it maintains the triumphalism of sublimity over beauty. In contrast, a theology such as Edwards' might inspire recognizes creation as participation in the divine perfections. Beauty is not confined to the plane of the merely sensible—as it is for Kant—and through beauty the plane of immanence opens to the infinite God. Beauty mediates the mystery of the God whose beauty it is and so always elicits further forms of consent through the infinite extension and diversification of contemplation, imagination, invention, acts of love, forms of community, speech, and art. To this beauty, sublimity, if one still wants to use the term, returns as beauty's inexhaustible depth.[12] Beauty, in this sense, sustains difference and demands it, but not as the Heraclitean flux in which difference merely cancels and never secures being.

Among the most-visited sites in Houston's museum district, the Rothko Chapel holds fourteen monumental paintings by Mark Rothko, nine arranged in three triptychs, the rest hung singly. Almost monochrome, these faintly textured paintings in black with nuances of plum and purple surround the hushed, windowless space of the panreligious chapel. They glory in their stern, sublime voiding of all religious particularity, a gesture of rejection to all symbols and revelations, the purportedly liberating rebuke of all forms. Overwhelming the speech, the image, the song, and the story, the silent void remains unimpressed. Interpreters recognize that here Rothko brings the sublime to a pitch of black, consuming all contours. These somber paintings mediate the ecumenical hospitality of a panreligious chapel, and the decision to commission them reflects a very significant interpretation of the world's faiths. The chapel relativizes the distinctive narratives, rituals, beliefs, ethics, and philosophies of those faiths before a voiceless beyond that gathers them all in its condescending indifference. Akin to the theological sublime, especially in its postmodern form, the paintings' setting represents a particular—and theologically particular—understanding of religious faith and of the relationship between the divine and the world as a place in which the divine is known. Another contrasting imagination of a panreligious space, more in the spirit of an Edwardean vision, would be a plaza on which some hundred various folk declaimed, sung, told stories, gathered in rituals, sat, stood, knelt in prayer or adopted postures of meditation, argued, exercised charity, made peace, exhorted, read scriptures, forgave, laid on hands, anointed, observed laws, made love and friendship, and from time to time rowed hideously. At least, this prospect acknowledges the seriousness of forms, of that knowing the divine that faiths claim.

For Christian faith and theology, certainly, the incomprehensibility of God and God's revelation must not be set off against one another. Doing so renders God's incomprehensibility either partial and, therefore, finite, or else absolute, and, therefore, seals the world within its own immanence. In this connection, Philip Dick's *VALIS* takes on a tragic aspect. The novel critiques the control and coercive power associated with the sublime and with Gnosticism, its ancient analogue. Furthermore, the duality of Horselover Fat and Phil both affirms and denies manifestation in order to maintain an unknowable and transcendent divine. Dick's world, however, remains so sundered from the source of revelation that knowledge of the transcendent comes in spite of the world and as always strange to it. Again, this dualism threatens either to render the divine as merely opposed to the worldly and so finite, or to close down revelation altogether. In Edwards' terms, the world of *VALIS* lacks beauty, the occasions of proportion that as consents to being mediate God's beauty.

Sublime unrepresentability must give way to the beautiful or be transformed within it. Until February 2012, this took just a short walk from the Rothko chapel. Near the University of St. Thomas, a glass and wood structure figured the shape of a small Byzantine chapel, decorated by frescoes in the apse and dome.[13] Saints and angels crowd the lower part of the dome beneath the head and shoulders of Christ; in the apse, the archangels Michael and Gabriel revere the

Virgin Mary, on whose chest appears an image of the Christ child. The angels and the saints bear the beauty of Christ, as does the Virgin. They radiate from him, show the distribution of his glory, drawing the viewer's eyes upward and inward from the floor below. Christ and the Virgin are painted on an eternal space of blue; they come from and return to an inexhaustible mystery, bright and not dark, visible and always more invisible. As an Orthodox hymn proclaims, "No one could describe the Word of the Father; but when he took flesh from you, O Theotokos, he accepted to be described, and restored the fallen image to its former beauty."[14] The face of humanity's being in and from God comes to light again, and so creation is restored and the forms of being recognized as revealing the plenitude of God's beauty. The science-fictional delight in imagining the many forms of being calls thus to the Christian imagination, too.

# NOTES

## INTRODUCTION

1 Despite the influence of Longinus' *On the Sublime*, see below, p. 16.

2 See, for instance, Lap-Chuen Tsang, *The Sublime: Groundwork towards a Theory* (Rochester, N.Y.: University of Rochester Press, 1998).

3 See below. pp. 59–60.

4 For a recent example of how discussion of the sublime still orbits the "high history," see Timothy M. Costelloe, ed., *The Sublime: From Antiquity to the Present* (Cambridge: Cambridge University Press, 2012).

5 Jürgen Habermas, *The Structural Transformation of the Public Sphere: An Inquiry into a Category of Bourgeois Society* (Boston: MIT Press, 1991), 14–26, 57–67.

6 Joseph Addison and Richard Steele, *Selections from "The Tatler" and "The Spectator"* (London: Penguin Classics, 1988); J. Aiken and A. L. Aiken, "On the Pleasure Derived from Objects of Terror; with Sir Bertrand, a Fragment," in *Miscellaneous Pieces in Prose* (Belfast: James Magee, 1774).

7 See, for instance, Jean-François Lyotard, "The Sublime and the Avant-Garde," in *The Inhuman: Reflections on Time* (Cambridge: Polity, 1993), 89–107.

8 George Slusser, "The Origins of Science Fiction," in *A Companion to Science Fiction*, ed. David Seed (Oxford: Wiley-Blackwell, 2005), 40.

9 Roger Luckhurst identifies these conditions as the following: universal literacy and primary school education; new cheap magazine formats; the democratization of scientific and technical education; and the widespread penetration of daily life by modern technologies. Luckhurst, *Science Fiction* (Cambridge: Polity, 2005), 16–17.

10 The cover is reproduced in Steve Holland et al., *Sci-Fi Art: A Graphic History* (Lewes, U.K.: ILEX, 2009), 47.

11 Lester del Rey, "Nerves," in *The Science Fiction Hall of Fame*, vol. 2A, *The Greatest Science Fiction Novellas of All Time Chosen by the Members of the Science Fiction Writers*, ed. Ben Bova (New York: Orb Books, 2009), 157. "Nerves" was published in 1942; del Rey expanded the novella into a full-length novel in 1956. For the biblical echoes, see, amongst others, Exod 19:15; 1 Kgs 19:11–14; Ps 121:1 (all KJV).

12 Richard Matheson, *The Shrinking Man*, new ed. (London: Gollancz, 2003), 172, 200.

13 The more felicitous word would be "sublimated," but using the technical psychoanalytical term would be confusing—not that there are not important connections. See Clayton Crockett, *Interstices of the Sublime: Theology and Psychoanalytic Theory* (New York: Fordham University Press, 2007).

14 Samuel R. Delany, *Babel-17* (London: Gollancz, 2010), 62.

15 On the term "social imaginary": "There is thus a *unity* of the total institution of society and . . . this unity is in the last resort the unity and internal cohesion of the immensely complex web of meanings that permeate, orient, and direct the whole life of the society considered, as well as the concrete individuals that bodily constitute society. This web of meanings is . . . the 'magma' of *social imaginary significations* that are carried by and embodied in the institution of the given society and that, so to speak, animate it." Cornelius Castoriadis, *World in Fragments: Writings on Politics, Society, Psychoanalysis, and the Imagination* (Stanford: Stanford University Press, 1997), 7; emphasis original. "Magma" is important here as a metaphor for a dynamic complex of meanings containing tensions, incompatibilities, developments, combinations, dominance, transformations, changing centers, and shifting margins. Thus, "that magma of social significations makes many forms of sociality possible, makes possible new construals of 'society.'" Graham Ward, *Cultural Transformation and Religious Practice* (Cambridge: Cambridge University Press, 2005), 163. For a science fiction metaphor for the "social imaginary," consider R. A. Lafferty's "silent radio," in "The Three Armageddons of Enniscorthy Sweeney," in *Apocalypses* (Los Angeles: Pinnacle Books, 1977), 266–80.

16 A 2001 survey indicated that about 30 percent of readers included science fiction in their reading and 16 percent of those did so regularly. Interestingly, the survey revealed no significant divide between men and women; it did suggest that there was a correspondence between higher rates of science fiction reading and those with higher educational attainments generally, as well as with those holding

further qualifications in science/mathematics. Put differently, there is an indication, if nothing more, that science fiction readers may be found in somewhat greater numbers among those likely to have more cultural influence in the area of science and technology and thus contribute to the cultural authority of its institutions, including educational and media representations.

17 "Chapter 7: Science and Technology; Public Attitudes and Public Understanding; Science Fiction and Pseudoscience," National Science Foundation, accessed June 11, 2013, http://www.nsf.gov/statistics/seind02/c7/c7s5.htm.

18 "Chapter 7: Science and Technology."

19 Home page for Newcastle Science City, accessed June 11, 2013, http://www.newcastlesciencecity.com/.

20 "Britain's Seven Super-cities Revealed—in Pictures," *Telegraph*, accessed June 11, 2013, http://www.telegraph.co.uk/finance/newsbysector/industry/8550490/Britains-seven-super-cities-revealed-in-pictures.html?image=1.

21 "Steve Todd—Newcastle Science Central," accessed June 11, 2013, http://www.newcastlesciencecentral.com/get-involved/science-central-campaign/steve-todd/ (no longer active).

22 Hugh Blair, cited in Roald Hoffmann and Iain Boyd Whyte, eds., *Beyond the Finite: The Sublime in Art and Science* (New York: Oxford University Press, 2011), 16–17.

23 This photograph also appears on the billboards surrounding the building site for the Newcastle "Science City" project. A few billboards to the left, there is a photograph of an Asian woman with her children. She says, with reference to Science City's employment policies, "As long as they [the children] are happy, I'm happy." This very traditional division of gender labor— ndeed, gender stereotyping—is interesting. With respect to gender, the billboards present the same mix of technological modernity and traditional domesticity as does much early science fiction. The technological sublime is thoroughly inflected with masculinity, as is much of the imagery associated with the science fiction sublime. That this is so in this location, and in spite of contemporary sensibilities, illustrates both how images come in complexes of association and just how enduring they can be.

24 Not all science fiction, of course, deploys the sublime for technological triumphalism; indeed a great deal does not, as may be gathered from the chapters below on the work of Lovecraft, Dick, and authors of science fiction "apocalyptic."

25 Stephen R. L. Clark, "Science Fiction and Religion," in Seed, *A Companion to Science Fiction*, 95–110; Farah Mendlesohn, "Religion

and Science Fiction," in *The Cambridge Companion to Science Fiction*, ed. Edward James and Farah Mendlesohn (Cambridge: Cambridge University Press, 2003), 264–75; Tom Woodman, "Science Fiction, Religion, and Transcendence," in *Science Fiction: A Critical Guide*, ed. Patrick Parrinder (New York: Longman, 1979), 110–30; James F. McGrath, *Religion and Science Fiction* (Eugene, Ore.: Pickwick, 2011).

26 Roger Zelazny, *Lord of Light* (New York: Eos, 2004), 287.

27 Adam Smith, "The Principles Which Lead and Direct Philosophical Enquiries; Illustrated by the History of Astronomy," in *Essays on Philosophical Subjects* (Dublin: Wogan, Byrne, et al., 1795).

28 *The Complete Poems of Hart Crane*, ed. Marc Simon (New York: Liveright, 1993), 44.

## CHAPTER 1

1 David E. Nye, *American Technological Sublime* (Boston: MIT Press, 1996), 246; emphasis added.

2 Quoted from a TripAdvisor review of Pacific Whale Foundation, Maui, Hawaii.

3 General works on the sublime, particularly on its eighteenth-century theorists, include James Kirwan, *Sublimity: The Non-rational and the Rational in the History of Aesthetics*, new ed. (New York: Routledge, 2005); David B. Morris, *Religious Sublime: Christian Poetry and Critical Tradition in Eighteenth-Century England* (Louisville: University Press of Kentucky, 1982); Peter de Bolla, *The Discourse of the Sublime: Readings in History, Aesthetics and the Subject* (Oxford: Basil Blackwell, 1989); Thomas Weiskel, *The Romantic Sublime: Studies in the Structure and Psychology of Transcendence* (Baltimore: Johns Hopkins University Press, 1976); Philip Shaw, *The Sublime* (London: Routledge, 2005); Samuel H. Monk, *The Sublime: A Study of Critical Theories in XVIII-Century England* (Ann Arbor: University of Michigan Press, 1960); Marjorie Hope Nicolson, *Mountain Gloom and Mountain Glory: The Development of the Aesthetics of the Infinite* (Seattle: University of Washington Press, 1997); Timothy M. Costelloe, ed., *The Sublime: From Antiquity to the Present* (Cambridge: Cambridge University Press, 2012); Hoffmann and Whyte, *Beyond the Finite*.

4 For exhibition information and fuller description, see the Richard Rigg exhibition description on the Baltic Centre for Contemporary Art website, *BALTIC*, accessed April 1, 2013, https://www.balticmill.com/whats-on/exhibitions/detail/richard-rigg.

5 There are too many examples to list, but, for the huts, see Sir Ernest

Waterlow, *The Lauterbrunnen Valley*, Switzerland, 1885–1910, Laing Gallery, Newcastle-upon-Tyne.

6 Richard Rigg exhibition description, *BALTIC*.

7 Ussher, Kant, and Coleridge—all of whom, in different ways, theorized the sublime—would agree. The mind, not its objects, makes sublimity. "No object of Sense is sublime in itself; but only as far as I make it a symbol of some Idea." *The Collected Works of Samuel Taylor Coleridge*, vol. 11, *Shorter Works and Fragments*, ed. H. J. Jackson and J. R. de J. Jackson (Princeton: Princeton University Press, 1995), 596–97.

8 Nicolson, *Mountain Gloom and Mountain Glory*, 35.

9 Nicolson, *Mountain Gloom and Mountain Glory*, 356–57. This is not to suggest no one before the eighteenth century ever peered over a precipice and went "Ooooh!"; even Poole included "stately" and "aspiring" on a short list for at least faint praise of the mountainous. The thrill, though, was not a culturally or ideologically elaborated experience; it lacked a cultural space in which to gather weight. The sublime's syllabus of wonder had to be learned; men and women had to be formed in these particular astonishments and in the significances they found there.

10 Adam Smith, *The Theory of Moral Sentiments*, reissue ed. (London: Liberty Classics, n.d.), 236.

11 That notions of the sublime lurk among the origins of science fiction has been noted by some historians of the genre, though with a rather narrow treatment of "sublimity" and no acknowledgment of its religious dimension. Oppositional accounts of "science and religion" have had annoying effects on science fiction histories as well as in much else. Philosophical discussions of the sublime in the twentieth century ignore science fiction, though James Kirwan makes an oblique reference. See Kirwan, *Sublimity*; Cornel Robu, "A Key to Science Fiction: The Sublime," *Foundation: The Review of Science Fiction* 42 (1988): 21–37; Brian W. Aldiss, *Billion Year Spree: The True History of Science Fiction* (New York: Doubleday, 1973); Istvan Csicsery-Ronay Jr., *The Seven Beauties of Science Fiction* (Middletown, Conn.: Wesleyan University Press, 2008).

12 G. Peyton Wertenbaker, letter to *Amazing Stories*, July 1926, cited in Paul Allen Carter, *The Creation of Tomorrow: Fifty Years of Magazine Science Fiction* (New York: Columbia University Press, 1980), 7.

13 John Dennis, *The Grounds of Criticism in Poetry* (London: Geo. Strahan, 1704).

14 M. John Harrison, *The Centauri Device* (New York: Doubleday, 1974), 74, 76.

15 Young, *Young's Night Thoughts*, 244, 250–51.

16 Harrison, *Centauri Device*, 161.

17 Harrison, *Centauri Device*, 87, 101.

18 We shall meet it again, for instance, in the work of Philip K. Dick and William Gibson. See below, pp. 131–34; 184–90.

19 The date of Longinus' work is disputed, but the present consensus places it within the first century.

20 Longinus, *On the Sublime*, trans. W. R. Roberts, in Hazard Adams, *Critical Theory since Plato* (San Diego: Harcourt Brace Jovanovich, 1971), 97. See also Longinus, *On the Sublime*, trans. William Smith (London: C. Whittingham, 1800), 37–38.

21 Adams, *Critical Theory since Plato*, 97.

22 The eighteenth century was the great period for philosophical interest in the sublime, theoretical interest in it waning during the nineteenth until, not too long ago, it could be described as a "moribund aesthetic" (Weiskel, *Romantic Sublime*, 6). Ironically, though, when that judgment was made in 1976, philosophical enthusiasm for the sublime was starting to revive rather vigorously. Whatever the vicissitudes of critical interest, sublimity as an aesthetic response and sublimity as a goal in painting, architecture, and writing has, since the late seventeenth century, burrowed deep into our cultural imagination, especially by way of Romanticism and its descendants. For the flourishing of interest in the sublime during the last thirty years, see especially, Jean-François Lyotard, *Lessons on the Analytic of the Sublime* (Stanford: Stanford University Press, 1994); Lyotard, *The Inhuman: Reflections on Time*, trans. Geoffrey Bennington and Rachel Bowlby (Cambridge: Polity, 1993); Slavoj Žižek, *The Sublime Object of Ideology* (London: Verso, 1989); Bolla, *Discourse of the Sublime*; Bill Beckley, ed., *Sticky Sublime*, illustrated ed. (New York: Allworth, 2001); Jeremy Gilbert-Rolfe, *Beauty and the Contemporary Sublime* (New York: Allworth, 1999).

23 Most scholarship dealing with the sublime in eighteenth-century Britain has given the lion's share of attention to Burke's *A Philosophical Enquiry into the Origins of the Sublime and Beautiful*. Since the vocational theme is less prominent in this text, the connection between sublimity and the "end of humanity" has not always received the attention it deserves.

24 John Dennis, *The Advancement and Reformation of Modern Poetry. . . .* (London: Rich Parker, 1701); Dennis, *Grounds of Criticism in Poetry*.

25 Young, *Young's Night Thoughts*; John Baillie, *An Essay on the Sublime* (London: R. Dodsley, 1747).

26 James Ussher, *Clio: Or a Discourse on Taste. Addressed to a Young Lady*, 3rd ed. (London: T. Davies, 1772).

27 The essays were published between June 19 and July 3, 1712. Addison and Steele, *Selections*, 364–406. Works on the sublime in the eighteenth century vary considerably in emphasis, purpose, and philosophical background and according to whether the interest is primarily on ways of achieving the sublime or on the psychology of the experience. Addison's interest is in the latter and its significance for the human vocation.

28 On the formation of the "public" and "public opinion," see Habermas, *Structural Transformation*. By 1712 London had three thousand coffee houses (32).

29 Habermas, *Structural Transformation*, 31–43.

30 Addison and Steele, *Selections*, 371.

31 Addison uses the term "sublime" only once, in a reference to Homer, but greatness is clearly synonymous with sublimity.

32 Addison and Steele, *Selections*, 371.

33 "Star Trek (All Opening Credits)," YouTube video, posted by "crouteru," August 22, 2011, http://www.youtube.com/watch?v=G4pKq0sEjuA&feature=youtube_gdata_player.

34 Addison and Steele, *Selections*, 371.

35 "Lorenzo" remains unknown, and he may well be a composite or typical figure. Young's own son, from whom he became estranged in later life, has been identified as "Lorenzo," but he was only eight when the poem was published. Even by eighteenth-century standards that is a little early to be hitting the bottle and running intellectually amok.

36 Young, *Young's Night Thoughts*, 240.

37 Young, *Young's Night Thoughts*, 240.

38 Addison and Steele, *Selections*, 393.

39 Addison and Steele, *Selections*, 369, 373.

40 For economic growth in the late seventeenth and early eighteenth centuries, see Frank O'Gorman, *The Long Eighteenth Century: British Political and Social History 1688–1832* (London: Hodder Arnold, 1997), 19–24, 108–18.

41 Addison and Steele, *Selections*, 368.

42 Addison and Steele, *Selections*, 368.

43 Terry Eagleton, *Reason, Faith, and Revolution: Reflections on the God Debate* (New Haven, Conn.: Yale University Press, 2009), 80.

44 Addison and Steele, *Selections*, 197–200.

45 On the problematic character of the epistemological role of sight in modernity, see Colin Gunton, *Enlightenment and Alienation* (Grand Rapids: Eerdmans, 1985), 33–44. The classical Christian concern with "contemplation" might, at first blush, seem another instance of privileging sight; however, contemplating God—as described,

for instance, by Origen in the East, or Bernard of Clairvaux in the West—embraced the whole range of "spiritual senses," and accorded "touch" and "taste" a primary place among them.

46 Addison and Steele, *Selections*, 378.

47 *Jean Baudrillard: Selected Writings* (Oxford: Polity, 2001), 33.

48 The classical account is that of Augustine, especially in *De nuptiis et concupiscentia*, though he, and much of the tradition after him, was too ready to settle for identifying concupiscence with specifically sexual desire. Paul Tillich, *Systematic Theology: Three Volumes in One* (Chicago: University of Chicago Press, 1967), 2:59–63.

49 Alastair Reynolds, *Chasm City* (London: Gollancz, 2008), 270.

50 Donald A. Wollheim, *The Universe Makers: Science Fiction Today* (New York: HarperCollins, 1971), 2.

51 Edmund Burke, *A Philosophical Enquiry into the Origins of the Sublime and Beautiful: And Other Pre-revolutionary Writings* (London: Penguin Classics, 1999).

52 David G. Hartwell, *Age of Wonders: Exploring the World of Science Fiction*, rev. ed. (New York: Walker, 1984), 46–47.

53 Damon Knight, cited in Hartwell, *Age of Wonders*, 54.

54 Wollheim, *Universe Makers*, 6.

55 Hartwell, *Age of Wonders*, 17.

56 Addison and Steele, *Selections*, 382; emphasis original.

57 Ann Radcliffe, *The Mysteries of Udolpho*, in *Complete Novels of Mrs. Ann Radcliffe* (London: Folio Society, 1987), 173–74, 176–77.

58 Addison and Steele, *Selections*, 399.

59 Larry Niven, *Ringworld*, new ed. (London: Gollancz, 2005), 109.

60 Burke, *Philosophical Enquiry*, 103.

61 Ussher, *Clio*, 123.

62 Dennis, *Grounds of Criticism in Poetry*, 87.

63 Young, *Young's Night Thoughts*, 213.

64 On experiences with and without "event structure," see Stewart Goetz and Charles Taliaferro, *Naturalism* (Grand Rapids: Eerdmans, 2008), 44–48.

65 Young, *Young's Night Thoughts*, 252.

66 Immanuel Kant, *The Critique of Judgement*, trans. James Creed Meredith (Oxford: Oxford University Press, 2006), 114–15.

67 Young, *Young's Night Thoughts*, 256.

68 Young, *Young's Night Thoughts*, 257–58.

69 Others managed their wonder within the bounds of reason, seeking a present balance between imagining and understanding. "Nothing is sublime," James Beattie warned, "that does not create in the mind a *pleasing* astonishment; and nothing can please a rational being,

but what is consistent with itself, and regulated by the standard of nature." "The true sublime," therefore, "is always natural and credible: but unbounded exaggerations, that surpass all proportion and all belief, are more apt to provoke laughter than astonishment." James Beattie, "Illustrations on Sublimity," in *Dissertations Moral and Critical* (London: W. Strahan & T. Cadell, 1783), 646, 620; emphasis original. Young might have retorted, "Says who?"

70 Addison and Steele, *Selections*, 375–76.

71 Addison and Steele, *Selections*, 370.

72 Baillie, *Essay on the Sublime*.

73 In arguing for an innate knowledge of God, Ussher departs from the Lockean philosophical inspiration of most writers on the sublime.

74 Ussher, *Clio*, 113.

75 Ussher, *Clio*, 128.

76 Ussher, *Clio*, 103.

77 Consistency is not a human trait. The theological tensions between the sublime and Christian theology are not a good measure of the place of the latter in a person's faith and practice. Young's account of Addison's death is a moving testimony to this. See Edward Young, *Conjectures on Original Composition* (London: A. Millar & R. and J. Dodsley, 1759), 102–4.

78 Addison and Steele, *Selections*, 401.

79 Julian May, *Jack the Bodiless* (New York: Knopf, 1992), 122–23.

80 May, *Jack the Bodiless*, 403.

81 For the introduction of the phrase, see Leo Marx, *Machine in the Garden: Technology and the Pastoral Ideal in America* (New York: Oxford University Press, 1964).

82 The most famous of the technological utopias is Edward Bellamy's *Looking Backward from 2000*, published in 1887. Others include King Camp Gillette, *The Human Drift* (1894); Thomas Kirwan, *Reciprocity (Social and Economic) in the Thirtieth Century, the Coming Cooperative Age* (1909); Henry Olerich, *Modern Paradise: An Outline or Story of How Some of the Cultured Will Probably Live, Work, and Organize in the Near Future* (1915); Fred M. Clough, *The Golden Age or the Depth of Time* (1923).

83 Ralph Waldo Emerson, *Emerson: Selected Essays* (London: Penguin Classics, 1982), 39.

84 Burke, *Philosophical Enquiry*, 113.

85 John Wilmerding, ed., *American Light: The Luminist Movement, 1850–1875; Paintings, Drawings, Photographs* (Washington, D.C.: National Gallery of Art, 1980), 77.

86 Marx, *Machine in the Garden*, passim, esp. chap. 4. For Britain, see the account of Coalbrookdale in F. D. Klingender and Arthur Elton,

*Art and the Industrial Revolution* (London: Paladin, 1972), 75–80. The perception of a harmony between nature and industry was not completely absent from British art; see Klingender and Elton, *Art and the Industrial Revolution*, 90.

87 Tench Coxe, cited Marx, *Machine in the Garden*, 160.

88 Tench Coxe, cited Marx, *Machine in the Garden*, 157.

89 Thomas Cole, *Expulsion from the Garden of Eden*, oil on canvas, 1828, Museum of Fine Arts, Boston.

90 Marx, *Machine in the Garden*, 194.

91 "Signs of the Times," in *Thomas Carlyle: Selected Writings* (London: Penguin Books, 1988).

92 Marx, *Machine in the Garden*, 186.

93 "Power, a Portfolio by Charles Sheeler," *Fortune*, December 1940; cited in David E. Nye, *American Technological Sublime* (Boston: MIT Press, 1996), 142.

94 E.g., the walls of Leicester County Jail (1825) and the front of Newgate (1770–1782); the arch for Euston Station (1836–1838); Metropolitan Tabernacle, London (1896–1899). See photographs and discussion in ed. H. J. Dyos and Michael Wolff, *The Victorian City: Images and Realities*, vol. 2 (London: Routledge & Kegan Paul, 1973), 431–49.

95 James Oppenheim, cited in Nye, *American Technological Sublime*, 107.

96 1905 and 1931 newspaper articles, cited in Nye, *American Technological Sublime*, 104, 105.

97 Nye, *American Technological Sublime*, 104–5, 107.

98 Lewis Mumford on New York, cited in Nye, *American Technological Sublime*, 192.

99 Nye, *American Technological Sublime*, 195.

100 Nye, *American Technological Sublime*, 85.

101 *The Complete Poems of Hart Crane*, ed. Marc Simon (New York: Liveright, 1993), 44.

102 Crane, *Complete Poems*, 56; the phrase is Walt Whitman's.

103 Nye, *American Technological Sublime*, 56.

104 Nye, *American Technological Sublime*, 21.

105 Baillie, *Essay on the Sublime*, 4.

106 Nye, *American Technological Sublime*, 28.

107 Nye, *American Technological Sublime*, 57.

108 Nye, *American Technological Sublime*, 132.

109 Nye, *American Technological Sublime*, 134.

110 E.g., Ignatius Donnelly, *Caesar's Column, a Story of the Twentieth Century* (1890); Adam Roberts, *The History of Science Fiction* (London: Palgrave Macmillan, 2007), 120. For an alternative, more sympathetic reading of Bellamy, by, perhaps significantly, an American scholar, see

Paul K. Alkon, *Science Fiction before 1900: Imagination Discovers Technology*, Studies in Literary Themes and Genres (Boston: Twayne, 1994), 107–15.

111 On Ford's factories, see Nye, *American Technological Sublime*, 129–32, 134.

112 Nye, *American Technological Sublime*, 227.

113 Nye, *American Technological Sublime*, 227; emphasis added.

114 "Correspondence with Dr. Bentley," in *Isaac Newton: Philosophical Writings* (Cambridge: Cambridge University Press, 2004), 95.

115 Newton, "Correspondence with Dr. Bentley," 96.

116 The term "physico-theological" referred to arguments drawn from observations of the natural world to support or interpret the claims of biblical revelation, such as—in addition to the existence, nature, and wisdom of God—the occurrence and extent of Noah's flood. At the time of "The Pleasures of the Imagination," the best known "physico-theological" writer was John Ray, also a member of the Royal Society. His popular physico-theological works were *The Wisdom of God Manifested in the Works of Creation* (1691) and *Three Physico-Theological Discourses* (1693). For a classic example of a mediation employing a pattern of ascent, see Augustine, *Confessions* 7.10.

117 Addison and Steele, *Selections*, 399.

118 *Isaac Newton*, 21. In *De Gravitatione*, Newton develops an account of "body" as a "portion of space" that God causes to be "impenetrable" as well as moveable from one part of space to another. Thus described, "it would have shape, be tangible and mobile, and be capable of reflecting and being reflected, and constitute no less a part of the structure of things than any other corpuscle" (*Isaac Newton*, 28). On Newton's account of space and divine omnipresence, see also Amos Funkenstein, *Theology and the Scientific Imagination from the Middle Ages to the Seventeenth Century* (Princeton, N.J.: Princeton University Press, 1989), 89–97.

119 According to Newton, "absolute space" is the emanative effect within which God knows the "real" position of all objects in their relation to one another in space, the latter being, as it were, the "sensorium" through which God knows creation. Absolute space is distinguished from "relative space," which is the ordering of objects as they appear to a finite observer.

120 Thomas Aquinas, *Summa Theologiae*, vol. 2, *Existence and Nature of God, 1a.2–11* (Cambridge: Cambridge University Press, 2006), 113–17.

121 *De Gravitatione*, in *Isaac Newton*, 26.

122 Thus, "absolute space," as an eternal emanation of God and necessary to God's perfection, gives God "inherent measure and dimension."

Geoffrey Gorham, "Early Scientific Images of God: Descartes, Hobbes, and Newton," in *Turning Images in Philosophy, Science, and Religion: A New Book of Nature*, ed. Charles Taliaferro and Jil Evans (New York: Oxford University Press, 2011), 40. Cf. "[In absolute space] there are everywhere all kinds of figures, everywhere spheres, cubes, triangles, straight lines . . . even though they are not disclosed to sight." Newton, *De Gravitatione*, 22.

123 On Newton's anti-Trinitarianism and his unpublished manuscripts, see Frank Edward Manuel, *The Religion of Isaac Newton* (Oxford: Clarendon, 1974), 42, 54–59.

124 Translation of Newton's manuscript in J. E. McGuire, "Newton on Place, Time, and God: An Unpublished Source," *British Journal for the History of Science* 11, no. 2 (1978), doi:10.1017/S000708740001654X.

125 Samuel Clarke, whose influential Boyle lectures brought Newtonianism to bear against all sorts and conditions of atheism, argues for space as a "mode" of the divine being. Space is "abstract immensity or infinity," again implying that finite entities exist in God as in a container. *Samuel Clarke: A Demonstration of the Being and Attributes of God; And Other Writings* (Cambridge: Cambridge University Press, 1998), 31, 123. Though, Clarke also denied that the being of God was divisible and argued that God was, in both substance and attributes, equally present at all points within infinite space, though not himself contained by space (35). At the time, Clarke was read as teaching that God was himself "spatial," or "extended substance without solidity." Anthony Collins, *A Discourse of Freethinking, Occasioned by the Rise and Growth of a Sect called Free-Thinkers* (London, 1713), 39. See also, *Samuel Clarke*, xvii, n. 6.

126 Cordwainer Smith, *The Rediscovery of Man: The Complete Short Science Fiction of Cordwainer Smith* (Framingham, Mass.: Nesfa, 1993), 161–62; emphasis added.

127 In 1741 the University of Cambridge received a bequest from Thomas Seaton, former fellow of Clare College, and rector of Ravenstone. The gift established a prize to be awarded each year for the best English poem on "one or other of the Perfections or Attributes of the Supreme Being," the ultimate purpose of the competition being to promote what "is most conducive to the honour of the Supreme Being and recommendation of Virtue." *Poems by Christopher Smart*, ed. Robert Brittain (Princeton, N.J.: Princeton University Press, 1950), 269–70. Seaton required that poems on other Christian themes—and he suggested "Death, Judgment, Heaven, Hell, and Purity of Heart"—not be invited until the matter of the Supreme Being "be exhausted."

128 Baillie, *Essay on the Sublime*, 21; emphasis in original.

129 Young, *Young's Night Thoughts*, 244. Christopher Smart—here, as elsewhere, eccentric to his age—knew better. Immensities are not the best token of God's immensity: "man at home, within himself, might find / The Deity immense" and, elsewhere, "conspicuous in the Linnet's throat." *Poems by Christopher Smart*, 92–93.

130 Ussher, *Clio*, 103.

131 The argument is not original to any of these writers. They are following John Locke. Locke, whose influence in Anglo-American modernity really does deserve the metaphor "immense," was a devout Christian who did very worrying things with the doctrine of God. We know God, Locke suggests, in the same way as we know anything else—that is, by reflection upon the ideas in our minds, the ultimate origin of which lies in sense experience. Thus, we know we exist, and Locke points out that if you really want to doubt that, just miss a meal or two, and your stomach will teach you what your skepticism will not. Our minds have also derived from experience ideas of the many objects of the world, of the various forces over which we have no control, and of the various powers we do possess—perception, will, knowledge, for instance. Intuitively, we also know that "nothing comes from nothing," and this forces us to conclude that, since we are not responsible for our own existence or that of the world, there must be an eternal being who is. Failing that, nothing would exist, since everything that has a beginning needs a cause of that beginning. Moreover, this eternal being must possess all it takes to create all that exists, inanimate, animate, and intelligent. We thus arrive at that "eternal, most powerful, and most knowing being" we call God. This idea of God, Locke tells us, is "complex," or, in other words, it is a composite of various ideas that we join together, including unity, power, knowing, willing, duration over time, and so on. What makes the various ideas elements in an idea of God is that we qualify them all with the notion of "infinity." How, though, do we get the idea of infinity? We do not have a perfectly clear or adequate idea, but we do a good enough job by removing the limits from ideas we do have. To get the idea "God," we join together the ideas of "Existence and Duration; of Knowledge and Power; of Pleasure and Happiness; and of several other Qualities and Powers, which it is better to have than to be without," then combine them all with the idea of infinity, which we get as soon as we realize that there's no end to the possibility of mentally tacking one length of rope onto another or extending one length of time by another. The principle is the same when it comes to less mathematically compliant attributes such as "wisdom"

or "power." We "enlarge" them in our imaginations until we arrive at the idea of unlimited wisdom or power. See Locke, *An Essay concerning Human Understanding* (London: Penguin Classics, 1998), 547–52.

132 Gorham, "Early Scientific Images," in Taliaferro and Evans, *Turning Images*, 37.

133 Burke, *Philosophical Enquiry*, 111, 112. Via Immanuel Kant, and especially within the twentieth century, this theological move issues in the sublime as an immanent power of negation, as "the unrepresentable."

134 Ussher, *Clio*, 126.

135 Cf. John Wesley's sermon "The Witness of the Spirit: Discourse 2," Wesley Center Online, accessed March 7, 2014, http://wesley.nnu.edu/john-wesley/the-sermons-of-john-wesley-1872-edition/sermon-11-the-witness-of-the-spirit-discourse-two/.

136 Newton, cited in Taliaferro and Evans, *Turning Images*, 38.

137 That might seem unfair or grossly exaggerated; after all, eighteenth-century critics largely upheld Milton's *Paradise Lost* as the sublime poem par excellence, and, surely, that refers us firmly, and more generally, back to the biblical story of salvation? Ironically, though, the search for sublimity led largely to passages dealing with the magnificence of creation, the glory of the Father as Creator, the horrors of Satan and his fall, and the Son's thunderous wrath upon the rebel angels. The sublime reading of Milton reinforced rather than resisted the truncation of biblical narrative.

138 Dennis, *Advancement and Reformation*, 120.

139 Young, *Young's Night Thoughts*, 240, 289.

140 Baillie, *Essay on the Sublime*, 6; emphasis in original.

141 "The Satan Pit," *Doctor Who—The Complete Second Series* (Sci-Fi Channel, 2007), all quotations, transcript.

142 Michael Hardt and Antonio Negri, *Empire* (Cambridge, Mass.: Harvard University Press, 2001), 73.

## CHAPTER 2

1 Holland et al., *Sci-Fi Art*, 30.

2 See, e.g., "The Fire Worshippers" (1837), in Martin Myrone, ed., *John Martin: Apocalypse* (London: Tate, 2011), 157.

3 Holland et al., *Sci-Fi Art*, 28. *Amazing Stories* was one of many—often short-lived—"pulp magazines." The term "pulp" derives from the cheap wood pulp used to make the paper for these magazines; higher quality paper was used for the "slicks." Early editions of *Amazing Stories* are now seemingly impossible to handle without their crumbling under even a gentle touch. I am, therefore, all the more grateful to

Liverpool for allowing me to enjoy them without armed supervision.

4 Hugo Gernsback has an ambiguous reputation. To his credit, he founded *Amazing Stories* as the first English-language magazine devoted entirely to science fiction. Gernsback also initiated the systematic promotion and cultivation of science fiction as a distinct genre. However, he paid his authors meanly, irregularly, and, occasionally, not at all. H. P. Lovecraft dubbed him Hugo the Rat; others stopped writing for him, or finally resorted to litigation. Michael Ashley, "Science Fiction Magazines," in Seed, *Companion to Science Fiction*, 64. Historians of science fiction have also weighed in, condemning Gernsback's taste and indifference to literary values, and condemning him for landing the genre with a stifling reputation for the juvenile and aesthetically inferior. He was, Brian Aldiss concluded, "one of the worst disasters ever to hit the science-fiction field." Aldiss, *Billion Year Spree*. See also, Edward James, *Science Fiction in the Twentieth Century* (New York: Oxford University Press, 1994). Nevertheless, as Michael Ashley has pointed out, Gernsback launched *Amazing Stories* against the odds, and he persisted in promoting the genre in new magazines, even after his bankruptcy in 1929. Gernsback's "genius" for making the most of an audience's enthusiasm popularized science fiction and introduced the writers "who brought science fiction through the Second World War." Ashley, *The Gernsback Days* (Holicong, Pa.: Wildside, 2004), 252, 254.

5 Ashley, *Gernsback Days*, 98; emphasis added. Ashley's study is a detailed and sympathetic assessment. While recognizing Gernsback's "financial mismanagement," he also suggests reasons for modifying judgments of the editor's knavery (253–54).

6 The author was Edmond Hamilton. Ashley, *Gernsback Days*, 129.

7 Ashley, *Gernsback Days*, 22–23. *Ralph 124C 41+* appeared in eleven installments, beginning in April 1911.

8 Hugo Gernsback, *Ralph 124C 41+*, 2nd ed. (New York: Frederick Fell, 1951), 10.

9 Gernsback, *Ralph 124C 41+*, 25; emphasis added.

10 Gernsback, *Ralph 124C 41+*, 32.

11 The novel evidences the American cultural imagination of the early twentieth century, at least before the Depression. *Ralph 124C 41+* fosters the heroic picture of the inventor and engineer; pride in the youthful energy and superiority of American invention and industry; and recognition of European decline—they have no aerial to match young Ralph's—and America's emergent international status and self-perceived role. On the other hand, women are firmly outside the sphere of the technoscientific power that is the only power

in Ralph's world; miscegenation is illegal, at least between Martians and humans; and the conjunction of races, of insiders and outsiders, native and alien, is a sure sign of imminent villainy.

12 Gernsback, *Ralph 124C 41+*, 196; emphasis added.

13 Significantly for the place allotted to women in science fiction, at least before the 1960s, the only chapters not to include these "info-dumps" are two brief episodes in which Alice is the main character.

14 Gernsback, "A New Sort of Magazine" (editorial), *Amazing Stories*, April 1926, 3. Verne comes closer than Poe or Wells, but only the short piece describing a day in the life of Mr. Fritz Napoleon Smith, a communications magnate in 2889, is much like Gernsback's fiction. Jules Verne, "In the Year 2889," in *In the Year 2889 and a Voyage in a Balloon* (New York: CreateSpace, 2010).

15 Gernsback, *Ralph 124C 41+*, 154.

16 This is clearer from the sales and the stories readers enthused over than from the letters Gernsback quoted in his editorials, such as the gentlemen who wanted all scientific facts printed in italics for emphasis. Gernsback, "Thank You" (editorial), *Amazing Stories*, May 1926, 99.

17 This appeared in the *Amazing Stories Annual*. Burroughs began the Barsoom series in 1911.

18 John Whiteclay Chambers II, *The Tyranny of Change: America in the Progressive Era, 1890–1920*, 3rd ed. (New Brunswick, N.J.: Rutgers University Press, 2000), 6–8.

19 "A Princess of Mars," in *The Works of Edgar Rice Burroughs*, ed. Raleigh St. Clair. Amazon Digital Services, 2009. Kindle edition.

20 "A Princess of Mars."

21 A version of *The Moon Pool* had first appeared in *All-Story Weekly* in 1918 and 1919. The longer, novel version was published in 1919. Gernsback serialized the latter in three installments.

22 Gernsback, *Amazing Stories*, May 1927, 111.

23 Abraham Merritt, *The Moon Pool* (Middletown, Conn.: Wesleyan University Press, 2004), 134–35.

24 Merritt, *Moon Pool*, 138.

25 Martin E. Marty, *Modern American Religion*, vol. 2, *The Noise of Conflict, 1919–1941*, illustrated ed. (Chicago: University of Chicago Press, 1991), chap. 5.

26 Merritt, *Moon Pool*, 56.

27 J. G. Frazer, *The Golden Bough: A Study in Magic and Religion* (London: Macmillan, 1967), 931.

28 Frazer, *Golden Bough*, 932. As opposed to the way in which magic projects onto phenomena features of the mental life of human beings.

29 Merritt, *Moon Pool.* Merritt includes this footnote on Murian religion, with its nicely ironic conclusion:

> I have no space here even to outline the eschatology of this people, nor to catalogue their pantheon. Siya and Siyana typified worldly love. Their ritual was, however, singularly free from those degrading elements usually found in love-cults. Priests and priestesses of all cults dwelt in the immense seven-terraced structure, of which the jet amphitheatre was the water side. The symbol, icon, representation, of Siya and Siyana—the globe and the up-striving figures—typified earthly love, feet bound to earth, but eyes among the stars. Hell or heaven I never heard formulated, nor their equivalents; unless that existence in the Shining One's domain could serve for either. Over all this was Thanaroa, remote; unheeding, but still maker and ruler of all—an absentee First Cause personified Thanaroa seemed to be the one article of belief in the creed of the soldiers—Rador, with his reverence for the Ancient Ones, was an exception. Whatever there was, indeed, of high, truly religious impulse among the Murians, thus far, the High God had. I found this exceedingly interesting, because it had long been my theory—to put the matter in the shape of a geometrical formula—that the real attractiveness of gods to man increases uniformly according to the square of their distance—W. T. G, p. 56.

30 Ernst Mach, *Popular Scientific Lectures*, trans. Thomas J. McCormack (Cambridge University Press, 2014), 224.

31 Ashley, *Gernsback Days*, 260.

32 D. D. Sharp, "The Eternal Man," in *The History of the Science Fiction Magazine*, vol. 1, *1926–1935*, ed. Michael Ashley (Chicago: Henry Regnery, 1976), 91–98.

33 Ashley, *Gernsback Days*, 154.

34 Ashley, *History of the Science Fiction Magazine*, 67–81.

35 Ashley, *History of the Science Fiction Magazine*, 153–71.

36 Bankrupt but unbowed, Gernsback sent a letter to his authors offering to publish the manuscripts still in his possession, in a "new and better" magazine and at the "regular space rates." The "new and better" magazine turned into *Air Wonder Stories*, *Science Wonder Stories*, *Science Wonder Quarterly*, and, in addition, a series of booklets he called the *Science Fiction Series*. Gernsback's radio company went to the Curtiss Aeroplane and Motor Company. Ashley, *Gernsback Days*, 134.

37 *Astounding Stories of Super-Science* was published by William Clayton and first edited by Harry Bates. The magazine quickly became known as *Astounding Stories* and, in 1938, was renamed as *Astounding Science-Fiction*.

38 Tremaine was editor of *Astounding* from late 1933. Michael Ashley, *Time Machines: The Story of the Science-Fiction Pulp Magazines from the Beginning to 1950*, collectors ed. (Liverpool: Liverpool University Press, 2001), 84–85.

39 For examples of responses to Tremaine's invitation, see Ashley, *Time Machines*, 84–86.

40 Albert I. Berger, *The Magic That Works: John W. Campbell and the American Response to Technolog* (San Bernardino, Calif.: Borgo, 1993), 34.

41 The implicit pessimism of the Stuart stories is admonitory. Campbell certainly thought little of "present human nature," but he was hopeful about the chances of changing the composition of the race overall by scientific leadership and good breeding. In a 1941 editorial, he wrote, presumably ignorant of the appalling irony, "Present human nature is a highly unsatisfactory combination of mulish obstinacy and monkey tendency to hunt each other in packs. A change for the better is (a) very possible and (b) highly desirable. A change for the worse is possible, but, all things considered, not too easy to conceive. You can't change human nature, unfortunately; that seem to be bred in the beast, but you can change the race; *that is happening right now*." Cited in Berger, *Magic That Works*, 161; emphasis added.

42 John W. Campbell, *A New Dawn: The Complete Don A. Stuart Stories* (Framingham, Mass.: Nesfa, 2003), 50, 51.

43 Campbell, *New Dawn*, 31.

44 Campbell, *New Dawn*, 32–33.

45 Michael E. Parrish, *Anxious Decades: America in Prosperity and Depression, 1920–1941* (New York: W. W. Norton, 1992), 29–46, 94–95, 164–66.

46 Campbell, *New Dawn*, 60.

47 Campbell, *New Dawn*, 101.

48 Campbell, *New Dawn*, 35, 36.

49 George Parkin Grant, *Time as History* (Toronto: Canadian Broadcasting, 1969).

50 Campbell, *New Dawn*, 154.

51 See below, pp. 79–95.

52 Campbell, *New Dawn*, 164.

53 Campbell, *New Dawn*, 209–32.

54 A "moral of the history of Dwranl," in Campbell, *New Dawn*, 56–57.

55 Campbell, *New Dawn*, 371.

56 Josiah Strong, *Our Country, Its Possible Future and Its Present Crisis*, cited in Martin E. Marty, *Modern American Religion*, vol. 1, *The Irony of It All, 1893–1919* (Chicago: University Of Chicago Press, 1987), 23–24, 29–30. *Our Country* was Strong's most widely read work. Published in

1885 and revised in 1891, this was a foundational text for the liberal modernism of early twentieth-century America. Strong was a significant influence upon Walter Rauschenbusch. By "science," Strong was thinking primarily of the social sciences, though very much as modeled after the natural: he was an admirer of Herbert Spencer. If such ecclesiastical hopes now seem merely silly, the ugly side should not be forgotten. For some, including Josiah Strong, "United States" meant the "Anglo-Saxon race," now ready to school the world in civilization. Unfortunately for the rest of the world, they were all too close to the truth, though not as they expected.

57 On Campbell's elitist politics, see Berger, *Magic That Works*, 159–76, 191–92. The editor of *Astounding* continued to believe that the greatest obstacle to achieving a technologically strenuous future was most of us. "The seed of the geniuses shall inherit the earth. And the stars, too, of course. The normal man of any given era is rejected by the whole immensity of the future." Normal man is still pesky enough, though, to derail the genius and return humanity to the sofa with a TV remote and buckets of ice cream. Campbell's solution was to restrict the vote to the educated and financially successful, and keep a tight elitist hold on politics until technology rendered politics and economics obsolete and society was safely in the hands of the scientists—again, a world not too far from *Ralph 124C 41+*.

58 Rauschenbusch crafted the most theologically sophisticated exposition of the "social gospel." In this context, "social gospel" refers at least as much to an emergent sensibility as to a movement, and those who identified themselves with the social gospel were politically diverse, their activism varying from very timid reformism to—though rather more rarely—socialism. They were united, though, in seeking to relieve the miseries and injustices of America's industrialism and rapid urban growth, such miseries as reached public notice through "muck-raking" journalists and books like Upton Sinclair's *The Jungle* and the novels of Theodore Dreiser. Rauschenbusch himself had worked as pastor in New York's overcrowded Hell's Kitchen district, and the experience informed his advocacy of a socialism achieved by gradual reforms and the progressive Christianization of society.

59 Walter Rauschenbusch, *A Theology for the Social Gospel* (New York: Macmillan, 1917), 69–76. Though Rauschenbusch's theology of those "super-personal" forces of sin is one of his most important contributions, his program for Christian action still turns on changing the attitudes and values of the wealthy. His heroes, therefore, are the factory owner revolted by his own child labor practices, or the financier who suddenly recognizes the poor in the stories of Jesus. These

are comparable to Campbell's solitary engineers whom he held up as paradigms despite an actually collaborative world of science.

60 "Our effort must rather be to preserve all the benefits which the elaboration of the productive machinery has worked out, but to make these benefits enrich the many instead of the few." Walter Rauschenbusch, *Christianity and the Social Crisis* (New York: Macmillan, 1907), 345.

61 Rauschenbusch, *Christianity and the Social Crisis*, 345.

62 As in "The Machine" series, esp, "The Invaders."

63 Rauschenbusch, *Theology for the Social Gospel*, 224.

64 Rauschenbusch, *Theology for the Social Gospel*, 227. To be fair, Rauschenbusch recognizes that he is being speculatively fanciful. However, he still fails to provide a Christian eschatology that does not involve labor "without end."

65 Rauschenbusch, *Theology for the Social Gospel*, 237.

66 Rauschenbusch, *Theology for the Social Gospel*, 102.

67 Rauschenbusch, *Theology for the Social Gospel*, 150–51.

68 Rauschenbusch, *Theology for the Social Gospel*, 148.

69 Rauschenbusch, *Theology for the Social Gospel*, 179–80.

70 Herman Melville, especially in *Moby Dick* and *The Encantadas*, had opposed natural and human sublimes. Ahab defies the whale with an elevation of the human will in terms of the technological sublime: "Naught's an obstacle, naught's an angle to the iron way!" During the second half of the nineteenth century, though, hardly anybody was reading Melville. Interestingly, though, interest in his work revived at the same time as the beginnings of *Amazing Stories* and *Astounding*.

71 A spectral horse's head, also the subject of debate as to its meaning, protrudes through a curtain over the woman's legs.

72 Martin Myrone, Christopher Frayling, and Marina Warner, *Gothic Nightmares: Fuseli, Blake and the Romantic Imagination* (London: Tate, 2006), 13.

73 Mrs. Radcliffe, cited in Patricia Meyer Spacks, *The Insistence of Horror: Aspects of the Supernatural in Eighteenth-Century Poetry* (Boston: Harvard University Press, 1962), 107; emphasis in original. Some eighteenth-century writers ignored the distinction, using "horror" and "terror" synonymously and appropriating both to a sublime reached by "mysterious horrors, undefined terrors" (97). Burke, of course, specifies terror as essential to the sublime. He also gave the examples of ghosts and goblins, identified by others as matter for horror.

74 Noel Carroll, *The Philosophy of Horror* (New York: Routledge, 1990), 240.

75 H. P. Lovecraft, *The Call of Cthulhu and Other Weird Stories*, Penguin Classics Deluxe ed. (London: Penguin Classics, 2011).

76 Some critics argue that Lovecraft's work stands outside the genre of science fiction. Lovecraft's credentials as a writer of science fiction rest, however, not on any deployment of technology, which plays little or no role in the tales, but on the intrusion of cosmic alien powers into the human world. Where technology does appear, as in the cylinders of living brains wired for a chat with Henry Akeley, it is repellent and uncelebrated. Maurice Levy has argued that, whereas science fiction is "basically a forward-looking genre," Lovecraft's stories are "essentially regressive," appealing to a "fabulous past," while his humanity is the victim not the agent of change. Levy, *Lovecraft: A Study in the Fantastic*, trans. S. T. Joshi (Detroit: Wayne State University Press, 1988), 79–80. This suggests that science fiction moves within a more optimistic and humanistic horizon than much of it would confirm. Levy's contrast also underestimates the role of science in Lovecraft's tales. Science, expressly contrasted with religion, is the decidedly privileged medium of rationality and future development. Though they might disagree on what counts as scientific evidence, Lovecraft and H. G. Wells have an equal regard for the unique cultural authority of science. Admittedly, scientific progress leads to appalling consequences in these stories. However, this is not because science encourages hubris or releases technological powers we have not wit to use: rather, the Lovecraftian scientist pitches us all over the abyss as a direct consequence of what is essential, and essentially good, about science. Lovecraft may have despised his contemporaries' trust in the blessings of the sciences and in the promises of technological prosperity, but he does so in the name of scientific knowing. Fritz Leiber had the measure of this in saluting Lovecraft as the "Copernicus of the horror story" who "shifted the focus of supernatural dread from man and his little world and his gods, to the stars and the black and unplumbed gulfs of intergalactic space." Leiber, "A Literary Copernicus," in *Discovering H. P. Lovecraft*, ed. Darrell Schweitzer, rev. exp. ed. (Holicong, Pa.: Borgo, 2001), 7. Lovecraft also contests Christianity very much along science-fictional lines. He does not oppose Christian faith as a modern pagan: Lovecraft was definitely not lusting after some more sensual or ecstatic worship. However, nor did he think some rationally chastened Christianity would be an improvement. Lovecraft is a familiar of the "warfare of science and religion," and he confidently serves the scientific lines that were mapped at the end of the nineteenth century in the popular writings of John Draper and Andrew White (John William Draper, *History of the Conflict between Science and Religion* [1874]; Andrew Dickenson White, *A History of the Warfare of Science with Theology in Christendom*

[1896]). On the influence of both of these texts, see James R. Moore, *The Post-Darwinian Controversies: A Study of the Protestant Struggle to Come to Terms with Darwin in Great Britain and America, 1870–1900* (Cambridge: Cambridge University Press, 1981), 19–100.

77 Lovecraft, *Call of Cthulhu*, 354.

78 Lovecraft, *Call of Cthulhu*, 354; cf. John 1:11.

79 H. P. Lovecraft, *Thing on the Doorstep* (London: Penguin Books, 2002), 329–30.

80 Lovecraft, *Call of Cthulhu*, 177–78.

81 Lovecraft, *Call of Cthulhu*, 14.

82 S. T. Joshi, *A Subtler Magick: The Writings and Philosophy of H. P. Lovecraft*, 3rd ed. (Berkley Heights, N.J.: Borgo, 1996), 77.

83 Lovecraft, *Call of Cthulhu*, 139.

84 Howard Phillips Lovecraft, *Supernatural Horror in Literature* (New York: Dover, 1973).

85 Lovecraft, *Call of Cthulhu*, 169.

86 Lovecraft, *Call of Cthulhu*, 167.

87 Lovecraft, *Call of Cthulhu*, 167.

88 Lovecraft, *Call of Cthulhu*, 167.

89 Lovecraft, *Call of Cthulhu*, 167.

90 Lovecraft, *Call of Cthulhu*, 167.

91 Hans Urs von Balthasar, ed., *Origen: Spirit and Fire—A Thematic Anthology of His Writings*, new ed. (Washington, D.C.: Catholic University of America Press, 2001), 37, 31. Origen is quoting Psalm 36:9.

92 "Revelation," of course, referring to the entire Bible, not to its last book.

93 See above, pp. 28–30.

94 Heraclitus (5 c. B.C.E.), in Guy Davenport, *7 Greeks* (New York: New Directions, 1995), 158.

95 On the Logos, see Alois Grillmeier, *Christ in Christian Tradition: From the Apostolic Age to Chalcedon (451)*, trans. John Stephen Bowden (Atlanta: John Knox, 1975), pt. 2; Walter Kasper, *The God of Jesus Christ* (New York: Crossroad, 1984), 179–82; John Michael Rist, *The Stoics* (Los Angeles: University of California Press, 1978), chaps. 6, 7; John Behr, *The Way to Nicaea*, The Formation of Christian Theology, vol. 1 (Crestwood, N.Y.: St. Vladimir's Seminary Press, 2001).

96 Lovecraft, *Call of Cthulhu*, 341.

97 Lovecraft, *Call of Cthulhu*, 344.

98 Lovecraft, *Call of Cthulhu*, 344.

99 Lovecraft, *Call of Cthulhu*, 344.

100 Lovecraft, *Call of Cthulhu*, 286.

101 Lovecraft, *Call of Cthulhu*, 155.

102 Lovecraft, *Call of Cthulhu*, 251.

103 Poul Anderson, *Tau Zero*, new ed. (London: Gollancz, 2006).

104 Ursula K. Le Guin, *The Dispossessed: An Ambiguous Utopia* (New York: Harper Paperbacks, 1994); Alastair Reynolds, *The Prefect* (London: Gollancz, 2008).

105 One of the "apocalyptic" novels discussed in chapter 5, Thomas Disch's *The Genocides*, comes closer to a Lovecraft tale in that the moral warning is irrelevant and the disaster bears no relation to the actions of human beings, who turn out to be just local pests demanding a good bug spray. Disch, though, does not reach for the metaphysical as does Lovecraft. His aliens are the old-fashioned kind.

106 "Facts concerning the Late Arthur Jermyn and His Family," in Lovecraft, *Call of Cthulhu*, 14–23.

107 "The inassimilable other" reminds us of Lovecraft's racism, expressions of which are frequent and frequently vicious. The "foreigners," "negroes," and "Asiatic hordes" with "their odious presence and twisted visages and stunted forms"—who appalled Lovecraft, especially during his short residence in New York—find themselves in the tales as the savage cultists, decadent human bloodlines, and hideous hybridities. Howard Phillips Lovecraft, *Lord of a Visible World: Autobiography in Letters*, ed. S. T. Joshi and David E. Schultz (Columbus: Ohio University Press, 2000), 180.

108 Lovecraft, *Call of Cthulhu*, 334.

109 Immanuel Kant, *Critique of Judgement*, 98; emphasis in original.

110 For a fuller account of Kant in relation to the science-fictional sublime, see pp. 198–99 below.

111 Julia Kristeva, *Powers of Horror: An Essay on Abjection* (New York: Columbia University Press, 1984).

112 Kristeva, *Powers of Horror*, 101.

113 Kristeva, *Powers of Horror*, 1; emphasis in original.

114 Lovecraft, *Call of Cthulhu*, 181.

115 Kristeva, *Powers of Horror*, 117.

116 Kristeva, *Powers of Horror*, 13.

117 Sigmund Freud, *The Uncanny*, trans. David McLintock (London: Penguin Classics, 2003), 123–62.

118 Freud, *Uncanny*, 150.

119 Interestingly, in Dante's *Inferno* the great triumvirate of betrayal—Judas, Brutus, and Cassius—are eternally chewed in the grinding mouth of Satan: destroyed, pulled apart, and still maintained—and never consumed.

120 Lovecraft, *Call of Cthulhu*, 328.

121 Lovecraft, *Call of Cthulhu*, 327.

CHAPTER 3

1 The full title is *Natural Theology; or, Evidences of the Existence and Attributes of the Deity; Collected from the Appearances of Nature.* It became a staple of clerical education throughout the nineteenth century, and was read widely by members of the laity as well, Charles Darwin among them.

2 William Paley, *Natural Theology* (Charlottesville, Va.: Ibis, 1986), 283.

3 "Natural selection," Darwin argued, "acts solely through the preservation of variations in some way advantageous." Charles Darwin, *The Origin of Species by Means of Natural Selection: The Preservation of Favored Races in the Struggle for Life* (London: Penguin Classics, 1982), 153.

4 Diana Donald and Jane Munro, *Endless Forms: Charles Darwin, Natural Science and the Visual Arts* (New Haven, Conn.: Yale University Press, 2009), 162.

5 Later, Watts revised his account of the painting. Not long before he started work on *Evolution*, he described the painting so as seemingly to withdraw the focus from human evolution, writing that "the intention of this picture is to convey in the language of symbol an idea of the passing of our planet from chaos to order." Barbara Bryant, "George Frederic Watts and Assistants: *Chaos* c. 1875–82," accessed August 30, 2013, http://www.tate.org.uk/art/artworks/watts-chaos-n01647/text-exhibition-catalogue-text.

6 Donald and Munro, *Endless Forms*, 162.

7 On the reception history of Darwinism, see Peter J. Bowler, *Evolution: The History of an Idea*, 3rd ed. (Los Angeles: University of California Press, 2003); Bowler, *Reconciling Science and Religion: The Debate in Early-Twentieth-Century Britain* (Chicago: University of Chicago Press, 2001); Moore, *The Post-Darwinian Controversies*; Edward J. Larson, *Evolution: The Remarkable History of a Scientific Theory* (New York: Modern Library, 2006).

8 Moore, *Post-Darwinian Controversies*, 224.

9 Patrick Geddes, ed., *The Evergreen: A Northern Seasonal*, vol. 1 (Edinburgh: T. Fisher Unwin, 1895), 11.

10 Geddes, *Evergreen*, 25.

11 *H. G. Wells: Early Writings in Science and Science Fiction*, ed. Robert Philmus and David Y. Hughes (Los Angeles: University of California Press, 1975), 209.

12 Darwin comments on retrogression to simpler forms of organization: "It is quite possible for natural selection gradually to fit an organic being to a situation in which several organs would be superfluous and

useless: in such cases there might be retrogression in the scale of organization." Chrles Darwin, *Origin of Species*, 221.

13 *H. G. Wells*, 219.

14 Bowler, *Reconciling Science and Religion*, 130–46; Moore, *Post-Darwinian Controversies*, 217–51.

15 H. G. Wells, *Selected Short Stories* (London: Penguin Books, 1965), 77–78.

16 T. H. Huxley, *Evolution and Ethics and Other Essays*, Project Gutenberg, n.d. PDF e-book, 5.

17 Wells, *Selected Short Stories*, 77–78.

18 Wells, *Selected Short Stories*, 76.

19 H. G. Wells, *The War of the Worlds*, paperback (London: Penguin Books, 1946), 51, 60.

20 Wells, *War of the Worlds*, 24–25.

21 Wells, *War of the Worlds*, 11.

22 Salvation by bacteria struck the American astronomer and novelist Garrett Serviss as such an affront to human, especially American, dignity that he rushed a sequel into print in which a counterattack is led by Thomas Edison in command of various scientists, including the British physicist Lord Kelvin. They build a whopping great space fleet and give Mars a lot more than a bad cold. Fittingly, the nonfictional Lord Kelvin was a strong opponent of evolution understood, in the manner of Wells and Huxley, as a blind, unguided process of natural selection.

23 *H. G. Wells*, 36.

24 Bowler, *Evolution*; Bowler, *Reconciling Science and Religion*, 168–70; Moore, *Post-Darwinian Controversies*, 185–87.

25 *H. G. Wells*, 37. Lamarck (1744–1829) proposed a clear directedness to evolution, a teleological favoring of the more complex. This was still popular among biologists in the 1890s; see Bowler, *Reconciling Science and Religion*, 142–46.

26 H. G. Wells, *The Island of Dr. Moreau* (New York: CreateSpace, 2010), 48, 47.

27 Wells, *Island of Dr. Moreau*, 81.

28 Wells also draws on the Swiftian tradition: like Gulliver, following his term in the land of the Houyhnhnms, when Prendick returns to "civilization," he sees the beast in his neighbors rather than the enlightened agents of reason.

29 *H. G. Wells*, 216–17. Wells' understanding of language is, admittedly, inadequate. He thinks of it in primarily technological terms, as enabling instruction, information, and collaborative work, rather

than as that which constitutes our subjectivity and constitutes it, from the ground up, as intersubjectivity.

30 *H. G. Wells*, 211.

31 Wells, *Selected Short Stories*, 83.

32 *H. G. Wells*, 218.

33 Huxley, *Evolution and Ethics*, 85.

34 Huxley, *Evolution and Ethics*, 85.

35 Huxley, *Evolution and Ethics*, 45.

36 Edwin Ray Lankester, *Degeneration: A Chapter in Darwinism* (London: General Books, 2010), 33.

37 Lankester, *Degeneration*, 60–61.

38 H. G. Wells, *The Food of the Gods and How It Came to Earth* (New York: General Books, 2010), 224–25.

39 H. G. Wells, *A Modern Utopia* (London: General Books, 2010), 11.

40 Wells' distinction between natural and social evolution is a secular and humanist dualism of spirit and matter. This dualistic interpretation, though, was not forced on Wells by his acceptance of Darwinian evolution. Darwin had proposed that the social traits Wells found opposed to natural selection were actually the product of that same selection working at the level of the social group, the group as a whole benefiting from the presence of these characteristics. Nor would Darwin have set the human off against the animal as regards the development of behaviors and characteristics valuable to a society, even when they rendered the individual itself vulnerable in terms of survival. Thus he applied the same selectionist logic both to the continuing existence of sterile members among colonies of social insects and to altruism in human communities. For an excellent discussion of Darwin's treatment of the dilemma posed for natural selection—which works through the selection of fitter individuals, by seemingly nonadaptive variations within social groups—see Timothy Shanahan, *The Evolution of Darwinism: Selection, Adaptation and Progress in Evolutionary Biology* (Cambridge: Cambridge University Press, 2004).

41 Wells, *Modern Utopia*, 96.

42 Wells, *Food of the Gods*, 247.

43 Wells, *War of the Worlds*, 75.

44 Speaking personally, having served my curacy in a neighboring parish, I have a certain perverse satisfaction in contemplating the destruction of Weybridge.

45 Norman Mackenzie and Jeanne Mackenzie, *The Life of H. G. Wells: The Time Traveller* (London: Hogarth, 1987), 313.

46 The novel went through thirteen editions before Christmas 1916, and Mr. Britling made his way into a good many English pulpits. Patrick

Parrinder, *H. G. Wells: The Critical Heritage* (London: Routledge & Kegan Paul, 1972), 236–38.

47 Parrinder, *H. G. Wells*, 310–13; Lovat Dickson, *H. G. Wells: His Turbulent Life and Times* (London: Pelican, 1972), 307, 314.

48 H. G. Wells, *God the Invisible King*, chap. 5, Project Gutenburg n.d.. PDF e-book.

49 H. G. Wells, *Mr. Britling Sees It Through*, Project Gutenburg n.d. PDF e-book, 327

50 Wells, *Mr. Britling*, 333.

51 Wells, *Mr. Britling*, 333.

52 Wells, *Mr. Britling*, 336.

53 Wells, *Mr. Britling*, 309.

54 Wells, *Mr. Britling*, 336.

55 Wells, *God the Invisible King*, 5.

56 Wells, *God the Invisible King*, 9.

57 Wells, *God the Invisible King*, 24.

58 Wells, *God the Invisible King*, 35.

59 Wells, *God the Invisible King*, 35.

60 Wells, *God the Invisible King*, 47.

61 Wells, *God the Invisible King*, 88.

62 Wells, *God the Invisible King*, 13.

63 See above, pp. 39–40.

64 In a late novel, *Death into Life*, Olaf Stapledon imagines a "Spirit of Man," very much along the lines of Wells' personal God. He comes into being with humanity, suffers the sorrows and pains of humanity, grows and learns, and yearns with humanity. "For him the whole ocean of human experience, far from being a chaos, formed a clear, though often self-conflicting pattern of his own self-knowledge and knowledge of the world." Olaf Stapledon, *Worlds of Wonder* (Holicong, Pa.: Wildside, 2009), 144. Stapledon's "spirit of Man," however, is clearly a metaphor for humanity in its striving toward spiritual expression.

65 Though now standardization has set in, in Stapledon's time the British billion, a million million, was equivalent to the current American trillion. Stapledon provided timeline diagrams at the end of both *Last and First Men* and *Star Maker* to represent the scale of his narrative canvas.

66 Olaf Stapledon, *Last and First Men* (London: Gollancz, 2000), xiv.

67 Cf. Darwin's notebook entry: "Man in his arrogance thinks himself a great work, worthy the interposition of a deity; more humble & I believe true to consider him created from animals." Cited in Shanahan, *Evolution of Darwinism*, 265.

68 Stapledon developed this scenario more fully in the sequel *Last Men in London*, published in 1932. The novel also provides more details of

the Neptunian life of the "Last Men," though, as a novel, it lacks the narrative interest and ingenuity of invention Stapledon achieved in *Last and First Men.*

69 Stapledon, *Last and First Men*, xix.

70 The term is Mikhail Bakhtin's. See M. M. Bakhtin, *The Dialogic Imagination: Four Essays* (Austin. University of Texas Press, 1982).

71 Olaf Stapledon, *Beyond the "Isms,"* Searchlight Books 16 (New York: Secker & Warburg, 1942), 67.

72 In *Star Maker*, Stapledon suggests a philosophy closer to "pan-psychism" in that even the nebulae possess mind; however, he still both emphasizes the contingencies that determine all sentient beings and their fates, and warns against any comforting notion that the cosmos is concerned for a particular form of mind. Olaf Stapledon, *Star Maker* (Middletown, Conn.: Wesleyan University Press, 2004), 213–18.

73 Stapledon, *Last and First Men*, 79, 113.

74 Stapledon, *Last and First Men*, 286.

75 In a decidedly unsettling example of sublime disruption, Stapledon assaults the intimate association of humanity with Earth. Not only does humanity migrate from Earth to Venus and, thereafter, to Neptune, but we are told that the Venerian and Neptunian periods are by far the greater portion of human history, the latter lasting for half the time within which human beings exist. They are terrestrial in their childhood.

76 Stapledon, *Star Maker*, 265.

77 Burke, *Philosophical Enquiry*, 165.

78 Stapledon, *Last and First Men*, 248.

79 Stapledon, *Last and First Men*, 285.

80 Stapledon, *Last and First Men*, 287–88.

81 Stapledon, *Beyond the "Isms,"* 68–69.

82 Stapledon, *Beyond the "Isms,"* 70, 71.

83 Stapledon, *Last and First Men*, xiv, 215.

84 Stapledon, *Last and First Men*, 72–78, 174–79.

85 Stapledon, *Last and First Men*, 126.

86 Stapledon's rejection of Christianity was fundamental, and it remained so all his life, despite Sam Moskowitz' claim that, shortly before his death, he had "accepted God . . . admitted the Cosmic Mind at last." Leslie A. Fiedler, *Olaf Stapledon: A Man Divided* (New York: Oxford University Press, 1983), 219.

87 Stapledon, *Last and First Men*, 115.

88 The absence of capitalization, when Stapledon discusses "spirit," is telling.

89 Stapledon, *Last and First Men*, 123; emphasis in original.
90 Stapledon, *Last and First Men*, 276–77.
91 Stapledon, *Last and First Men*, 288.
92 Anonymous, *The Cloud of Unknowing and Other Works* (London: Penguin Classics, 2002).
93 Stapledon, *Last and First Men*, 287.
94 Stapledon, *Last and First Men*, 288.
95 Stapledon, *Last and First Men*, 303.
96 Stapledon, *Last and First Men*, 303.
97 Stapledon, *Last and First Men*, 91.
98 Stapledon, *Last and First Men*, 232. At first blush it is hard not to read this passage as ironic. However, the use of Stapledon's key musical metaphor, one with which he concludes the novel, makes that unlikely.
99 Stapledon, *Last and First Men*, 232.
100 Fyodor Dostoyevsky, *The Brothers Karamazov* (London: Folio Society, 1964), 275.
101 Stapledon, *Last and First Men*, 304.
102 Stapledon, *Last and First Men*, 304.
103 Caldy Hill in West Kirby, not too far from Liverpool. See Stapledon, *Star Maker*, 283.
104 Stapledon, *Star Maker*, 7.
105 Stapledon, *Star Maker*, 260.
106 1 Cor 13:13.
107 Stapledon, *Star Maker*, 212.
108 Stapledon, *Star Maker*, 223.
109 Stapledon, *Star Maker*, 212.
110 Stapledon, *Star Maker*, 227.
111 Stapledon, *Star Maker*, 228.
112 Dante Alighieri, *Paradiso* (New York: Bantam Classics, 1986), sec. Canto XXXIII, 52–54.
113 Alighieri, *Paradiso*, sec. Canto XXXIII, 124–26.
114 Stapledon, *Star Maker*, 232.
115 Stapledon, *Star Maker*, 246–47.
116 Stapledon, *Star Maker*, 233.
117 Whitehead gave his Gifford Lectures, *Process and Reality*, in 1927–1928.
118 Stapledon, *Star Maker*, 233.
119 Stapledon, *Star Maker*, 233.
120 In an appendix to *Star Maker*, Stapledon refers to an "infinite" number of creations, which suggests that we should not take the description within the novel of an "ultimate creation" too restrictively. However, this comment appears in the rubric for a circular diagram that

continues to represent the progress from immature, through mature, to ultimate cosmos. This may hint at an infinite series of cycles, however not necessarily involving a "recurrence of the same." The theological implications remain, though. Stapledon has carefully bound his Star Maker to a process, and that he is the immanent ground and outcome of an infinite number of creative processes does not bring the Star Maker any closer to the transcendence argued for the God of traditional Christian theism—which, of course, is entirely consistent with Stapledon's philosophy and polemic.

121 Stapledon, *Star Maker*, 255.

122 Stapledon, *Star Maker*, 257.

123 William Desmond, *God and the Between* (Oxford: Wiley-Blackwell, 2007), 287. Thomas Aquinas, *The Summa Theologiae of St. Thomas Aquinas: Latin-English Edition, Prima Pars, Q. 1–64* (Scotts Valley, Calif.: CreateSpace, 2009), 1.4.2, pp. 44–55 (reference is to part, question, and article).

124 Stapledon, *Star Maker*, 256.

125 Stapledon, *Star Maker*, 256.

126 Burke, *Philosophical Enquiry*, 111.

127 Burke, *Philosophical Enquiry*, 111.

128 Mackenzie and Mackenzie, *Life of H. G. Wells*.

129 Stapledon, *Star-Maker*, 228.

## CHAPTER 4

1 "*Metropolis* Restored: Watch a New Version of Fritz Lang's Masterpiece," *Open Culture*, accessed September 11, 2013, http://www.openculture.com/2012/07/imetropolisi_restored_watch_a_new_version_of_fritz_langs_masterpiece.html.

2 "Nature" here, as "the inherent force that directs either the world or human beings or both" and "nature" as "the material world itself, taken as including or not including human beings." Raymond Williams, *Keywords: A Vocabulary of Culture and Society* (London: Fontana, 2010), 219.

3 Elizabeth Gaskell, *Mary Barton* (London: Folio Society, 2004), 5–7. The passage provides a very full survey of rural blessings, all set in contrast to Mancunian miseries.

4 Of course, where this contrast is culturally forceful, intimations of the enigmatic otherness it frequently serves to obscure may still be recognized. John Clare's bird poems, for example, both invoke the metaphor of nature as blessed retreat from culture ("Ah, happy songster, man can seldom share / A spot so hidden from the haunts of

care" ["The Reed-Bird"]) and hint that difference of being beyond the happy coordination of culture and nature ("she wakes her jarring noise / to the unheeding waste" ["The Fern-Owl's Nest"]). John Clare, *Bird Poems*, ed. Peter Levi (London: Folio Society, 1980), 99, 95.

5 Raymond Williams, *Problems in Materialism and Culture* (London: Verso Books, 1996), 83. See also Heidegger's famous description of nature as a "standing reserve" in a technological culture. Martin Heidegger, *The Question Concerning Technology, and Other Essays* (New York: Harper Perennial, 1982).

6 For a nice example of the humor: "The door refused to open, it said, 'Five cents, please.' . . . 'What I pay you,' he informed it, 'is in the nature of a gratuity, I don't *have* to pay you.' 'I think otherwise,' the door said, 'Look in the purchase contract you signed when you bought this conapt. . . . You discover I'm right,' the door said. It sounded smug." Philip K. Dick, *Ubik*, 1st Vintage Books ed. (New York: Vintage Books, 1992), 23–24.

7 Philip K. Dick, *The Simulacra* (New York: Vintage Books, 2002); Dick, *Now Wait for Last Year* (New York: Voyager, 2009); Dick, *The Penultimate Truth*, new ed. (London: Gollancz, 2005).

8 Fritz Leiber, *Gather, Darkness!* 1548 paperback ed. (London: New English Library, 1966); Frank Herbert, *Dune*, 2nd ed. (London: Hodder Paperbacks, 1982).

9 Philip K. Dick, *Blade Runner (Do Androids Dream of Electric Sheep?)*, new ed. (London: Gollancz, 1999), 20.

10 Dick, *Do Androids Dream*, 7.

11 Dick, *Do Androids Dream*, 2, 3.

12 Dick, *Do Androids Dream*, 14.

13 Dick, *Do Androids Dream*, 47.

14 Dick, *Do Androids Dream*, 41.

15 Dick, *Do Androids Dream*, 18.

16 Dick, *Do Androids Dream*, 170.

17 Dick, *Do Androids Dream*, 174.

18 Dick, *Do Androids Dream*, 184.

19 Dick, *Do Androids Dream*, 200.

20 Dick, *Do Androids Dream*, 201.

21 Dick, *Do Androids Dream*, 155.

22 Dick, *Do Androids Dream*, 201.

23 Dick, *Do Androids Dream*, 205.

24 Dick, *Do Androids Dream*, 207.

25 Dick, *Do Androids Dream*, 211.

26 Dick, *Do Androids Dream*, 212.

27 Mark 10:13-15.

28 Dick, *Do Androids Dream*, 214.

29 Dick, *Do Androids Dream*, 207.

30 Philip K. Dick, *Time Out of Joint*, new ed. (London: Gollancz, 2003); Dick, *Penultimate Truth*; Dick, *Dr. Bloodmoney* (New York: Vintage Books, 2002).

31 *The Three Stigmata of Palmer Eldritch* was published in 1965, three years before *Do Androids Dream*.

32 Umberto Rossi, *The Twisted Worlds of Philip K. Dick: A Reading of Twenty Ontologically Uncertain Novels* (Jefferson, N.C.: McFarland, 2011), 178.

33 The term "bildungsroman" is appropriate here, I would argue. Even though these are not "coming of age" stories, they do involve the maturing—albeit ambiguous, as one would expect from Philip Dick—of a sensitive character who is at odds with his social role but achieves a different, more humanly adequate, relationship to others through enduring a series of crises.

34 Philip K. Dick, *The Three Stigmata of Palmer Eldritch*, new ed. (London: Gollancz, 2003), 204; emphasis in original.

35 My summary straightens out a narrative that is more hilariously complicated and enjoys rather more convoluted time shifts and virtual-reality jumps.

36 Thierry de Duve and Doreet LeVitte Harten, eds., *Heaven* (London: Hatje Cantz, 1999), 10.

37 Dick, *Palmer Eldritch*, 45; and, of course, Heb 11:1 (KJV).

38 Dick, *Palmer Eldritch*, 41; cf. 1 Cor.

39 Cf., in the case of *soma*, the exhortation that sin should not reign in "your mortal body [*soma*]" or offer "your bodies [*somata*] as a living sacrifice." Rom 6:12; Rom: 12:1. Rudolf Bultmann, *Theology of the New Testament*, vol. 1, trans. K. Grobel (London: SCM Press, 1971), 192–203.

40 Dick, *Palmer Eldritch*, 48.

41 Dick, *Palmer Eldritch*, 43, 46.

42 This a recurrent theme in Dick's novels. Alternative realities of this compensatory kind feature an obsessive concern with authenticity and exactness of reproduction. In addition to Ragle Gumm, mentioned above, there is, for example, Virgil Ackerman's recreation of his boyhood hometown (Dick, *Now Wait for Last Year*).

43 Dick, *Palmer Eldritch*, 41, 37. In both these versions, eucharistic language is significantly distorted. The distinction between "accidents" and "substance," as in the doctrine of transubstantiation, did not separate the accidents of bread and wine from the substance of the body and blood of Christ, as when the colonist Fran suggests that translation only involves the "appearances." In the sacrament, "the

very body of Christ exists." Ironically, but in keeping with his position on an axis that opposes him to Christ, Palmer Eldritch provides the more accurate account of transubstantiation when comparing it with the relationship between his virtual-reality avatar and his substantial presence. On the other hand, the presence of Christ in the sacrament is not an unqualified presence but a presence that is also an absence and necessarily so. The biblical narratives and symbols associated with Jesus' ascension intimate an abiding presence of one who "goes to the Father," has now "ascended," is not "to be clung to," is present "through the Spirit," and will "come again." Sacramental presence, therefore, is not immediacy but the presence of Jesus who has "ascended into heaven," and is received now in the form of his absence. We have, therefore, an abiding distance, an otherness mediated in a sacrament that resists the narcissistic temptation toward a full immediate and absorbing presence. Receiving the Eucharist means assenting to a presence that is also a loss: the Lord is here as the one who is still to come. In contrast, the underlying structure of Martian debate upon the sacred served by Can-D is an opposition between presence and absence. The "orthodox" view, the strong interpretation, claims a full presence, an impossible immediacy, conditional upon an absence from bodies that are left behind as abject "husks."

44 Dick, *Palmer Eldritch*, 176.

45 Dick, *Palmer Eldritch*, 212.

46 Dick, *Palmer Eldritch*, 187.

47 Dick, *Palmer Eldritch*, 193; emphasis in original.

48 Dick, *Palmer Eldritch*, 192. Eldritch's stigmata recall the futurist aesthetic of sublime mechanical violence, as in Duchamp-Villon's *Le Grand Cheval* (1914), in which the horse's anatomy is enthusiastically transformed through "its mechanical correlative: connecting rod, axle, gears, and piston." Didier Ottinger, ed., *Futurism* (London: Five Continents Editions, 2009), 210. See also F. T. Marinetti, "Geometric and Mechanical Splendour, and the Numerical Sensibility, 1914," in *Futurist Manifestos*, ed. Umbro Apollonio (London: Tate, 2009), 154–59. And, on the dystopian side, Jacob Epstein's *Rock Drill* should be viewed with Palmer Eldritch in mind. Mark Antliff and Vivien Greene, eds., *The Vorticists: Manifesto for a Modern World* (London: Tate, 2011), 19, 96, 97.

49 Dick, *Palmer Eldritch*, 86, 94.

50 Dick, *Palmer Eldritch*, 202.

51 Dick, *Palmer Eldritch*, 204.

52 Dick, *Palmer Eldritch*, 224, 225–30.

53 Dick, *Palmer Eldritch*, 213.

54 Burke, *Philosophical Enquiry*, 85–87. Of course, the sublime is interpreted variously in relation to self-preservation. For Kant, see below, pp. 71–72, 198–99.

55 Nye, *American Technological Sublime*. See also, Ellul, *Technological Society*; and, more recently, Lyotard, *Inhuman*, 8–23.

56 Harlan Ellison, "I Have No Mouth, and I Must Scream," in *Dreams with Sharp Teeth* (New York: Quality Paperback Book Club, n.d.), 33.

57 Dick, *Palmer Eldritch*, 220.

58 Dick, *Palmer Eldritch*, 149.

59 Dick, *Palmer Eldritch*, 149.

60 Jung's essay "Transformation Symbolism in the Mass" was an important influence on Dick's thinking at the time of writing *Palmer Eldritch*. The various references to eucharistic doctrine, however, show that influence less directly than does the spiritual crisis and moral development of Barney Mayerson. In interpreting the symbolism of the Mass, Jung analyses "sacrifice" and its role in the process of individuation. As we "individuate," Jung argues, the "self" overcomes the resistances of the "ego" to become, in the ego, at least partially self-conscious. The "self" is the unconscious ground of the ego, pressing toward consciousness. The ego, however, desiring to maintain its illusory primacy and control, dreads becoming more fully conscious. As Jung describes it, becoming self-conscious is a sacrificial drama, one symbolic complex of which is the Christian narrative of incarnation. The ego allows itself to be displaced, its self-preserving drive checked by the disclosure of the self, revealed as the larger psychic environment from which the ego originated. The self, for its part, submits to the passage from unconscious totality to partial consciousness within the ego, feeling "in some sort" the ego's sacrifice as "a sacrifice of itself." C. G. Jung, *Psychology and Western Religion (from Vols. 11, 18 Collected Works)*, trans. R. F. C. Hull (Princeton, N.J.: Princeton University Press, 1984), 158. Mayerson's voluntary exile to the wretchedness of Mars follows the contours of Jung's analysis: a self-sacrifice proceeding from a moral choice not mandated by a "collective moral standard" mediated by the Freudian superego. There is, in consequence, a loss of moral bearings, a measure of bewilderment about motive, and distress at the personal cost. Under these circumstances, the sacrifice appears as an act of the self, an attainment of individuation whereby the ego both is dethroned and comes to itself, to a psychic fullness that is always present but resisted. This "proper self" is an inwardness that informs the ego but with which the ego can never catch up or render wholly present.

61 Dick, *Palmer Eldritch*, 218; emphasis in original.

62 Dick uses the language and mythology of classical Gnosticism, as found in the Nag Hammadi scriptures, drawing especially on the Valentinian works and explicitly citing the tractate *On the Origin of the World*.

63 Wilhelm Schneemelcher, *New Testament Apocrypha*, vol. 2, *Writings Relating to the Apostles*, rev. ed. (Louisville, Ky.: Westminster John Knox, 2003), 808.

64 On March 16, 18, and 20, Philip K. Dick experienced a series of visions, surprisingly extended in time. In the first, "frightening vortexes of light" swirled about his bed, and, in the second, he was treated to "hundreds of thousands" of "perfectly formed modern abstract paintings." In both cases, the visions lasted around eight hours. Later, Dick described the first vision as releasing him "from every thrall, inner and outer." Over the following months, Dick was the subject of several paranormal events and further visions that he interpreted as revelatory and, at least to a certain extent, healing. For the description, see the July 1974 letter quoted in Lawrence Sutin, *Divine Invasions: The Life of Philip K. Dick* (New York: Harmony Books, 1990), 213–14. Dick turned the last eight years of his life into a test site for interpretations and validations of these visions and their associated experiences. This interpretative pilgrimage was, not surprisingly, "circular": the insights, often contradictory, frequently shifting in conceptuality and symbolic range, shaping the remembered experiences and nurturing future ones. Before his death in 1982, the pages of his "Exegesis" notebooks, the primary outlet for his speculations, had piled up into their thousands. He also wrote four novels, one of which, the posthumously published *Radio Free Albemuth*, was an early version of *VALIS*, though very different in form and content. The other novels are *The Divine Invasion* and *The Transmigration of Timothy Archer*, published in 1981 and 1982 respectively. All these novels turn around the events of "2-3-74" and may be read for their contribution to Dick's evolving interpretation of his visions. The reading proposed here, though, has a quite different purpose, which is to place *VALIS* in relation to the science-fictional sublime, concentrating on the novel's appropriation of gnostic myth and imagery in terms that transpose "gnosis" into "information." *VALIS* is, after all, a novel and deserves reading in its own terms, not as evidence for Dick's intellectual or religious biography, and not as the first in a "trilogy," of formally quite disparate works, despite certain themes resonant of 2-3-74. That said, I am not denying the importance of the works for Dick's biography or the interest of reading his final novels as a trilogy.

An interesting example of sifting Dick's later works for an underlying theological position—in this case, a traditional Christianity with heterodox elements—is Gabriel McKee's *Pink Beams of Light from the God in the Gutter: The Science Fictional Religion of Philip K. Dick* (Lanham, Md.: University Press of America, 2003). Umberto Rossi offers a careful reading of the whole trilogy, finding in *The Transmigration of Timothy Archer* answers to questions first posed in *VALIS*. Rossi, *Twisted Worlds*.

65 *Philip K. Dick: VALIS and Later Novels; A Maze of Death / VALIS / The Divine Invasion / The Transmigration of Timothy Archer* (New York: Library of America, 2009), 177.

66 Dick, *VALIS and Later Novels*, 178.

67 Dick, *VALIS and Later Novels*, 385.

68 *The Three Forms of Thought*, in Marvin Meyer, ed., *The Nag Hammadi Scriptures: The Revised and Updated Translation of Sacred Gnostic Texts Complete in One Volume*, international ed. (New York: HarperOne, 2008), 730.

69 See Giovanni Filoramo, *A History of Gnosticism*, new ed. (Oxford: Wiley-Blackwell, 1992); Hans Jonas, *The Gnostic Religion*, 3rd ed. (Boston: Beacon, 2001); Birger A. Pearson, *Ancient Gnosticism: Traditions and Literature* (Minneapolis: Fortress, 2007).

70 *The Secret Book of John*, in Meyer, *Nag Hammadi Scriptures*, 114.

71 David is not present for the viewing.

72 The plot of *Valis* partially reprises that of Dick's posthumously published *Radio Free Albemuth*.

73 Dick, *VALIS and Later Novels*, 347.

74 Dick, *VALIS and Later Novels*, 350.

75 Prov 8:29-34.

76 The appendix to *VALIS*, made up of the passages from Fat's exegesis quoted during the novel, is discussed below. This appendix provides—despite what might be taken as a promise in its title, *Tractates Cryptica Scriptura*—no synthesis but a provocation to further branching interpretation.

77 Luciano Floridi, *Information: A Very Short Introduction* (New York: Oxford University Press, 2010), 71.

78 On the different forms and functions of information, see Floridi, *Philosophy of Information*, chap. 15.

79 Dick, *VALIS and Later Novels*, 342.

80 Dick, *VALIS and Later Novels*, 255.

81 *On the Origin of the World*, in Meyer, *Nag Hammadi Scriptures*, 206. See also, for instance, *The Tripartite Tractate*, in Meyer, *Nag Hammadi Scriptures*, 85; *Secret Book of John*, in Meyer, *Nag Hammadi Scriptures*,

116; *The Second Discourse of the Great Seth*, in Meyer, *Nag Hammadi Scriptures*, 479.

82 Meyer, *Nag Hammadi Scriptures*, 204.

83 Dick, *VALIS and Later Novels*, 228. Cf. Meyer, *Nag Hammadi Scriptures*, 206.

84 Meyer, *Nag Hammadi Scriptures*, 74.

85 Meyer, *Nag Hammadi Scriptures*, 207.

86 Dick, *VALIS and Later Novels*, 283.

87 Dick, *VALIS and Later Novels*, 254–55.

88 Dick, *VALIS and Later Novels*, 338.

89 Dick, *VALIS and Later Novels*, 331.

90 Dick, *VALIS and Later Novels*, 350–51; cf. Prov 8.

91 Dick, *VALIS and Later Novels*, 335.

92 Dick, *VALIS and Later Novels*, 337, 356; 355–57; 342.

93 Desmond, *God and the Between*, 223.

94 Dick, *VALIS and Later Novels*, 363–64.

95 *The Gospel of Truth*, in Meyer, *Nag Hammadi Scriptures*, 44.

96 *Tripartite Tractate* and *The Gospel of Truth*, in Meyer, *Nag Hammadi Scriptures*, 76, 44. See also, "In the uprightness of our love, we are innocent, pure, and good, and we have the mind of the Father in an ineffable mystery." *Second Discourse of the Great Seth*, in Meyer, *Nag Hammadi Scriptures*, 482.

97 Dick, *VALIS and Later Novels*, 343; emphasis in original.

98 A threat analogous to the maze in which the Lamptons claim that they lost themselves along with their fellow travellers from the Albemuth star system.

99 Dick, *VALIS and Later Novels*, 286–87, 292.

100 Dick, *VALIS and Later Novels*, 350.

101 W. H. C. Frend, *The Rise of Christianity* (London: Darton, Longman & Todd, 1984), 229–307; David Braake, "Self-Differentiation among Christian Groups: The Gnostics and Their Opponents," in *The Cambridge History of Christianity,* vol. 1, *Origins to Constantine*, ed. Margaret Mary Mitchell, Frances M. Young, and K. Scott Bowie (Cambridge: Cambridge University Press, 2006), 62–84.

102 Dick, *VALIS and Later Novels*, 355–56.

103 Meyer, *Nag Hammadi Scriptures*, 207.

104 Dick, *VALIS and Later Novels*, 384.

## CHAPTER 5

1 The quotation in the heading for this section is from Captain Beefheart, *Spotlight Kid/Clear Spot* (Warner, 2006).

2 As in James Blish, *The Triumph of Time* (New York: Avon Publications, 1958); discussed below.

3 The apocalyptic subgenre is often divided into "apocalyptic" and "postapocalyptic" novels. "Apocalyptic" novels and stories focus on the disaster itself, on causes, character, and impact; the "postapocalyptic" tell of life in the aftermath of cataclysm. In practice, that is a fuzzy distinction. Most apocalyptic novels anticipate or describe the beginnings of life after the "big one," whatever it is, and whether it comes in a flash or grinds us all down over generations. By the same token, in stories generally classed as postapocalyptic, the originating catastrophe shadows their circumstances and shapes the plot.

4 On the use of the term "apocalypse," cf. Klaus Koch, *The Rediscovery of Apocalyptic: A Polemical Work on a Neglected Area of Biblical Studies and Its Damaging Effects on Theology and Philosophy*, Studies in Biblical Theology 22 (London: SCM Press, 1972).

5 "Apocalyptic" did not secure the same abiding interest in Judaism after the second century, partly because of Christian enthusiasm. Apocalyptic ideas, however, are found in the Talmud, and themes, e.g., from 1 Enoch, became important within medieval Jewish mysticism. See *Encyclopedia Judaica*, vol. 3 (Jerusalem: Keter, 1972), s.v. "Apocalypse."

6 More recently, scholars have traced apocalyptic elements in other faiths, including Islam, contemporary Buddhism in Japan, and Native American religion, as well as in secular political movement, and in non-Western popular culture. In literary and cultural theory, "apocalyptic" has been appropriated, against itself, in the form of "end-time-without-judgment," a strategy of undermining hegemonic cultural orders, to create an opening in the name of the "others" a culture excludes.

7 Myrone, *John Martin: Apocalypse*, 156.

8 Campbell's poem was published in 1823, three years before Shelley's novel. For the full text, see Thomas Campbell, "'The Last Man' by Thomas Campbell," *Romantic Circles*, published October 1, 1997, http://www.rc.umd.edu/editions/mws/lastman/campb.htm.

9 Rev 6:16.

10 This is not, of course, a question of the medium but of the demands of the sublime; painting is quite capable of symbolic richness; indeed the Pre-Raphaelites provide Victorian examples.

11 The full title is *The Sacred Theory of the Earth: Containing an Account of the Original of the Earth and of All the General Changes Which It Hath Already Undergone or Is To Undergo Till the Consummation of All Things* (London: Printed by R. N. for Walter Kettilby, 1697).

12 Burnet, *Sacred Theory*, 47; emphasis in original.

13 See, Nicolson, *Mountain Gloom and Mountain Glory*.

14 In their turn, theological attacks on Burnet's theory reinforced the modern sublime by disputing his slur upon the existing state of geological reality. Mountains, insisted John Ray (the influential "physico-theologian"), are of providential design and not the wretched consequence of punitive catastrophe. They are "most proper for the putting forth of Plants; yielding the greatest Variety, and the most luxuriant Sorts of Vegetables," while earthquakes warn human beings of their imminent moral accountability before God. Herbert Croft drew upon sublimity itself in defending an original world of crag and cave. Mountain scenery, especially when set next to the sea, "represent unto us the infinite Power and Majesty of God." With this, the Bishop of Hereford turned the sublime against Burnet, disputing the theology by conceding the aesthetic. For the controversy, see Nicolson, *Mountain Gloom and Mountain Glory*, 255–68.

15 Burnet, *Sacred Theory*, 52.

16 Greg Bear, *The Forge of God* (London: Tor Books, 2001), 457.

17 Young, *Young's Night Thoughts*.

18 Hoxie Neale Fairchild, *Religious Trends in English Poetry*, vol. 1 (New York: Columbia University Press, 1949), 119.

19 Hill, cited in Fairchild, *Religious Trends*, 449.

20 "Most Surprizing Scenes . . ." comes from the preface to Young's "A Poem on the Last Day," cited in Morris, *Religious Sublime*, 117; "Worldliness and Other-Worldliness: The Poet Young," in *The Essays of "George Eliot,"* ed. Nathan Sheppard (New York: Funk & Wagnalls, 1883), 236. Eliot's condemnation intimates one theological problem with the sublime, especially for a faith the center of which is the Word made flesh: "In Young we have the type of that deficient human sympathy, that *impiety toward the present and the visible*, which flies for its motives, its sanctities, and its religion, to the remote, the vague, and the unknown" (256; emphasis in original).

21 Ciaran Cronin, *A Companion to Victorian Poetry*, ed. Richard Cronin, Antony Harrison, and Alison Chapman (Malden, Mass.: Wiley-Blackwell, 2002), 35.

22 Edward Henry Bickersteth, *Yesterday, To-Day, and For Ever: A Poem in Twelve Books* (New York: Robert Carter & Bros., 1875), 352. A contemporary review begins with the irresistibly silly, "the poem opens very naturally, describing the narrator's death" (8).

23 This summary is apt to my purposes but shows nothing of the richness of Miller's narrative.

24 Walter M. Miller Jr., *A Canticle For Leibowitz* (London: Gollancz, 2013), 336.

25 Wolfhart Pannenberg, *Jesus: God and Man* (Louisville, Ky.: Westminster John Knox, 1982), 69.

26 Greg Bear, *Blood Music* (London: Gollancz, 2008), 262.

27 Bear, *Blood Music*, 239.

28 Thomas M. Disch, *The Genocides* (New York: Vintage Books, 2000), 4, 12.

29 In *War of the Worlds*, Wells compares Martian invasion to British imperialism. *The Genocides* invites an analogous comparison with the Holocaust, though it is never made explicitly.

30 That the mean-spirited and blundering Neil meets an unpleasant end is no surprise, but that he dies relieving his "pent-up lusts" on the severed head of the elderly "Alice Nemerov R.N." tips from savagery into tasteless black comedy. Disch, *Genocides*, 135.

31 Disch, *Genocides*, 113.

32 Disch, *Genocides*, 143. This development reverses the pattern of a widespread mythologem according to which humanity originated under the earth's surface and the primal ancestors made their way by stages, up to the "outer world." Claude Lévi-Strauss, *The Jealous Potter*, trans. Bénédicte Chorier (Chicago: University of Chicago Press, 1988), chaps. 8, 9; Mircea Eliade, *Myths, Dreams and Mysteries: The Encounter between Contemporary Faiths and Archaic Realities* (New York: Harper & Row, 1975), chap. 7.

33 Disch, *Genocides*, 30.

34 Disch, *Genocides*, 146.

35 Disch, *Genocides*, 145.

36 Andersen's "fierce, unreasoning Calvinism" (Disch, *Genocides*, 38), it should be stressed, is a grotesque caricature of Reformed theology, and an all-too-common one, even if it has had some "real world" examples.

37 Disch, *Genocides*, 38.

38 Disch, *Genocides*, 145.

39 Ps 103:16.

40 The Gramineae (also known as Poaceae) are the world's fifth-largest plant family, with over ten thousand species. Christopher's choice of disaster is very canny and a good example of an effective but understated use of science in science fiction. Loss of the grasses would devastate the food economy and leave billions starving. Root vegetables cannot be grown as widely; fish and other forms of food from seas and rivers are also limited in access and volume. Christopher does

not mention these explicitly, but Gramineae includes plants used for more than food, too: pampas grass, bamboo, reeds.

41 Potatoes, of course, are not a grass and, therefore, become the agricultural hope of the novel. Christopher does not mention another, at least, global possibility. Soybeans are legumes, not grass, so perhaps soybeans, which were imported into Europe during the Second World War to offset food shortages, might modify the novel's assessment of disaster. That said, soybeans do not grow in Yorkshire!

42 John Christopher, *The Death of Grass* (London: Penguin Modern Classics, 2009), 77.

43 On the "buffered self," see Charles Taylor, *A Secular Age* (Cambridge, Mass.: Harvard University Press, 2007), 27–89..

44 Christopher, *Death of Grass*, 116.

45 Christopher, *Death of Grass*, 160.

46 There is one passing, and sarcastic, reference to a "parson." Christopher, *Death of Grass*, 94.

47 Christopher, *Death of Grass*, 104.

48 Christopher, *Death of Grass*, 105.

49 Christopher, *Death of Grass*, 195.

50 Christopher, *Death of Grass*, 194.

51 Samuel Johnson, *The History of Rasselas: Prince of Abyssinia*, ed. Gilbert Phelps (London: Folio Society, 1975), 128–30.

52 The order of writing is rather different, with the "prequel," *They Shall Have Stars* (1957), which introduces "spindizzies" and "anti-agathic drugs," published second, and a further novel, *A Life for the Stars* (1962), set prior in time to *Earthman, Come Home* (1955), the first to be completed.

53 Blish, *Triumph of Time*, 47.

54 Blish, *Triumph of Time*, 59.

55 Blish, *Triumph of Time*, 157–58.

56 Blish, *Triumph of Time*, 130.

57 Blish, *Triumph of Time*, 65.

58 Blish, *Triumph of Time*, 156.

59 Blish, *Triumph of Time*, 107.

60 Blish, *Triumph of Time*, 138.

61 Blish, *Triumph of Time*, 158.

62 Blish, *Triumph of Time*, 136.

63 Blish, *Triumph of Time*, 56.

64 Blish, *Triumph of Time*, 153.

65 Hans Urs von Balthasar, *Theo-Drama: Last Act v. 5; Theological Dramatic Theory* (San Francisco: Ignatius, 1988), 397–98.

66 Karl Rahner, *Hearers of the Word: Laying the Foundation for a Philosophy of Religion* (New York: Continuum, 1997), 53.

67 Stapledon, *Beyond the "Isms,"* 67.

68 The weakness of the doctrine of the Trinity within eighteenth- and nineteenth-century theology has much to do with the plausibility of denying personality to God. See William C. Placher, *The Domestication of Transcendence: How Modern Thinking about God Went Wrong* (Louisville, Ky.: Westminster John Knox, 1996), 164–78; Michael J. Buckley, *At the Origins of Modern Atheism* (New Haven, Conn.: Yale University Press, 1987).

69 For an understanding of "person" that permits analogy with God's "infinite" personality, see *The Collected Works of Samuel Taylor Coleridge,* vol. 15, *Opus Maximum*, ed. Thomas MacFarlane (Princeton, N.J.: Princeton University Press, 2002), 166–213; Desmond, *God and the Between*, 191–204, 281–340; Huw Parri Owen, *Christian Theism: A Study in Its Basic Principles* (Edinburgh: T&T Clark, 1984), chap. 1.

70 George Zebrowski, *The Omega Point Trilogy* (New York: Ace Science Fiction, 2002), 294.

71 Zebrowski remained diffident about the philosophy itself, insisting that the main attraction was "an entertaining conflict and a strong emotional conviction." However, from the last chapters of *The Omega Point* and throughout *Mirror of Minds*, the ideas determine the story even at the expense of suspense and character. Zebrowski, *Omega Point Trilogy*, 295.

72 Zebrowski's philosophical sources also include Leibnitz, Nietzsche, and Bergson. The two latter give him language for an evolving universe, and Leibnitz the concepts of "monadic structure." More importantly, all three help him make his a radical distinction between appearance and reality, the external surface and its spiritual inwardness. De Chardin and Schopenhauer, however, seem to me to be the most significant of his conversation partners.

73 Zebrowski, *Omega Point Trilogy*, 207.

74 The relationship between worlds as produced by the force-center and worlds as the externality of minds is unclear. Zebrowski probably derived the duality from Schopenhauer's distinction between the "Will" and the eternal "Ideas" that inform the particulars of the phenomenal world, the "world as representation."

75 Zebrowski, *Omega Point Trilogy*, 291, 273.

76 Miroslav Volf, "Enter into Joy!" in *The End of the World and the Ends of God*, ed. J. C. Polkinghorne and Michael Welker (London: SCM Press, 2000), 256–78; Karl Rahner, *Theological Investigations,* vol. 4, *More Recent Writings* (London: Helicon, 1966), 323–46; Wolfhart

Pannenberg, *Systematic Theology*, vol. 3 (Grand Rapids: Eerdmans, 1991), 555–79; Jürgen Moltmann, *Theology of Hope: On the Ground and the Implications of a Christian Eschatology* (London: SCM Press, 2002); Walter Kasper, *Jesus the Christ* (New York: Paulist, 1976), 125–60.

77 Pierre Teilhard de Chardin, *The Human Phenomenon: A New Edition and Translation of "Le Phenomene Humain"* (Brighton, U.K.: Sussex Academic, 2003), 30–32.

78 Zebrowski, *Omega Point Trilogy*, 207. The relationship between tangential energy and entropy is more complex in de Chardin, given his conviction that tangential energy is "constantly increasing" (Teilhard de Chardin, *Human Phenomenon*, 31) but without violating the second law of thermodynamics. This, not surprisingly, was one of the claims for which de Chardin was sharply attacked.

79 Zebrowski, *Omega Point Trilogy*, 217.

80 For Schopenhauer, Zebrowski's inspiration here, both the beautiful and the sublime offer us the chance of a solace that lifts us out of the phenomenal to the timeless "Ideas." The sublime is distinctive, however, as it forces us to still our wills in relation to the threatening aspects of its material focus—that is, the chances of falling off the cliff or into the cataract. See Kirwan, *Sublimity: The Non-rational and the Rational in the History of Aesthetics*, new ed. (London: Routledge, 2005), 97–102; Kathleen Higgins and Robert C. Solomon, *The Age of German Idealism: Routledge History of Philosophy,* vol. 6, new ed. (London: Routledge, 2003), 345–53.

81 Hans Moravec, *Robot: Mere Machine to Transcendent Mind* (New York: Oxford University Press, 1998), 167.

82 Zebrowski, *Omega Point Trilogy*, 273.

83 To be fair, Teilhard de Chardin, who so influenced Zebrowski, maintained the traditional refusal to identify "nature" and "grace" at this point: the kingdom of God is not a "natural" goal but "comes down" from God. It exceeds all evolutionary possibilities (Teilhard de Chardin, *Human Phenomenon*, 214n*; here, Teilhard argues his respect for the traditional affirmation of humanity's final goal as a "supernatural" one: "the presence at the head of the world of *something still higher, in its line*, than the Omega Point"; emphasis in original). However, de Chardin, while understanding "spirit" as "born within and . . . a function of matter," also anticipated the final "detachment" of spirit "from its material matrix." He thus left us with another "monism of mind." Pierre Teilhard de Chardin, *Christianity and Evolution* (New York: Mariner Books, 2002), 108; Teilhard de Chardin, *Human Phenomenon*, 206. The evolutionary ladder, thus kicked away, includes all the plant and animal life, now revealed as originally necessary but ultimately

dispensable. An adequate Christian eschatology cannot afford such instrumentalization, nor the spiritual liquidation of matter.

84 Way back in the fourteenth century, Julian of Norwich had grasped that, from the beginning, our physicality was made complicit with eternity: "Our sensuality is founded in nature, in mercy, and in grace, and this foundation enables us to receive gifts which lead us to endless life. For I saw very surely that our substance is in God, and I also saw that God is in our sensuality, for in the same instant and place in which our soul is made sensual, in that same instant and place exists the city of God, ordained for him without beginning. He comes into this city and will never depart from it." *Julian of Norwich: Showings*, ed. James Walsh (New York: Paulist, 1978), 287.

85 William Gibson, *Neuromancer* (New York: Ace, 1984), 30.

86 Gibson, *Neuromancer*, 5, 51.

87 Gibson, *Neuromancer*, 52.

88 Gibson, *Neuromancer*, 168.

89 Gibson, *Neuromancer*, 52.

90 Gibson, *Neuromancer*, 6.

91 Gibson, *Neuromancer*, 258.

92 Gibson, *Neuromancer*, 6.

93 Gibson, *Neuromancer*, 203.

94 Gibson, *Neuromancer*, 172.

95 Gibson, *Neuromancer*, 173.

96 Gibson, *Neuromancer*, 173.

97 Georges Bataille, *Theory of Religion* (New York: Zone Books, 2006), 19.

98 Gibson, *Neuromancer*, 56.

99 Gibson, *Neuromancer*, 239.

100 Gibson, *Neuromancer*, 109–10.

101 Gibson, *Neuromancer*, 270.

102 Gibson, *Neuromancer*, 270.

103 This may seem ironic or even perverse given that recent, postmodern philosophical interpretations of the sublime have claimed it as a means to "make war upon totality" (Jean-François Lyotard, *The Postmodern Condition: A Report on Knowledge* (Manchester: Manchester University Press, 1984), 82. The evidence of this chapter aside, though, the nihilism of postmodern interpretations of sublimity precipitates human beings into a radical equivocity without escape, arguably an especially hopeless totality.

CHAPTER 6

1 Alfonso Cuarón, *Gravity*, Drama, Sci-Fi, Thriller (2013).

2 IMDb's page for *Gravity* has an example of the poster; see "Pictures & Photos from Gravity," accessed November 21, 2013, http://www.imdb.com/media/rm741451264/tt1454468.

3 Christian eschatology, of course, affirms bodiliness in the doctrine of resurrection. Much Western eschatology, though, especially in popular modern forms, has obscured this affirmation or dispensed with it altogether. See Pannenberg, *Systematic Theology*, vol. 3; Polkinghorne and Welker, *End of the World*.

4 E.g., see "Gravity Trailer (Main Trailer)," video, IMDb, accessed November 21, 2013, http://www.imdb.com/video/imdb/vi2340006169/.

5 Quoted from an IMDb member's review of *Gravity*.

6 Recently, the old chestnuts of this sorry polemic have been served up yet again. Only willful boneheadedness accounts for this revival, especially by the likes of Richard Dawkins. Dawkins, *The God Delusion* (London: Mariner Books, 2008).

7 The image is T. H. Huxley's.

8 Nye, *American Technological Sublime*, 85.

9 Blish, *Triumph of Time*, 86.

10 Clark, "Science Fiction and Religion," in Seed, *Companion to Science Fiction*, 95–110; Farah Mendlesohn, "Religion and Science Fiction," in Edward James and Farah Mendlesohn, eds., *The Cambridge Companion to Science Fiction* (Cambridge: Cambridge University Press, 2003), 264–75.

11 C. S. Lewis is, of course, most famous here but, also, rather untypical given the level of allegorizing. Writers whose work is informed by their Christian vision, but who do not allegorize or use literature as a direct vehicle for theological teaching, include R. A. Lafferty, Cordwainer Smith, and Gene Wolfe.

12 Locke, *An Essay concerning Human Understanding*, 549. The definition of "theism" here is controversial in that the term is often used simply to differentiate or associate Christian understanding of God with monotheistic tradition such as Judaism, Islam, and Sikhism; e.g., Owen, *Christian Theism*; David Bentley Hart, *The Experience of God: Being, Consciousness, Bliss* (New Haven, Conn.: Yale University Press, 2013). For present purposes, however, "theism" provides a convenient way of drawing attention to the difference between the Christian doctrine of God as developed over the first fifteen hundred years of Christianity and the theological changes associated especially with early Modernity and the Enlightenment.

13 For Clarke, see *Samuel Clarke*, 1–92.

14 René Descartes, "Meditations on First Philosophy," 2.37, in *Meditations & Other Writings* (London: Folio Society, 2012), 15–92.

15 As regards transcendence, cf., on Aquinas: "Theism, as it is commonly understood, tends to emphasize the language of distinction (God as an independent reality above and apart from the world), while Thomas seems to favor the language of participation in which distinction and identity are found inseparably linked together." Rudi A. te Velde, *Aquinas on God: The 'Divine Science' of the "Summa Theologiae"* (Burlington, Vt.: Ashgate, 2006), 172.

16 On the historical development, see Placher, *Domestication of Transcendence*; Charles Taliaferro, *Evidence and Faith: Philosophy and Religion since the Seventeenth Century* (Cambridge: Cambridge University Press, 2005).

17 See above, chap. 3.

18 Baillie, *Essay on the Sublime*, 6; emphasis in original.

19 Kant, *Critique of Judgement*, 98; emphasis in original.

20 William Desmond, *Art, Origins, Otherness: Between Philosophy and Art* (Albany: State University of New York Press, 2003), 82; emphasis in original.

21 Johann Gottlieb Fichte, "On the Foundation of Our Belief in a Divine Government of the Universe," in *Nineteenth-Century Philosophy*, ed. and trans. Patrick L. Gardiner (New York: Free Press, 1969), 25.

22 Young, *Young's Night Thoughts*, 240, 289.

23 Burke, *Philosophical Enquiry*, 112; emphasis added.

24 Robert W. Jenson, *America's Theologian: A Recommendation of Jonathan Edwards* (New York: Oxford University Press, 1992), chap. 2.

25 Edwards, *Scientific and Philosophical Writings*, The Works of Jonathan Edwards Series, vol. 6, ed. W. Anderson (New Haven, Conn.: Yale University Press, 1980), 332–38.

26 Roland Andre Delattre, *Beauty and Sensibility in the Thought of Jonathan Edwards: An Essay in Aesthetics* (New Haven, Conn.: Yale University Press, 1968), chap. 3.

27 Addison and Steele, *Selections*, 371.

28 Addison and Steele, *Selections*, 376.

29 Addison and Steele, *Selections*, 375–76.

30 Young, *Young's Night Thoughts*, 244.

31 Ussher, *Clio*, 102.

32 Burke, *Philosophical Enquiry*, 184; cf. 147.

33 Burke, *Philosophical Enquiry*, 177.

34 Burke, *Philosophical Enquiry*, 185; emphasis added.

35 Burke, *Philosophical Enquiry*, 110.

36 Edmund Burke, *Reflections on the Revolution in France: And on the Proceedings in Certain Societies in London Relative to That Event*, ed. Conor Cruise O'Brien (London: Penguin Books, 1986), 182.

37 Kant, *Critique of Judgement*, 125; cf. Immanuel Kant, *Observations on the Feeling of the Beautiful and the Sublime*, ed. John T. Goldthwait (Berkeley: University of California Press, 2003), 78–96.

38 Friedrich Schiller, *Aesthetical and Philosophical Essays* (Charleston, S.C.: Bibliobazaar, 2007), 154. "Liberty, with all its drawbacks, is everywhere vastly more attractive to a noble soul, than good social order without it—than society like a flock of sheep, or a machine working like a watch. This mechanism makes of man only a product; liberty makes him the citizen of a better world" (153).

39 Carter Ratcliff, "The Sublime Was Then: The Art of Barnett Newman," in Beckley, *Sticky Sublime*, 215.

40 Terry Eagleton, *The Ideology of the Aesthetic* (Oxford: Wiley-Blackwell, 1991), 59.

41 Edwards, *Scientific and Philosophical Writings*, 2–36.

42 Edwards, *Religious Affections*, ed. John Edwin Smith, The Works of Jonathan Edwards Series, vol. 2 (New Haven, Conn.: Yale University Press, 1959), 95; Edwards, *Typological Writings*, ed. Wallace E. Anderson, Mason I. Lowance, and David H. Watters, The Works of Jonathan Edwards Series, vol. 11 (New Haven, Conn.: Yale University Press, 1993), 56.

43 Edwards, *Letters and Personal Writings*, ed. John Edwin Smith, The Works of Jonathan Edwards Series, vol. 16 (New Haven, Conn.: Yale University Press, 1980), 793.

44 Edwards, *Sermons and Discourses, 1734–1738*, ed. John Edwin Smith, The Works of Jonathan Edwards Series, vol. 19 (New Haven, Conn.: Yale University Press, 1980), 565.

45 Edwards, *Ethical Writings*, The Works of Jonathan Edwards Series, vol. 8, ed. P. Ramsey (New Haven, Conn.: Yale University Press, 1989), 424.

46 Edwards, *Ethical Writings*, 34.

47 Edwards, *Scientific and Philosophical Writings*, 202.

48 Jacques Maritain, *A Preface to Metaphysics: Seven Lectures on Being* (London: Sheen and Ward, 1948), 25; see also Velde, *Aquinas on God*, 133.

49 Edwards, *Scientific and Philosophical Writings*, 332.

50 Delattre, *Beauty and Sensibility*, 98.

51 Kari Weil, *Thinking Animals: Why Animal Studies Now?* (New York: Columbia University Press, 2012), 31.

52 Edwards, *Scientific and Philosophical Writings*, 333.

53 Edwards, *Scientific and Philosophical Writings*, 336.

54 Edwards, *Scientific and Philosophical Writings*, 336. Thus, later in "The Mind," he writes, "When we spake of excellence in bodies we were obliged to borrow the word 'consent' from spiritual things" (362).

55 Edwards, *Scientific and Philosophical Writings*, 336; Edwards' distinction between primary and secondary sometimes appears to correspond to the beauties of bodies as opposed to those of minds. However, in *The Nature of True Virtue*, he argues that there is a secondary beauty in immaterial matters, too, in the affairs of friendship, social concert, and the like. The difference lies in that the heart and mind, in the case of primary beauty, consent to individual beings in the light of "being-in-general" or being as God himself in the perfections of his eternal life and his self-communication in creation.

56 Edwards, *Typological Writings*, 54.

57 Edwards, *Scientific and Philosophical Writings*, 336.

58 Edwards, *Scientific and Philosophical Writings*, 365.

59 Edwards, *Scientific and Philosophical Writings*, 364.

60 Edwards, *Scientific and Philosophical Writings*, 362.

61 Edwards, *Scientific and Philosophical Writings*, 335. Edwards' ontology is often described as Neoplatonist, but the empiricist aspect of his thought, with its stress on particular existents as occasions of God's perfections of being communicated *ad extra*, marks a decisive difference of theological significance as regards individual bodily creatures. Cf.: "For Edwards, unlike Neoplatonism, spiritual realities, at whatever levels of the hierarchy of being, are embodied in the material dimension of actual entities. That is, the material dimension as such of particular beings embodies in a physical way the ultimate spiritual reality. Every entity in the world is somehow intended to be a spatio-temporal repetition of God's glory at whatever level that entity may be." Sang Hyun Lee, *The Philosophical Theology of Jonathan Edwards*, expanded ed. (Princeton, N.J.: Princeton University Press, 2000), 249.

62 *The Philosophy of Jonathan Edwards: From His Private Notebook*, ed. Harvey G. Townsend (Eugene, Ore.: Wipf & Stock, 2009), Misc. 850, p. 82.

63 Edwards, *Scientific and Philosophical Writings*, 338.

64 Edwards, *Scientific and Philosophical Writings*, 337.

65 Cf.: "Reality is a community of minds; and it is an actual community, that is, one engaged in communication. . . . The world of bodies is the *between* of their communication, the perspectival field in which persons can come together while each remaining an *other* from all the others. The world of bodies is what God thinks in order to think a *communal plurality* of consciousnesses, who are to think and feel each other's thoughts and feelings while yet remaining plural." Jenson, *America's Theologian*, 32; emphasis in original.

66 Edwards, *Scientific and Philosophical Writings*, 305.

67 Delattre, *Beauty and Sensibility*, 69. At this point, again, Edwards is closer to Aquinas than to the Neoplatonists.

68 Addison and Steele, *Selections*, 368; Burke, *Philosophical Enquiry*, 85–87.

69 Nye, *American Technological Sublime*, 56; Crane, *Complete Poems*, 44.

70 Edwards, *Ethical Writings*, 445.

71 Edwards, *Ethical Writings*, 432–33.

72 On Augustine and Aquinas, see Richard Viladesau, *Theological Aesthetics: God in Imagination, Beauty, and Art* (New York: Oxford University Press, 2013), 105–17.

73 Edwards, *Ethical Writings*, 521.

74 Edwards, *Ethical Writings*, 435; emphasis in original. For a contemporary doctrine of God that, along similar lines, understands divine self-sufficiency as entire and unqualified but also inherently self-communicating, see Desmond, *God and the Between*.

75 On occasion, Edwards appears to contradict his assertions of the uniqueness of God's being and, therefore, of the difference between Creator and creature: thus, "many have wrong conceptions of the difference between the nature of the Deity and created spirits. The difference is no contrariety, but what naturally results from his greatness and nothing else. . . . So that if we should suppose the faculties of a created spirit to be enlarged infinitely, there would be the Deity to all intents and purposes," Misc. 135 (Edwards, *Miscellanies*, The Works of Jonathan Edwards, ed. Thomas A. Schafer, vol. 13 [New Haven, Conn.: Yale University Press, 1980], 113). The suggestion of an "infinite enlargement" that reaches to a point of identity between God and creation is reminiscent of God's subliming across the Atlantic. The difference, however, between Edwards and the effusions of Young or the analogies of Baillie, lies in Edwards' metaphysics. "Greatness," though often related to the metaphor of size, consists for Edwards in the degree of being—an archangel, as Edwards points out, has a greater degree of being than a flea—but God's degree of being is the infinity of entire fullness of being, sole source and sole self-subsistence. The point Edwards is making about created spirits being enlarged infinitely concerns the reality of creatures as the emanations or communications of God's being *ad extra*. If creatures are such communications, there can be no question of *contrariety*. Edwards' eschatology confirms this and also his retention of the radical difference: an eternal, asymptotic progression respects both the likeness, the communication *ad extra*, and the eternal distinction that is such that the uniting and beautifying never ends.

76 God alone "in metaphysical strictness and propriety is." Edwards, *Scientific and Philosophical Writings*, 364. For the accusation of pantheism,

see Michael James McClymond and Gerald R. McDermott, *The Theology of Jonathan Edwards* (New York: Oxford University Press, 2012), 109.

77 The forms and instances of beauty greatly vary, "yet it is manifest that there is no greater, and no other variety in it, than in the internal and essential glory of God itself." Edwards, *Ethical Writings*, 529.

78 Edwards, *Sermons and Discourses*, 414, 419. Cf. Addison and Steele, *Selections*, 364–70.

79 Edwards, *Ethical Writings*, Misc. 198, p. 717.

80 John Freke, *A Treatise on the Nature and Property of Fire. In Three Essays. I. Shewing the Cause of Vitality, and Muscular Motion; with Many Other Phaenomena; II. On Electricity; III. Shewing the Mechanical Cause of Magnetism; and Why the Compass Varies in the Manner It Does* (London: W. Innys & J. Richardson, 1752), 12. Of course, quite a few did doubt it—Edwards was not alone in doing so, as he knew from his reading of Ralph Cudworth and Henry More—but the mechanistic model quickly became culturally and scientifically normative and managed to outlast both Romantic protest and, also in the early nineteenth century, scientific advances that discredited it.

81 Edwards, *Scientific and Philosophical Writings*, 216.

82 *Selected Philosophical Papers of Robert Boyle*, ed. M. A. Stewart (New York: Hackett, 1991), 139; emphasis in original.

83 Boyle, *Selected Philosophical Papers*, 139.

84 *Robert Boyle: A Free Enquiry into the Vulgarly Received Notion of Nature*, ed. Edward Davis and Michael Hunter (Cambridge: Cambridge University Press, 1996), 13.

85 Boyle, *Selected Philosophical Papers*, 18–53, 138–39.

86 Edwards, *Scientific and Philosophical Writings*, 211.

87 Edwards, *Scientific and Philosophical Writings*, 215.

88 Edwards, *Original Sin*, ed. Clyde A. Holbrook, The Works of Jonathan Edwards Series, vol. 3 (New Haven, Conn.: Yale University Press, 1970), 402; emphasis in original.

89 Edwards, *Scientific and Philosophical Writings*, 348, 353.

90 Edwards, *Scientific and Philosophical Writings*, 216.

91 On beauty and "replication," see Elaine Scarry, *On Beauty and Being Just* (London: Duckworth, 2006), pt. 1.

92 *Philosophy of Jonathan Edwards*, 193–95.

93 Misc. 182, Edwards, *Miscellanies*, 328–29.

94 Misc. 182.

95 Edwards, *Ethical Writings*, 452.

96 Edwards, *Scientific and Philosophical Writings*, 381.

97 Most famously, in the "Spider papers." Edwards, *Scientific and Philosophical Writings*, 163–69.

98 Edwards distinguishes between humans and animals in a traditional way. Animals are passive receivers, not active in knowing: "A very great difference between men and beasts is that beasts have no voluntary actions about their own thoughts, for it is in this only that reasoning differs from mere perception and memory. It is the act of the will in bringing its ideas into contemplation, and ranging and comparing of them in reflection and abstraction. The minds of beasts, if I may call them minds, are purely passive with respect to all their ideas; the minds of men are not only passive, but abundantly active." *Scientific and Philosophical Writings*, 374. Contemporary animal studies has thrown a great deal of doubt on such a stark divide between humans and animals, and especially on the entire passivity of animal cognition. Edwards however, and in a hugely important insight, insists that human knowledge of God is intuitive and not primarily discursive: it is an immediate and felt knowing, before it is an object of reflection. Animal knowing may not be reflective in the same fashion as human cognition, but that does not prevent what might be called animal forms of "religious experience." Edwards writes,

> It is evident therefore by this, that the way we come by the idea or sensation of beauty, is by immediate sensation of the gratefulness of the idea called "beautiful"; and not by finding out by argumentation any consequences, or other things that it stands connected with; any more than tasting the sweetness of honey, or perceiving the harmony of a tune, is by argumentation on connections and consequences. And this manner of being affected with the immediate presence of the beautiful idea depends not, therefore, on any reasonings about the idea, after we have it, before we can find out whether it be beautiful, or not; but on the frame of our minds whereby they are so made that such an idea, as soon as we have it, is grateful, or appears beautiful. (*Ethical Writings*, 619)

99 *Philosophy of Jonathan Edwards*, Misc. 749, p. 86. The paragraph is worth quoting in full:

> We have all reason to think that this first cause of all things, that is the cause of all perception and intelligence in the world, is not only not an unintelligent, unknowing, and insensible being, but that he is infinitely the most intelligent and sensible being of all; that he is more perceiving than any; that his perception is so much more sensible and lively and perfect; that created minds are in comparison of him like dead, senseless, unperceiving substances; and that he

infinitely more exceeds them in the sensibility and life and height (if I may so speak) of his perception than the sun exceeds the planets, in the intensive degree of his brightness, as well as the bulk or extent of his shining disk. And as he is more sensible, so he is as I may express it more voluntary than created minds. He acts more of himself, infinitely more purely active, and in no respect passive, as all created minds are in a great measure passive in their acts of will. And the acts of will are more voluntary. Though there be no proper passions as in created minds, yet voluntariness is exercised to an infinitely greater height. The divine love, which is the sum of all the exercises of the divine will, is infinitely stronger, more lively and intense, as not only the light of the sun, but his heat, is immensely greater than that of the planets whose light and heat is derived from him.

100 Edwards, *Sermons and Discourses*, 565–68.

101 *Philosophy of Jonathan Edwards*, 258.

102 For the term "agapeic" here, I am indebted to William Desmond's metaphysics. The theme runs throughout his work, but see, in particular, Desmond, *Being and the Between* (Albany: State University of New York Press, 1995), chaps. 10–13; Desmond, *Perplexity and Ultimacy: Metaphysical Thoughts from the Middle* (Albany: State University of New York Press, 1995), chaps. 4 and 6.

103 Stanley A. Weinbaum, "A Martian Odyssey," in *The Oxford Book of Science Fiction Stories*, ed. Tom Shippey (New York: Oxford University Press, 1992), 74; emphasis added.

104 Weinbaum, "Martian Odyssey," in Shippey, *Oxford Book of Science Fiction*, 78.

105 Weinbaum, "Martian Odyssey," 78; emphasis in original.

106 Joanna Russ, "Towards an Aesthetic of Science Fiction," in *Visions of Wonder: The Science Fiction Research Association Anthology*, ed. David G. Hartwell, Milton T. Wolf, and Science Fiction Research Association (New York: Tor Books, 1996), 556.

107 Stapledon, *Last and First Men*, 136.

108 Stapledon, *Last and First Men*, 137.

109 For "sociophobics," see Douglas E. Cowan, *Sacred Terror: Religion and Horror on the Silver Screen* (Waco, Tex.: Baylor University Press, 2008).

110 Stapledon, *Last and First Men*, 276–77.

111 Samuel Taylor Coleridge, *Biographia Literaria; Or, Biographical Sketches of My Literary Life and Opinions*, ed. James Engell and Walter Jackson Bate (Princeton, N.J.: Princeton University Press, 1984), 304–5.

112 C. J. Cherryh, *The Deep Beyond: Cuckoo's Egg/Serpent's Reach* (New York: DAW Books, 2005).

113 Cherryh, *Deep Beyond*, 306.
114 Cherryh, *Deep Beyond*, 230–31.
115 Cherryh sets up a parallelism between humanity and hive by way of Kontrin, betas, and azi, on the one hand, and hive-mother, workers, and warriors, on the other. The parallelism is ironic in that only through violence and manipulation can human beings form a likeness to the hive, and that only a wretched one. The traditional science fiction aversion to hive minds is, therefore, both included—as a self-destructive possibility for humans—and rejected in the complex relationship with the majat.
116 Edwards, *Scientific and Philosophical Writings*, 362.
117 John Milbank, Graham Ward, and Edith Wyschogrod, *Theological Perspectives on God and Beauty* (Harrisburg, Pa.: Trinity, 2003), 62.

CONCLUSION

1 See above, pp. 158–60.
2 Adams, *The Education of Henry Adams* (Mineola, N.Y.: Dover, 2002), 286.
3 Douglas Adams, *The Restaurant at the End of the Universe* (London: Pan Books, 2009), 88.
4 Kant, *Critique of Judgement*, 106.
5 John R. Betz, "Beyond the Sublime: The Aesthetics of the Analogy of Being (Part One)," *Modern Theology* 21, no. 3 (2005): 387; emphasis added. I owe a considerable debt to Betz' analysis at this point.
6 Kant, *Critique of Judgement*, 124; Betz, "Beyond the Sublime," 385.
7 Jean-François Lyotard, "The Interest of the Sublime," in *Of the Sublime: Presence in Question; Essays by Jean-François Courtine, Michel Deguy, Eliane Escoubas, Philippe Lacoue-Labarthe, Jean-François Lyotard, Louis Marin, Jean-Luc Nancy, Jacob Rogozinski* (Albany: State University of New York Press, 1993), 124.
8 Jean-François Lyotard, *The Postmodern Explained: Correspondence, 1982–1985* (Minneapolis: University of Minnesota Press, 1993), 13.
9 Betz, "Beyond the Sublime," 389.
10 Clayton Crockett, *A Theology of the Sublime* (New York: Routledge, 2001), 389.
11 Louis K. Dupre, *Religious Mystery and Rational Reflection: Excursions in the Phenomenology and Philosophy of Religion* (Grand Rapids: Eerdmans, 1998), 93. The phrase "dazzling darkness" comes from Henry Vaughan's poem "Night."
12 John R. Betz, "Beyond the Sublime: The Aesthetics of the Analogy of Being (Part Two)," *Modern Theology* 22, no. 1 (2006): 33–34; William

Desmond, *Desire, Dialectic, and Otherness: An Essay on Origins* (New Haven, Conn.: Yale University Press, 1987), 146–63.

13 The frescoes were returned to Cyprus in February 2012.

14 Henry Karlson, "The Triumph of Orthodoxy," *Vox Nova* (blog), February 28, 2009, http://vox-nova.com/2009/02/28/the-triumph-of-orthodoxy/.

# BIBLIOGRAPHY

## SCIENCE FICTION TEXTS AND FILM

Adams, Douglas. *The Hitchhiker's Guide to the Galaxy*. London: Pan Books, 2009.

———. *The Restaurant at the End of the Universe*. London: Pan Books, 2009.

Anderson, Poul. *Tau Zero*. New ed. London: Gollancz, 2006.

Asimov, Isaac. *Foundation and Empire*. London: Panther Science Fiction, 1971.Edgar Asimov, Isaac, George Zebrowski, and Martin H. Greenberg, eds. *Creations: The Quest for Origins in Story and Science*. New York: Crown, 1983.

Bear, Greg. *Blood Music*. London: Gollancz, 2008.

———. *Eon*. London: Tor Books, 1991.

———. *The Forge of God*. London: Tor Books, 2001.

Bester, Alfred. *The Demolished Man*. New York: Vintage, 1996.

———. *The Stars My Destination*. London: Gollancz, 2010.

Blish, James. *Cities in Flight*. Science Fiction Book Club. New York: Nelson Doubleday, 1970.

———. *The Triumph of Time*. New York: Avon, 1958.

Bradbury, Ray. *The Martian Chronicles*. Rev. ed. New York: Doubleday, 1958.

Brunner, John. *The Sheep Look Up*. London: Benbella Books, 2003.

Burroughs, Edgar Rice. *The Works of Edgar Rice Burroughs*. Edited by Raleigh St. Clair. Amazon Digital Services, 2009. Kindle edition. See esp. "A Princess of Mars."

Campbell, John W. *A New Dawn: The Complete Don A. Stuart Stories*. Framingham, Mass.: Nesfa, 2003.

Cherryh, C. J. *The Deep Beyond: Cuckoo's Egg/Serpent's Reach*. New York: DAW Books, 2005.

Christopher, John. *The Death of Grass*. London: Penguin Modern Classics, 2009.
Clarke, Arthur C. *Childhood's End*. New York: Harcourt, Brace & World, 1953.
———. *The Collected Stories of Arthur C. Clarke*. New York: Orb Books, 2002.
Clement, Hal. *Mission of Gravity*. New York: Doubleday, 1954.
Cuarón, Alfonso. *Gravity*. Drama, Sci-Fi, Thriller, 2013.
Delany, Samuel R. *Babel-17*. London: Gollancz, 2010.
———. *Stars in My Pocket Like Grains of Sand*. Middletown, Conn.: Wesleyan University Press, 2004.
Del Ray, Lester. "Nerves." In *The Science Fiction Hall of Fame*. Vol. 2A, *The Greatest Science Fiction Novellas of All Time Chosen by the Members of the Science Fiction Writers*, edited by Ben Bova, 88–158. New York: Orb Books, 2009.
Dick, Philip K. *Blade Runner (Do Androids Dream of Electric Sheep?)*. New ed. London: Gollancz, 1999.
———. *Dr. Bloodmoney*. New York: Vintage Books, 2002.
———. *Now Wait for Last Year*. New York: Voyager, 2009.
———. *The Penultimate Truth*. New ed. London: Gollancz, 2005.
———. *Philip K. Dick: VALIS and Later Novels; A Maze of Death / VALIS / The Divine Invasion / The Transmigration of Timothy Archer*. New York: Library of America, 2009.
———. *The Simulacra*. New York: Vintage Books, 2002.
———. *The Three Stigmata of Palmer Eldritch*. New ed. London: Gollancz, 2003.
———. *Time Out of Joint*. New ed. London: Gollancz, 2003.
———. *Ubik*. 1st Vintage Books ed. New York: Vintage Books, 1992.
Disch, Thomas M. *The Genocides*. New York: Vintage Books, 2000.
*Doctor Who—The Complete Second Series*. Sci-Fi Channel, 2007.
*Dollhouse: Season One*. Twentieth Century Fox, 2009.
Ellison, Harlan. *Dreams with Sharp Teeth*. New York: Quality Paperback Book Club, n.d. See esp. "I Have No Mouth, and I Must Scream."
England, George Allan. *Darkness and Dawn*. Edited by Andrew Sly. Kindle Books, 2005. Originally published in 1912.
Gernsback, Hugo. "The Magnetic Storm." *Amazing Stories*, July 1926.
———. *Ralph 124C 41+*. 2nd ed. New York: Frederick Fell, 1951.
Gibson, William. *Count Zero*. New York: Ace Books, 1987.
———. *Mona Lisa Overdrive*. London: Voyager, 1995.
———. *Neuromancer*. New York: Ace, 1984.
Harrison, Harry. *The Deathworld Trilogy: Three Novels*. New York: Nelson Doubleday, 1968.
Harrison, M. John. *The Centauri Device*. New York: Doubleday, 1974.

Herbert, Frank. *Dune*. 2nd ed. London: Hodder Paperbacks, 1982.
King, John Robert. *Bruno Lipshitz and the Disciples of Dogma*. London: Gollancz, 1976.
Lafferty, R. A. *Apocalypses*. Los Angeles: Pinnacle Books, 1977. See esp. "The Three Armageddons of Enniscorthy Sweeney."
Le Guin, Ursula K. *The Dispossessed: An Ambiguous Utopia*. New York: Harper Paperbacks, 1994.
———. *The Left Hand of Darkness*. New York: SFBC Science Fiction, 2004.
Leiber, Fritz. *Gather, Darkness!* 1548 paperback ed. London: New English Library, 1966.
Leinster, Murray. *First Contacts: The Essential Murray Leinster*. Framingham, Mass: New England Science Fiction Association, 1998.
Lovecraft, H. P. [Howard Phillips]. *The Call of Cthulhu and Other Weird Stories*. Penguin Classics Deluxe ed. London: Penguin Classics, 2011.
———. *The Dreams in the Witch House: And Other Weird Stories*. London: Penguin Classics, 2004.
———. *Thing on the Doorstep*. London: Penguin Books, 2002.
Lucas, George. *Star Wars Episode IV: A New Hope*. DVD. Twentieth Century Fox Home Entertainment, 2006.
Matheson, Richard. *I Am Legend*. London: Tor Books, 2007.
———. *The Shrinking Man*. New ed. London: Gollancz, 2003.
May, Julian. *Jack the Bodiless*. New York: Knopf, 1992.
McCaffery, Larry, ed. *Storming the Reality Studio: A Casebook of Cyberpunk and Postmodern Science Fiction*. Durham, N.C.: Duke University Press, 1992.
Merritt, Abraham. *The Moon Pool*. Middletown, Conn.: Wesleyan University Press, 2004.
Niven, Larry. *Ringworld*. New ed. London: Gollancz, 2005.
Orwell, George. *Nineteen Eighty-Four*. London: Folio Society, 2003.
Priest, Christopher. *Inverted World*. London: Gollancz, 2008.
Prucher, Jeff, ed. *Brave New Words: The Oxford Dictionary of Science Fiction*. Oxford University Press, 2007.
Reynolds, Alastair. *Chasm City*. London: Gollancz, 2008.
———. *The Prefect*. London: Gollancz, 2008.
Scott, Ridley. *Blade Runner*. Drama, Sci-Fi, Thriller, 1982.
———. *Blade Runner: The Final Cut*. 2-Disc Special Edition. DVD. Warner Home Video, 2007.
Sharp, D. D. "The Eternal Man." In Ashley, *History of the Science Fiction Magazine*. Vol. 1, 91–98.
Shelley, Mary Wollstonecraft. *The Last Man*. London: Hogarth, 1985.
Shippey, Tom, ed. *The Oxford Book of Science Fiction Stories*. New York: Oxford University Press, 1992.

Silverberg, Robert, ed.. *The Science Fiction Hall of Fame: The Greatest Science Fiction Stories of All Time*. New York: Avon Books, 1971.

Smith, Cordwainer. *The Rediscovery of Man: The Complete Short Science Fiction of Cordwainer Smith*. Framingham, Mass.: Nesfa, 1993.

Stapledon, Olaf. *Beyond the "Isms,"* Searchlight Books 16. New York: Secker & Warburg, 1942.

———. *Last and First Men*. London: Gollancz, 2000.

———. *Last and First Men / Last Men in London*. London: Penguin, 1973.

———. *Odd John and Sirius*. New York: Dover, 1972.

———. *Star Maker*. Middletown, Conn: Wesleyan University Press, 2004.

———. *Worlds of Wonder*. Holicong, Pa: Wildside, 2009.

Stapledon, Olaf, and Robert Crossley. *An Olaf Stapledon Reader*. Syracuse, N.Y.: Syracuse University Press, 1997.

Stewart, George R. *Earth Abides*. New York: Del Rey, 2006.

Verne, Jules. *In the Year 2889 and a Voyage in a Balloon*. New York: CreateSpace, 2010. See esp. "In the Year 2889."

Vernon, Conrad, and Rob Letterman. *Monsters vs. Aliens*. 1-Disc. DVD. DreamWorks Home Entertainment, 2009.

Vogt, A. E. van. *Slan: A Novel*. New York: Orb Books, 1998.

Weinbaum, Stanley A. "A Martian Odyssey," in Shippey, *Oxford Book of Science Fiction*, 70–94.

Wells, H. G. [Herbert George]. *The Food of the Gods and How It Came to Earth*. New York: General Books, 2010.

———. *The Island of Dr. Moreau*. New York: CreateSpace, 2010.

———. *Mr. Britling Sees It Through*. Accessed April 27, 2011. http://www.gutenberg.org/ebooks/14060.

———. *Selected Short Stories*. London: Penguin Books, 1965.

———. *The War of the Worlds*. London: Penguin Books, 1946.

Whedon, Joss, and John Cassaday. *Astonishing X-Men*. Vol. 1. New York: Marvel Comics, 2004.

Wyndham, John. *The Chrysalids*. London: Folio Society, 2010.

Zebrowski, George. *The Omega Point Trilogy*. New York: Ace Science Fiction, 2002.

Zelazny, Roger. *Lord of Light*. New York: Eos, 2004.

## CHRISTIAN THEOLOGY, SCIENCE FICTION, AND THE SUBLIME

Abbott, H. Porter. *The Cambridge Introduction to Narrative*. Cambridge: Cambridge University Press, 2002.

Adams, Hazard. *Critical Theory since Plato*. San Diego: Harcourt Brace Jovanovich, 1971.

Adams, Henry. *The Education of Henry Adams*. Mineola, N.Y.: Dover, 2002.
Adams, Marilyn McCord. *Horrendous Evils and the Goodness of God*. Cornell Studies in the Philosophy of Religion. Ithaca: Cornell University Press, 2000.
Addison, Joseph, and Richard Steele. *Selections from "The Tatler" and "The Spectator."* London: Penguin Classics, 1988.
Aiken, J., and A. L. Aiken. "On the Pleasure Derived from Objects of Terror; with Sir Bertrand, a Fragment." In *Miscellaneous Pieces in Prose*, 57–65. Belfast: James Magee, 1774.
Aldiss, Brian W. *Billion Year Spree: The True History of Science Fiction*. New York: Doubleday, 1973.
Alexandria, St. Cyril of. *On the Unity of Christ*. Translated by John Anthony McGuckin. Crestwood, N.Y.: St. Vladimir's Seminary Press, 1995.
Alighieri, Dante. *Paradiso*. New York: Bantam Classics, 1986.
Alkon, Paul K. *Science Fiction before 1900: Imagination Discovers Technology*. Studies in Literary Themes and Genres. Boston: Twayne, 1994.
Anonymous. *The Cloud of Unknowing and Other Works*. London: Penguin Classics, 2002.
Antliff, Mark, and Vivien Greene, eds. *The Vorticists: Manifesto for a Modern World*. London: Tate, 2011.
Apollonio, Umbro, ed. *Futurist Manifestos*. London: Tate, 2009.
Aquinas, Thomas. *Compendium of Theology*. Translated by Richard J. Regan. New York: Oxford University Press, 2009.
———. *Summa Contra Gentiles: Book One; God*. Notre Dame, Ind.: University of Notre Dame Press, 1991.
———. *The Summa Theologiae of St. Thomas Aquinas: Latin-English Edition, Prima Pars, Q. 1–64*. Scotts Valley, Calif.: CreateSpace, 2009.
———. *Summa Theologiae*. Vol. 2, *Existence and Nature of God; 1a. 2–11*. Cambridge: Cambridge University Press, 2006.
Ashfield, Andrew, and Peter de Bolla. *The Sublime: A Reader in British Eighteenth-Century Aesthetic Theory*. Cambridge: Cambridge University Press, 1996.
Ashley, Michael. *The Gernsback Days*. Holicong, Pa.: Wildside, 2004.
———, ed. *The History of the Science Fiction Magazine*. Vol. 1, *1926–1935*. Chicago: Henry Regnery, 1976.
———, ed. *The History of the Science Fiction Magazine*. Vol. 2, *1936–1945*. Chicago: NTC/Contemporary, 1976.
———, ed. *The History of the Science Fiction Magazine*. Vol. 3, *1946–1955*. Chicago: Contemporary Books, 1977.
———. "Science Fiction Magazines." In Seed, *Companion to Science Fiction*, 60–76.

———. *Time Machines: The Story of the Science-Fiction Pulp Magazines from the Beginning to 1950*. Collectors ed. Liverpool: Liverpool University Press, 2001.

Augustine. *Confessions*. London: Penguin Classics, 1961.

Badmington, Neil, ed. *Posthumanism*. London: Palgrave Macmillan, 2000.

Baillie, John. *An Essay on the Sublime*. London: R. Dodsley, 1747.

Bakhtin, M. M. *The Dialogic Imagination: Four Essays*. Austin: University of Texas Press, 1982.

Bal, Mieke. *Narratology: Introduction to the Theory of Narrative*. 2nd rev. ed. Toronto: University of Toronto Press, 1997.

Balthasar, Hans Urs von, ed. *Origen: Spirit and Fire—A Thematic Anthology of His Writings*. New ed. Washington, D.C.: Catholic University of America Press, 2001.

———. *Scandal of the Incarnation: Irenaeus against the Heresies*. San Francisco: Ignatius, 1990.

———. *Theo-Drama: Last Act v. 5; Theological Dramatic Theory*. San Francisco: Ignatius, 1988.

Bataille, Georges. *Theory of Religion*. New York: Zone Books, 2006.

Baudrillard, Jean. *Jean Baudrillard: Selected Writings*. Oxford: Polity, 2001.

Beattie, James. "Illustrations on Sublimity." In *Dissertations Moral and Critical*, 605–55. London: W. Strahan & T. Cadell, 1783.

Beckley, Bill, ed. *Sticky Sublime*. Illustrated ed. New York: Allworth, 2001.

Behr, John. *The Way to Nicaea*. The Formation of Christian Theology. Vol. 1. Crestwood, N.Y.: St. Vladimir's Seminary Press, 2001.

Berger, Albert I. *The Magic That Works: John W. Campbell and the American Response to Technology*. San Bernardino, Calif.: Borgo, 1993.

Betz, John R. "Beyond the Sublime: The Aesthetics of the Analogy of Being (Part One)." *Modern Theology* 21, no. 3 (2005): 367–411.

———. "Beyond the Sublime: The Aesthetics of the Analogy of Being (Part Two)." *Modern Theology* 22, no. 1 (2006): 1–50.

Bickersteth, Edward Henry. *Yesterday, To-Day, and For Ever: A Poem in Twelve Books*. New York: Robert Carter & Bros., 1875.

Bolla, Peter de. *The Discourse of the Sublime: Readings in History, Aesthetics and the Subject*. Oxford: Basil Blackwell, 1989.

Bowler, Peter J. *Evolution: The History of an Idea*. 3rd ed. Los Angeles: University of California Press, 2003.

———. *Reconciling Science and Religion: The Debate in Early-Twentieth-Century Britain*. Chicago: University of Chicago Press, 2001.

Boyle, Robert. *Robert Boyle: A Free Enquiry into the Vulgarly Received Notion of Nature*. Edited by Edward Davis and Michael Hunter. Cambridge: Cambridge University Press, 1996.

———. *Selected Philosophical Papers of Robert Boyle*. Edited by M. A. Stewart. New York: Hackett, 1991.

Braake, David. "Self-Differentiation among Christian Groups: The Gnostics and Their Opponents." In Mitchell, Young, and Bowie, *The Cambridge History of Christianity*. Vol. 1, *Origins to Constantine*, 62–84.

Browne, Thomas. "Hydriotaphia, Urne-Burial." In *The Voyce of the World*. Folio Society, 2008, 115–56.

Buckley, Jerome H. *The Triumph of Time: A Study of the Victorian Concepts of Time, History, Progress, and Decadence*. Cambridge, Mass.: Belknap, 1966.

Buckley, Michael J. *At the Origins of Modern Atheism*. New Haven, Conn.: Yale University Press, 1987.

Bull, Malcolm. *Apocalypse Theory and the Ends of the World*. Oxford: Blackwell, 1995.

Bultmann, Rudolf. *Theology of the New Testament*. Vol. 1. Translated by K. Grobel. London: SCM Press, 1971.

Burke, Edmund. *A Philosophical Enquiry into the Origins of the Sublime and Beautiful: And Other Pre-revolutionary Writings*. London: Penguin Classics, 1999.

———. *Reflections on the Revolution in France: And on the Proceedings in Certain Societies in London Relative to That Event*. Edited by Conor Cruise O'Brien. London: Penguin Books, 1986.

Burnet, Thomas. *The Sacred Theory of the Earth: Containing an Account of the Original of the Earth and of All the General Changes Which It Hath Already Undergone or Is To Undergo Till the Consummation of All Things*. London: Printed by R. N. for Walter Kettilby, 1697.

Burtt, E. A. *Metaphysical Foundations of Modern Science: A Historical and Critical Essay*. Rev. ed. New York: Routledge & Kegan Paul, 1951.

Carlyle, Thomas. *Thomas Carlyle: Selected Writings*. London: Penguin Books, 1988. See esp. "Signs of the Times."

Carroll, Noel. *The Philosophy of Horror*. New York: Routledge, 1990.

Carter, Paul Allen. *The Creation of Tomorrow: Fifty Years of Magazine Science Fiction*. New York: Columbia University Press, 1980.

Castoriadis, Cornelius. *The Imaginary Institution of Society*. Boston: MIT Press, 1998.

———. *World in Fragments: Writings on Politics, Society, Psychoanalysis, and the Imagination*. Stanford, Calif.: Stanford University Press, 1997.

Cavallaro, Dani. *Cyberpunk and Cyberculture: Science Fiction and the Work of William Gibson*. London: Continuum , 2000.

———. *The Gothic Vision: Three Centuries of Horror, Terror, and Fear*. Rev. ed. London: Continuum , 2005.

Chambers, John Whiteclay, II. *The Tyranny of Change: America in the Progressive Era, 1890–1920*. 3rd ed. New Brunswick, N.J.: Rutgers University Press, 2000.

Clare, John. *Bird Poems*. Edited by Peter Levi. London: Folio Society, 1980.

Clark, Stephen R. L. "Science Fiction and Religion." In Seed, *Companion to Science Fiction*, 95–110.

Clarke, Samuel. *Samuel Clarke: A Demonstration of the Being and Attributes of God; And Other Writings*. Cambridge: Cambridge University Press, 1998.

Clute, John, and Peter Nicholls. *The Encyclopedia of Science Fiction*. London: Orbit, 1999.

Coleridge, Samuel Taylor. *Biographia Literaria; Or, Biographical Sketches of My Literary Life and Opinions*. Edited by James Engell and Walter Jackson Bate. Princeton, N.J.: Princeton University Press, 1984.

———. *Coleridge's Writings: On the Sublime*. Edited by David Vallins. London: Palgrave Macmillan, 2003.

———. *The Collected Works of Samuel Taylor Coleridge*. Vol. 11, *Shorter Works and Fragments*, edited by H. J. Jackson and J. R. de J. Jackson. New York: Routledge, 1995.

———. *The Collected Works of Samuel Taylor Coleridge*. Vol. 15, *Opus Maximum*. Edited by Thomas MacFarlane. Princeton, N.J.: Princeton University Press, 2002.

Collins, Anthony. *A Discourse of Freethinking, Occasioned by the Rise and Growth of a Sect called Free-Thinkers*. London, 1713.

Costelloe, Timothy M., ed. *The Sublime: From Antiquity to the Present*. Cambridge: Cambridge University Press, 2012.

Courtine, Jean-François. *Of the Sublime: Presence in Question; Essays by Jean-François Courtine, Michel Deguy, Eliane Escoubas, Philippe Lacoue-Labarthe, Jean-François Lyotard, Louis Marin, Jean-Luc Nancy, Jacob Rogozinski*. Albany: State University of New York Press, 1993.

Cowan, Douglas E. *Sacred Terror: Religion and Horror on the Silver Screen*. Waco, Tex.: Baylor University Press, 2008.

Crane, Hart. *The Complete Poems of Hart Crane*. Edited by Marc Simon. New York: Liveright, 1993.

Crockett, Clayton. *Interstices of the Sublime: Theology and Psychoanalytic Theory*. New York: Fordham University Press, 2007.

———. *A Theology of the Sublime*. New York: Routledge, 2001.

Cronin, Ciaran. *A Companion to Victorian Poetry*. Edited by Richard Cronin, Antony Harrison, and Alison Chapman. Malden, Mass.: Wiley-Blackwell, 2002.

Crossley, Robert. *Olaf Stapledon: Speaking for the Future*. Syracuse, N.Y.: Syracuse University Press, 1994.

Csicsery-Ronay, Istvan, Jr. *The Seven Beauties of Science Fiction*. Middletown, Conn.: Wesleyan University Press, 2008.

Cunningham, Conor. *Darwin's Pious Idea: Why the Ultra-Darwinists and Creationists Both Get It Wrong*. Grand Rapids: Eerdmans, 2010.

Darwin, Charles. *The Origin of Species by Means of Natural Selection: The Preservation of Favored Races in the Struggle for Life*. London: Penguin Classics, 1982.

Davenport, Guy. *7 Greeks*. New York: New Directions, 1995.

Davies, Brian. *The Thought of Thomas Aquinas*. New York: Oxford University Press, 1993.

Dawkins, Richard. *The God Delusion*. London: Mariner Books, 2008.

Delattre, Roland Andre. *Beauty and Sensibility in the Thought of Jonathan Edwards: An Essay in Aesthetics*. New Haven, Conn.: Yale University Press, 1968.

Dennis, John. *The Advancement and Reformation of Modern Poetry. A Critical Discourse. In Two Parts. The First, Shewing That the Principal Reason Why the Ancients Excel'd the Moderns in the Greater Poetry, Was Because They Mix'd Religion with Poetry. The Second, Proving That by Joyning Poetry with the Religion Reveal'd to Us in Sacred Writ, the Modern Poets Might Come to Equal the Ancient by Mr. Dennis*. London: Rich Parker, 1701.

———. *The Grounds of Criticism in Poetry*. London: Geo. Strahan, 1704.

Descartes, René. "Meditations on First Philosophy." In *Meditations & Other Writings*. London: Folio Society, 2012, 15–92.

Desmond, William. *Art, Origins, Otherness: Between Philosophy and Art*. Albany: State University of New York Press, 2003.

———. *Being and the Between*. Albany: State University of New York Press, 1995.

———. *Desire, Dialectic, and Otherness: An Essay on Origins*. New Haven, Conn.: Yale University Press, 1987.

———. *God and the Between*. Oxford: Wiley-Blackwell, 2007.

———. *Perplexity and Ultimacy: Metaphysical Thoughts from the Middle*. Albany: State University of New York Press, 1995.

Dick, Philip K. *The Exegesis of Philip K. Dick*. Edited by Jonathan Lethem and Pamela Jackson. London: Gollancz, 2012.

Dickson, Lovat. *H. G. Wells: His Turbulent Life and Times*. London: Pelican, 1972.

Dionysius the Areopagite. *Pseudo-Dionysius: The Complete Works*. New ed. New York: Paulist, 1993.

Donald, Diana, and Jane Munro. *Endless Forms: Charles Darwin, Natural Science and the Visual Arts*. New Haven, Conn.: Yale University Press, 2009.

Donne, John. *John Donne: The Complete English Poems*. Edited by J. Smith. Folio Society, 2005. See esp. "Satire 3."

Dostoyevsky, Fyodor. *The Brothers Karamazov*. London: Folio Society, 1964.

Dupre, Louis K. *Religious Mystery and Rational Reflection: Excursions in the Phenomenology and Philosophy of Religion*. Grand Rapids: Eerdmans, 1998.

Duve, Thierry de, and Doreet LeVitte Harten, eds. *Heaven*. London: Hatje Cantz, 1999.

Eagleton, Terry. *The Ideology of the Aesthetic*. Oxford: Wiley-Blackwell, 1991.

———. *Reason, Faith, and Revolution: Reflections on the God Debate*. New Haven, Conn.: Yale University Press, 2009.

Edwards, Jonathan. *Ethical Writings*. Edited by P. Ramsey. The Works of Jonathan Edwards Series. Vol. 8. New Haven, Conn.: Yale University Press, 1989.

———. *Images or Shadows of Divine Things*. Edited by Perry Miller. New Haven, Conn.: Yale University Press, 1977.

———. *Letters and Personal Writings*. Edited by John Edwin Smith. The Works of Jonathan Edwards Series. Vol. 16. New Haven, Conn.: Yale University Press, 1980.

———. *Miscellanies*. The Works of Jonathan Edwards. Edited by Thomas A. Schafer, vol. 13 [New Haven, Conn.: Yale University Press, 1980].

———. *Original Sin*. Edited by Clyde A. Holbrook. The Works of Jonathan Edwards Series. Vol. 3. New Haven, Conn.: Yale University Press, 1970.

———. *The Philosophy of Jonathan Edwards: From His Private Notebook*. Edited by Harvey G. Townsend. Eugene, Ore.: Wipf & Stock, 2009.

———. *Religious Affections*. Edited by John Edwin Smith. The Works of Jonathan Edwards Series, Vol. 2. New Haven, Conn.: Yale University Press, 1959.

———. *Scientific and Philosophical Writings*. Edited by W. Anderson. The Works of Jonathan Edwards Series. Vol. 6. New Haven, Conn.: Yale University Press, 1980.

———. *Sermons and Discourses, 1734–1738*. Edited by John Edwin Smith. The Works of Jonathan Edwards Series. Vol. 19. New Haven, Conn.: Yale University Press, 1980.

———. *Typological Writings*. Edited by Wallace E. Anderson, Mason I. Lowance, and David H. Watters. The Works of Jonathan Edwards Series. Vol. 11. New Haven, Conn.: Yale University Press, 1993.

Eliade, Mircea. *Myths, Dreams and Mysteries: The Encounter between Contemporary Faiths and Archaic Realities*. New York: Harper & Row, 1975.

Eliot, George. *The Essays of "George Eliot."* Edited by Nathan Sheppard. New York: Funk & Wagnalls, 1883. See esp. "Worldliness and Other-Worldliness: The Poet Young."

Ellul, Jacques. *The Technological Society*. New York: Vintage Books, 1964.

Emerson, Ralph Waldo. *Emerson: Selected Essays*. London: Penguin Classics, 1982.

Fairchild, Hoxie Neale. *Religious Trends in English Poetry*. Vol. 1. New York: Columbia University Press, 1949.

Fara, Patricia. *Newton: The Making of Genius*. New York: Columbia University Press, 2004.

Fauvel, John, Raymond Flood, Michael Shortland, and Robin Wilson. *Let Newton Be!* New York: Oxford University Press, 1990.

Featherstone, Mike, and Roger Burrows, eds. *Cyberspace/Cyberbodies/Cyberpunk: Cultures of Technological Embodiment*. London: SAGE, 1996.

Fichte, Johann Gottlieb. "On the Foundation of Our Belief in a Divine Government of the Universe." In *Nineteenth-Century Philosophy*, edited and translated by Patrick L. Gardiner, 24–45. New York: Free Press, 1969.

Fiedler, Leslie A. *Olaf Stapledon: A Man Divided*. New York: Oxford University Press, 1983.

Filoramo, Giovanni. *A History of Gnosticism*. New ed. Oxford: Wiley-Blackwell, 1992.

Floridi, Luciano. *Information: A Very Short Introduction*. New York: Oxford University Press, 2010.

———. *The Philosophy of Information*. Oxford: Oxford University Press, 2013.

Fortey, Richard. *Life: An Unauthorized Biography*. London: Folio Society, 2008.

Frazer, J. G. *The Golden Bough: A Study in Magic and Religion*. London: Macmillan, 1967.

Frei, Hans W. *The Eclipse of Biblical Narrative: A Study in Eighteenth and Nineteenth Century Hermeneutics*. New Haven, Conn.: Yale University Press, 1980.

Freke, John. *A Treatise on the Nature and Property of Fire. In Three Essays. I. Shewing the Cause of Vitality, and Muscular Motion; with Many Other Phaenomena; II. On Electricity; III. Shewing the Mechanical Cause of Magnetism; and Why the Compass Varies in the Manner It Does*. London: W. Innys & J. Richardson, 1752.

Frend, W. H. C. *The Early Church: From the Beginnings to 461*. 4th ed. London: SCM Press, 2003.

———. *The Rise of Christianity*. London: Darton, Longman & Todd, 1984.

Freud, Sigmund. *The Uncanny*. Translated by David McLintock. London: Penguin Classics, 2003.

Funkenstein, Amos. *Theology and the Scientific Imagination from the Middle Ages to the Seventeenth Century*. Princeton, N.J.: Princeton University Press, 1989.

Gaskell, Elizabeth. *Mary Barton*. London: Folio Society, 2004.
Geddes, Patrick, ed. *The Evergreen: A Northern Seasonal*. Vol. 1. Edinburgh: T. Fisher Unwin, 1895.
George, Marie I. *Christianity and Extraterrestrials? A Catholic Perspective*. New York: Universe, 2005.
Geraci, Robert. *Apocalyptic AI: Visions of Heaven in Robotics, Artificial Intelligence, and Virtual Reality*. New York: Oxford University Press, 2010.
Gilbert-Rolfe, Jeremy. *Beauty and the Contemporary Sublime*. New York: Allworth, 1999.
Goetz, Stewart, and Charles Taliaferro. *Naturalism*. Grand Rapids: Eerdmans, 2008.
Gorham, Geoffrey. "Early Scientific Images of God: Descartes, Hobbes, and Newton." In Taliaferro and Evans, *Turning Images in Philosophy, Science, and Religion*, 25–45.
Graham, Elaine. *Representations of the Posthuman: Aliens and Others in Popular Culture*. Manchester: Manchester University Press, 2002.
Grant, George Parkin. *Technology and Empire: Perspectives on North America*. Toronto: House of Anansi, 1983.
———. *Time as History*. Toronto: Canadian Broadcasting, 1969.
Grillmeier, Alois. *Christ in Christian Tradition: From the Apostolic Age to Chalcedon (451)*. Translated by John Stephen Bowden. Atlanta: John Knox, 1975.
Gunn, James, Marleen S. Barr, and Matthew Candelaria. *Reading Science Fiction*. London: Palgrave Macmillan, 2008.
Gunton, Colin. *Christ and Creation*. Grand Rapids: Eerdmans, 1993.
———. *Enlightenment and Alienation*. Grand Rapids: Eerdmans, 1985.
Habermas, Jürgen. *The Structural Transformation of the Public Sphere: An Inquiry into a Category of Bourgeois Society*. Boston: MIT Press, 1991.
Haraway, Donna. *The Haraway Reader*. New York: Routledge, 2003.
Hardt, Michael, and Antonio Negri. *Empire*. Cambridge, Mass.: Harvard University Press, 2001.
Hart, David Bentley. *The Beauty of the Infinite: The Aesthetics of Christian Truth*. Grand Rapids: Eerdmans, 2004.
———. *The Experience of God: Being, Consciousness, Bliss*. New Haven, Conn.: Yale University Press, 2013.
Hartwell, David G. *Age of Wonders: Exploring the World of Science Fiction*. Rev. ed. New York: Walker, 1984.
Hartwell, David G., Milton T. Wolf, and Science Fiction Research Association, eds. *Visions of Wonder: The Science Fiction Research Association Anthology*. New York: Tor Books, 1996.
Hassan, Ihab. *Postmodern Turn: Essays in Postmodern Theory and Culture*. Columbus: Ohio State University Press, 1988.

Hayles, N. Katherine. *How We Became Posthuman: Virtual Bodies in Cybernetics, Literature, and Informatics* Chicago: University of Chicago Press, 1999.

Hegel, Georg Wilhelm Friedrich. *Early Theological Writings*. Translated by T. M. Knox and Richard Kroner. Chicago: Chicago University Press, 1948.

———. *Introductory Lectures on Aesthetics*. Translated by Bernard Bosanquet. London: Penguin Classics, 1993.

Heidegger, Martin. *The Question Concerning Technology, and Other Essays*. New York: Harper Perennial, 1982.

Herzfeld, Noreen. *In Our Image: Artificial Intelligence and the Human Spirit*. Theology and the Sciences. Minneapolis: Augsburg Fortress, 2000.

Hetherington, Norris S. *Cosmology: Historical, Literary, Philosophical, Religious, and Scientific Perspectives*. New York: Routledge, 1993.

Himes, Michael J., ed. *Finding God in All Things: Essays in Honor of Michael J. Buckley, S.J.* New York: Herder & Herder, 1996.

Hoffmann, Roald, and Iain Boyd Whyte, eds. *Beyond the Finite: The Sublime in Art and Science*. New York: Oxford University Press, 2011.

Holland, Steve, Alex Summersby, Steve White, Toby Weidmann, Adrian Faulkner, and Tim Muray. *Sci-Fi Art: A Graphic History*. Lewes, U.K.: ILEX, 2009.

Holmqvist, Kenneth and Jaroslaw Pluciennik, *Infinity in Language: Conceptualization of the Experience of the Sublime*. Cambridge, Mass.: Cambridge Scholars, 2008.

Horn, S.D.S. Stephan, and Cardinal Christoph Schönborn. *Creation and Evolution: A Conference with Pope Benedict XVI in Castel Gandolfo*. San Francisco: Ignatius, 2008.

Hughes, Thomas P. *Human-Built World: How to Think about Technology and Culture*. Chicago: University Of Chicago Press, 2005.

Huxley, T. H. *Evolution and Ethics and Other Essays*. Project Gutenberg, n.d.

Jacob, Margaret C. *Newtonians and the English Revolution 1689–1720*. New York: Cornell University Press, 1976.

James, Edward. *Science Fiction in the Twentieth Century*. New York: Oxford University Press, 1994.

James, Edward, and Farah Mendlesohn, eds. *The Cambridge Companion to Science Fiction*. Cambridge: Cambridge University Press, 2003.

Jenson, Robert W. *America's Theologian: A Recommendation of Jonathan Edwards*. New York: Oxford University Press, 1992.

———. *Systematic Theology*. Vol. 1, *The Triune God*. New York: Oxford University Press, 2001.

Johnson, Samuel. *The History of Rasselas: Prince of Abyssinia.* Edited by Gilbert Phelps. London: Folio Society, 1975.

Jonas, Hans. *The Gnostic Religion*. 3rd ed. Boston: Beacon, 2001.

Joshi, S. T. *H. P. Lovecraft: The Decline of the West*. Berkley Heights, N.J.: Borgo, 1991.

———. *A Subtler Magick: The Writings and Philosophy of H. P. Lovecraft*. 3rd ed. Berkley Heights, N.J.: Borgo, 1996.

Julian of Norwich. *Julian of Norwich: Showings*. Edited by James Walsh. New York: Paulist, 1978.

Jung, C. G. *Psychology and Western Religion (from Vols. 11, 18 Collected Works)*. Translated by R. F. C. Hull. Princeton, N.J.: Princeton University Press, 1984.

Kant, Immanuel. *The Critique of Judgement*. Translated by James Creed Meredith. Oxford: Oxford University Press, 2006.

———. *Critique of Practical Reason*. Translated by Lewis White Beck. London: Macmillan, 1956.

———. *Lectures on Philosophical Theology*. Translated by Allen W. Wood and Gertrude M. Clarke. New York: Cornell University Press, 1986.

———. *Observations on the Feeling of the Beautiful and the Sublime*. Edited by John T. Goldthwait. Berkeley: University of California Press, 2003.

Kasper, Walter. *The God of Jesus Christ*. New York: Crossroad, 1984.

———. *Jesus the Christ*. New York: Paulist, 1976.

Kelly, J. N. D. *Early Christian Doctrines*. Rev. ed. New York: HarperOne, 1978.

Kirwan, James. *Sublimity: The Non-rational and the Rational in the History of Aesthetics*. New ed. New York: Routledge, 2005.

Klingender, F. D., and Arthur Elton. *Art and the Industrial Revolution*. London: Paladin, 1972.

Koch, Klaus. *The Rediscovery of Apocalyptic: A Polemical Work on a Neglected Area of Biblical Studies and Its Damaging Effects on Theology and Philosophy*. Studies in Biblical Theology 22. London: SCM Press, 1972.

Kristeva, Julia. *Powers of Horror: An Essay on Abjection*. New York: Columbia University Press, 1984.

Kubrick, Stanley. *2001: A Space Odyssey*. DVD. Warner Home Video, 2007.

Lankester, Edwin Ray. *Degeneration: A Chapter in Darwinism*. London: General Books, 2010.

Larson, Edward J. *Evolution: The Remarkable History of a Scientific Theory*. New York: Modern Library, 2006.

Lee, Sang Hyun. *The Philosophical Theology of Jonathan Edwards*. Expanded ed. Princeton, N.J.: Princeton University Press, 2000.

Lévi-Strauss, Claude. *The Jealous Potter*. Translated by Bénédicte Chorier. Chicago: University of Chicago Press, 1988.

Levy, Maurice. *Lovecraft: A Study in the Fantastic*. Translated by S. T. Joshi. Detroit: Wayne State University Press, 1988.

Livingston, James C., and Francis Schussler Fiorenza. *Modern Christian Thought*. Vol. 2, *The Twentieth Century*. 2nd rev. ed. Minneapolis: Fortress, 2006.

Locke, John. *An Essay concerning Human Understanding*. London: Penguin Classics, 1998.

Longinus. *On the Sublime*. Translated by William Smith. London: C. Whittingham, 1800.

Lovecraft, Howard Phillips [H. P.]. *Lord of a Visible World: Autobiography in Letters*. Edited by S. T. Joshi and David E. Schultz. Columbus: Ohio University Press, 2000.

———. *Supernatural Horror in Literature*. New York: Dover, 1973.

Lubac, Henri de. *Catholicism: Christ and the Common Destiny of Man*. San Francisco: Ignatius, 1988.

———. *The Discovery of God*. Grand Rapids: Eerdmans, 1996.

———. *The Faith of Teilhard de Chardin*. London: Fowler Wright Books, 1967.

Luckhurst, Roger. *Science Fiction*. Cambridge: Polity, 2005.

Lyotard, Jean-François. *The Inhuman: Reflections on Time*. Translated by Geoffrey Bennington and Rachel Bowlby. Cambridge: Polity, 1993. See esp. "The Sublime and the Avant-Garde."

———. *Lessons on the Analytic of the Sublime*. Stanford, Calif.: Stanford University Press, 1994.

———. *The Postmodern Explained: Correspondence, 1982–1985*. Minneapolis: University of Minnesota Press, 1993.

Lyotard, Jean-François, G. Bennington, and B. Massumi. *The Postmodern Condition: A Report on Knowledge*. Manchester: Manchester University Press, 1984.

Mackay, Donald M. *Information, Mechanism and Meaning*. New ed. Boston: MIT Press, 2004.

Mackenzie, Norman, and Jeanne Mackenzie. *The Life of H. G. Wells: The Time Traveller*. London: Hogarth, 1987.

Manuel, Frank Edward. *The Religion of Isaac Newton*. Oxford: Clarendon, 1974.

Marinetti, F. T. "Geometric and Mechanical Splendour, and the Numerical Sensibility, 1914." In Apollonio, *Futurist Manifestos*, 154–59.

Maritain, Jacques. *A Preface to Metaphysics: Seven Lectures on Being*. London: Sheed & Ward, 1948.

Marty, Martin E. *Modern American Religion*. Vol. 1, *The Irony of It All, 1893–1919*. Chicago: University Of Chicago Press, 1987.

———. *Modern American Religion*. Vol. 2, *The Noise of Conflict, 1919–1941*. Illustrated ed. Chicago: University of Chicago Press, 1991.

Marx, Leo. *Machine in the Garden: Technology and the Pastoral Ideal in America*. New York: Oxford University Press, 1964.

Mascall, Eric Lionel. *He Who Is*. Rev. ed. London: Darton, Longman & Todd, 1967.

McClymond, Michael James, and Gerald R. McDermott. *The Theology of Jonathan Edwards*. New York: Oxford University Press, 2012.

McGrath, James F. *Religion and Science Fiction*. Eugene, Ore.: Pickwick, 2011.

McGuire, J. E. "Newton on Place, Time, and God: An Unpublished Source." *British Journal for the History of Science* 11, no. 2 (1978). doi:10.1017/S000708740001654X.

McKee, Gabriel. *The Gospel according to Science Fiction: From the Twilight Zone to the Final Frontier*. Louisville, Ky.: Westminster John Knox, 2007.

———. *Pink Beams of Light from the God in the Gutter: The Science Fictional Religion of Philip K. Dick*. Lanham, Md.: University Press of America, 2003.

Mendlesohn, Farah. "Religion and Science Fiction." In James and Mendlesohn, *Cambridge Companion to Science Fiction*, 264–75.

Meyer, Marvin, ed. *The Nag Hammadi Scriptures: The Revised and Updated Translation of Sacred Gnostic Texts Complete in One Volume*. International ed. New York: HarperOne, 2008. See esp. *The Gospel of Truth*; *On the Origin of the World*; *The Second Discourse of the Great Seth*; *The Secret Book of John*; *The Three Forms of Thought*; and *The Tripartite Tractate*.

Midgley, Mary. *Evolution as a Religion: Strange Hopes and Stranger Fears*. 2nd ed. London: Routledge, 2002.

———. *Science as Salvation: A Modern Myth and Its Meaning*. London: Routledge, 1992.

Milbank, John, Graham Ward, and Edith Wyschogrod. *Theological Perspectives on God and Beauty*. Harrisburg, Pa.: Trinity International, 2003.

Mitchell, Margaret Mary, Frances M. Young, and K. Scott Bowie, eds. *The Cambridge History of Christianity*. Vol. 1, *Origins to Constantine*. Cambridge: Cambridge University Press, 2006.

Moltmann, Jürgen. *Coming of God: Christian Eschatology*. Minneapolis: Augsburg Fortress, 2004.

———. *Theology of Hope: On the Ground and the Implications of a Christian Eschatology*. London: SCM Press, 2002.

Monk, Samuel H. *The Sublime: A Study of Critical Theories in XVIII-Century England*. Ann Arbor: University of Michigan Press, 1960.

Moore, James R. *The Post-Darwinian Controversies: A Study of the Protestant Struggle to Come to Terms with Darwin in Great Britain and America, 1870–1900*. Cambridge: Cambridge University Press, 1981.

Moravec, Hans. *Mind Children: The Future of Robot and Human Intelligence*. Boston: Harvard University Press, 1988.

———. *Robot: Mere Machine to Transcendent Mind*. New York: Oxford University Press, 1998.

Morley, Simon, ed. *The Sublime*. London: Whitechapel Art Gallery, 2010.

Morris, David B. *Religious Sublime: Christian Poetry and Critical Tradition in Eighteenth-Century England*. Louisville: University Press of Kentucky, 1982.

Mumford, Lewis. *Pentagon of Power: The Myth of the Machine*. New York: Harcourt, 1970.

———. *Technics and Civilization*. Chicago: University of Chicago Press, 2010.

Myrone, Martin, ed. *John Martin: Apocalypse*. London: Tate, 2011. See esp. "The Fire Worshippers."

Myrone, Martin, Christopher Frayling, and Marina Warner. *Gothic Nightmares: Fuseli, Blake and the Romantic Imagination*. London: Tate, 2006.

Newport, Kenneth. *The End All around Us: The Apocalypse and Popular Culture*. Millennialism and Society. London: Equinox, 2009.

Newton, Isaac. *Isaac Newton: Philosophical Writings*. Cambridge: Cambridge University Press, 2004. See esp. "Correspondence with Dr. Bentley"; and *De Gravitatione*.

Nicolson, Marjorie Hope. *Mountain Gloom and Mountain Glory: The Development of the Aesthetics of the Infinite*. Seattle: University of Washington Press, 1997.

Nieuwenhove, Rik van, and Joseph Wawrykow, eds. *The Theology of Thomas Aquinas*. Notre Dame, Ind.: University of Notre Dame Press, 2010.

Noble, David F. *The Religion of Technology: The Divinity of Man and the Spirit of Invention*. London: Penguin, 1999.

Nye, David E. *American Technological Sublime*. Boston: MIT Press, 1996.

O'Gorman, Frank. *The Long Eighteenth Century: British Political and Social History 1688–1832*. London: Hodder Arnold, 1997.

Olson, Richard G. *Science and Religion, 1450–1900: From Copernicus to Darwin*. Baltimore: Johns Hopkins University Press, 2006.

O'Regan, Cyril. *Gnostic Apocalypse: Jacob's Boehme's Haunted Narrative*. Albany: State University of New York Press, 2002.

———. *Gnostic Return in Modernity*. Albany: State University of New York Press, 2001.

Ottinger, Didier, ed. *Futurism*. London: Five Continents Editions, 2009.

Owen, Huw Parri. *Christian Theism: A Study in Its Basic Principles*. Edinburgh: T&T Clark, 1984.

Pacini, David S. *Cunning of Modern Religious Thought*. Minneapolis: Augsburg Fortress, 1986.

Paley, William. *Natural Theology*. Charlottesville, Va.: Ibis, 1986.

Pannenberg, Wolfhart. *Jesus: God and Man*. Louisville, Ky.: Westminster John Knox, 1982.

———. *Systematic Theology*. Vol. 3. Grand Rapids: Eerdmans, 1991.

Parrinder, Patrick. *H. G. Wells: The Critical Heritage*. London: Routledge & Kegan Paul, 1972.

———, ed. *Science Fiction: A Critical Guide*. New York: Longman, 1979.

Parrish, Michael E. *Anxious Decades: America in Prosperity and Depression, 1920–1941*. New York: W. W. Norton, 1992.

Pattison, George. *Routledge Philosophy Guidebook to the Later Heidegger*. London: Routledge, 2000.

Pauw, Amy Plantinga. *The Supreme Harmony of All: The Trinitarian Theology of Jonathan Edwards*. Grand Rapids: Eerdmans, 2002.

Pearson, Birger A. *Ancient Gnosticism: Traditions and Literature*. Minneapolis: Fortress, 2007.

Pelikan, Jaroslav. *The Christian Tradition: A History of the Development of Doctrine*. Vol. 1, *The Emergence of the Catholic Tradition*. Chicago: University Of Chicago Press, 1975.

Placher, William C. *The Domestication of Transcendence: How Modern Thinking about God Went Wrong*. Louisville, Ky.: Westminster John Knox, 1996.

Polkinghorne, J. C., and Michael Welker, eds. *The End of the World and the Ends of God*. London: SCM Press, 2000.

Porter, Roy, ed. *The Cambridge History of Science*. Vol. 4, *The Eighteenth Century*. Cambridge: Cambridge University Press, 2003.

Punter, David. *A Companion to the Gothic*. Oxford: Wiley-Blackwell, 2001.

Radcliffe, Ann. *The Mysteries of Udolpho*. In *Complete Novels of Mrs. Ann Radcliffe*. London: Folio Society, 1987.

Rahner, Karl. *Hearers of the Word: Laying the Foundation for a Philosophy of Religion*. New York: Continuum , 1997.

———. *Theological Investigations*. Vol. 4, *More Recent Writings*. London: Helicon, 1966.

Ratcliff, Carter. "The Sublime Was Then: The Art of Barnett Newman." In Beckley, *Sticky Sublime*, 211–39.

Rauschenbusch, Walter. *Christianity and the Social Crisis*. New York: Macmillan, 1907.

———. *A Theology for the Social Gospel*. New York: Macmillan, 1917.

Ray, John. *Three Physico-Theological Discourses*. 3rd ed. St. Paul's Church-yard, London: William Innys (Printer), 1713.

Reid, Robin Anne. *Arthur C. Clarke: A Critical Companion*. Westport, Conn.: Greenwood Press, 1997.

Ricoeur, Paul. *The Symbolism of Evil*. Boston: Beacon, 1986.

Rist, John Michael. *The Stoics*. Los Angeles: University of California Press, 1978.

Roberts, Adam. *The History of Science Fiction*. London: Palgrave Macmillan, 2007.

Robinson, James, ed. *Nag Hammadi Library in English: The Definitive Translation of the Gnostic Scriptures, Complete in One Volume*. 3rd rev ed. New York: HarperOne, 2000.

Robu, Cornel. "A Key to Science Fiction: The Sublime." *Foundation: The Review of Science Fiction* 42 (1988): 21–37.

Rossi, Umberto. *The Twisted Worlds of Philip K. Dick: A Reading of Twenty Ontologically Uncertain Novels*. Jefferson, N.C.: McFarland, 2011.

Russ, Joanna. "Towards an Aesthetic of Science Fiction." In Hartwell, Wolf, and Science Fiction Research Association, *Visions of Wonder*, 555–63.

Scarry, Elaine. *On Beauty and Being Just*. London: Duckworth, 2006.

Schiller, Friedrich. *Aesthetical and Philosophical Essays*. Charleston, S.C.: Bibliobazaar, 2007.

Schmidt, Lawrence E., and Scott Marratto. *The End of Ethics in a Technological Society*. Montreal: McGill-Queen's University Press, 2008.

Schneemelcher, Wilhelm. *New Testament Apocrypha*. Vol. 1, *Gospels and Related Writings*. Louisville, Ky.: Westminster John Knox, 2006.

———. *New Testament Apocrypha*. Vol. 2, *Writings Relating to the Apostles*. Rev. ed. Louisville, Ky.: Westminster John Knox, 2003.

Scholes, Robert. *Structural Fabulation: Essay on Fiction of the Future*. Notre Dame, Ind.: University of Notre Dame Press, 1975.

Schweitzer, Darrell, ed. *Discovering H. P. Lovecraft*. Rev. exp. ed. Holicong, Pa.: Borgo, 2001.

Seed, David, ed. *A Companion to Science Fiction*. Oxford: Wiley-Blackwell, 2005.

Segal, Howard P. *Future Imperfect: Mixed Blessings of Technology in America*. Boston: University of Massachusetts Press, 1994.

———. *Technological Utopianism in American Culture*. Chicago: University of Chicago Press, 1985.

Segal, Robert A., June K. Singer, and Murray Stein, eds. *The Allure of Gnosticism: Gnostic Experience in Jungian Psychology and Contemporary Culture*. Chicago: Open Court, 1995.

Shanahan, Timothy. *The Evolution of Darwinism: Selection, Adaptation and Progress in Evolutionary Biology*. Cambridge: Cambridge University Press, 2004.

Shaw, Philip. *The Sublime*. London: Routledge, 2005.

Slusser, George. "The Origins of Science Fiction." In Seed, *Companion to Science Fiction*, 27–42.

Smart, Christopher. *Poems by Christopher Smart*. Edited by Robert Brittain. Princeton, N.J.: Princeton University Press, 1950.

Smith, Adam. "The Principles Which Lead and Direct Philosophical Enquiries; Illustrated by the History of Astronomy." In *Essays on Philosophical Subjects*. Dublin: Wogan, Byrne, et al., 1795.

———. *The Theory of Moral Sentiments*. Reissue ed. London: Liberty Classics, n.d.

Spacks, Patricia Meyer. *The Insistence of Horror: Aspects of the Supernatural in Eighteenth-Century Poetry*. Boston: Harvard University Press, 1962.

Stableford, Brian. *The Sociology of Science Fiction*. Holicong, Pa.: Borgo, 2007.

Stapledon, Olaf. *Beyond the "Isms."* Searchlight Books 16. New York: Secker & Warburg, 1942.

———. *The Opening of the Eyes*. London: Methuen, 1954.

Sussman, Herbert L. *Victorians and the Machine: The Literary Response to Technology*. Boston: Harvard University Press, 1969.

Sutin, Lawrence. *Divine Invasions: The Life of Philip K. Dick*. New York: Harmony Books, 1990.

Suvin, Darko. *Positions and Presuppositions in Science Fiction*. Kent, Ohio: Kent State University Press, 1988.

Suvin, Darko, and Robert M. Philmus. *H. G. Wells and Modern Science Fiction*. Cranbury, N.J.: Bucknell University Press, 1977.

Szerszynski, Bronislaw. *Nature, Technology and the Sacred*. Oxford: Wiley-Blackwell, 2005.

Taliaferro, Charles. *Evidence and Faith: Philosophy and Religion since the Seventeenth Century*. Cambridge: Cambridge University Press, 2005.

Taliaferro, Charles, and Jil Evans, eds. *Turning Images in Philosophy, Science, and Religion: A New Book of Nature*. New York: Oxford University Press, 2011.

Taylor, Charles. *A Secular Age*. Boston: Harvard University Press, 2007.

———. *Sources of the Self: The Making of the Modern Identity*. New ed. Cambridge: Cambridge University Press, 1992.

Teilhard de Chardin, Pierre. *Christianity and Evolution*. New York: Mariner Books, 2002.

———. *The Human Phenomenon: A New Edition and Translation of "Le Phenomene."* Humain. Brighton: Sussex Academic, 2003.

Tillich, Paul. *Systematic Theology: Three Volumes in One*. Chicago: University of Chicago Press, 1967.

Tillotson, John. *A Seasonable Vindication of the B. Trinity; Being an Answer to This Question, "Why Do You Believe in the Doctine of the Trinity?"* London: B. Aylmer, 1697.

———. *A Sermon Concerning the Unity of the Divine Nature and the Blessed Trinity*. London: B. Aylmer & W. Rogers, 1696.

Tindal, Matthew. *Christianity as Old as Creation or the Gospel: A Republication of the Religion of Nature*. Facsimile of 1730 ed. New York: Garland, 1978.

Torrance, Thomas F. *Christian Theology and Scientific Culture*. New York: Oxford University Press, 1982.

———. *Trinitarian Faith: Evangelical Theology of the Ancient Catholic Church*. New York: Continuum, 1993.

Traherne, Thomas. *Selected Poems and Prose*. London: Penguin Books, 1991.

Tsang, Lap-Chuen. *The Sublime: Groundwork towards a Theory*. Rochester, N.Y.: University of Rochester Press, 1998.

Ussher, James. *Clio: Or a Discourse on Taste. Addressed to a Young Lady.* 3rd ed. London: T. Davies, 1772.

Velde, Rudi A. te. *Aquinas on God: The 'Divine Science' of the "Summa Theologiae."* Burlington, Vt.: Ashgate, 2006.

Vernier, J. P. "Evolution as a Literary Theme in H. G. Wells' Science Fiction." In *H. G. Wells and Modern Science Fiction*, edited by Darko Suvin and Robert Philemus, 70–89. Princeton, N.J.: Associated University Presses, 1979.

Viladesau, Richard. *Theological Aesthetics: God in Imagination, Beauty, and Art*. New York: Oxford University Press, 2013.

Voegelin, Eric. *Science, Politics, Gnosticism*. Washington, D.C.: ISI Books, 2005.

Volf, Miroslav. "Enter into Joy!" In Polkinghorne and Welker, *End of the World*, 256–78.

Walpole, Horace. *The Castle of Otranto: A Gothic Story*. London: Folio Society, 1976.

Ward, Graham. *Cultural Transformation and Religious Practice*. Cambridge: Cambridge University Press, 2005.

———. *Theology and Contemporary Critical Theory*. 2nd ed. London: Palgrave Macmillan, 2000.

Warrick, Patricia. *The Cybernetic Imagination in Science Fiction*. Boston: MIT Press, 1980.

Weil, Kari. *Thinking Animals: Why Animal Studies Now?* New York: Columbia University Press, 2012.

Weiskel, Thomas. *The Romantic Sublime: Studies in the Structure and Psychology of Transcendence*. Baltimore: Johns Hopkins University Press, 1976.

Wells, H. G. [Herbert George]. *God the Invisible King*. Accessed April 27, 2011. http://www.gutenberg.org/ebooks/1046.

———. *H. G. Wells: Early Writings in Science and Science Fiction*. Edited by Robert Philmus and David Y. Hughes. Los Angeles: University of California Press, 1975.

———. *A Modern Utopia*. London: General Books, 2010.

Wesley, John. "The Witness of the Spirit: Discourse 2." The Wesley Center Online. Accessed March 7, 2014. http://wesley.nnu.edu/john-wesley/the-sermons-of-john-wesley-1872-edition/sermon-11-the-witness-of-the-spirit-discourse-two/.

Wiener. *The Human Use of Human Beings: Cybernetics and Society*. New ed. Boston: Da Capo, 1988.

Williams, Raymond. *Keywords: A Vocabulary of Culture and Society*. London: Fontana, 2010.

———. *Problems in Materialism and Culture*. London: Verso Books, 1996.

Wilmerding, John, ed. *American Light: The Luminist Movement, 1850–1875; Paintings, Drawings, Photographs*. Washington, D.C.: National Gallery of Art, 1980.

Winner, L. *Autonomous Technology: Technics-out-of-Control as a Theme in Political Thought.* New ed. Boston: MIT Press, 1977.

Wollheim, Donald A. *The Universe Makers: Science Fiction Today*. New York: HarperCollins, 1971.

Woodman, Tom. "Science Fiction, Religion, and Transcendence." In Parrinder, *Science Fiction: A Critical Guide*, 110–30.

Young, B. W. *Religion and Enlightenment in Eighteenth-Century England: Theological Debate from Locke to Burke*. New York: Oxford University Press, 1998.

Young, Edward. *Conjectures on Original Composition*. London: A. Millar & R. and J. Dodsley, 1759.

———. *Young's Night Thoughts; or, Thoughts on Life, Death, and Immortality*. New York: Worthington, 1889.

Žižek, Slavoj. *The Sublime Object of Ideology*. London: Verso, 1989.

# INDEX